The Diva's Mouth

Rosa at home, 1922. Chicken Tetrazzini, peach Melba, pasta Ponselle. *(Photo courtesy of the Theatre Museum V&A.)*

The Diva's Mouth

BODY, VOICE,
PRIMA DONNA POLITICS

SUSAN J. LEONARDI

AND

REBECCA A. POPE

Rutgers University Press

New Brunswick, New Jersey

Library of Congress Cataloging-in-Publication Data

Leonardi, Susan J.
    The diva's mouth : body, voice, prima donna politics / Susan J.
Leonardi and Rebecca A. Pope.
       p.   cm.
    Includes bibliographical references (p.) and index.
    ISBN 0-8135-2303-6 (cloth : alk. paper). — ISBN 0-8135-2304-4
(pbk. : alk. paper)
    1. Women singers. 2. Music and society. I. Pope, Rebecca A.
II. Title.
ML400.L46 1996
783.6—dc20

96-12979
CIP
MN

British Cataloging-in-Publication information available

Portions of chapter 3 appeared in somewhat different form as "The Diva Doesn't Die:
George Eliot's *Armgart*" in *Criticism* 32.4 (Fall 1990): 469–483. Bits of chapter 2
appeared in very different form as "To Have a Voice: The Politics of the Diva" in
Perspectives on Contemporary Literature 13 (1987): 65–72.

Manufactured in the United States of America

For

Jeanette and Ralph
(almost) Perfect Parents

and

Julian, Benedicta, Allegra, and Jakob
(still straight but otherwise) Perfect Offspring

CONTENTS

Acknowledgments

Brigitte, Benita, Cecilia, Frederica, Teresa, Kiri, Kathleen, Leontyne, Marilyn, Dawn, June, Jessye, and Julianne: if not for you . . .

$\mathcal{M}$ore practically and less euphonically, we thank the University of California at Davis, the University of Chicago, the University of Maryland at College Park, and Georgetown University for travel funds that allowed us to consult collections beyond our home libraries and try out early versions of some of this material at conferences. The Graduate Research Board and the English Department at the University of Maryland gave Susan a teaching-free year for research and writing. Colleagues, friends, and students kindly brought us material we would not otherwise have seen, patiently offered computer advice, generously stayed enthusiastic when our own enthusiasm waned, and heroically listened without looking bored when we droned on about divas. Among them are Linda Coleman, Theresa Coletti, Maureen Corrigan, Jane Donawerth, Robin Evans, Ruth Fassinger, Michael Foley, Sandra Greer, Marcia Harrison, Nigella Hillgarth, Lynne Hirschfeld, Mary Anne Hoopes, Linda and Michael Hutcheon, Julie Johnson, Dianna Johnston, Linda Kauffman, Carol Kent, Katie King, Joyce Kornblatt, Sue Lanser, Paula McDowell, Jan Montefiore, Karen Oosterhaus, Carla Peterson, Joanna Raczynska, Joyce Raynor, Pierre Riches, Edith and Don Rothchild, Catherine Schuler, Craig Seymour, Debbie Shaller, Seth Silberman, Bruce Smith, Kyna Taylor, Norma Tilden, Patricia Tollefson, Lauren Voloshen, Josephine Withers, and the members of Susan's No Limits group, especially Patricia Dubroof, who lent us Doña Diva. And thanks to Dan Vellosa at Louisiana Express for good humor and endless refills of caffeine.

(Ethnically constructed to desire the vendetta, we here resist the temptation to list institutions and individuals who strew stones in our path; publishing well—we tell ourselves and our numerous large-muscled, hot-tempered, well-armed siblings—is revenge enough.)

Special thanks to Gordon Davis, who understands obsessions, who talks diva better than anyone, and who cheerfully slogged through the original six-hundred-page manuscript to keep us from making even more—and more egregious—opera errors than we probably have. Finally, thanks to those academic colleagues—and to Leslie Mitchner, our editor—who understand that there comes a time in the (perverse) course of academic life when girls just want to have fun.

The Diva's Mouth

I think I've had one of the most beautiful lyric soprano voices
I've ever heard. I'm mad about my voice. It was gorgeous.
I loved it so much that from time to time
I used to take out one of my best crystal glasses,
sip a little champagne and toast it.
—Leontyne Price

Program Notes

*I*n the opening frames of Annie Lennox's 1992 video, *Diva,* we see a light-rimmed rectangle with the letters DIVA shining onto the screen. It could be a marquee, an appropriate announcement of the appearance of a figure as exalted as the prima donna. But the lights are dim neon, the sign itself on the shabby side. Perhaps this diva is not an opera star at all but a singer in a second-rate Las Vegas casino. Or worse. The sign looks, when you stop to think about it, suspiciously like a vanity license plate. Self-promotion of a nobody. What the elusiveness of the sign suggests is underscored by the unpromising appearance of the promised goddess: she is not on stage, not surrounded by the opulence and excitement of a theater or concert hall, but alone, in front of her mirror, herself her only audience. How the mighty have fallen, the divas declined.

Each generation of diva admirers has made similar complaints. Divas just aren't as wonderful, glamorous, dramatic, imposing as they used to be. Nor are their voices as elastic, warm, versatile, full, compelling. We might say, if we were cranky purists, that even the word "diva" has been debased, from its origin in the female pantheon to its current mundaneness, "pop diva" or "disco diva" its most frequent incarnation. Recent publications have referred to Sandra Bernhard as "the diva of comedy," Estee Lauder as a "make-up diva," Ivana Trump as a "shopping network diva," and Martha Stewart as the "Diva of Domesticity"; a book review describes a character as a "consummate trailer park diva." Such wanton proliferation.[1]

Not only has every female star, singer, and artist been dubbed diva, but, we note, high-ranking businesswomen and, well, some pretty low-ranking women, too. And not just women. There are now drag queen divas, snap divas, voguing divas (they were there all along, but we didn't hear much about them until RuPaul and Jennie Livingston and Madonna). And not all the drag queen divas are glamorous these days, either. A Washington, D.C., bar devotes Wednesdays to "Drag Freak Bingo" emceed by "Bingo Divas" Beate, Biannca, and Babette, their look best described as thrift-store seventies. Indeed there's something both decidedly common and decidedly queer about divas today. (It's not an accident, we think, that the diva proliferates in popular and middle-brow culture at the same time that there is more media focus on gays and lesbians. One can read this as another example of the way the icons and artifacts of various lesbian and gay cultures—like black leather, voguing, earrings for men and hiking boots for women—are appropriated and domesticated by mainstream [straight] popular culture.)

Of course, the association between divas and queers is hardly new. One of the most common stereotypes of the gay male is the opera queen, the diva worshiper, and one of the most circulated anecdotes of opera history is the story of the young woman so madly infatuated with diva Mary Garden that after Garden's secretary refused her access to the diva's dressing room, she shot herself in the head; she was found clutching to her breast a photograph of the great singer. Such "mad infatuation"—the phrase used by the young woman's mother—characterizes (less violently and less tragically, one hopes) the lesbian diva fan and the opera queen as well. Both madness and infatuation (at least when the object of such infatuation is obviously beyond reach) are, of course, unacceptable conditions in the civilized adult; combined with queerness they're unbearable. And thus are born academic studies like this one, the unacceptable passions from which they spring discreetly cloaked in measured cadences, the cloaks discreetly closeted by careful footnotes, fetishes of the repressed.

Two academic critics, both queer, both diva-mad, have, however, recently unclothed their passions, offering readers (with diffidence, embarrassment, anguish, defensiveness, how otherwise?) a salutary look (with footnotes, how otherwise?) into the personal obsessions that both fuel and constitute their pleasures and their scholarship. Wayne Koestenbaum in *The Queen's Throat: Opera, Homosexuality, and the Mystery of Desire* and Terry Castle in "In Praise of Brigitte Fassbaender (A Musical Emanation)" announce themselves ("come out" is a phrase both use) as diva worshipers, even though, as Castle admits, "at best, the diva-worshipper is a kind of parody-adult, a maker of silly sounds and fatuous conceits—a sort of gurgling, burbling semi-idiot" (201). The only thing more embarrassing than being a diva worshiper, Castle opines, is being a *female* diva worshiper, that perverse creature for whom "to enthuse over the voice is, if only subliminally, to fancy plumping down in bed with its owner" (201).

While we, respectable academics that we fancy ourselves, would like to shield ourselves from suspicions of gurgling, burbling semi-idiocy, we nevertheless recognize the erotic component to our fascination with divas, both exalted and common, and the significance of that eroticism in our own scholarship. It is the conviction of that significance that urges us to participate, by way, first of all, of these autobiographical program notes, in what seems to us an important conversation about women's voices, love, and work.

We began the public conversation at the 1992 convention of the Modern Language Association, when we gave a joint presentation to commemorate the tenth anniversary of *Tulsa Studies*. The topic of the panel was women collaborators, our contribution a dialogue offering some descriptive models of collaboration using our own experience of thinking and writing together—experience that is by the time of *this* writing much more extensive.[2] One of our starting places was Wayne Koestenbaum's first book, *Double Talk*, on male collaboration. One of his claims there, at least about the nineteenth-century writers he's examining, is that "men who collaborate engage in metaphorical sexual intercourse and . . . the text they balance between them is alternately a child of their sexual union, and a shared woman" (3). Although we don't find this model of collaboration particularly applicable to our own work, we like the book very much, in part because Koestenbaum explores, as so few others have, the erotics of collaboration.

It is interesting and, we think, not coincidental that the book on male collaboration was followed by one on divas. That is, although both Koestenbaum and Castle present their diva worship as solitary obsessions, both take pains as well to see these obsessions in the context of a community of obsessors—for Koestenbaum opera queens, for Castle lesbian diva fans. (There is no convenient term for the latter, though we might call them diva-flappers, in honor of the Gerry-Flappers, who, as Castle notes, "waited every night at the stage door of the Met for Geraldine Farrar in the teens and twenties, casting flowers and love-notes in her direction" [206].)

Although Koestenbaum uses phrases like "the solitary operatic feast, the banquet for one, onanism through the ear" (*QT* 30) to describe his own early, "antisocial" devouring of opera recordings, and although he claims that opera queens are "rarely" nice to one another, he admits that their "anger is a form of flirtation" and a sign of "too much in common" (*QT* 39). Castle's confession is determinedly idiosyncratic, but she revels in the "comforting" discovery "that even in the realm of perversity, one can find compatriots and companions-at-arms"(202). Diva worship, then, in both its history and its current manifestations, seems very much a collaborative as well as a solitary activity.

The models for collaborative activity that we offered to our audience—quilt making, cooking, having a conversation, part singing (though not diva worshiping)—were all, we acknowledged, inadequate, partly because they did not take into account the erotics of work in general and of collaborative work in particular. We see ourselves at one extreme of the collaborative spectrum, since we are lovers as well as collaborators, but we see also our own concrete erotic connection as—in part, of course—the literalization of the erotic always inherent in the collaborative process and our concrete collaborative projects as the literalization of the collaboration always inherent in the erotic process. Collaborators, to put it less ponderously, are always in some sense lovers, and lovers in some sense collaborators. This particular collaboration has its roots in both our erotic relationship and our diva-flapping. We tell the story in hopes of suggesting some of the labyrinthine and subterranean connections among the components, in hopes of eliciting other experiences of such connections, in hopes of corroborating and elaborating Koestenbaum's and Castle's narratives of sex and sound.

The collaborative "we" here changes to "I" because I (Susan), officially designated storyteller of the family, am temporarily taking over. Besides, to a large extent I was the author of the ensuing plot, Rebecca, for the most part, playing the role of resisting reader. We met in Oxford, both graduate students working on dissertations, both temporarily living in the Somerville College graduate house: Rebecca had been at Somerville College for her M.Phil. and had returned for a summer; my dissertation was on Somerville women before the First World War, and I had a three-week summer grant to do some on-site research. My project began in a love affair with Somervillian and novelist Winifred Holtby and ended, one might say, in a love affair with a more contemporary Somervillian. By dedicating the resultant book to "the women of Somerville," I could include them both. But I'm getting ahead of my story.

Not long before the trip to Oxford, I had purchased and been dazzled by my first diva recording—Leontyne Price's *Nuit d'été*. Rebecca had just bought her first season subscription to the Lyric Opera of Chicago and was mad about Kiri Te Kanawa. We had no equipment on which to play music, but we talked about our discoveries with the enthusiasm of recent initiates. We also talked about divas in books, especially about Daniel Deronda's mother, a figure we both found among the most moving, in spite of the brevity of her appearance, in the nineteenth-century novel, love for which was something else we had in common. It might make an interesting book, I suggested—though we weren't quite sure what "it" was. By the end of the three weeks we were mad about each other. (The implication that the whole of this whirlwind courtship took place over and through operatic conversations is merely a convenient autobiographical fiction. We also talked a lot about food. But food, of course, is diva territory as well—peach Melba, chicken Tetrazzini, pasta.)

When I got back to California, I did two things. First, I wrote out my preliminary thoughts about literary divas, presented them at a conference, got them in print. Just to let Rebecca know I was serious. (Nothing, I think, like love to spur one on to new heights of productivity. Especially when said love is two thousand miles away.) Second, I bought all the available Kiri Te Kanawa recordings (at that time, fortunately for my graduate student finances, quite limited) and even managed to find one that Rebecca didn't know about, a Kiwi recording from Kiri's early days as a New Zealand folk singer. I brought it to her when I visited Chicago in December, diva gift, first of many.

Excitement over Kiri's voice (we call her Kiri; we have, after all, spent a lot of time with this woman) was barely distinguishable from excitement over one another's bodies. And who had time for distinctions anyway?

Within the next few years, we saw Kiri in concert in Chicago (when I visited Rebecca), in *Der Rosenkavalier* in San Francisco (when Rebecca visited me), and in *The Marriage of Figaro* at Ravinia (another visit to Chicago, these passions becoming increasingly expensive); we met in New York for a Kiri concert to celebrate my fortieth birthday (no, we cannot excuse our excess on grounds of youth and inexperience). We felt like jet setters, stood in line for Kiri's autograph, felt like groupies, let her rich warm voice feed our passion for her and for each other, admitted sheepishly that we'd sleep with her if we could. And we talked about the book. I offered Rebecca this long-term project—it was, after all, a book we could write only after we finished our dissertations, if we ever finished our dissertations—as an incentive to think of "us" as a long-term project. The diva book as seduction. Maybe we could even use it as a ploy to interview Dame Kiri. (She turned us down.)

Rebecca agreed to the collaboration, and only to the collaboration, having convinced herself before she met me that she needed to try out the straight world or, more accurately, to try out for a straight role in the only world she knew. But I think we both realized that the "yes" had resonances beyond the book, that the collaborative process would be, for us— incorrigible head people—one way of working through the confusing and threatening things we felt for and about one another, and that the subjects of the book would somehow bring us together in a less confusing and threatening (because so closely allied with art and imagination, our safety zones) but no less real physicality. While I'm not sure that we could make a case for Kiri Te Kanawa's "homovocality," I think we vaguely sensed what Terry Castle so elegantly expresses about "her" divas: "By the liberating way that *she* desires—by the bold ardor of her own 'homovocal' exaltation—a singer like Fremstad or Fassbaender becomes a collective emblem: a poignant, often thrilling token of homoerotic possibility" (237).

When I got an East Coast job offer, we talked for the first time about living together. There were complications. Major ones, like children. Minor ones, like wondering if any relationship could survive new jobs, new part of the country, new family configuration all at once. But, we reasoned, calmly, sensibly, disingenuously, if we're going to be writing the diva book, it would be so *convenient*. The diva book the deciding factor.

We've settled in, traded jet setting on Q-class flights and frequent flyer miles for a flat in the D.C. suburbs that we shared, until they started college, with two of my four children. Our (we return now, story time over, to the joint narrator) passion for Kiri has waned over the years (her fault, we claim, those crossover recordings so ill-suited to her voice, that Christmas album so downright embarrassing, her interviews so mindless), Koestenbaum and Castle's suggestion that true diva worshipers must choose a diva and stick to her, notwithstanding. Our current rave, whom we know of at this writing only from recordings and one concert appearance, is Cecilia Bartoli (an inevitable choice, perhaps, given that both of us come from Italian-American families; she sings to us when we eat pasta, which is several times a week), but Jessye Norman, Dawn Upshaw, Kathleen Battle, Julianne Baird (who readily agreed to an interview, has been generous with her time, and undoubtedly thinks that this book will never see print), and Frederica von Stade claim a fair share of our love, loyalty, and CD collection.

And we're expanding our range, amazed by the proliferation of and happily seduced by full-throated, in-your-face, stop-at-nothing pop 'n' rock divas, rap queens, girl groups, riot grrrls. We bring them to bed with us, revel in their variety, rejoice in their abundance, worry that there are so many voices, so little time. In response to voices, old and new, operatic and pop, we do what we do best. Read about them, think about them, talk about them, write about them, put them in historical and literary contexts. Aestheticize them, intellectualize them, appropriate them, subordinate them. Make them, some might say, boring. Make them, our students will accuse, political.

We're political animals; living in the D.C. area, of course, exacerbates existing tendencies. Hopeless left-wing flailers, utopianists (more you than me, Rebecca groans), revolutionaries, cynics, thoroughly compromised middle-class hedonists (it's a humble flat but it's well located and we're addicted to olive oil, porcini mushrooms, and our new Honda), pacifists when we aren't adding to our hit list (Rush Limbaugh, Jesse Helms, Newt Gingrich), vegetarians when we aren't savoring smoked salmon, socialists when we aren't checking on our mutual funds, Italian-Americans who have worked hard to eradicate traces of our families' emigrant roots—except for the hit list and the pasta and our household saints and the farmhouse-in-Tuscany fantasy and our occasionally extravagant prose and Cecilia (no, it's worse than that: Rebecca's Italian grandfather's idea of recreation was having her grandmother read him opera libretti)—we live out the very contradictions and hypocrisies we try to expose in our work. We politicize everything, even, our students say—angry, irritated, disgusted—sex and art.

To write, then, about the *politics* of the diva is to see that figure in a variety of erotic and artistic contexts, to explore her significance for a variety of writers, readers, listeners, admirers, detractors, lovers, to wonder about the complex gender politics inherent in the diva stereotype, the proto-feminist and feminist reworking of that stereotype, the complicated sexual politics inherent in opera, the feminist and queer reworking of those politics, the implicit gender and sexual politics of the diva who, with a powerful voice and from a position reached by incredible discipline and steely ambition, sings traditional love lyrics and dies a sacrificial death or who, alternatively, even alternately, dons trousers and sings traditional love lyrics to another woman, the explicit gender and sexual politics of the diva who, in fantastical gown, pin-stripe suit, torn-up jeans, nothing at all (nothing, that is, but blood smeared lavishly across her naked chest), screams protest, advocates violent action, denounces whites, rails against men, masturbates on stage. We dwell in complication.

"At the opera," Wayne Koestenbaum asks, "what does your body do?" (*QT* 39). From the knotty and naughty but relatively abstract concerns just enumerated, we return to the material and the concrete. This is very much a book about bodies. A book about body parts. Fragile throats, open mouths, powerful lungs, swollen epiglottises, larynxes on the edge, pierced ears, notes from the chest, notes from the head, heaving breasts, bared breasts, bound breasts, snipped testicles, clipped frenums. It's a book about muscles, hair, fat, blood, sweat, and secretions. Elisabeth Söderström, in her autobiography *In My Own Key*, insists that "my job is sweat, phlegm, and dirty feet" (2). A diva in a detective novel, Barbara Paul's *Prima Donna at Large*, wants to talk about saliva. "It's an unpleasant subject, I know, but it's one of those very real problems singers have to worry about. Singing opera makes all sorts of demands on the human body, and saliva accumulates in the mouth as a result of all the *pushing* you have to do. . . . That's why the first few rows of the audience sometimes see one singer spraying another—which makes love duets particularly hazardous" (210).

When you hear a diva sing, what does your body do? (The Ayatollah Khomeini knew—he banned public singing.) In an 1897 review for the *Nebraska State Journal*, the young Willa Cather reveals a little of her own enthusiastic and physical response to the great diva Emma Calvé singing Carmen: "Good heavens! The outrageous way in which she wheedled and bewitched and flirted with the audience in those trills! You felt as if you should have brought a chaperone" (Curtin 410). What, one wonders, did Cather's body do when she listened to Emma Calvé? Perhaps the same thing that the narrator in Marcia Davenport's *Of Lena Geyer* does; he claims that you listen to Geyer "with everything from your ears to your sexual organs" (39). And what does the diva's body do? Diva Agnes Baltsa, one of her friends says, is "erotically excited by being on stage" (Matheopoulis 246), and Christa Ludwig elaborates on such excitement: "Pouring out the full voice and unleashing that torrent of sound over a full orchestra is . . . almost orgiastic [does she mean 'orgasmic'?], like making love" (290). The opera house, it appears, positively throbs with desire. The performance constructs a vast circuit of erotic exchange.

It's a book about sex.

In the film version of *The Joy Luck Club*, a husband's cruel infidelity is signified by his affair with a diva, face cold, sensual, unreadable as she looks at the rejected wife. In *Diva* Jules rushes to a prostitute after a concert and asks her to wear the diva's stolen gown. In *The Lisbon Traviata*

Mendy puts a diva on his stereo for lovemaking. Koestenbaum links the diva to his gayness, Castle to her lesbianism.

It's a book about sexuality, dangerous and deviant.

What the diva wears is a subject of great import. Witness Jules's theft of his diva's gown. The loving descriptions of diva dress on Met broadcasts. Yves Saint-Laurent's sartorial tributes to Maria Callas. Frances Alda's brag that if she ever has "any repenting to do, it won't be in sackcloth and ashes [but] in trailing grey chiffon cut by somebody who has an inspiration about gores, and folds, and trailing drapery" (Alda 136). Beverly Sills's dictum: "Prima donnas do not wear inexpensive outfits" (Sills ix). The silk, leather, and fur designer fashions, most with trousers, that Tina Rossi sports in *Dolly and the Singing Bird*. The fantastic headdress on Annie Lennox's diva—and her pin-stripe suit. The trouser role. Sexologist Krafft-Ebing wrote that divas "who appear in male attire on stage by preference" may "nearly always be suspected" of "uranism" (Smith-Rosenberg 269). In *M. Butterfly*, the diva's femininity is only dress deep. Geraldine Farrar in a 1913 interview with Willa Cather explains her "shocking" refusal to wear gloves on stage: "I can't sing if I feel my clothes. I don't wear stays and would like to sing without any clothes" ("Three" 38). Early divas, including Geraldine Farrar and Olive Fremstad, designed their own costumes. Fremstad "practically [made] them" (Cather, "Three" 47).

It's a book about clothes.

What we're confessing here—the most embarrassing confession of all—is that the topic has both overwhelmed and eluded us. We are still trying to figure out how a book that began as a fairly straightforward study of the diva as she appears in nineteenth- and twentieth-century Anglo-American texts became a book about politics, bodies, sex, sexuality, clothes. How a book, that is, that initially seemed so manageable became so impossible. Well, we said at first, looking in dismay at the proliferation of material, there are just more literary divas than we at first imagined. And, indeed, there were.

And then it became more and more difficult to separate the literary divas from their real-life counterparts, in part because the real life divas began to seem as fictional, as constructed, as the literary ones, their very lives put together, piece by piece, from narrative conventions. The diva, we realized, even when we give her a recognizable name—Maria Callas, Joan Sutherland, Marilyn Horne, Leontyne Price, Marian Anderson—is not so much a person as a position, a condition, a situation. We tried hard not to get distracted by the obvious parallels and extensions: the fictionality of our own lives, the positionality of our own selves, the varying roles we both perform. We tried but we failed.

But most of all, the diva herself—constructed, fictional, conditional as she is—is larger (or louder) than life and much more fragile. The canvas on which we work seems too small for her, our brushes too crude and clumsy. Chameleon, protean, vampiric, dramatic, regal, seductive, powerful, manipulative, ambitious, generous, life-enhancing, life-altering, extravagant, she won't sit still for us. A Study in Hyperbole, we'd call her portrait, if we could ever finish it.

Susan wears a tiny pin (another diva gift)—a woman singing, mouth open wide, arms extended (embracing the world or crushing it?), hair sticking straight out in snake- or staff-like strands, extravagant gown striped and flowered. We call her the screaming diva. But we know that it's not only she who's screaming. In trying to portray her (frame her?), some strange identifications or reversals have taken place. Our mouths have begun to scream, our gestures to inflate. Our clothes have become costumes, our prose taken on a certain operatic breathlessness.

"Opera," says Koestenbaum, "has the power to warn you that you have wasted your life. You haven't acted on your desires" (*QT* 44). Okay, we've been warned. What scares us, of course, is that listening to the diva will turn us—not into stone, though she has been portrayed as a Medusa, but—into a seething mass of unacceptable, uncontainable, and inexpressible desires.

Yeah. So lucky us.

Mostly, though, it's a book about books.

It is not, alas, a book about opera. And the worst of it is, as Frances Alda says of her own autobiography, "there isn't any ending to this story, in which every day may introduce a new chapter" (307).

Overture

Let's give them something to talk about.
—Bonnie Raitt

$\mathcal{W}$hile composing *The Marriage of Figaro* Mozart took time out for a commission from Emperor Joseph II; the result, performed for the emperor on February 7, 1786, was *Der Schauspieldirektor* (*The Impresario*), a one-act comedy with music set to a libretto by Gottlieb Stephanie the younger. It is a tale of dueling divas. Madame Herz and Mademoiselle Silberklang both sing arias for a theater manager who is putting together a company.[1] He hires them both, and for the same salary. Mademoiselle Silberklang can accept financial parity, but she demands top billing; she must be the *prima* donna. Madame Herz protests, of course. As the conflict escalates, we quickly see that there is a vast difference between the singers themselves and the women they have just portrayed in their arias. The woman of Madame Herz's aria is all romance and conventional womanhood—she laments that she and her lover must part; she wonders how she can live without him. The woman of Mademoiselle Silberklang's aria declares that she finds her happiness in her lover's gaze, that nothing is so dear to her as he. The two divas perform these "true women" beautifully, but it is difficult to imagine either Silberklang or Herz languishing in love, depending on a man, or taking less than what she thinks is her due.

The aria contest over, Mademoiselle Silberklang's "I am the prima donna" is countered by Madame Herz's bitchy "Yes, . . . in *your* opinion," and their duet becomes a trio when the tenor, Monsieur Vogelsang, enters the fray and pleads with them to listen to reason.[2] Soon both divas are singing "I am the prima donna" alternately. The phrase starts a note higher on each repetition; to what heights, Mozart's music seems to ask, will this rivalry escalate? After the tenor argues that "no artist should decry another, this degrades their art," the capricious divas reverse themselves and compete to withdraw their claims, only to shift again and reassert them *sotto*

voce. All the while, of course, the music—beautiful, harmonious part singing—has been imposing a harmony that seems to envelop and override the
divas' conflict. This continues in the final *vaudeville*, in which all three
sing together, "Artists must always strive to achieve excellence, but to give
the preference to oneself . . . makes the greatest artist small." By the close,
then, the divas are playing another part, the noble and selfless artists. But
we suspect that these performances, like their truce, will soon end.

The difference between the two strong-willed, self-satisfied prima
donnas and the pining, passive women they impersonate in their arias dramatizes the pervasive disjunction between women singers and the roles
they sing, especially women's roles in the late-eighteenth- and nineteenth-
century operatic repertory. But of course, Mozart's divas are not "real singers," historical singers, but as much characters as the women they play, as
stereotyped as the pining lovers in their prima donna nastiness, competitiveness, and egomania. And they are sisters not so much to historical divas
as to other divas in opera, like Puccini's Tosca, Janáček's Elina Makropulos,
Strauss's Prima Donna, and Argento's Julianna Bordereau.

In Jacques Offenbach's opera *The Tales of Hoffmann*, the poet
Hoffmann drinks in a tavern while *Don Giovanni* is being performed at the
opera house next door. He appears to be unhappily in love with the prima
donna, aptly named Stella. Hoffmann offers to tell the assembled company
the tales of his three great loves (and losses); Stella, it is implied, embodies
them all.

The first, Olympia, is a singing mechanical doll with whom Hoffmann, mistaking her for a flesh-and-blood woman, falls in love. Only after
her two evil inventors have a falling out, and one smashes the doll to
pieces, does Hoffmann wake from his fantasy. The second, Giulietta, is a
Venetian courtesan who seduces Hoffmann and steals his soul. The third,
young and innocent Antonia, must, according to her father and Hoffmann,
her suitor, give up singing to avoid aggravating her consumption. The evil
Dr. Miracle tries to convince her otherwise and finally succeeds when he
makes a portrait of her dead mother, a diva, seem to come alive and urge
Antonia to sing. She does, and she dies. His tales told, the drunken
Hoffmann passes out. Stella comes looking for him and, finding him unconscious, leaves with Lindorf, another admirer. As she exits, she tosses at
the poet's feet a rose from her bouquet.

Hoffmann's three loves, as Catherine Clément has argued before us,
epitomize traditional, stereotypical representations of the diva.[3] Like Giulietta, she is seducing siren and whore. Like Olympia, she is a product pro-

duced by men as a vessel for men's voices. What the diva can't be, as Antonia's narrative makes clear, is wife, good woman, true woman. Divahood kills womanhood. Antonia succumbs to the diva's temptation; divahood corrupts virtue.

We open this book with examples of operas about opera divas because such works so neatly and economically raise the issue of how divas are represented and because they make clear that divas are representations, constructions. Talk is the primary action of *The Tales of Hoffmann*; a man, a poet, tells stories about women, especially women who sing. The narrative strategy lays bare the extent to which traditional representations of the diva—as siren or vessel or some combination of both; as corrupt, monstrously selfish, ruthlessly competitive; as destructive and deadly—are masculinist fantasies that have little to do with flesh-and-blood women. The tradition goes back at least as far as another, earlier poet, Homer, and his archetypal siren tale. We call this tradition "masculinist" (although we worry that this term will prompt readers to think we are arguing—we are not—something essentialist, such as "all men represent the diva one way and all women another"), because it consistently figures the woman with a voice as dangerous and "unnatural." In that way, it seeks to reinforce traditional gender categories and the compulsory heterosexuality those categories support.

An operatic example of this tradition is Janáček's *The Makropulos Case* (1923),[4] in which diva Elina Makropulos lives—what a nightmare!—for three hundred years. Like many of the singers in our study, this vampiric diva and her "stupendous" voice seduce men to their destruction and women to perversion. An old man who "left everything behind" for her has become "half-witted"; another man screams that he loves her so much "I could tear the flesh from my bones"; a third (whose name, Janek, echoes the composer's own) kills himself "on [her] account." She, besides, steals Janek from Krista, an aspiring diva who is herself in love with Makropulos and who has renounced Janek in imitation of her ambitious, unwomanly idol. Most frightening of all, the diva doesn't give a damn. While Janek's father rails at her for his son's death, she combs her hair and comments, "Pooh! the number of men who kill themselves!" Nor does she—doubly, triply unnatural woman—care about the "many thousands of my brats / . . . scampering around the world." Although she refuses to use the potion that will keep her alive for another three hundred years, the now old and ugly diva tries to entice Krista—with promises of fame and Voice—to use it instead. Perverse even in death, she lures other women to the unnatural life that is divahood. The diva's final words, the final words of the opera, "Our Father," suggest repentance but also make clear, unwittingly perhaps, the very source of the nightmare/fantasy.

Not surprisingly, most of the literary divas in this tradition—from Homer's Sirens to Cain's Veda to the divas in a novel coauthored by opera singer Robert Merrill—appear in texts written by men. In the chapter "Singing His Mind Away," we look at this masculinist representational tradition, not in opera but in texts, mostly novels and poetry, mostly Anglo-American, from the nineteenth and twentieth centuries. In a chapter on divas in film, "Divas Do the Movies," we examine how film narratives about opera singers borrow and reinscribe the features of this tradition.

Stella the diva, as diva, is a field for the projections of others, most particularly the masculine imagination's fantasies about singing women. What Clément's admittedly short reading of the opera tends not to admit is the potential for critique, the possibility that the narrative is turning back on itself, in the opera's dramatization of this process of projection. For most of the opera, as Clément notes, Stella—the "real" diva—is off stage, of less importance to the romantic poet and to the opera than his own fantasies of her. Clément demonstrates how *The Tales of Hoffmann* participates in what she shows to be the masculinist perspective of nineteenth-century opera itself—"the great masculine scheme . . . thought up to adore, and also to kill, the feminine character" (6). But in her eagerness to make this case, she smooths over the opera's complications and complexities. What, we wonder, is Stella thinking? Is she being the capricious slut of the masculinist tradition when she leaves with Lindorf, or is her switch a sign that she is not as enthralled to the myths of romantic love as the poet himself? Does she leave for sex or does she just need a ride home? And what of the rose, tossed at Hoffmann's feet? Might it suggest that the real prima donna of the scene is Hoffmann, not Stella?

In other words, what Clément wants to see as a relentlessly monologic narrative—nineteenth-century opera replays and displays the death or undoing of women, and the women who play those women are themselves constructed as *femmes fatales*—we and other resisting listeners see as potentially dialogic. Stella doesn't sing and barely speaks, but neither does she die. Her silence can, of course, be placed in the service of Clément's claims, but she lives to sing another day; she has escaped the fate of Olympia and Antonia. What we argue in this study is that (roughly, generally) it is not until women start writing about divas that Stella gets to speak and sing, that the diva gets to talk back. We suggest further that it is the very ambiguity of her appearance in the opera's closing scene that opens for us, resisting readers, the possibility of imagining Stella speaking for herself, not speaking Hoffmann's or the librettist's lines, not speaking or singing, as Olympia does, the words of another who is male.

The diva, that is, becomes a field for the projections and identifications of others, but not all of these others are, as Offenbach's Hoffmann and the masculinist representational tradition might tempt us to believe, heterosexual men. There is ample evidence of these projections and identifications. From the nineteenth century on, Anglo-American women writers, and a few (good) men, have given us divas very different from the prima donnas of the masculinist tradition and in such number that, we argue, these texts constitute a counterdiscourse to that masculinist tradition. These writers see possibilities for the diva figure that Clément does not. Certain subcultures of gay men, as has long been recognized, find in the diva a field for their fantasies, projections, and identifications; Wayne Koestenbaum's *The Queen's Throat* operatically elaborates his; Jonathan Demme's *Philadelphia* includes a scene (about which we have mixed feelings) in which the Tom Hanks character enacts and tries to explain his passion for opera while playing a Callas recording. Contrary to what this scene may imply, critic Michael Moon makes clear that for some gay men these identifications are not just with the diva's passionate and determined overreaching, with the diva as icon of brilliantly burning self-consumption, or with her emotional pain: "One happy aspect of the story of my own and many other gay men's formations of our . . . body images is that the fat, beaming figure of the diva has never been entirely absent from . . . our fantasies of ideal bodies; . . . the diva's body has never lost its representational magnetism for us as an alternative body-identity fantasy, resolutely embodying as it does the otherwise almost totally anachronistic ideal, formed in early nineteenth-century Europe, of the social dignity of corpulence" (216).[5] The recent work of Terry Castle and Elizabeth Wood has begun the process of uncovering a tradition of lesbian diva worship and identification.[6] Our study charts some of this territory, from writer Willa Cather, whose interest in divas we examine at length in "The Sirens Avenged," to the lifelong female companions of both the "real" historical divas and literary divas we discuss in "The Sirens Avenged" and "Diva Truths, Diva Lies, Diva Lives," and finally to the Derivative Duo, a lesbian couple who do lesbian-feminist opera parody, and whose work we couple with "gay" male writer E. F. Benson's comic *Lucia* novels in "The Diva's Mouth: A Comic Interlude." The profusion and variety of all this fantasy, identification and projection suggests that there is more to the story of opera and its divas than Clément captures.

How can so many find so much in the diva if most of the operatic repertory and much opera history sings only one song about its female characters and the women who portray them? As we have suggested, opera's representations and representations of opera and its divas are more variously voiced than Clément allows, and further, this "dialogism," to use Bakhtin's term, opens up other points of identification and fields for projection, especially for those viewers/listeners who don't have access to the privileges of heterosexual masculinity. Women, lesbian and straight, and gay men have a long history of finding such places in even the most relentlessly sexist and heterosexist narratives; they must for their own survival. Yes, many operas offer as entertainment and make spectacular an old, deadly, and ideological narrative about women that depends on masculinist fantasies and serves masculine interests. But the ending that kills the Other, though powerfully privileged and overdetermined, is not the only place of identification. Even as that ending offers to viewers/listeners a lesson they already know, that otherness is a punishable offense, it cannot shut down the possibility of fantasized alternatives. Indeed, some of these narratives offer fairly clear places, sites, clues for their own undoing—the survival of Stella or the very irresistibility and *persistence* of Elina Makropulos— signs of an alternative, unspoken but imaginable, narrative.

And then there's the music. Carmen dies, but oh, her arias! Clément suggests that opera's beautiful music lulls the critical faculties to sleep; it is for her a sort of reverse siren song that allows the unconscious to consume pernicious representations. Historian Paul Robinson offers an alternative reading of the relations between the diva and the music she sings, and he argues that both the music and the female voice itself have the potential to redress the operatic plot's narrative of female subordination and submission. "Perhaps the single most important musical fact about opera's female victims," Robinson writes, "is that they sing with an authority equal to that of their male oppressors. Opera is built on one of the great natural equalities, the equality of men's and women's voices. Women can sing as loudly as men, their voices embrace as large a range as those of men and they have the advantage of commanding the heights where they can emit sounds of unparalleled incisiveness," evidence for Robinson "that women in opera are rarely experienced as victims. Rather, they seem subversive presences in the patriarchal culture, since they so manifestly contain the promise—or the threat—of women's equality" (3).

When the diva sings, at what does your heart leap? If you're a woman, it might be what Robinson calls the "vocal assertiveness" of the female voice (3), or its preeminence (it is the highest voice), strength, and authority.

It is in these complexities, complications, and exceptions to the masculinist tradition Clément lays out that we situate our study. But we begin, in the first chapter, "Pieces and Breeches," by qualifying Robinson's claim of "the great natural equalities." Opera may be built on that equality, but it wasn't built on men's and women's voices equally. The first operatic divinities were castrated men who sang in the soprano and alto registers, first in the church and later on the opera stage, to the complete exclusion of women from the opera stage in Rome and the Papal States and to the limitation and hindrance of women singers' careers in most European states (except perhaps France, which was less affected by the rage for castrati). Women's soprano voices were assumed inferior, in part because the majority of female singers were not *trained* as well as the castrati.

(Similarly, in the nineteenth century, the voices of African-American women were consistently judged to be inferior when in reality they were, of course, simply less trained; these women did not have the same access to good teachers nor to the opera house itself that white women did. This lack of opportunity and therefore visibility may be one reason that there are so few fictional representatives of black opera divas, why, despite the existence of African-American opera singers, the "opera diva" as a cultural icon is consistently constructed as white. Contemporary African-American writers seem less inclined to explore issues of voice by featuring opera singers than jazz, blues, or gospel divas, traditions rooted in African-American culture. Examples of this tradition are Pilate in Toni Morrison's *Song of Solomon*, Joy in Marsha Hunt's eponymous novel, Zora in Terry McMillan's *Disappearing Acts*, and Shug Avery in Alice Walker's *The Color Purple*; we hope that someone will give this tradition the scholarly attention it deserves. Finally, while the opera diva can be read as a figure of white privilege, she is also consistently othered, as we show, along ethnic rather than racial lines. She is most often constructed, especially in the masculinist tradition, as Italian, as, in other words, a dark caucasian who is excessive, transgressive, stupid, loud-mouthed.)

In "Pieces and Breeches" we show how the stereotypes associated with the prima donna—vanity, competitiveness, self-absorption—were originally applied to castrati and how the castrati phenomenon affected women singers' access to training and roles. We suggest as well that as the practice of castrating boys waned in the eighteenth century, women singers inherited from the castrati not only their operatic roles and the public's fascination, adulation, and censure but also the role of serving as opera's premier figure of gender and sexual ambiguity, reversal, and disorder. Only when the castrati were gone can we say that opera recognized (was forced to recognize?) the "equality" between men's and women's voices, and we argue that the symbolic significance of this shift was not lost on two of the nineteenth century's greatest women writers, George Sand and George Eliot. In the opera house, women's voices were not only heard but celebrated. In the opera house women were not only needed but, with the passing of the castrati, positively irreplaceable—as women, as artists, as professionals. In the opera house women's voices thus had authority, or displayed, in Robinson's terms, (the promise of) equality.

After a survey of the masculinist tradition in chapter 2, "Singing His Mind Away," we open chapter 3, "The Sirens Avenged," with an extended look at George Eliot's verse drama *Armgart*,[7] which we see as one of the earliest texts in an alternative, revisionary representational tradition that we lay out in that chapter. Many years ago, in *Literary Women* Ellen Moers recognized the importance of the diva figure for Eliot, Sand, and Cather, but we make wider claims than she in discussing their texts as early examples of a specific representational tradition (there are so many diva novels we are tempted to call them a subgenre) that extends from the mid-nineteenth century to the present and is, further, a fairly explicit counterdiscourse to the masculinist tradition that figures divas as sirens or vessels or both. Most women writers, and a few men, offer a very different—we want to say, deliberately different—diva. Their texts explore what it means for a woman to "have a voice." Voice becomes there a metaphor of and vehicle for female empowerment both on stage and off—for, that is, "voice" in every sense of that word. In other words, we are most interested in how these representations construct the diva's voice as a political instrument. Some of the narratives in this tradition see the voice in more essentialist terms than we do, but even as these texts see the voice as authentic self-expression, for example, they discuss this expression in political terms. For us, essentialist and performative notions of the diva's voice intersect at the site of the social and political.

Most divas in texts by women are dedicated to their work, sometimes to the exclusion of sexual relationships. Unlike Olympia and du Maurier's Trilby, they are self-made women. Outside of detective novels, we can't think of any novel since *Robinson Crusoe* that devotes so many pages to the protagonist's work as Cather's *Song of the Lark* and Marcia Davenport's *Of Lena Geyer*. Seductive and hypersexual in the masculinist tradition, the diva here has little time for or interest in romance, little time or energy for sex. She is less interested in seducing and harming men than in securing a share of traditionally masculine power and privilege for herself and other women. In other words, while masculinist discourse is preoccupied with what the diva and her voice do to men, the counterdiscourse is concerned with what the diva does for women. The diva's voice is a political force. It asserts equality and earns authority in the public, masculine world (one reason that, of course, masculine discourse must diminish it, other it, confine it, label it and the woman who possesses and wields it as "unnatural" or "demented"). It also serves to connect the diva with other women. Again and again in these texts the diva's voice moves and transforms women (and a few men), gives them (or helps them to "discover" in themselves) new vision, strength, desire.[8]

We are not arguing in this study that the diva's voice serves as a metaphor for some kind of essential or authentic unified selfhood. While many of the texts we discuss flirt with such a notion, there is throughout these narratives, as there is in diva discourse in general, oppositional, deconstructive talk about voice loss and breakage, as well as self-alienating rhetoric about "the voice" and its vulnerability, that counters essentialist conceptions of the voice. Singers constantly confess/complain that their voices are not fully under their control. Historical singer Emma Calvé even referred to hers as a "visitor" in her 1922 autobiography: "I do not know why it stays with me, except that I have 'entreated it' kindly, and that I have tried not to be an unworthy hostess" (249). The religious language that permeates the passage from which this is excerpted may at first seem to imply that although the voice may not be essential, it might be transcendent, but this passage opens a chapter called "Health and Hygiene," which links again the voice with the physical, the material, the worked for. This reluctance fully to essentialize the voice is of a piece with the revisionary tradition's general tendency, most obvious in these texts' repeated stress on performance, to see the human being as constructed subject. The logical end of this conception of the subject, we argue in the final chapters of this study, can be seen in the work of three contemporary singers outside the operatic tradition who consciously construct themselves, and are constructed by others, in the tradition of the operatic diva.

(A theoretical throat clearing, with apologies to literate readers. A survey of the diva representations we discuss in this book may seem to imply that we are in fact constructing two conflicting strands of counter-discursive representations: on the one hand a, to many theorists dated, feminist one, which presents the diva as an icon of powerful womanhood and thereby flirts with an essentialism that we should, to be up-to-date, reject, in part because it recalls pre-poststructuralist Anglo-American feminist criticism; and, on the other, a queer reading of the diva as an icon of performativity. To our eyes, the diva may have the potential to mediate these conflicting theoretical positions. At any rate, we resist the neatness of these distinctions and the categories on which they are based. First, an icon is an icon, after all, and second, women writers, as we show, were talking about the diva's performativity long before academics began talking about performativity. Third, lesbian and gay identifications of the diva are multiple—not just with her performativity but with her large body, with her anguish and triumph, and with her empowered marginality.

Finally, we are uneasy about the neatness of the very essentialist/constructionist distinctions we nevertheless employ. We have sympathy with David Halperin's acknowledgment, "I don't think there's any way that I, or anyone else who grew up in bourgeois America when I did, could ever believe in what I'm saying [i.e., that homosexuality and heterosexuality are cultural constructs] with the same degree of conviction with which I believe, despite everything I've said, in the categories of heterosexuality and homosexuality" (53). In other words, though intellectually committed to theories of cultural construction—at least as incredibly valuable heuristic tools [like good literature, they make the familiar strange, and therefore "seeable"]—we, given our own cultural construction, "believe" in the category of woman and so, like many of the women writers we discuss, take pleasure in the diva as figure of powerful, independent womanhood.)

$\mathcal{A}$s we have suggested, both the masculinist and the revisionary traditions agree that the diva makes visible the seams and fissures of a culture's gender and sexual ideology. A quick look at how the female singer's throat has been figured and read illustrates the diva's power to disrupt traditional gender categories and oppositions.

From antiquity to the scene in *Truth or Dare* in which Warren Beatty wants Madonna's throat examined off camera, the female singer's throat has consistently been linked with her vagina.[9] On the other hand, the diva's throat has also been repeatedly figured in phallic terms. Of soprano Angelica Catalani (1779–1848) a contemporary marvels, "Her throat seems endowed (as has been remarked by medical men) with a power of expansion and muscular motion by no means usual." (Pleasants 111). Assessing Jenny Lind's voice, her contemporary Henry Chorley commented on "the disproportions of her organ" (1:305). And finally, there is, of course, the convention of talking about a singer's "vocal endowment."

These figural and rhetorical dissonances are symptomatic of the diva's power to disrupt traditional gender oppositions. She has a loud voice in the public world;[10] she quite literally wears the pants. In the masculinist tradition this makes her man-eating and man-aping. In her discussion of the "lesbian phallus," a notion that resonates with our phallicized diva, Judith Butler quotes Lacan's reading of Freud's description of a threatening female mouth: "the abyss of the feminine organ from which all life emerges . . . in which everything is swallowed up and no less the image of death in which everything comes to in the end" (*Bodies That Matter* 258–259). The diva dentata.

Women writers have a different vision of the singer's throat. Eliot's Armgart declares that she carries her revenge in her throat and speculates that if she had not had a voice she might have become a murderer. Throat here is not consuming abyss but vessel for anger and vehicle for empowerment.[11]

As the diva—by virtue of her social positioning as the exception to feminine silence and powerlessness and by the fact that she performs both femininity and masculinity—unsettles gender oppositions, so she breaks down another disciplinary and normative opposition, the hetero/homo opposition. If you are female, how do you describe what your body does when you hear the diva sing? If you are a diva, how do you represent your relations with your longtime female companion? Female eroticism is an inextricable part of the opera world, and as many of these chapters show, the world of divas and diva worshipers, both "real" and fictional, is a realm of unstable gender relations, diffuse desires, and "chaotic" sexualities.

What fun, we think. But not everyone sees upsetting sexual categories as harmless, or fun, or freeing. The forces that demand compulsory heterosexuality still reign. "Diva Truths, Diva Lies, Diva Lives" looks at the life narratives, autobiographies and biographies, of historical singers to isolate the conventional representations and conventions of representing the diva in these genres while paying particular attention to the way lesbianism serves as a locus for a set of issues, insinuations, and denunciations that often follow women on the stage, women exposed in a public (man's) role. In these texts, issues of gender and genre intersect in ways that mark historical shifts in the ideology of gender and sexuality. Writing early in the twentieth century, Luisa Tetrazzini proudly acknowledges her ambition and disinterest in romance in the manner of the fictional divas of the period by Cather and Davenport; she constructs her autobiography using the conventions of the boy's adventure story. But divas (especially white divas) who came of age professionally shortly after World War II respond to that era's greater ambivalence about women working outside the home by working hard to construct themselves as accidental divas, as "natural women" reluctantly famous and relentlessly heterosexual.

Diva biographies and autobiographies, especially more recent ones, have commonalities, ideologically and rhetorically, with more popular genres. Opera began as an elite form, the entertainment of dukes and princes. In the late eighteenth and early nineteenth centuries the audience became increasingly middle-class. Today, ticket prices may be increasingly out of reach for many middle-class opera lovers, but opera is as close as the television set—via either public broadcasting or the video store down the street. Is opera elite or popular entertainment today? Or is it both? Surely the holders of season boxes at the Met are not the same fans who go to hear Luciano Pavarotti, miked, at a football stadium. We want to suggest that as opera seems these days to cross boundaries between elite and popular entertainment in a way that calls these categories into question, so too do divas. There are so many divas, both sirenic and feminist, in one genre of popular fiction, the detective novel, that we devote an entire chapter to them, "Divas, Death, and Detectives." In "Divas Do the Movies," we trace some of the history of "real" divas who moved from the opera stage to the sound stage and look, as well, at films about divas. Like opera and its divas, divahood has escaped its elite precincts and "descended" to the realm of pop music and culture. We close our study with a look at three divas, pop and pomo, who quite explicitly evoke, invoke, exploit, refute, rework the stereotypes of opera's prima donna. (The) Madonna constructs herself as whore, as siren, while Annie Lennox, in the tradition of more recent diva autobiographers, works in her *Diva* recording and video to construct herself as both not-a-diva and not-Madonna. We give the final word to singer-composer Diamanda Galas, who explicitly claims that her voice is a political instrument. Dubbed the "diva of disease" by the press, she has written and performed an operatic requiem, *Plague Mass*, for persons in what she calls the "AIDS community."[12] In that piece and others, she pushes her three-and-one-half octave operatically trained voice to the edge of ruin as she screams out her protest, personal and political, at the intolerable number of AIDS-related deaths that have touched her life. A timely and appropriate culmination to the history of the diva figure we sketch here, Galas is a singer who understands that all performance is politics and who appropriates the power of the siren, not to seduce but to protest, not to destroy but to mourn, not to charm but to defy the institutionalization of intolerance.

(A concluding theoretico-methodologico, somewhat boring, post-script, which we invite readers to skip: the diva is consistently figured as promiscuous, and we acknowledge that our critical method in this book is likewise sluttish. As we have suggested in this introduction, and as we suggest in other places in this text, our subject, representations of the diva, can play a role in a number of theoretical debates. We have tended not to exploit the moments in our text when this becomes clear, tended not to expand these moments into occasions for more full-fledged interventions in those debates. The primary business of this book is to demonstrate how widespread a cultural icon the diva is and to track her significance in different modes of cultural production and for persons variously socially situated, and we therefore argue extensively from example. [Others can, perhaps with the help of what we lay out in this text, use the diva for more extended and explicit theorizing.] Current theoretical work has been essential to this enterprise, and we trust that our academic colleagues see the extent to which we have benefited from the theoretical work of others, but we tend to use such work situationally, tactically rather than strategically, taking the theoretical work that best helps us to construct a fertile reading of a given representation or aspect of diva history and to explore as many of its complexities as possible. Sometimes this means using in the same book, sometimes in the same chapter, work by scholars who represent opposing positions in various important theoretical debates.)

A colleague left a message on our answering machine: "I have a student paper here that spells 'prima donna' 'pre-Madonna.'" It is to the pre-Madonna divas that we now turn.

CHAPTER 1

Pieces and Breeches

*For even though the typical diva is usually perceived
to be exotic and larger than life, and even though the
nightingale is a small, drab bird, comparisons between
the two would seem to be inevitable, given the heavenly
quality of the nightingale's voice. Isn't Hans
Andersen's story "The Nightingale" truly a paean to his
love for Jenny Lind? And wasn't Adelina Patti reported
to have eaten, every night before retiring, a sandwich
containing the tongues of twelve nightingales?*
—Kathryn Davis, The Girl Who Trod on a Loaf

*F*or the soundtrack of the film *Farinelli, Il Castrato*, The Institute for Musical and Acoustic Research in Paris re-created the sound of a castrato by electronically combining the voices of a male countertenor and a female soprano.[1] In a nice historical irony, the castrato sound described by contemporary listeners as ethereal, otherworldly, disembodied, superhuman is now produced quite literally out of body—and electronic "morphing" is, of course, a much less painful way of creating the sound than the original process by which castrati were produced. Lovers and scholars of the voice have long lamented the loss of the castrato voice and expressed curiosity to hear it (even as they point out that they are not advocating a return to castration). *Farinelli, Il Castrato* may provide the closest approximation to the castrato sound that they will ever hear. We doubt that many of the curious and nostalgic will like it; after all, voice lovers have been arguing over the merits of the technological engineering of voices since the birth of the gramophone.[2]

Castrati, then, with their ethereal and otherworldly voices, were the first operatic "divinities"; they were also the first singers to be abused and stereotyped. If we think of a diva as a star soprano or mezzo given to tantrums, vanities, and all manner of other excesses, then the first divas were castrati. If we think of a diva as a figure who disrupts, through her voice and the freedoms it gives her, the binary oppositions of the traditional sex-gender system, then the castrato, with his high, feminine register and his masculine vocal power, is an apt precursor. Women singers seem to have inherited the prima donna stereotypes from castrati just as they inherited many of their roles—roles both operatic, like Gluck's Orpheus, and cultural, as transgressive figures who blur boundaries and refuse discipline.[3]

Women, in the shape of the Medusa, also inherited the responsibility for castration, but the first castrato seems untraceable. "The origin of the castrati is shrouded in mystery," begins Angus Heriot's history (9). Attempting to locate the Italian city where castrations were performed, Charles Burney reports that he was repeatedly sent on to the next city. The Milanese sent him to Venice, the Venetians to Bologna, where he was directed to Florence, and then to Rome, and finally to Naples (312). We have thus no first castrato, and a cultural silence surrounds his creation. It is as if castrati were, like God, always already there, occupying the place/moment of primal sex and gender fluidity before the fall into a normative code of sex-gender difference. How else to account for contemporary descriptions of the castrato voice as high like a woman's, strong like a man's and also otherworldly, superhuman, disembodied? Simultaneously celebrated and othered, revered and reviled, the castrato was central to the reinforcement of a system of sex and gender division precisely because he was constructed as someone outside that system.

In place of the Medusa myth as the originary narrative for male castration, we are tempted to argue that the original "castrating females" (and also "castrated"—Jesus, after all, spoke of eunuchs for the kingdom of heaven) were those patriarchs in skirts, the popes. Castration was, perhaps, the price patriarchy paid to keep women silent and its authority intact. "As in all congregations of God's people, women should keep silent at the meeting," St. Paul advised the Corinthians (I Cor. 14.33–34), and his namesake Pope Paul IV (1555–1559) codified Paul's advice by officially banning women from singing in St. Peter's. Church choirs depended on boys and adult male falsettists to sing soprano and alto parts, but as monody gave way to increasingly complicated polyphony, more powerful voices and mature musicians (especially singers who would not be lost once their voices changed) were needed for upper-register parts. A Spanish castrato is said to have entered the Sistine Chapel choir in 1562; the pope formally authorized recruitment of castrati for the papal choir in 1589, but the Church did not officially acknowledge that some of its sopranos were castrati until 1599 (Rosselli 34). This lag in time between employment—some early castrati probably passed as falsettists[4]—and official acknowledgment is characteristic of the Church's attitudes about and dealings with castrati. By banning women from singing in churches and supporting centuries-old arguments that they should be kept off the public stage as well, the Church created the market for castrati even as it officially condemned the practice of castration and threatened excommunication for anyone known to perform the operation.[5] Yet, arguing that victims of the practice should not be further victimized, the Church gave the most promising boys brought to it the best musical training available in its own conservatories. Historians estimate that at the height of this practice four thousand boys on the Italian peninsula were castrated annually. Only a small number achieved major careers in opera or the church. Most spent their days singing and/or teaching in provincial churches; many lost their voices (some didn't have any to begin with) and were forced to return to their villages.

By the early seventeenth century, castrati were singing in both chapels and courts throughout Italy and southern Germany (Rosselli 34), but it was as singers of the then nascent form of opera that they gained their greatest celebrity and, for a lucky few, great wealth. In the eighteenth century, 70 percent of male opera singers were castrati (Heriot 31). The undisputed stars of opera from the mid-seventeenth to the mid-eighteenth century ("Long live the knife, the blesssed knife," screamed frenzied fans), castrati were celebrated and abused—as half-men, capons, geldings, and monsters of vanity, extravagance, and bad temper—from Naples to London.

Until the morphing of Farinelli, we had only texts, contemporary accounts, through which to hear/imagine what Koestenbaum calls the castrati's "scandalous vocal plenitude" and to understand the rage for their voices (*QT* 159). These accounts repeatedly stress the startling mixture of choirboy sweetness and adult power in the voice, as well as its strength, flexibility, and brilliance. During an 1891 visit to the Sistine Chapel, soprano Emma Calvé heard one of the last castrati, Mustapha. "He had an exquisite high tenor voice, truly angelic, neither masculine nor yet feminine in type—deep, subtle, poignant in its vibrant intensity. . . . He had certain curious notes which he called his fourth voice—strange, sexless tones, superhuman, uncanny!" she wrote (64). (Fascinated, she asked him to teach her this "fourth voice" technique, and after three years of work she was finally able to duplicate it.) Phallic economies generally uphold bigger as better, but in the case of the castrato, the procedure that usually kept his endowment smaller than average also insured the retention of his small boyhood larynx with its thin folds. This kept the voice flexible and agile as well as high, even as the body matured and gained greater lung capacity. Lacking some of the hormones that send the body signals to stop growing, castrati were often taller than average—in a number of contemporary caricatures they tower over other figures, huge phallic pillars ironically unmanned. Thanks to a combination of physiology and training they were also barrel-chested; some castrati could, it was said, hold a note for a minute or longer.

This combination of agility and power produced a voice capable of extraordinary vocal pyrotechnics. The age of the castrato was the age of the greatest florid singing, an era that cheered improvisation and embellishment and privileged voice over text and dramatic continuity. The castrato's voice was the spectacle. Responding to both the supply of singers and the public taste, most eighteenth-century composers of vocal music wrote for castrati, and this music, both sacred and operatic, is "some of the most glorious and challenging music ever written for the human voice" (Oberlin 18). Mozart, for example, wrote the soprano showpiece *Exultate Jubilate* for the castrato Rauzzini.

Two features—we think they are related—of the castrato story are of special interest to us: the satire and abuse heaped on castrati, much of which precedes and parallels the accusations later made against divas, and early opera's cross-gender casting, which often called for castrati to sing women's roles. Such prima donna stereotypes as vanity, luxury, temper, unreasonableness, competitiveness, and licentiousness were common accusations against castrati, and the castrati who lived up to these stereotypes are, of course, generally better remembered than their less excessive brethren. Castrati rivalries as intense as that between divas Faustina Bordoni and Francesca Cuzzoni sometimes turned an opera into a singing competition. Farinelli and Bernacchi transformed a 1727 performance of Orlandini's *La Fedelta Coronta* into a spectacle of dueling arias. After Farinelli sang a cadenza in which he pulled out all the stops, Bernacchi stepped up and in his aria duplicated all Farinelli's ornaments—singing them better than Farinelli did—and added extra of his own for good measure. The castrato Caffarelli was known for dueling off stage with swords and was famous for his tantrums and on stage deportment; in 1741 he was thrown in jail for "disturbing the other performers, acting in a manner bordering on lasciviousness with one of the female singers, conversing with the spectators in the boxes from the stage, ironically echoing whichever member of the company was singing an aria, and finally refusing to sing in the *ripieno*" (quoted in Christiansen, *Prima Donna* 34–35). Marchesi was famous for his vanity.

He demanded that a favorite aria written expressly for him be interpolated into every opera in which he performed (not an uncommon practice; so many singers demanded the inclusion of such signature pieces that they were called "suitcase arias"), and also required that his first entrance always be on horseback and accompanied by trumpet fanfare. Striking here is the way these gestures of excess were so clearly (and more completely than would ever be possible in our era, given as it is to dramatic continuity) part of the performance. Vanity and competitiveness were staged. "Castrato," like "prima donna," was a role to play.

Castrati generally sang two sorts of roles, the "first man" roles of *opera seria*—noble lovers, warriors, rulers—which exploited the ethereal and superhuman sound of the castrato voice, and women's roles *en travesti*. In Rome and the Papal States, where women were banned from the public stage until the close of the eighteenth century, female characters were always played by castrati—except when women pretending to be castrati managed to fool the examining priest with a strap-on. (Such a passing woman could have been cast as a woman who was required, through various machinations of plot, to masquerade as a man for part of the opera.) There were castrati who specialized in female parts, and a few even crossdressed off the stage as well. Some of these were hearty heterosexuals: by arriving for assignations in costume, a castrato named Consolino is said to have carried on an affair with a married woman without arousing her husband's suspicion (Heriot 27).

In places where women were allowed to perform in public theaters—at the cost of being thought courtesans, of course—cross-gender casting could be even more elaborate. Early opera privileged the high voice, no matter the sex of the body producing it. First man parts were generally soprano roles, sung either by castrati or, especially after 1700, women *en travesti*. Historian John Rosselli argues that this stress on the high voice had as much to do with deeply rooted cultural values as passing fashion: "'Soprano' means 'higher,' a notion not taken lightly by a society that was at once hierarchical-minded and used to displaying hierarchical order in forms perceived by the senses" (34). Traditional gender hierarchies could be reinscribed within this high-low vocal hierarchy, however; the original casting of Monteverdi's *L'Incoronazione di Poppea* had the male singers, sopranos, singing in a higher range than that of the female singers. With the addition of women singers, then, baroque opera provided even greater opportunity for gender play and reversal than Elizabethan drama. Male sopranos regularly played Venus and Cleopatra, and women played heroes like Achilles. This is not to say that all these gender reversals, which reveal the usually hidden gap between anatomical sex and gender performance, were necessarily progressive; theatrical cross-dressing can recuperate as easily as it can challenge a culture's gender ideology.[6]

Rome, wrote Casanova, "forces every man to become a pederast" (Heriot 55). The occasion for the observation was a 1762 trip to Rome during which he saw a performance by a castrato:

> In a well-made corset, he had the waist of a nymph . . . his breast was in no way inferior, either in form or beauty, to any woman's; and it was above all by this means that the monster made such ravages. Though one knew the negative nature of this unfortunate, curiosity made one glance at his chest, and an inexpressible charm acted upon one, so that you were madly in love before you realized it. . . . When he walked about the stage during the *ritornello* of the aria he was to sing, his step was majestic and at the same time voluptuous; and when he favoured the boxes with his glances, the tender and modest rolling of his black eyes brought a ravishment to the heart. It was obvious that he hoped to inspire the love of those who liked him as a man, and probably would not have done so as a woman. (Heriot 54–55)

Casanova anticipates contemporary theorists by suggesting that the homosocial bonds through which masculine power is solidified and sustained depend on inciting and structuring homoerotic desire, desire between men for men. He understands that the performance context here exemplifies and enacts cultural ideals and structures. The singer's breast "was in no way inferior . . . to any woman's," and yet every one knows that this is a man. The spectator watches a performance of Womanhood, a cultural ideal and ideological construction. Casanova looks to the castrato's breast and not his groin because the castrato himself is a fetish. In other words, what is on display here is the possibility that men can substitute for women, that men can be better women than women can. As Casanova's desire for the castrato implies, woman's presence is unnecessary; as the castrato's desire for male desire makes clear, this is an exchange between men—about women, about their possible superfluity—that bonds men.

Not surprisingly, castrati were regularly accused of tempting others to practices that would fall under our current term of "homosexuality."[7] Producers of that "disembodied voice" were relentlessly figured as all body. Castrato sex lives, like those of women in general and divas in particular, were the subject of much public interest. That castrati often occupied a woman's place on stage might have invited some of this; the association of actresses with licentiousness preceded castrati by centuries, and this taint was perhaps transferred to them. But of course persons who appear to lack phallic erotic power, who are assumed to have little or nothing to show, are always the subject of talk, especially talk that constructs them as threats. (We think here of Michael Jackson, a male singer with a high voice who is simultaneously constructed as figuratively castrated—gay, feminine, unable to manage marriage—and as monstrously predatory.)

As a man with a high voice, the castrato was a disrupter of gender categories even before he donned a dress; he was also figured as a disrupter of the opposition between different-sex/same-sex eroticisms that gender oppositions help to enforce.[8] Worries that castrati recruited other men to same-sex erotic practices paralleled worries that women would find them irresistible. Supposedly "sexless," the castrato was also cast as sexual virtuoso, a figure of excessive and polymorphous sexuality. Such anxiety underpins *Il Castrato*, a monody composed for castrato voice by Fabrizio Fontana in which the singer claims that the absence of testicles enhances sexual performance (Rosselli 50). Charles Ancillon's *Eunuchism Display'd*, published in London in 1718 from a French original, offers itself as a response to a report that a young woman, having fallen in love with a castrato, desired to marry him; it warns that such marriages "could not but be attended with dismal Consequences." Like so much anti-castrato discourse, Ancillon's text labors to construct the castrato as not-a-male and to convince readers that he has nothing to offer. (Of course the cultural irony here, an irony that generates much of the anxiety these texts try to address, is precisely that male power and privilege rests on next to nothing, on only a few small anatomical bits.) But, as Beth Kowaleski-Wallace points out, the worry fueling the polemic is the possibility that "nothing" might just be what women want: "The imagined sexual liaison of the castrato and woman introduces the possibility of a non-phallic, female sexual pleasure which is not linked to reproduction" (158); loving a castrato might just be the first step down the slippery slope to Sapphism.[9]

Not only might women want nothing (except their own sexual autonomy), but they might themselves do the spending—on opera tickets, on wax figures or miniatures of the castrato of the moment, on gifts for their favorite castrato.[10] In a pamphlet attributed to the famous courtesan Teresia Constantia "Con" Phillips published in London in 1735, "The Happy Courtezan: Or, the Prude demolish'd An Epistle from the celebrated Mrs.

C—— P——, to the Angelic Signior Far——n——lli," the speaker plots a
fantasy in which she and Farinelli run off and enjoy together the treasures
lavished on him by the "Prudes," women who desire him precisely because
he is a few pieces short of a "whole man."

> They know, that safe with thee they may remain,
> Enjoy Love's pleasures yet avoid the Pain:
> Each, blest in thee, continue still a Maid;
> Nor of a tell-tale Bantling be afraid:
> This, by Experience, know the Prudes full well,
> Who're always virtuous, if they never swell.
>
> . . . .
>
> Eunuchs can give uninterrupted Joys,
> Without the shameful curse of Girls and Boys:
> The violated Prude her shape retains,
> A vestal in the publick Eye remains.

As the "who're"/whore wordplay implies, the castrato's paradoxical status
as man/not-man is transferred to the woman, who, with him, can be a virtuous, even Vestal, whore. Castrato sexuality is as much a breakdown of
moral categories as gender categories. From a woman's perspective, the
castrato offers a scandalous sexual as well as vocal plenitude: painless
physical joys "uninterrupted" and the possibility of retaining one's virtue
while having the freedom and pleasure of throwing it away.

> Well-knowing Eunuchs can [the Prudes'] Wants supply,
> And more than Bragging Boasters satisfy;
> Whose Pow'r to please the Fair expires too fast,
> While F——lli stands it to the last.

Not-man is transformed—by his lack—into Superman, and only supermen
can hope to keep up with women's larger appetites.

Some scholars have taken for granted that Phillips penned the poem;
most have not. Penciled at the bottom of the catalog card for "The Happy
Courtezan" in the Folger Shakespeare Library, whose copy we quote here,
is an anonymous note declaring that the author of the pamphlet is certainly
not Phillips and that the attribution is satiric. Who wrote this note, and on
what evidence, we wonder. A long-ago scholar who reasoned that Phillips
would not make herself part of the joke? A librarian reluctant to entertain
the possibility that a woman, even a courtesan, could speak and fantasize

so boldly and baldly about what women want? We lament that Phillips probably didn't write the lines but take pleasure in the fantasy that she did.

One woman who knew what she wanted, and wanted a castrato, was Dorothy Maunsell, who married the castrato Giusto Tenducci and, in 1768, published an account of their persecution by her enraged father. As Heriot notes, the narrative, with its persecuted and confined heroine and arrogant gentry, reads like a Richardson novel (186). Mrs. Tenducci's representation of herself also recalls those Richardsonian heroines who make it nearly impossible to tell how much naiveté and how much (unconscious?) calculation figure in both their actions and self-presentations. According to the text, her father forcibly separated the couple shortly after their marriage. The family accused Tenducci of seducing and kidnapping her and had him thrown into prison; she was similarly confined against her will in a private home by persons associated with her father. After Tenducci was released from prison, her father tried to make it impossible for him to see his wife or to earn a living.

Dorothy Tenduccci introduces her narrative by claiming that "the punishment has far exceeded the fault: for whatever errors may have supposed to have been committed, are of the kind which generally meets with some indulgence" (3). She closes by accusing her father of "persecuting me with all the rigor due to the most heinous crimes, and still more unjustly pursuing, with an implacable spirit of resentment, a person innocent of every fault, but that of having complied with my request and inclination" (66). Elopement being, as Dorothy Tenducci suggests, a fairly common transgression, readers who come to her narrative without knowing who, or more to the point "what," Tenducci is will no doubt sympathize with her sense that her father has grossly overreacted. And readers of *A True and Genuine Narrative of Mr. and Mrs. Tenducci* won't learn that Tenducci is a castrato, because his wife never mentions it; the "fault"—whether one reads it as lacking testicles or marrying someone so lacking—is not, then, from one perspective a "common" one. Dorothy Maunsell's female reluctance to be the object of male sexuality seems a more common "fault" than her culture is willing to acknowledge, however. By eliding Tenducci's castration and concentrating on clearing him of the accusation that he is a seducer, the text reclaims full vigorous "manhood" for him while implying that castration is too small a thing to be mentioned, and too small a thing to keep them from legal marriage.

Castrati were often described as "unnatural," but in this text it is the enraged and controlling patriarch who, according to his daughter, is the source of the perverse and unnatural. Readers should be alarmed "to see in our persons the law of the land trampled upon; the authority of M———y influenced, and perverted, to serve the private and unnatural revenge of individuals" (66). Her father might have argued that his efforts were, rather, to renaturalize his daughter, to make her appear "natural," as an innocent who had been exploited rather than a woman who "unnaturally" asserted her own will. At one point, the family tricks Tenducci into turning her letters over to them, letters that, according to the narrative, clearly show that the elopement was her idea. Without the letters, Tenducci cannot defend himself against the charge of seduction and kidnapping. Dorothy Tenducci's narrative stands in the place of the lost letters by repeatedly stressing her desire for the castrato and her will to marry him. "Here (I blush to own it!) I gave him greater encouragement than was perhaps consistent with prudence; but I was very young, inexperienced, and overcome with the strength of my attachment," she writes of their first meetings (5–6). A short time later, her father and friends urged on her "a marriage which was perfectly disagreeable to me. I persisted in refusing, and they in tormenting me to comply"; meeting Tenducci a short time later, she finds "every tender sentiment, which I had formerly felt, was again renewed; and these conspired with thoughts of avoiding a marriage for which I had conceived the greatest horror and aversion, to bring me to the determination of marrying Tenducci, sooner than I otherwise should have done. This design I immediately imparted to him, and ordered that every necessary preparation should be made with the greatest expedition"(6). Loving a castrato is again represented as a way to attain, and maintain, sexual autonomy.

Figure of gender disruption, the castrato, by his presence, makes possible gender reversals. In *A True and Genuine Narrative* the castrato, rather than the young woman, is apparently carried off. Like Con Phillips's Prudes, Dorothy Tenducci knows what she wants and makes sure she gets it. Her father's rigorous persecution and his attempt to cast her as victim rather than agent suggest that he understands his daughter's actions as a threat to the phallic power and traditional gender relations on which his own status as patriarch depends.

A final reversal: Dorothy Tenducci later had two children, which Tenducci claimed were his. Did the castrato finally fail to satisfy or was he Superman? Did Dorothy Tenducci get what she wanted but not what she expected? Tenducci himself claimed that his castration had been incomplete, which ironically made him complete.

Dorothy Tenducci writes that her desire for Tenducci grew in response to his help in the cultivation of her singing voice. Frustration with the obstacles placed in the way of fulfilling that desire and the need to voice publicly what her father would censor—that she desired the castrato—led her to take up her pen, to find and cultivate her own narrative voice. Loving Tenducci, in other words, turned her into a writer. Other women writers have also found in the castrato a vehicle for the exploration and disruption of traditional gender, class, and sexual categories and hierarchies.[11] In Fanny Burney's *Cecilia* (1782), the young heroine, on the verge of social and sexual adulthood, hears the famous castrato Pacchierotti (historical singers figure prominently in fictional narratives that feature castrati and divas): "She found herself by nothing so deeply impressed as by the plaintive and beautiful simplicity with which Pacchierotti uttered the affecting repetition of *sono innocente!*" (61–62).

Cecilia's own pleasure and desire lead her to become a secret watcher of the pleasure of another: "She could not avoid taking notice of an old gentleman . . . and during the songs of Pacchierotti he sighed so deeply, that Cecilia, struck by his uncommon sensibility to the power of the music, involuntarily watched him, whenever her mind was sufficiently at liberty to attend to any emotions but her own" (62). Both male and female listener give themselves up to the castrato, figure of disruption and reversal. The scene functions primarily to connect Cecilia and the old gentleman, who figures as a sort of moral monitor in the novel. He tends to watch spectacles—theatrical and social—from the margins, a privileged place of epistemological power. But the triangular relation the scene constructs makes possible a series of gender as well as specular inversions. The castrato occupies the traditionally feminine role of spectacle on display; in the privacy thus created for the woman, she experiences, for a moment, the masculine prerogative of being the agent rather than the object of the gaze and in that way places the man she watches, the old gentleman, in the same feminine subject position as the castrato.

Burney knew Pacchierotti and carried on a correspondence with him. In her analysis of their relationship, Kowaleski-Wallace speculates that Burney found in the castrato a model for the social construction of gender and an image of her own position as a woman writer: "Like him, the woman writer could be said to experience a culturally induced handicap. . . . Like him as well, she finds in those adverse circumstances the conditions which will produce great art" (163). The identification is not with his castration as such, Kowaleski-Wallace argues, but with his social positioning and status as spectacle: "What matters is not the fact of his 'mutilation' but the resulting social perception which invests so much erotic energy in his body at the expense of his soul" (163).

We glimpse here some of the reasons that women writers have been interested in the castrato and that their treatment of him may sometimes differ from the nostalgic preoccupation with injury, lack, loss, and effeminization that pervades male-authored texts like *Sarrasine* and *S/Z*. It is hard to be anxious over the vulnerability of phallic power if one is often on the wrong end of it, hard to mourn the loss of a phallic privilege one has never had, nor even, perhaps, wished for. Anti-castrato discourse demonized and marginalized the castrato in order to reinforce the traditional gender and sexual codes destabilized by both his existence and the responses of others to him. But the castrato can also serve as a vehicle for exploring what it's like to be constructed and confined by those codes or, alternatively, what pleasures and pains are available to those who live, by choice or necessity, outside those codes.

Vernon Lee (pseudonym of Violet Paget) is known best among music scholars for her study of Italian music and theater, *Studies of the Eighteenth Century in Italy* (1887), and among literary critics for her fiction. She brings these interests together in her ghost story "A Wicked Voice" (1890), about a composer, a disciple of Wagner named Magnus, who is haunted by, and finally falls in love with, the voice of the famous eighteenth-century castrato Zaffirino. An expert on eighteenth-century music, Magnus keeps secret his motivation: he has studied the period the better to hold it in contempt. He wants the public to know him as a "follower of the great master of the Future" rather than the "miserable singing masters of the past" (196). Over the course of the story, Magnus becomes obsessed with the haunting voice—he hears it all around him and in his head when he is trying to work—and finally realizes that "this voice was what I cared most for in all the world" (234). This recognition leads not to reconciliation but, apparently, to madness. The close of the tale finds Magnus, like Keats's knight, alone and palely loitering, longing to hear the voice again.

The tale can be read in a number of ways: as a story about the return of the repressed past, as an attempt to conjure up the bewitching and destabilizing power of the castrato voice for a readership who in 1890 had little chance of hearing it, or as an attack on Wagner, whose music Lee considered decadent, by constructing his disciple as an invert who falls in love with a voice that he repeatedly describes as "swelling," "piercing," and, in a more Paterian vein, "delicate, voluptuous . . . strange, exquisite" (234).[12] All these readings depend on taking Magnus at his word and seeing the voice as the source of his madness. But there are other strains on Magnus's psyche, the strain, for example, of leading a double life. Magnus is not just obsessed by the voice but revolted by this obsession. To find "sweet beyond words" what he held in contempt—"For what is the voice but the Beast calling, awakening that other Beast sleeping in the depths of mankind"— both shocks and shames Magnus, who has a reputation to protect (234, 198). He thus remains a closet lover of the voice. He speaks of suffering from a "moral malaria" (the phrase resonates with other conservative tropes that figure homosexuality as a moral pathology), but Magnus suffers from another moral disorder as well, hypocrisy. Paget was herself erotically attracted to women and lived at a time, the late nineteenth and early twentieth centuries, when medical and psychiatric discourses worked to solidify homoerotic feelings into a pathologized identity. From this perspective, it may be tempting to argue that the story is a symptom of Paget's own internalized homophobia; we see it, rather, as an allegory for the surprise (for some people, the discomfort) of recognition—of experiencing a desire one is supposed to be "superior" to, of finding oneself desiring what one has a deep (culturally schooled) investment in not desiring.

Paget's story closes with Magnus desiring the voice and feeling as though he has lost his inspiration: "I can never lay hold of my own inspiration. My head is filled with music which is certainly by me, since I have never heard it before, but which still is not my own, which I despise and abhor" (237). We don't learn whether Magnus ever comes to claim as his own the music in his head that he knows is by him, whether he comes to reconcile his passion with the identity he has constructed for himself. The tale only suggests the work that reconciliation will take, the obstacles it must overcome, the strong possibility that recognition can lead to paralysis as easily as it can free the subject to compose a new identity.

The castrato continues to be an attractive protagonist for women writers, but in Anne Rice's historical novel *A Cry to Heaven* (1982) the homoerotic has lost its frightening or maddening face. Tonio Treschi, possessed of a beautiful soprano voice and member of the Venetian ruling class, is forcibly castrated by his estranged and vengeful father and sent off to Naples with Guido Maffeo, a castrato singing master in Venice scouting for voices. Under Guido's tutelage, Tonio becomes a brilliant and famous singer; he also becomes Guido's lover.

As in so many other castrato narratives, Tonio's condition becomes the pretext for his, and the text's, meditation on masculinity. Shortly before his death, Tonio's grandfather tells him that manhood is performative:

"Make up your mind, Tonio, that you are a man . . . behave as if it were absolutely true and all else will then fall into place" (185). But knowing that gender is performative—Tonio not only acts the man while he is still a boy, but later, on stage, acts the woman as well—doesn't save Tonio from being haunted by the conventional codes of manhood. Knowing that he is seen as a half-man, he carries a stiletto and sometimes uses it. Nor does knowing that gender is a set of cultural prescriptions free Tonio from the code of masculine revenge and Oedipal violence: at the close of the novel, he sneaks back into Venice disguised as a woman and kills his father.

Through most of the novel, all Tonio can think of are his losses. His physical loss means social losses: of male privilege and of his place among the ruling elite of Venice. Guido offers him an alternative reading of his situation. After Tonio refuses the advances of a cardinal who is acting as their patron, Guido is impatient with his scruples and advises him to return to the cardinal and give him what he wants. Tonio accuses Guido of treating him as if he were "nothing but a whore from the streets," and Guido responds: "If you were a whore, you wouldn't be in this house, you wouldn't be fed and sheltered by the Cardinal. You are a castrato. . . . I would do it without hesitation if he wanted it from me" (356). Horrified and disgusted, Tonio accuses him of having "no honor, no creed, no decent sentiments":

> "Yes, yes, yes!" Guido said. . . . "Make me out a demon if you will,
> I tell you the configurations you place on all these things are lovely
> and meaningless. You are not bound by the rules of men. You are a
> castrato. You can do these things." (356–357)

Despite Tonio's appeals to Guido's love for him, Guido refuses to invest in sexual coupling its traditional meanings of privilege and exclusivity, and therefore reinforce the possessiveness this construction engenders:

> "Where is the dishonor in giving this man what he asks of you when
> you will not be diminished in the slightest?. . . If you were a virgin
> girl you could plead that, but he would never have asked that of you.
> He is a holy man. And were you a man, . . . you could claim an aver-
> sion whether you felt it or not. But you are neither of these, and you
> are *free*, Tonio, free. There are men and women who dream every
> night of their lives for such freedom! And it's yours by your nature
> and you cast it away." (357, Rice's emphasis)

Constructed as an exception to the sex-gender system, the castrato is, as we have seen, paradoxically central, the exception on which the rule depends, both before and outside. As in her better-known series of vampire novels, Rice uses characters who inhabit the margins in order to explore the freedoms and possibilities there. Unlike Tonio, whose preoccupation with the status of his "manhood" suggests that he is still caught in the grip of discourses that cast him out as other, Guido sees that the margins are places of possibility, including the possibility of recognizing that because sexual categories are socially constructed so, too, is the meaning of sex. Tonio can only see Guido's advice as mercenary, but Guido understands that monogamy and romantic love are features of the same system as "manhood." When Tonio argues that their coupling was motivated by love and passion, Guido responds, "So love him then! . . . Go and love him for this little while and there will be passion, too" (357). Tonio goes, and there is, in the end, passion and love with the cardinal that supplements, rather than endangers, the passion and love he has with Guido.

To be not-a-man, *A Cry to Heaven* suggests, is not necessarily a bad thing. But, as Guido implies, neither is it the same thing as being a woman. Tonio's mother, caught between Carlo and Tonio, drinks herself to death. One woman does, however, manage to create a space of freedom for herself, a young Englishwoman named Christina, a professional painter. When Tonio sleeps with her (Rice's castrati can have erections; indeed, they have many), he is surprised to learn that the widow is a virgin. We are less surprised; she had married an old man for whom she probably served as token of his continued phallic potency in exchange for a celibate marriage. Childlessness insures the freedom to paint; widowhood gives her social position and a certain amount of social freedom. At the novel's close, Tonio, having dispatched his father, is on his way back to Christina and Guido: "Before the sun rose he would be with [them]. And for the first time they would be truly together" (530). What makes such a clichéd and sentimental ending still interesting is that Tonio goes back to both Christina and Guido. The castrato becomes the figure for both sexual diversity and for what we might call relational diversity. Other people may dream with envy of their sexual freedoms, but the castrati are also free of the claustrophobia of the couple, a possibility few of the rest of us have the intellectual and psychological freedom to entertain.

*O*ur focus above on the castrati as the first operatic divinities, the first "divas," and on their literary legacy does not mean that women did not become opera singers of renown during the eighteenth century, only that their celebrity was overshadowed by that of the castrati. There were well-known and accomplished female singers in Italy as early as the sixteenth century; some were noblewomen who had been encouraged to learn music as a way of filling their time and increasing their attractions; others were women of lesser rank who had nonetheless established themselves as singers in the courts. Few of these *cantatrice da camera* were willing to move from the private venue of the courts to the stages of public opera houses. The centuries-old assumption that women who displayed themselves on stage must be prostitutes—in eighteenth-century Naples, according to Benedetto Croce, the terms "virtuosa" and "prostitute" were almost synonymous (Ellison 14)—kept many women singers, protective of their respectability, from performing on the public stage and generally worked to impede the progress of women in opera.

Commentators, while acknowledging that many early opera singers were not courtesans, tend to focus on the singers who were, or singers who, if not technically courtesans, were more protective of their pleasure than of their respectability. Giulia di Carlo, for example, dubbed by wags the "Madonna del Bordello," was "a naturally brilliant singer," Heriot assures his readers, who ruined her voice and looks with her off-stage activities and died, in poverty and disgrace, of course, in 1696 (28–29).[13] While the mistresses of powerful men did often take up singing, in palaces and on public stages, these courtesan-singers should also be seen in the wider context of an era and culture in which artists were generally dependent on patrons, which was structured to make male protection a necessity for women, and in which women often lacked the dowry necessary for marriage or admission to a convent. Before the eighteenth century, options for most women singers were limited to the court or convent, but "between [the court] and the nunnery lay an ambiguous zone where a woman might get occasional lucrative opera engagements, at the cost of being deemed a courtesan or else of having again and again to be certified as respectable" (Rosselli 61–62). The effect of these pressures, Rosselli points out, was a "need for highly placed male protection. A number of women singers could be straightforwardly described as courtesans; these by definition had their protectors. The others needed protectors to establish (what for many of them was probably true) that they were not courtesans" (62).

Singers throughout the eighteenth century often depended on court patronage and were often victims of tyranny and exploitation. During the 1770s, Gertrude Mara signed a contract to be a court singer for Frederick the Great, who later kept her under surveillance and threw her into prison to prevent her marriage. He finally allowed her to marry only on the condition that she remain in Berlin. Her attempts to get herself dismissed were unsuccessful, and she became reluctant to perform. Once, when she claimed that she was too ill to sing, Frederick sent dragoons to get her. (Canceling performances on pleas of indisposition is, of course, a prima donna stereotype, but there is evidence that behavior almost always read as duplicitous and willful was for some women singers grounded in physiological necessity. Performing and touring are hard on the body. And a woman's hormonal fluctuations can affect the quality of the voice; thus developed the custom of menstruating singers wearing a rose to signal to their audiences that they were not, thanks to their period, in top voice.)

The status of women singers did begin slowly to improve in the eighteenth century. Accomplished singers like Faustina Bordoni, Vittoria Tesi, and Francesca Cuzzoni gained respect as skillful musicians (and, in the case of Faustina and Cuzzoni, infamy as "prima donnas"); social and legal structures that inhibited women from managing their own careers began to loosen. Italian opera became increasingly internationalized, and singers like Faustina and Cuzzoni made their way to London. Handel hired both of them for an opera there and thus set the stage for one of the greatest diva rivalries in opera history, a rivalry that culminated, the story goes, in their having a fistfight on stage. Fashionable London was fiercely divided between their respective partisans, and riots broke out in the theater and its environs. Few women, however, gained the fame and fees of Cuzzoni and Faustina. For most of the eighteenth century, women singers were still in the shadow of the castrati. Indeed, there are tales of rivalries between castrati and women singers as intense as those between women singers. When English soprano Nancy Storace and Marchesi, one of the last great castrati, appeared together Storace matched his famous signature fioritura, called "la bomba di Marchesi." Marchesi threatened to quit if the management did not fire Storace, which they did. Caterina Gabrielli fared better when she sang with Pacchierotti in Sicily. Midway through one of her arias, the castrato, declaring himself unworthy to be on the same stage with such a singer, burst into tears and left the stage.

These small victories, which demonstrated to those willing to listen that women could be accomplished singers, did not, however, win the war of celebrity. The public was fascinated by the exotic quality of the castrato voice, a quality women were said to be unable to duplicate. In addition, as Vernon Lee notes, because "the male singer was at once more respectable and more thoroughly artistic than the singing actress, it was he who had all the social advantages to himself" (*Studies* 119). The male castrato was "more thoroughly artistic" in large measure because women did not have the same opportunities for rigorous conservatory training that the castrati did. Women's lack of opportunity for first-rate training did not, of course, stop criticism that they were untrained. Women singers were, for example, repeatedly criticized—to the effect, perhaps, of constructing them as the worst offenders—for using inappropriate ornamentation that ignored musical context, a singing sin not confined to women. Marcello, in his satire on opera, "Teatro alla Moda," claims that when a female singer gets a new part she takes it to her maestro "so that he may write in the passages, the variations, the beautiful ornaments, etc.—and Maestro Crica, without knowing the first thing about the intentions of the composer . . . will write . . . in the empty spaces of the bass staff everything he can think of, and in very great quantity" (Heriot 31).

Pier Francesco Tosi's famous singing manual *Observations on the Florid Song* counsels students to avoid the example of women singers in the matter of ornament and imitation. We quote from an English translation published in London in 1743: "If, out of particular Indulgence to the sex, so many female Singers have the Graces set down in writing, one that studies to become a good Singer should not follow the Example; whoever accustoms himself to have things put in his mouth, will have no invention, and become a Slave to his Memory" (88). Women who showed they could sing were thus diminished again, accused of a poverty of creativity and musicality. Since conservatory training was not easy to come by, perhaps women could learn through observation and imitation, but Tosi forecloses this way of learning as well: "If many of the female Singers (for whom I have due respect) would be pleased to consider, that by copying good ones, they are become very bad ones, they would not appear so ridiculous on the Stage for their Affectation in presuming to sing the *Airs* of the Person they copy, with the same Graces. In this great Error. . . . they seem to be govern'd by instinct, like the inferior Creatures, rather than by Reason" (153). What is really worrying the castrato Tosi, however, is not that women will slavishly copy male singers, or even each other, but that male students will imitate women: "If the Complaisance, which is due the fair Sex, does not excuse the abuse of copying when it proves prejudicial to the Profession, what ought one then to say of those Men, who, instead of inventing, not only copy others of their own Sex, but also Women?" he asks, and answers, "Foolish and Shameful!" (154). Indeed, Tosi's text can be read as a defense of singing as a manly art and a defense against the advances of female singers in the profession. Not only are women offered as the exemplary model of bad singing, they are positioned as the *origin* of bad singing: "The unwearied Study of Youth is sure to overcome all Obstacles that oppose, though Defects were sucked in with our Mother's Milk" (82).[14]

Observations on the Florid Song appeared in England in 1743, the same decade that the number of castrati began to decline. Historians offer a number of reasons for their diminishing number and waning popularity in the second half of the eighteenth century. An economic revival in Italy during the 1730s may have convinced parents that such desperate measures as castration were no longer necessary to insure a son's future security (Rosselli 54–55). A decline in the number of religious orders in Italy during the century, and the dissolution of others with the coming of the French, may have also contributed to lowering the number of trained castrati available to sing in opera. Other developments repeatedly cited for the dimming of the castrati's fortunes are Gluck's reforms and a general shift away from the castrati's vocal specialty, florid singing; the decline of *opera seria* and comic opera's greater investment in realism; the attempts of various Napoleonic governments in Italy to outlaw castration. Finally, changes in political thinking during the second half of the eighteenth century—the increasing rejection of aristocratic tyranny and the championing of individual liberties—tended to cast castrati as an embarrassing sign of aristocratic excess and decadence. The solidifying of gender roles and categories as signs of innate, "natural," and complementary difference over the course of the eighteenth and nineteenth centuries probably didn't help the castrati either. By the 1820s the supply of castrati was so small that composers began to write the romantic male lead in the tenor register, and the soprano/alto/tenor/bass casting we are familiar with began to take hold. Not surprisingly, castrati lasted longer in the church than on the opera stage. Vellutti sang his final London performance in 1829, but Alessandro Moreschi was associated with the Sistine Chapel into the twentieth century.

Female sopranos stepped into the breach, and, in some cases, the breeches. Increasingly better trained,[15] some by castrati teachers, women appropriated many of the castrati roles even as composers began to concentrate on writing for the *female* soprano voice. "Women became the fulcrum of romantic opera," Cori Ellison notes; "this was the age of Leonore, of Norma, of Fides, and great interpreters materialized to enflesh these heroines with unprecedented dignity and strength—Maria Malibran, Giudetta Pasta, Pauline Viardot and many others" (37). Thus the age of the castrato gave way to the age of the diva.

The transformation of opera into a business contributed in large measure to the rise of the diva, who gained unprecedented celebrity and, of course, fees in the nineteenth century. Aristocratic patronage was no longer necessary if a woman were to have a career. Growing numbers of opera houses on both sides of the Atlantic increased the demand for singers and fueled the development of an international star system that depended on promotion and publicity (P. T. Barnum managed Jenny Lind's first American tour in 1850). Better communications and the development of the railroad allowed singers to pick up engagements more easily and to move from theater to theater more quickly; indeed, the railroad made what we now think of as the concert tour possible. Accomplished women singers took advantage of the market for their services; they demanded ever-higher fees and became increasingly shrewd in constructing and managing their careers. Some nineteenth-century singers even managed their own opera companies. Louis XVIII gave singer Angelica Catalani a grant and a theater with which to start a company, but the venture was a disaster, in part because Catalani, who liked to bill herself as "*prima cantatrice del mondo*," made sure that no singer who could rival her ever sang on her stage. In the United States, soprano-impresarias, including the well-known soprano Clara Louise Kellog, managed, with more success than Catalani, some of the best-known touring opera companies (Dizikes 261–262). Because American opera companies generally refused to cast blacks, African-American singers who wanted a stage as well as a concert career had to join or start traveling performance companies. Often billed as "the Black Patti," Sissieretta Jones toured with "Black Patti's Troubadours," which performed a comedy sketch followed by a vaudeville section and closed with scenes from popular operas complete with costume and scenery (Story 14).

The nineteenth century was the golden age of diva worship. Between the decline of the castrato and the rise of the tenor in the latter part of the nineteenth century and the early twentieth, the reigning celebrities of the opera stage were almost exclusively female. The postperformance bouquet for the diva, a practice begun by Malibran's fans, is a convention still with us today, but other more extravagant conventions of frenzied admiration have now died out. Nineteenth-century fans often unharnessed the horses from the diva's carriage and after her performance pulled the carriage from the theater to her hotel themselves. Sometimes she was serenaded there. Venetians named a theater after Malibran during her 1832 tour, but when she dared to sing Norma, a role owned by Pasta, at La Scala in 1834, her life was threatened and, during the second performance, the audience rioted; admiration and violent partisanship went hand in hand. Pasta was in the audience for Malibran's Norma, and we wonder whether either woman remembered the passionate note the adolescent Maria had sent to her idol years before: "If I were near you, you would have neither face nor body, because I would eat all of you. Love me, love me as I love you" (Christiansen, *Prima Donna* 72). Malibran was on safer ground in England and France, and when she died in Manchester at the tragically young age of twenty-eight, fifty thousand people turned out for a glimpse of her cortege. Perhaps the most famous diva worshiper of the century was Queen Victoria, who during her youth wrote often and effusively in her diary about Giulia Grisi (she preferred Grisi to Malibran) and later supported the careers of such well-known singers as Pauline Viardot, Emma Albani, and Jenny Lind, and, significantly, African-American singers Elizabeth Taylor-Greenfield and Marie Selika.[16] The young princess first heard Grisi as Anna Bolena and remarked in her diary, "I was VERY MUCH AMUSED INDEED"; Victoria's mother—not, it appears, particularly concerned by her daughter's gushing devotion—invited Grisi to sing at a concert planned to celebrate the princess's sixteenth birthday (St. Aubyn 46).

Nineteenth-century diva fervor reached its peak in the career of Jenny Lind, an exemplary career for anyone interested in divas or in the links between classical music and commerce or in Victorian prudery and hypocrisy. Lind, Henrietta Sontag, and Adelina Patti are conventionally grouped by commentators as the "nightingales" or, less kindly, the "warblers." Their voices were pure and silvery, angelic, without much vibrato and without much color or emotional range. We might say that the nightingales were the assertion of Victorian True Womanhood (Lind was famous for performing in white gowns; a typical nightingale role was Donizetti's tragically victimized Lucia) after the fiery, willful, and risk-taking Romantic diva epitomized by Malibran and Pasta and their Normas and Medeas.

Long before she submitted herself to Barnum's publicity machine, Lind had carefully constructed a public persona as an anti-diva who, unlike her sister divas, was religious and morally upright (some said smug and sanctimonious), shy and modest, reluctant of fame and longing for her Swedish home—as a singer, in other words, whose thoughts and actions were as pure as her voice. Lind appears to have understood that the public's interest in a diva extended to her private life and constructed an off-stage persona that reversed conventional expectations; the public expected scandal so she provided virtue. In other words, she provided middle-class ticket buyers with a model of their own ideals. The shrewdness of this image suggests the extent to which Lind was, in good diva fashion, calculating and ambitious.

If divas are in some sense fantasy figures, so are anti-divas. Lind signed a hasty contract for her London debut with the manager of Drury Lane, Alfred Bunn. A short time later she tried to get out of it—a very diva thing to do, of course—by modestly claiming that she wasn't good enough for London: "I possess neither the personal advantages, the assurance, nor the charlatanism of other *prime donne*," she wrote (Christiansen, *Prima Donna* 102). Charlatanism indeed, for while she was negotiating for a release from Bunn, she signed a more lucrative contract for a season at Covent Garden with his chief competitor, Benjamin Lumley. Even then, however, she refused for a long while to travel to London. Bunn later sued and won damages, but the delays in her first London appearance generated great publicity for her and helped ticket sales. When Lind finally performed she was received with wild enthusiasm. Some observers suspected calculation behind Lind's vacillation and modest reluctance. Henry Chorley, her contemporary and a chronicler of the Victorian music scene, notes, "The game of suspense was never more artfully played. . . . For months the mind of that opera-world . . . was irritated and kept alive, by tales of mysterious vacillations, persuasions, negotiations . . . and all this after the treaty had been signed and sealed!—By whom all this machinery was originated, it is of no consequence here to examine. It had racked our Opera-world into a state of fever; and elevated it into a firm faith, moreover, that that which had cost so much trouble to secure must be, indeed, something unspeakably precious" (I:301–302).

Lind's extraordinary London reception was nothing compared to what Barnum was able to engineer for her 1850 American concert tour. Her European triumphs were well known in the United States, and Barnum capitalized on the public's knowledge by planting stories that further romanticized and exoticized her; it was rumored that she was secretly married to an English duke and that she had no ears beneath her severely dressed hair (Christiansen, *Prima Donna* 106). There's something both fitting and ironic in the fact that it was Barnum, that master of the freak show, who invented what we might call diva marketing. Of course, since the days of the castrati, an element of the "freak" had been inherent in the appeal of the opera star. To speak of the diva as gloriously extraordinary is a polite way of acknowledging that she is something of a freak. Further, her ambition, power, and distance from conventionally silent and passive womanhood make the diva as much a curiosity and freak as that convention of the freak show the bearded lady, and in very similar terms. That Barnum's product here is not the openly acquisitive Patti, who threw temper tantrums on stage, or the ruthlessly competitive Grisi, but Lind the anti-diva, True Woman as reluctant diva, is both ironic and apt; it reminds us that True Womanhood is not only a performance, but a freakish one at that.

Lind landed in New York, where thirty thousand people turned out for her arrival. Her landing was a strategically managed spectacle: banners flew, and flowered arches transformed the gangplank into a stage worthy of a great diva's entrance. Barnum further capitalized on the fervor he had created by auctioning off tickets to Lind's first performance in each city. And there were other ways to commodify and profit from Jenny Lind. As in England, various products appeared on the market with her name or picture printed on them: Jenny Lind clothing, opera glasses, and jewelry were, perhaps, to be expected, but there were also Jenny Lind greeting cards, Jenny Lind sausages, even a Jenny Lind cigar (an honor she shares with Tetrazzini) and a Jenny Lind whistling—"singing"—teakettle.

Lind found the pace exhausting, conditions often uncomfortable, and some of Barnum's tactics objectionable to her moral sensitivities. After singing nearly one hundred concerts she asked to be released from her contract, and Barnum agreed. Managing her own tour, she continued to sing concerts at a slower pace, but public interest began to wane. Her mid-tour marriage to a Jewish pianist nine years her junior did little for her image as chaste innocent. Reports of her bad temper and brusque treatment of people who came to see her began to leak out. At every stop she was besieged at her hotel by fans (many of them passionate young women—one even dressed up as a maid in order get a glimpse of her idol), by people who wanted jobs, and by strangers who, having heard of her celebrated charity, sought some for themselves or others. In this way, Lind became the victim of the "Saint Jenny" persona she had constructed earlier in her career. Writing a hundred years later, Henry Pleasants summarizes, "The legendary Jenny Lind was her own masterpiece. . . . The public was taken in, and so were most of her friends and acquaintances; but so, also, was she" (198).[17]

Other divas in the nineteenth century and, of course, in our own century have inspired similar, if perhaps not quite so extravagant, adulation. Never far from fame, however, is notoriety, and, as we have seen, divas acquired plenty of that as well: they were, after all, women who had in the most literal and material and undeniable way a voice. A long tradition of silenced women could not help but make this voice a threat to the entire culture. In the next chapter we look at two related constructions of the diva that attempt to manage this threat: the diva as siren and the diva as cipher, the diva as man-eater and the diva as vessel for a man's voice.

CHAPTER 2

Singing His Mind Away

My movie company is Siren films.
You know what a Siren is, don't you?
A woman who leads men to their deaths.
—Madonna

The Lady Kirke has a vital warning for Odysseus and company:

> Square in your ship's path are Seirenes, crying
> beauty to bewitch men coasting by;
> woe to the innocent who hears that sound!
> He will not see his lady nor his children
> in joy, crowding about him, home from sea;
> the Seirenes will sing his mind away
> on their sweet meadow lolling. There are bones
> of dead men rotting in a pile beside them.
> *(The Odyssey* 12.33–41)

The only way to avoid this fate is to plug one's "ears / with beeswax kneaded soft" (12.43–44) or, as Odysseus himself chooses, to be tied to the mast of the ship. What Odysseus hears is, indeed, seductive: "lovely voices in ardor" (12.192), urging him to give in to their "Sweet coupled airs" (12.156) and "purling" notes "like honey twining from her throat and my throat" (12.161–162). Lolling, ardor, coupled, honey—all words that suggest the sexual nature of the bewitchment. The sirens' voices, that is, are sensual, sexual voices, luring men from their proper women, their Penelopes and Micaelas, and to their death. The voices are, quite literally, irresistible; only physical means—the earwax to block out the voice entirely or the ropes to prevent escape—can restrain the tempted.

The category of the *femme fatale*, to which the siren belongs, has been the subject of many scholarly studies, and the deadly woman herself has been the subject of an endless number of narratives—from Homer to the latest killer-woman film thriller—as feminist critics have pointed out

48

since the seventies. But it is the diva, the woman with a voice—huge, sexy, powerful, relentless—who is the literal heir to sirenic power and sirenic threat. Since the diva became a presence in the world of art and entertainment in the eighteenth century, she has been a presence as well in fictional narratives, which almost always associate her with her Homeric antecedents and almost always suggest that she shares, though sometimes unwittingly, their lethal allure. Such voices with their attendant power can be, of course, both feared and desired, both denounced and celebrated, both repressed and promoted—often in the same text. It is hardly surprising that a woman with so much *physical* power—what does your body do when a diva sings?—over so many people creates anxiety and ambivalence, or that she becomes, for many writers, the sign of femininity itself, and by extension the sign of otherness.

The texts we discuss in this chapter illustrate both the common representations of the diva figure and some of the fictional possibilities for dealing with the anxieties she generates. We call this tradition of representing female singers as man-destroying sirens or, at the other extreme, as devoiced and passive vessels for the voices of men (many narratives combine the two) the "masculinist" tradition because such narratives tend to reinscribe traditional gender oppositions and present women as creatures in need of control and confinement (or, as many of these narratives have it, male "protection"). Most of these texts are by male writers—as most of the narratives we look at in the next chapter are by female ones—but we are not positing here a rigid opposition between these representations or arguing for some essential difference between the writings of men and women. While, as we demonstrate in the next chapter, many women writers reclaim, defend, celebrate, and rewrite the diva figure as she is presented in the texts we discuss here, the most disturbing and most gratuitously evil diva in our study appears in a novel by a woman. While many male writers express palpable fear and loathing of the diva, E. F. Benson, as we will see later, has created one of the most generous, good-hearted, and independent.

We are all, as contemporary theorists have made clear, products of many, sometimes conflicting, ideologies—ideologies that become flesh, in all their contradictions, in the stories we tell. In Vera Brittain's first novel, for example, the melodramatic *The Dark Tide* (1923), poor Daphne's cad of a husband falls helplessly in love with an opera singer, Lucia. When the seduction begins, Lucia is, predictably, playing Carmen, that consummate operatic siren. The seduced Sylvester leaves Daphne, who has just given birth to a sickly child, for his diva. Lucia is thus set up as a siren figure from whom we expect stereotypical sirenic behavior. But Lucia then visits Daphne, because, she realizes, Daphne "had doubtless been through a very hard time—like most women who expected men to be reasonable" (294). Lucia, that is, seeks out her "rival" because Daphne is naive and in pain. And the diva does not taunt the rejected wife but consoles her: "One day I shall tire of him, just as I expect he will tire of me. I will love as it pleases me, but I will not lose my freedom" (297). Daphne *has* lost her freedom, and Lucia comes to stand, albeit ambivalently, for an alternative to the constricting contract of marriage. The sexual aggression and promiscuity always associated with women on the stage becomes for a moment a heady assertion of control and power. It is almost as though Brittain, having bought into the diva-as-siren, suddenly looked at her again and saw in her the possibility for a new narrative, a narrative more consonant with Brittain's own budding feminism.

While the diva's about-face isn't particularly convincing, it illustrates on the level of plot the collision of two quite different ideologies, two quite different ways of looking at a woman with a voice. In a very broad sense, these two ways are the subject of this study. But neither way is simple. (A siren, for example, can attract with evil intent, can attract with good intent, or can attract without any intent at all—without even knowing the power of her voice.) And neither of these ways is ever untouched by the other. Texts in which divas appear almost always evince admiration for the singer's power, even when they portray such power as deadly, almost always evince fear, even when they portray such power as beneficent.

Most of the early and Victorian diva fictions in the masculinist tradition represent the diva as corrupted by her profession but "naturally" sympathetic and womanly—if sometimes possessed of odd masculine tendencies and always of extraordinary, if usually unconscious, sirenic talent. It is not until the twentieth century that, responding perhaps to a social order threatened by the New Woman and later women's liberation movements, the diva comes to resemble more closely her Homeric sisters, deliberately luring victims, usually men, to her sensual lair—her body—and systematically picking their bones. Unlike the sirens who sing to Odysseus, however, and who sing and seduce together (their song is "our song"), the divas in the texts we discuss here have little sense of sisterhood. They sing alone, often rejected by other women—the situation in most of the nineteenth century texts—or, most blatantly in twentieth century texts, in competition with them for men, for roles, for riches, for fame.

This specific and specifically brutal kind of competition is the subject of both *Mawrdew Czgowchwz*, a 1975 novel by James McCourt, and

The Divas, a 1978 novel by Met baritone Robert Merrill and music critic Fred Jarvis. In the former, the rising diva Mawrdew is pitted against the past-her-prime diva Neri—who in her prima donna frenzies spits "every vile . . . Sicilian curse and oath" (33). Mawrdew's followers, so enamored of the siren that they stage a hunger strike, are pitted against Neri's passionate followers, the Sicilian Neriacs, one of whom, "raging in obscene Sicilian," curses Mawrdew and causes the loss of her voice (99). This parodic and camp fairy tale, though tongue-in-cheek, illustrates well the narrative of diva rivalry as well as the narrative of "the other" so prevalent in diva texts. While it may seem evenhanded enough to set Czech against Sicilian—both outsiders in New York—it is revealed later that Mawrdew is not Czech at all but Irish, a kind of civilized home girl in comparison to the "Fascist" Sicilian barbarians (133). The fairy tale ends happily: the Irish lass with her "voice beyond voices" triumphs over her temperamental rival. The good diva is rewarded with decades of "Mawrdolatry" and rewarded as well with a suitable mate. The "majestic goddess" Mawrdew is parodic of the hyperbole of the opera world, but the viciousness of the rivalry and the displacement of the evils of divahood onto the ethnic other disturb the jollity of the tale and its parodic force.

  The Divas, a more realistic fiction, also places such rivalry at the center of its plot. Three divas participate in a contest to find the fairest goddess of them all for a lucrative position as a television commentator: "Three sopranos in full sail, scratching and scheming. . . . Each one a piranha." While the three divas have beautiful voices, they are some of the nastiest characters in fiction. Carla, opera singer, porno star, and "sorceress" (161), seduces Sandy (the Paris figure, giver of the golden apples) and deliberately becomes pregnant by him; this seduction is part of a pattern: she got her first role, Micaela in *Carmen*, "without any agent or audition" by seducing the conductor (102). Gloria, an overweight alcoholic, screams vulgar and vicious homophobic epithets at opera personnel. Knowing that she'll say things so outrageous that she'll lose any chance for the golden apple, Elizabeth encourages Gloria to drink. Elizabeth has besides lured a man from his wife and children: "It was almost as if Elizabeth . . . were a hurricane and Paul, innocently lying in her path, had been devastated" (269). He dies from the stress of it all. When Elizabeth sees a way to destroy Carla, the narrator describes her expression, which could well be the expression of any of these singing monsters: "The women of the French Revolution sitting in glee around the guillotine must have betrayed themselves with such a look as the blade whirred downward" (181).

Piranhas, terrorists, killers, the women sabotage one another at every opportunity. Elizabeth has learned her Machiavellian ways from her idol, a diva of the previous generation, who taunted her, "You'll never have the problem of a man leaving his wife for you" (270). What Elizabeth learns, that is, from her predecessor, is the importance of being a siren. And lest we find hope in the new-generation soprano, Bonnie, who emerges at the end of the novel, we discover that the opera sponsor is "manacled to her merest whim," since she indulges "in some practices which even the most obliging of [his] previous mistresses had balked at" (380). The cycle of seductive and destructive divas goes on and on, broken for the individual diva only by true love. Gloria, for example, pines after her first husband, whom she divorced to advance her career. Her persistent love for this simple, working class, uneducated man saves her from the extremes of nastiness (unless one counts her relentless homophobia; the text does not) that her sister divas achieve. Elizabeth's one redeeming quality, the text makes clear, is that she loved Paul, the man she destroyed. And Carla is transformed by falling in love with Sandy.

The rhetoric surrounding Carla's transformation via a therapeutic heterosexual romance is instructive: "[She] suddenly found herself thinking about vacuum cleaners and wax polishes. . . . She was in the terminal throes of becoming a normal woman" (286). The implication, of course, is that the divas' overweening ambition puts them beyond the pale of normal womanhood, that divahood is a kind of gender pathology. "Why have a baby?" Carla asks early in the novel. "She had Paolo [her gay husband]. And together they had a career" (109); Elizabeth admits that if she had a "squalling infant" she would "bundle it up and leave it on the nearest church doorstep" if the infant didn't "further her professional interests" (176). Elizabeth's hypothetical baby is only, of course, hypothetically abandoned, but the very specter of a woman giving up her child firmly establishes her as the consummate unnatural woman.

Unnatural women, in turn, naturally associate themselves or are associated with other "unnaturals," here, as in many diva narratives, homosexuals. Carla's husband is a gay man absolutely unable to have sex with his wife. Traditional gender oppositions work to support the hetero/homo opposition, so Carla's transformation from unnatural diva to natural (that is, vacuum-wielding) woman requires that she move from perverse Paolo to straight Sandy. The novel's cure for sirenhood is the embrace of both the vacuum cleaner and the "proper" erotic object. But Paolo is by no means the only gay man in the novel. Gloria's diatribe against homosexuals is only one of her many diatribes directed against "the fag clique" (56) that has, according to her, taken over the opera world. While Gloria is, when the novel opens, a failed woman whose "sagging mounds of breast, . . . Santa Claus belly, . . . [and] thighs packed with fat" repel, she later loses weight, cuts down on her drinking, and becomes, in comparison to her rivals, the good diva (14). She gets the golden apple in spite of the fag clique, thus justifying her husband's judgment that "Gloria was, well, too good and too professional to appeal to their adore-the-misfit syndrome" (56). When, that is, the diva is portrayed as a real woman, a womanly woman, the onus of the unnatural is displaced onto the other; the singer is pitted against the other if she's a good diva, allied with the other if she's a bad one, a misfit.

Siren, Faustess, whore, babykiller, misfit, the unrepentant diva is a woman manqué, and, as with each of the divas in this chapter, it is the inextricable collusion of her voice and her sexuality that generates her unnatural, unwomanly ambition and that becomes the instrument of destruction for any man who foolishly forgets to fill his ears with wax.

This inextricability clearly marks the cruel siren Veda—a name that is almost an anagram of "diva"—in James Cain's 1941 novel *Mildred Pierce*. Veda's mother is the eponymous heroine, a feisty, aggressive woman whose main fault is her overweening love for her talented and nasty daughter. Though Veda's cruelty precedes her divahood, the text suggests that her evil "nature" and her musical genius are of a piece. Her music teacher implies as much to Mildred. "Are you insinuating," Mildred asks, "that my daughter is a snake?" "No," Treviso replies (in Italian-American dialect embarrassing to contemporary readers), "is a coloratura soprano, is much worse . . . a coloratura soprano, love nobody but own goddam self. . . . Is . . . worse than all a snake in a world." He lays out the trajectory of a diva's life: "All a coloratura crazy for rich pipple. . . . All borrow ten t'ousand bucks, go to Italy, study voice, never pay money back. . . . Sing in grand opera, marry a banker, get da money. Got da money, kick out a banker, marry a baron, get da title. 'Ave a sweetie on a side" (319). All the claims here come to pass, in spirit if not in specific detail. After shamelessly using her mother for publicity, the nasty singer—figured, like the divas in *The Divas*, as snake or worse—runs off with her mother's upper-class husband. In typical siren fashion, that is, the diva (or diva-to-be) lures young men to their ruin and older ones from their wives.

Significantly, it is Mildred Pierce who, despite her daughter's abuse and the warnings of others, succumbs most thoroughly to Veda's charms. Mildred in fact acts toward Veda "less like a mother than a lover" (310), an observation borne out by a strange scene late in the novel in which Mildred "knelt beside the bed . . . took the lovely creature in her arms and kissed her, hard, on the mouth. . . . She wanted to stay, to blow through the holes in Veda's pajamas" (335). When Veda sings at the Hollywood Bowl, "little quivers" go through her mother, and they keep "going through her the rest of the night," a night that is "the climax of Mildred's life" (345).

The diva who attracts and ruins men with her siren song lures women as well. And when she does, these lurings become, as we will see, clear sites of perversion in masculinist narratives.

The sirenic diva lives on in contemporary fiction, apparently immune to the influence of the women's movements of the seventies and eighties. Lili Schneider, in Judith Gould's 1992 potboiler *Forever*, is quite explicitly "an enchantress. . . . A siren" (1) and a "ruthless, power-hungry bitch" (142). This characterization is thoroughly supported by the trajectory of Lili's life, which begins with "your typical corny success story": on opening night the star meets with an accident, and her understudy, Lili, must take her place. "Needless to say, she wowed 'em. . . . Hollywood couldn't have plotted it better" (137). The novel thus calls up the stereotypical diva narrative and exaggerates it until it and the consummately evil diva (by far exceeding Gloria, Carla, Elizabeth, and Veda) who is its subject would strain the credulity even of Hollywood. Lili, it turns out, planned that accident, the first of many murderous acts toward her rivals. The darling of Hitler, who arranges "her marriage to one of his gay, opera-buff friends" (140), she redeems herself after the war by marrying a Brit and becoming Lady Hughes-Coxe.[1] At the height of her career, she fakes her death in order to become part of a medical experiment, carried out by a Nazi physician, to preserve youth indefinitely. Here diva narrative meets vampire narrative meets Janáček's *Makropulos Case*: the experiment requires the daily sacrifice of a child, and by the time the plot is uncovered, thousands of children have been killed.

The story, hyperbolic and unbelievable as it is, calls on several common motifs of the siren narrative besides her stunning beauty, heavenly voice, predatory selfishness, and endless bitchiness, or, as the text puts it by way of introducing her, "Lili with the face of an angel. Lili with the voice of the nightingale. Lili with the body of a whore" (1). The association of the diva with gay men, the (deadly) rivalry with other divas, the diva's concern with costume ("Lili had custom-made mannequins of her body at . . . all the world's greatest couturiers" [411]), and, of course, her tendency to sleep her way to the top are all motifs that appear, as we will see, with great frequency in diva narratives.

Perhaps the most disturbing motif, however, and also a very common one, is the association of the diva with the racially other. This, too, is an association that we will explore further in the context of some of the nineteenth-century novels in this tradition, but its appearance here deserves comment. Lili and her rich protectors several times call upon a professional assassin known as the Ghost (recalling the Opera Ghost in *Phantom of the Opera*) to eliminate anyone who suspects that the diva is still alive or that children are disappearing. The Ghost is never "he" or "she," but revelation of the Ghost's identity confirms what the careful reader has suspected: the Ghost is a greedy and cunning black woman, a prostitute. The Ghost thus seems to be a foil for Lili, who is fabulously famous while the Ghost is utterly anonymous, perfectly Aryan while the Ghost is black, living in incredible luxury while the Ghost haunts the streets. But in many ways the Ghost is actually Lili's double. She commits the murders that Lili needs to survive; she has, like Lili, "the body of a whore," host to impermissible desires; she is ambitious, cunning, chameleon; she sings her siren songs as she leads her unsuspecting victims to their deaths.

She is thus a sort of death diva who makes clear the deadliness of divahood, the fatal consequences—to the diva herself and to the victims of her voice—of showing "too much talent," being "a tad too aggressive and ambitious." "There's a reason prima donnas are called prima donnas—right?" a minor character observes (135). His question could be the epigraph for this study—or the epitaph for the dead divas strewn across the pages of these narratives. At the close of *Forever*, both Lili and her Ghost die violent and much deserved deaths, the vampiric/Faustian desire for eternal youth properly punished.

Not all diva novels are so unsympathetic to the diva herself, yet even diva heroines with whom a text clearly sympathizes often appear as sirens who lead good men to their doom or who lure them away from more deserving women. This representation is, we suggested, most prevalent in nineteenth-century texts. In George Meredith's *Sandra Belloni* (1864), for example, the eponymous diva has "an incomprehensible attractiveness" to the caddish Wilfred, a young man of higher social station (86). She falls in love with him, and much of the novel describes the waxing and waning of that relationship. But she lures others as well, among whom is the brave and virtuous Merthyr, whose sister believes that the singer "exercised some fatal fascination" over her poor brother (308). Another man makes explicit her kinship to the sirens when he cries, "Put me in a boat, and let her sing on, and all may end!" (450).

Belloni herself recognizes that "diva" is a position of power. At one point when Wilfrid has left her, she says, "'Yes; now, as I am *now*, he can abandon me': But how if he should see her and hear her in that hushed hour when she was to stand as a star before men?" (315). The pronoun shift is important. The power, that is, is not a particularly personal one; it resides in the voice itself, exercised publicly. And it is a power that very few women can hope to attain. "You shall have more rule zan twenty Queens— forty!" one of her early promoters promises (158).

For much of the novel, Sandra Belloni's voice is gone. During this time men pass her without noticing her; the "numerous indifferent faces . . . tell her she had lost her power" (330). She wanders the country-side, following a flock of sheep, listening to their "piteous noise," and "thinking curiously of the something broken that appeared to be in their throats. By-and-by, the thought flashed in her that they were going to be slaughtered" (333). She is thinking as well, of course, of her own broken voice and recognizing that the loss of power leaves her, like the sheep, like most women, vulnerable to a hostile world.

Significantly, the other women in this novel—and in most of the nov-els we discuss in this chapter—do not respond to the siren's song. Wilfrid's sisters, for example, fix on her boot-lace, not on her remarkable voice (11). And Methyr's sister cannot understand what her heroic and brilliant brother sees in the singer: "Herself always! . . . This is among the mysteries of Provi-dence to me, that one so indifferent to others should be gifted with so inex-plicable a power of attraction" (377). Women's ability to ignore the siren suggests, of course, the sexual element in the devotee's attraction to the diva. When women in these novels can't ignore her, they are (depending on the vocabulary available to the writer and social constructions of sexuality cir-culating during the time of composition) figured as women with Sapphic tendencies, as inverts, as lesbians. But women's bewilderment about the diva's power seems also to be, in part, a result of the diva's difference from other women. In all of these novels, the diva, or the young girl who is to become a diva, acts in ways that other girls or women do not act. She ap-pears freer, more spontaneous; her upbringing has been unconventional (one or both of her parents, usually her mother, is dead); she is oblivious to fash-ion (Sandra Belloni's "boot-lace hanging loose" [10]) or she creates her own; she does not put others first. She acts, in fact, rather "manly." At one point, for example, Sandra Belloni puts on Wilfrid's cap, a simple gesture but one that occasions serious, if facetious, narrative comment: "As soon as [a girl] puts on her brother's hat, she gives him a manly nod. The same philosopher who fathers his dulness on me, asserts that the modern vice of fastness . . . is bred by apparently harmless practices of this description" (47).

In other words, the diva-to-be is already a gender bender, a potential pervert, a cross-dresser—and cross-dressing has its effects. Divahood is ever a gender disorder.[2] In his cap, Wilfrid proclaims, she is "a charming boy"; another character says admiringly that "she is half man" (310). In the sequel to this novel, *Vittoria* (1867), a woman asks the diva bitterly, "Are you only half a woman, that you have no consciousness of your power [over men]?" (280). Another woman hates her for being "a woman who attracted all men . . . who never appealed to forgiveness" (427). What the men love and the women hate, then, is the "masculine" in Sandra Belloni, and the text itself uses that "masculine," which the men find charming, admirable, and eventually heroic, to isolate her from other women, to claim that what is best in her is indeed her masculinity. At the same time, however, she is presented as intensely feminine. Sandra Belloni's obsession with the unworthy Wilfrid is unrelenting and inexplicable. To remain at his side, she gives up a chance to study abroad and revels in her sacrifice: "This renunciation of a splendid destiny for Wilfred's sake seemed to make her worthier of him" (159). The text, then, stresses the diva's femininity, but femininity alone could hardly make her the subject of nearly a thousand pages. "She might have many of the littlenesses of which women are accused; for Art she promised unspotted excellence; and, adorable as she was by attraction of her sex, she was artist over all" (334). What makes her interesting, we presume, is this combination of feminine littleness and masculine greatness, a combination that is perhaps the source both of these writers' fascination with the diva and of the very definition of "diva" in a culture in which the "divine" and the "feminine" seem mutually exclusive.

The diva's relationship to divinity—or the impossibility of that relationship—is most thoroughly explored in George Moore's *Evelyn Innes* (1898) and *Sister Teresa* (1901), texts that, of all the novels in this chapter, most sympathetically and most idiosyncratically portray the singer. Evelyn Innes, that is, is not a stereotypical prima donna but a fully developed subject with a complex interior life that eventually leads her to give up the stage, renounce her lovers, and enter a convent—to become Sister Teresa. So carefully is she crafted that in the transition from diva to nun she remains a consistent and convincing (insofar as consistent can *be* convincing) self. The result is the location of corruption and unbridled sensuality in divahood itself or in the voice that makes divahood inevitable, rather than in the girl or woman who becomes a diva. The novels try valiantly to maintain this untenable distinction by their very separation of the heroine—and of her narrative itself—into Evelyn Innes and Sister Teresa.

Like many aspiring divas, Evelyn Innes is a child without a mother. Her father has "made of her an excellent musician, able to write fugue and counterpoint," but he has neglected to develop her mother's heritage, her voice (*EI* 6). Her voice is, nonetheless, a beautiful and powerful one. Like Sandra Belloni's, men cannot resist it, or her, and one of the most desirable of them, rich and handsome Lord Owen Asher, volunteers to take her to Paris for voice lessons. Several important issues, implicit in all these novels, are made explicit here. First, if Evelyn, a girl without mother or means, wants to develop her voice, she has no choice but to accept Asher's or someone else's offer. A diva must go abroad for training; such travel and training require funds. Second, she cannot marry her patron; married women do not sing in public. Owen is explicit about this: "Lady Asher as Kundry! Could anything be more grotesque? . . . But he might marry her five or six years hence, for there was no reason why she should continue singing 'Isolde' and 'Brünnhilde' till she had no shred of voice left. . . . In the full blaze of her glory she might become Lady Asher" (*EI* 69).[3]

Third, such patronage presumes a sexual relationship. There is never any question that if she goes to Paris with Asher, she will be not only his project but his mistress. And finally, even once the diva has established herself (or been established) and is earning money, she needs an escort and protector. She therefore needs a man. Not, of course, a husband, since that would preclude a career on the opera stage. She needs, then, a lover. Unlike most of these diva-heroines, Evelyn sees this clearly at several points in the novel: "She could not remain on the stage without a lover. . . . It was no use for her to deceive herself!" (*EI* 231). "She ought to send them both away. . . . But could she remain on the stage without a lover? Could she go to Bayreuth by herself?" (*EI* 328). The questions are rhetorical; the answer, obviously not.

The young woman who, after a retreat at a convent, thought she might become a nun, first becomes a diva and struggles thereafter with the moral code of her upbringing and inclination and the practical code that dictates her artistic life. The text sympathizes. It recognizes her dilemma; it does not brand her a sinner or trivialize the decisions she must make. She feels early in the first novel that she *could* renounce her art, but later sees that "her art was not merely a personal sacrifice. In the renunciation of her art she was denying a great gift that had been given to her by Nature . . . for the admiration of the world" (*EI* 91). The dilemma, that is, is real. And of a piece with that of George Eliot's Dorothea Brooke. What does a young girl do with a great gift? That Evelyn's favorite saint is Teresa of Avila, that she herself becomes, unsuccessfully, Sister Teresa, suggests, with Eliot, that the nineteenth-century female genius has less of a chance than her sixteenth-century counterpart.

At the end of *Evelyn Innes* and the beginning of *Sister Teresa*, the diva uses her great gift for another purpose. She sings benediction in her convent, which is on the brink of bankruptcy, in order to attract donors. She has at this point renounced her lovers, given up the stage, stopped seeing her friends, stripped herself of her fine clothes and jewels, and thrown away her sensual music. But even this singing in the service of God brings nothing but unhappiness and destruction. The music brings in money but also brings distraction from prayer, jealousy among the nuns, and a philosophical schism in the community. Evelyn's voice is, besides, the direct cause of one genuinely holy nun leaving the convent and Evelyn's own near-fatal illness, as well as the indirect cause of the death of the good prioress. Yet Evelyn herself, as readers have never doubted and as the text firmly asserts in the person of the wise and ailing prioress, is "very good" and desires goodness "ardently" (*ST* 209).

What is going on here?

In spite of Evelyn's basic "goodness," she is, nonetheless, a fallen woman; she has fallen into both sexuality and ambition, and the novel implies that there can be no complete return to some primal pre-diva state. When she first contemplates Paris with Owen Asher, for example, she thinks "with a thrill of pleasure that it would be much more exciting to run away with him than to be married to him" (*EI* 62). She succumbs to temptation not only, then, out of economic necessity but also out of a desire for pleasure. After she enters the convent, she thinks several times that she would be a better nun if it were not for her sexual past. The men with whom she has had sexual relationships keep invading her prayers and infecting her thoughts. Sex and spirituality seem unable to inhabit the same space, especially if that space is a female one.

Ambition, too, has indelibly marked the aspiring nun. It makes her, for example, renounce motherhood. "I don't want children," Evelyn declares, "I want to sing" (*EI* 87). Refusal to bear children, as we have seen, marks the woman and her ambition as unnatural. Early in *Evelyn Innes*, her father is disturbed to hear her sing *Faust* and to hear her argue that Faust's "was a beautiful and human aspiration" (81). Identification with Faust and his "aspiration" is impermissible for a woman, a sign of culpable ambition, of forbidden straying from her path. Marguerite must be her role in this opera.

There are other signs that Evelyn's ambition makes her long for the impossible. When she returns home after years on the opera stage, a boy has just quit her father's choir. "I wish I could take the place of the naughty boy," Evelyn says. Not only does her father immediately reject the proposal, but Evelyn herself recognizes its futility. She has, after all, heard the voices of both boys and castrati,[4] "soprano voices of a rarer and more radiant timbre than any woman's sexful voice" (*EI* 232). Women are, witness the quality of their voices, doomed by their sexuality from achieving anything truly spiritual. Even the nuns in *Sister Teresa*, asexual women that most of them are, are silly and childish. "Am I going to spend the whole of my life," Sister Teresa/Evelyn wonders at one point, "with these women who are no better than children?" (191). Their spiritual aspirations, perhaps because such aspirations are themselves masculine, have led them nowhere. And this is reflected in their voices, "not the clear, sexless voice of boys" but "women's voices, out of which sex had faded like colour out of flowers . . . weak and feeble" (*EI* 421). Women's voices, then, are either "sexful" and seductive or faded and "pathetic." Evelyn's desire to replace the boy, to become a boy, to take on the ethereal, spiritual "sexless voice of boys" is itself a kind of hubris, or at least impermissible ambition.

Sexuality and ambition are not easily separable in most diva narratives. Here their inextricability is emphasized by the repetition of Evelyn's attachment to men. All her musical striving is filtered through them—her father, whom she calls "her ultimate judge" (*EI* 257), her lovers, Owen Asher and Ulick, and finally Monsignor Mostyn, largely responsible for her religious vocation. The point is not made subtly: "Her own desire of art had been inseparably linked to her desire to please men. Three days ago she had looked down from the organ loft to see if there were any men among the congregation, knowing she would not sing so well if she were only singing to women" (*ST* 9). One of her fellow nuns observes that "a man always comes before everyone else, whether she is on the stage or in a convent" (*ST* 152).

The nun, Sister Mary John, is critical here. And a feminist reader, taking Sister Mary John's point—and viewpoint—might be tempted to see the text as critical of a too male-dependant woman. But this seems not to be the case: Sister Mary John rails because *she* wants to come "before everyone else" in Sister Teresa's heart. The woman, that is, who objects to another woman's male-centeredness is figured as an invert (though the word is never used). Sister Mary John realizes with "horror" that "it was since love of Evelyn had begun in her that passionate love of Christ, which was her vocation . . . had declined. She must choose between Christ and Evelyn," who is a "sensible pleasure" (*ST* 153). Sister Mary John has, it is clear both to herself and to readers, transformed her "passionate love of Christ" to a passionate love of Evelyn Innes and her amazing, sensual, sexual voice.

Other characters note Sister Mary John's transformation as well and appear to recognize that her desires are erotic. Sister Mary Hilda, for example, who has always had qualms about Evelyn's becoming a nun, mentions to the prioress "another matter on which I would not speak if speech could be avoided. It is a matter so delicate that I fear, whatever words I use, my words will misinterpret my meaning"; the words Sister Mary Hilda chooses are balanced and neutral: Sister Mary John is "absorbed in [Evelyn's] influence," such that it is "impossible not to notice it" (*ST* 161). Homoeroticism is here the love that cannot speak its name, the nameless horror. Another nun is similarly attracted, but most of the nuns respond to Evelyn more predictably, more "femininely," much as the other women in *Sandra Belloni* and *Vittoria* respond to Sandra Belloni: they are "jealous of Evelyn's voice," and "they resented the [masculine] attention that always hummed around Evelyn in the parlour" (*ST* 164). These feminine women are, then, immune to the attractions of Evelyn's voice and body; it is Sister Mary John who suffers most from the great longing, perhaps because she is already a woman with "inverted" tendencies.

Unlike the other nuns, Sister Mary John, already—in a convent where male names are rare—masculinized by her name, "continue[s] to slouch . . . , to cross her legs, to swing her arms, to lean forward and interrupt when she was interested in the conversation" (*EI* 441). Later we see the eccentric nun in "enormous boots" that look "like men's boots" (*EI* 470). The novels thus figure Sister Mary John in every way as masculinized, as, that is, an invert, and it is Evelyn's voice that brings out that potential. The two women are much thrown together because Sister Mary John directs the convent choir. Eventually, Sister Mary John asks to be transferred to another convent to remove herself from the temptation of Evelyn's presence. When she leaves, Evelyn asks, "Won't you kiss me before you go?" Sister Mary John's response, "It will be better not," underscores their difference (*ST* 168). For the latter, a kiss, even at a moment when it's clear they will never see each other again, could never be just a kiss, a simple gesture of friendship and farewell. While Evelyn herself is devoid of any intention to seduce her friend, she did practice, after all, a profession that requires "months . . . seeking the exact rhythm of a phrase intended to depict and to rouse a sinful desire" (*EI* 433).

The text thus works to separate the woman Evelyn and the diva,[5] the one innocent, the other inevitably guilty, guilty not only of rousing a sinful desire in men but of rousing it in women as well. Evelyn the woman wonders why "the Church [has] not placed stage life under the ban of mortal sin" (*EI* 329), and her mentor, Monsignor Mostyn, says that "the virtuous actress is like a false light, which instead of warning vessels from the rocks entices them to their ruin" (*EI* 330). Again, the diva is figured as siren, and the siren is, in the end, appropriately punished, even though there are voices in these texts, sympathetic voices like the young composer Ulick, that rail against the incipient Philistinism of Mostyn and of Evelyn herself.

Evelyn Innes struggles with her vocation for most of *Sister Teresa*. At one point both she and her superiors decide that she must leave the convent—they because "she has been a source of distraction to us all," and she because thoughts of her life as a diva overwhelm her and elicit doubts not only about her calling but about the dogmas of faith as well (161). Her behavior becomes more and more bizarre and irrational. She has a breakdown, and it seems certain she will die. But something worse happens: she loses her voice, and although she has opportunities to leave the now oppressive life of the convent, she doesn't—"something had broken in her" (234). We are left with a Sister Teresa silenced and passive, quite different from the passionate Evelyn Innes, diva par excellence. Her silence and passivity are such that the novel ends not with its eponymous protagonist at all but with another diva, a minor character, wondering about her own future. It is difficult not to read this ending, this passivity unto erasure, as fit retribution for Evelyn's short stint as a diva, as, that is, "an agent of the sensual passion" (*EI* 329).

A somewhat later text, James Huneker's *Painted Veils* (1920), rejects the naive and sympathetic diva of Moore's narrative and illustrates the (by that time) wider cultural currency of the ideas of Freud and the sexologists. Like Moore's, this novel offers a diva who is siren to both men and women, but it is much more explicit about the nature of the seductions. And the diva herself, unlike Evelyn Innes, is wholly unrepentant of her irregular life, proudly perverse. The diva—Esther, Easter, and Istar at various points in the novel—both recognizes and exploits her role as siren. Needing money for training abroad, she thinks of a rich heiress, Allie Wentworth, who is, like Sister Mary John, "a masculine creature," affecting "a mannish cut of clothes," "hair closely cut," and "a hooked walking stick" (70); Allie becomes her constant companion. The main character of the novel and Easter's first lover, Ulick (his name suggesting, like the similarities between the divas' names, a "modern," that is, consciously informed by the sexologists, reworking of *Evelyn Innes*) is so hopelessly haunted by the ambitious and calculating diva that her cruel teasing of him leads to a stroke and eventual death. Among the other men she lures to harm is seminarian Milt, whom she drives to drink and debauchery. But she, like Evelyn, is not only a seducer of men; she systematically sets out to ensnare the helpless Mona, Milt's sister and Ulick's second love, after which she insinuates herself into the relationship between Ulick and a sweet young courtesan, Dora. Plied by Easter with highballs, Dora watches her "with ravished vision" (292). When Ulick suggests that Dora go to bed, she replies, "Yes but not with you . . . my boy" (292). Both Mona and Dora join Istar's "girls" who "sprawl" in "luxurious divans" and commit, we presume, "the sweet sin of Sappho" (309).

To be a diva is, all these narratives suggest, to be already corrupt and/or corrupted. But, as we have seen, in many earlier texts there is a stage prior to divahood in which the young singer is innocent, spontaneous, appealingly on the brink of becoming a woman. Her voice, untrained and therefore "natural," is seductive, and though she is innocent of any intent to seduce, her influence on her audience, who often hear her quite by accident, is usually profound. Hearing Sandra Belloni sing in the countryside changed Wilfred's life and, indeed, the lives of all the men around her. But perhaps the purest example of this stage—pure because we see her *only* then—is William Wordsworth's Solitary Reaper. Not only does she have no intent to seduce her audience, she never even discovers that she *has* an audience. The speaker listens to her "voice so thrilling" (12), but he can't understand her words; she is singing, we presume, in a Scottish dialect that he doesn't know. But in the end he doesn't really mind not knowing, the better to hear the song so typically Wordsworthian, "melancholy" (6) in tone and humbly rural and common in theme:

> Or is it some more humble lay,
> Familiar matter of today?
> Some natural sorrow, loss, or pain,
> That has been, and may be again? (17–24)

In the end, the "theme" is not the most important part of this musical experience. "Whate'er the theme, the Maiden sang / As if her song could have no ending" (25–26); it is the singer's passion ("the Vale profound / Is overflowing with the sound" [7–8]) and her persistence that move him.

Her theme is not in itself of great significance, then, because the speaker himself can, as he shows, supply the theme. He can also compensate for the song's ephemerality—another Wordsworthian theme: "The music in my heart I bore,/ Long after it was heard no more" (31–32). There's a finality in the passive "was heard no more" that suggests as well the singer's own loss of voice or even her death, and reminds us that we have never heard the voice, that we have only the poem that stands in for it, that displaces it from the start. By this time, in other words, her voice is no longer relevant; what persists is the music in the "heart" of the poet. He, too, is mortal, but, unlike the singer, he has the means to immortality; he can make a poem of her voice. And he does, "The Solitary Reaper." The poet thus makes into persistent and enduring art not only the singer, not only the "sound" (7) that exceeds the power and beauty of the "Nightingale" (9) and the "Cuckoo" (14), but his own hearing of it, his own appreciation of it, his own imaginative supplying of its themes, his own further meditation on persistence itself. Here the memorializing agenda of so much of Wordsworth's work is explicitly gendered. His poem takes the place of her ephemeral song even as it constructs her as she who must disappear; the death of her voice is the necessary precondition of his art, but his art has always already constructed her voice.

This cursory reading of the poem introduces an important motif that more explicit diva narratives elaborate: the appropriation of the female voice by the male artist—singer, poet, painter, general genius.[6]

There are clear strains of this motif in many diva novels, including *Sandra Belloni*, which opens with a scene strikingly similar to that of "The Solitary Reaper," and *Evelyn Innes*, which announces that Evelyn is "the instrument, he [Owen Asher] the hand that played upon it" (127). Evelyn herself sees the tremendous difference Asher has made in her life—"She would have been nothing without him"—and often submerges her voice in his, "saying exactly what he would say" (175). Evelyn is perhaps most "played upon" by Ulick, the genius composer, who becomes an extension of her musician father. "Sometimes her father and Ulick began an argument, her sympathies alternated between them; she spoke very little, preferring to listen"(317). She listens; she absorbs; she suppresses her own voice. What they teach takes on life in her singing. It is from Ulick, for example, that she learns to see the superficiality of Asher—embodied in the competent but undistinguished songs he writes—and to broaden her musical and spiritual horizons. And we have already seen how Monsignor Mostyn plays upon the earnest and "good" young singer.[7]

George du Maurier's *Trilby* (1895) and Gaston Leroux's *The Phantom of the Opera* (1911) offer the most extreme versions of the tale of the appropriation of the female voice by the male genius. Although the divas in *Trilby* and *Phantom* are in some ways as much sirens as the divas we discussed earlier, both of these novels, unlike *Evelyn Innes*, present the singer *primarily* as a woman without a voice of her own, a woman whose singing reflects, like the young woman's singing in "The Solitary Reaper," the mind, thought, intelligence of a man who is the true artist, poet, genius. And they do this much more literally than Wordsworth's poem: in *Trilby*, the man behind the diva's throne is a mesmerizer and sings through her; in *Phantom*, the true but twisted genius is a ventriloquist. The power of the siren is thus significantly diluted, the diva reduced to a puppet and subsequently punished, when appropriate, for her departures from the Victorian ideal, one of which departures is, of course, the very act of becoming a diva.

On the surface, for example, Trilby's death seems gratuitous; her brief and brilliant career as the most astonishing singer the world has known is forced on her by the evil Svengali. But the sweet and loving young woman had siren tendencies before she fell under his influence; her "one shortcoming," says the narrator, aside from the perfectly understandable and feminine ones like jealousy, is that she loved too many. The narrator, to make his story more acceptable (in case "the Young Person . . . should happen to pry into these pages when her mother is looking another way"), pronounces that judgment in Latin, "Quia multum amavit" (49), making clear that the loving is physical, that Trilby—she is grammatically the active lover—seduces. Unwittingly perhaps, even innocently, but she seduces nonetheless. And at the end of the novel, when she has lost her voice, her spirit, and possibly her mind, this has not changed: "Tuneless and insane, she was more of a siren than ever" (383).

In fact, Trilby's "one shortcoming" seems inextricable from her femaleness—"she followed love for love's sake only . . . as she would have followed art if she had been man" (50). Trilby is thus doomed from the beginning, a doom suggested in her first appearance; she was "clad in the gray overcoat of a French infantry soldier . . . her toes lost . . . in a huge pair of male slippers" (14). The male costume and quasi-male appearance

("She would have been a singularly handsome boy" [16]) suggest a forbidden appropriation of male prerogatives even before we, or the susceptible male characters, realize that she also has appropriated the male, the active, sexual role. Though her behavior—aside from this odd tendency to cross-dress—during the course of the novel is exemplary, she *has loved* too many and has besides posed nude for several painters. She is not, as Little Billee's mother impresses on her so forcefully, of "unblemished character" (180); marriage to Little Billee is therefore out of the question. In good operatic, Traviatic mode, Trilby agrees with Mrs. Bagot and promises never to see Billee again—with operatic, Traviatic consequences.

Trilby is thus from the first a combination—not always consistent—of the bad woman and the good woman. She has loved, she has exposed her body, but she gives all this up for Billee and his friends. She dresses like a boy, but this, too, changes under the influence of the good young Englishmen—she "went less into the open air. And she let her hair grow" (126). She loves where she should not but sacrifices her one chance at happiness by giving up Billee. As Mrs. Bagot so clearly sees, however, no amount of present virtue erases past vice, even as past vice fails to protect present virtue from the machinations of others. The very passivity that Trilby learns under the tutelage of Billee and the boys, the very femininity that she acquires, makes her susceptible to Svengali's mesmerizing influence.[8]

Among the young English artists in the novel—Billee and his friends—Trilby is not artist but art object, "the Venus Anadyomene from top to toe" (346); Billee draws her foot, and an artist's cast of her feet fetches enormous sums. For Svengali, the musical artist, Trilby is the mouthpiece. As Elaine Showalter notes, "Many critics have pointed to the way that Trilby's body is mutilated and fetishized by various male artists in the story, who reduce her to the perfect foot, larynx or mouth" (xvi). The narrative describes her as "just a singing-machine—an organ to play upon . . . the unconscious voice that Svengali sang with" (441). Significantly, she has no singing voice of her own. The first time we hear her sing, she is so out of tune, her voice so croaky and cracked, that she becomes the object of ridicule. Her performance after Svengali dies is "the most lamentable grotesque performance ever heard out of a human throat!" (365), eliciting "shouts of laughter, hoots, hisses, cat-calls, cock-crows" (364). In other words, Trilby's own voice is not simply ordinary or mediocre, it is terrible and tuneless, and the text takes great pain to emphasize this difference between Trilby before and Trilby after Svengali. In fact, as one of the characters remarks at the end, there are *two* Trilbys, the vibrant, tone-deaf, completely unambitious and unassuming Trilby and Trilby the diva, a "Trilby of marble, who could produce wonderful sounds—just the sounds [Svengali] wanted, and nothing else—and think his thoughts and wish his wishes" (441).[9] Interestingly, both Trilbys share absolute devotion to men, the first to Billee and his friends, and the second, the "Trilby of marble," to her Pygmalion (an avowed woman-hater in the Greek myth); both Trilbys mirror the male master, the male artist. When Billee first meets her, her eyes seemed "to reflect only a little image of himself" (40), while Trilby's love for Svengali is "just his own love for himself . . . reflected back on him as from a mirror" (441).

The text works to portray Billee and Svengali as opposites, but Trilby's susceptibility, which constitutes her very femaleness, puts her in similar relationship to both. Trilby's falling under the influence of Svengali seems a response to her falling (granted, somewhat differently) under the influence of Billee—who has "for the singing woman an absolute worship." Billee, the narrator informs us, "would have been an easy prey to the sirens! Even beauty paled before the lovely female voice. . . . The nightingale killed the bird of paradise" (59). Trilby is beautiful, but can't "tell a C from an F" until she is mesmerized by Svengali. La Svengali, man-made diva, is "the greatest contralto . . . the world has ever known" (439) and, as such, the clear embodiment of a man's desire: Billee is "especially in thrall to the contralto—the deep low voice that . . . soars all at once into a magnified angelic boy treble" (59). When Trilby becomes La Svengali, then, she becomes Billee's fantasy, every man's fantasy, the text implies, the perfect combination of nightingale and bird of paradise. But, of course, such perfection has its price, as every Faustian narrative assures us. There is a difference, though, between the Faustian narrative and *Trilby*, a gender difference. Once Trilby falls into femininity—as she must—she can do nothing so active, nothing so evil as selling her soul. Instead, evil befalls her; Svengali enthralls her and replaces her soul with his. When the diva sings, the narrator tells us, she seems to say, "What does the composer count for . . . when I am the singer; for I am *Svengali*; and you shall hear nothing, see nothing, think of nothing, but *Svengali, Svengali, Svengali*" (310). This Faustian sentiment not only figures the diva as egomaniac but in its collapse of Svengali and La Svengali—already a name implying Trilby's possession by male genius—suggests the complete replacement of the woman by the man. And this is the ultimate fantasy of this text, no matter how much the situation is eventually decried, no matter what its tragic consequences.

Billee, too, must die—for, perhaps, his unswerving devotion to the siren. But he must die as well to echo the fate of Svengali, to whom he is so intimately related through the body of Trilby. Both men are artists, geniuses in their respective fields; both use Trilby—Billee as model (though, modest youth that he is, he only draws her foot), Svengali as mouthpiece. But Billee and Svengali are linked in another way as well—their Jewish blood. Billee has in his "winning and handsome face . . . a faint suggestion of some possible very remote Jewish ancestor—just a tinge of that strong, sturdy, irrepressible, indomitable blood which is of such priceless value in diluted homeopathic doses, like the dry white Spanish wine called montejo, which is not meant to be taken pure" (6). Svengali, on the other hand, illustrates the consequences of this blood "taken pure." His "heavy, languid lustreless black hair," "bold, beady Jew's eyes" (60), and "long, thick, . . . Hebrew nose" (324) make him "offensive to the normal Englishman" (12) and reflect his moral degradation, a condition attributed to his Jewish blood: "Being an Oriental Israelite Hebrew Jew, he had not been able to resist the temptation of spitting in [Billee's] face, since he must not throttle him to death" (356). It is only, it seems, the restraining forces of civilization (here defined by the British Billee and friends) that can moderate Jewish blood "taken pure." Billee's "tinge" of Jewish blood suggests again his consanguinity with Svengali and suggests as well Svengali as a sort of dark double to the English hero and the embodiment of the artistic temperament, fueled quite literally by Jewish or otherwise foreign blood, run amok. Svengali, of course, is the novel's clearest genius and most powerful artist, his power and genius the source of his initial attraction for Trilby and perhaps for the thousands of readers who found him, no doubt, both compelling and repulsive. Only allied with his dark, foreign power does Trilby attain fame and fortune.

We look at these passages not because anti-Semitism is an exceptional sentiment in the Victorian novel but because virulent ethnic stereotyping is so prevalent in diva novels. Most often it is Jews and Italians—their passions always just barely under control—who are so stereotyped, and many times the two are conflated. In *Trilby*, for example, one of the two "human nightingales" of the century is Glorioli, a "swarthy foreigner" with an Italian name and a Sephardic heritage. Usually it is the diva herself who is "foreign," and though Trilby is Irish, La Svengali thoroughly takes on the "foreign" identity of Svengali, her inspiration.

The Phantom of the Opera (1911) by Gaston Leroux is a gentler, less extreme—in both plot and ideology—version of *Trilby*. The diva Christine

Daaé does not die, merely marries and stops singing. Unlike Svengali, the Phantom is not completely unsympathetic; he has had a hard life—"we must needs pity the Opera Ghost" (264).[10] Unlike Trilby, Christine is an extremely promising singer—"those who heard her prophesied that she would be the greatest singer in the world"—even before the Phantom appears (54). But after her father's death, "suddenly, she seemed to have lost, with him, her voice, her soul, her music" (54). While Christine, like Trilby, has a faithful suitor, the villain is not linked to him in any obvious ways, nor is the Phantom an overt scapegoat for xenophobic sentiments.

Christine, however, like Trilby, falls under the spell of a man with a voice—"oh, such a lovely man's voice" (45)—and so opens herself up to doubts about her virtue (Trilby, of course, has entirely forfeited claims to virtue from the beginning; her attachment to Svengali is more relapse than original fall). Christine's suitor, Raoul, is concerned and suspicious: "To think that he had believed in her innocence, in her purity!" he muses (86). He asks her confidante, "Is Christine still a good girl?" (85). "No, no, you have driven me mad!" Raoul says to the young diva at one point. "When I think that I had only one object in life: to give my name to an opera wench!" (94). "Opera wench" suggests not only Christine's questionable virtue but that of other women associated with the opera. In other words, the diva is tainted by divahood itself, regardless of the relative innocence of the young woman. But perhaps it is womanhood that is suspect, Raoul suggests, in another formulation of his distress: "He had loved an angel and now he despised a woman!" (88). As Christine's voice has ascended from the human to the angelic, she has fallen, in Raoul's eyes, from angel to woman. And the fall is a sexual one.

Raoul's suspicions are unfounded, of course, and Christine's virtue is rewarded by escape from the monster and the happy-ever-after reunion with Raoul. But Christine's virtue here, though equated by Raoul with virginity, encompasses more. Not only is Christine sexually pure, she is untainted by other marks of divahood, marks clearly enunciated in the text's description of her rival, the Spanish Carlotta, a "celebrated, but heartless and soulless diva" (72), who works "with all her might to 'smother' her rival" (71). Like most of the more modern divas we have seen, then, Carlotta is ambitious, envious, and ruthless. And she is suitably punished: she croaks during a performance and becomes a laughingstock. It is the Opera Ghost who metes out this punishment, a development that suggests his benevolence and good judgment, traits that emerge at the novel's close.

Even more interesting, though, is the timing of the punishment. The diva is singing the role of Marguerite in *Faust*, though her ambition makes Faust himself her real prototype; she is "certain of herself . . . certain of her voice and her success, fearing nothing" (77). This certainty, confidence, and fearlessness ally themselves with Faustian hubris—and have similar consequences. When Carlotta begins to triumph in this new role, she makes a serious mistake: she "flung herself into her part without restraint of modesty" (77). While her certainty of success is itself a lack of modesty in one sense of that word, "flung" and "without restraint" suggest the lack of sexual modesty as well, a suggestion confirmed by the disapproving comment that follows: "She was no longer Margarita, she was Carmen" (77). Of the role of Marguerite, "*chaste et pure*," with "*une ame innocent*" (*Faust* 3.4), Carlotta makes a Carmen, the flauntingly sexual, the promiscuous, unrestrained, independent singer of siren songs.

Christine, modest and loving, presents an obvious contrast. And to her, so much more suitable to it in every way, the part of Marguerite—in the wake of Carlotta's croaking and the subsequent crashing of the opera chandelier—falls. But Christine is charmingly innocent of the Opera Ghost's machinations to get her the part: "I don't know how it was that Carlotta did not come to the theater that night nor why I was called upon to sing in her stead," she says (117). In other words, Christine has a spectacular operatic success but has resorted to no dirty tricks. Her ambition is muted by modesty, her rise to the top orchestrated by forces outside not only her control but even her awareness. While Carlotta fills the opera house with her fans and does everything she can, in good prima donna fashion, to undermine her rival, Christine plays her lesser parts and waits, while the Phantom acts in her stead.

One of her lesser parts is Siebel in *Faust*, the youth devoted to Marguerite; Christine looks "charming in her boy's clothes" (75), but she is clearly meant for something more womanly than this, just as she is meant, in her real life, for something more womanly than the opera house stage. Christine Daaé is, that is, the model diva: she has no voice of her own but is the vessel for male genius; success comes to her without political effort, and she happily gives it all up to be with her one true love. Christine's happy fate rewrites the fate of the operatic Marguerite, who, too, succumbed to the charming voice of a supernatural man. When her brother goes off to war, he mourns that he must leave his parentless sister without a protector. Unprotected, unwatched, she falls in love with Faust, is abandoned by him, goes mad, and dies (though she manages to save her soul). In the last act, the chorus recognizes the cause of her tragedy: "*Ou*

trouverai-je un protecteur"—where will I find a protector—for the innocent? (5.4). Christine, well on her way to the same tragic fate, has the faithful Raoul to keep vigil over her virginity and to rescue her from the opera
underworld where the Phantom, in his most Faustian mode, keeps her.

There's not much difference, the text suggests, between the world of
the opera and the underworld of the opera. In both, Faustian ambition
reigns; in both, the innocent go unprotected. To preserve, or restore, virtue,
young divas like Trilby and Christine Daaé must leave that world and embrace domesticity among their own kind. Opera, that is, is always foreign,
always permeated with the Other—Italians, Jews, Spaniards, artists, geniuses, homosexuals. The consequence of this atmosphere of otherness on
innocent young womanhood is made clear when the Opera Ghost has lured
Christine to his apartment, where he writes his "music . . . so terrible that it
consumes all those who approach it." He insists that she sing a duet with
him, he Othello, she Desdemona. "Love, jealousy, hatred, burst out around
us in harrowing cries," Christine narrates. "Erik's black mask made me
think of the natural mask of the Moor of Venice. He was Othello himself"
(127). When she rips off his mask, there is more of the Moor underneath:
"four black holes of its eyes, its nose, its mouth . . . , the mighty fury of a
demon" (128).

Erik's color is black throughout the novel; here most explicitly his
color suggests race and its association with the dangers of difference.
Desdemona the white, the pure, the innocent, cannot survive the extreme
anger of the dark foreigner, just as Christine and Trilby cannot survive the
mighty fury of their respective devotees. France is Erik's birthplace, but
like Svengali the Jew he is a cosmopolitan figure, who "crossed the whole
of Europe" (261), spent time in Persia, and moved to Constantinople before
returning to the Paris opera house. These world travelers are, like opera itself, infected by foreign ways, Latin ways, Jewish ways, Gypsy ways, Eastern ways.

Without protection, without a protector, even the most modest of
young women catch the viruses that hover in the nicks and crannies of the
opera house. In a rare burst of self-assertion early in the novel, Christine
lashes out at her loyal protector, Raoul: "I am mistress of my own
actions . . . you have no right to control them and I beg you to desist henceforth" (101). A modern reader cheers her on, but the passage implies that
she oversteps herself: she says this "haughtily" and, readers understand, un-
truthfully, since shortly afterwards she admits that she is "no longer mistress of myself: I had become his [Erik's] thing!" (118). A preference for

the exotic over the homely, the ambitious over the humble, the sensual over the chaste, the showy over the modest, the assertive over the submissive, voice over silence—these are the viruses, their origins (like the "origins" of all our most feared diseases) securely, conventionally, located elsewhere, against which the female singer who chooses the opera stage can have no defenses.

The virus metaphor seems particularly apt for a profession that relies so thoroughly on the body. And it is perhaps this very reliance on the unreliable body—subject as it is to disease, decay, and violence of every sort—that renders divahood suspect. The novels themselves are clear about the intimate connection between the diva and her body and often make a certain part of the anatomy, usually but not always the throat, a sign of divahood. In *Evelyn Innes*, for example, Owen Asher remarks to Evelyn, "Your throat is too thick, you have the real singer's throat" (114). She has, that is, not a normal woman's throat but one that is excessive at best, deformed at worst. The diva is, by physical definition, abnormal, deformed, excessive.[11] Treviso in *Mildred Pierce* carefully examines Veda: "I see dees deep chest, dees big bosom, dees 'igh nose, dees big antrium sinus in front of face. . . . I see what come once in a lifetime only—a great coloratura" (320). Veda describes the examination: "He went all over me with instruments, little wooden hammers . . . on my knuckles, and caliper things that went over my nose, and gadgets with lights . . . that went down my throat" (335). The voice of the diva can, it seems, be ferreted out like a rare virus by its unusual physical symptoms, depending as it does on a certain degree of abnormality—sign, of course, of the diva's own distance from the "normal" woman—for its strength and beauty. No wonder, then, that it and the profession to which it most logically leads are always under suspicion. No wonder, then, that masculinist discourse seeks to quarantine the woman with a voice, to confine her in the pathological for fear that divahood is contagious. The frenzied adulation of Adelina Patti was called by some of her contemporaries the "Patti epidemic" (Dizikes 225).

But it is, of course, just this fear and suspicion on the part of the powers of conventional order and discipline that make the diva a figure full of potential and fascination for writers and artists, mostly but not exclusively women, who are suspicious of conventional order, writers and artists who would locate pathology not in bodies or the body's desire but in social discourses and institutions. We turn now to texts that redress the siren and the voiceless vessel narratives, that present divas as self-made women, women who work.

CHAPTER 3

The Sirens Avenged

DIVAS IN A DIFFERENT KEY

"Poor wretch!" she says of any murderess—
"The world was cruel, and she could not sing:
I carry my revenges in my throat."
—George Eliot, *Armgart*

During the nineteenth century, women's interest in divas was not limited to the fandom of Queen Victoria or the adolescent gushing of the proto–Gerry-Flappers who besieged Jenny Lind. In a tradition that runs roughly parallel to the masculinist tradition we looked at in chapter 2, the diva begins to appear frequently in women's writing. In 1865, for example, Ellen Creathorne Clayton published *Queens of Song*, a collection of narratives of the lives of well-known eighteenth- and nineteenth-century divas dedicated to diva Pauline Viardot. The dedication illustrates a pattern that we have found repeatedly in women's relations to the diva's voice: the diva's voice motivates another woman to discover and use her own (here, narrative) voice. In its five-hundred-plus pages, Clayton's book labors to redress prima donna stereotypes. We see singers abused by husbands and fathers; we see the sacrifices they made and the hard work they did to develop their voice; we see the many relatives and friends they supported with their singing. Clayton's was not the only nineteenth-century text inspired by and memorializing Viardot. A friend of both George Sand and George Eliot, Viardot is the model for both Sand's *Consuelo* and Eliot's *Armgart* and is, as well, one of the first of a long line of historical divas who served as models for the singers in women's writing.

George Eliot: The Diva Doesn't Die

If, following Clément, we see the woman who sings Carmen or Tosca as participating in and collaborating with an art form that rehearses and passes from one generation to another a masculinist gender code, then the number of divas in nineteenth- and twentieth-century women's writing is at first glance surprising. Since so many operas depend on "the submission or death of the woman for the sake of narrative closure" (McClary, "Foreword" ix), and the women who play these roles, the prima donnas, are reputed, as we have seen, to be rather deadly themselves, the diva would seem a figure for the woman writer to avoid rather than privilege.

Divas in women's texts, however, tend to redress prima donna stereotypes and revise the representations of female singers we find in many texts by men, to recoup for women themselves the woman who has, in every sense of the word, a "voice." Sand, Eliot, and later women writers understood that the diva's "voice" could serve as both a mode of and metaphor for female empowerment in a culture that traditionally placed women on the side of silence. It is in this context that most women writers have placed their female singers and privileged the diva as the woman who has, preeminently and indisputably, gained a voice. The diva in this tradition is neither femme fatale nor happy handmaiden to what is finally a male muse. She is, rather, a hardworking woman more interested in music than marriage, in empowering women than seducing men. She garners the attention, admiration, and respect of the world with her singing voice, a voice that, after the era of the castrati, men cannot reach, usurp, or displace. Moreover, thanks to this singing voice she has a "voice" in the music she makes, in her own destiny, and in the larger world. Her privileged status as a female success in a male realm gives her license to probe, revise, and even reject the traditional gender code.

George Eliot's Armgart serves as an early example. This eponymous heroine of a verse drama—written during a break in the composition of *Middlemarch*—is renowned for her portrayal of Orpheus in Gluck's opera. At the height of her career she becomes ill, loses her singing voice, and must give up the stage and teach singing to earn a living. The work has been neglected by critics, and most of the commentary that we do have reads it in the context of the novels, seeing Armgart as simply another of Eliot's egoists in need of chastening or as another of her angry and frustrated female artists.[1] While it is revealing to so contextualize Armgart, stopping here inhibits us from seeing the extent of Armgart's difference from other Eliot heroines and her revisionary force. Given Eliot's interest in and knowledge of music, readings of the poem and the heroine remain incomplete until we take into account Eliot's friendship with Viardot and her use of Gluck's *Orpheus and Eurydice*. Opera historians have long cited it as a major departure from the static conventionality and overelaborated virtuosity, including the florid singing of the castrati, of eighteenth-century opera. Its rejection of received conventions of form and its privileging of the archetypal poet-musician Orpheus make it an appropriate vehicle for Armgart, a consummate vocal artist who refuses traditional social forms and conventional gender roles.

Working during an age of transition from castrati to tenors and women *en travesti* in first man roles, Gluck produced two versions of *Orpheus*, one for castrato (1762) and one for tenor (1774). By the nineteenth century women were singing the castrato version of Orpheus, acting and singing, in other words, the incarnation of beautiful and powerful music. This change participated, of course, in the wider shift in opera away from castrati and to tenors or women *en travesti* in first man parts. We noted earlier that a castrato *en travesti* can be read as a recuperative and conservative figure even though cross-dressing, by opening to view the gap between sex and gender, works against essentialist notions of gender. We want to suggest here that a reversal in who performs whom makes a political difference, that when women dress up like men they are indeed dressing "up," toward power, and that such a strategy has the possibility of becoming political critique. When women perform the manly part, the gender hierarchy that was reaffirmed in Casanova's reading of the castrato is destabilized. Women, in the socially inferior postion by virtue of a gender ideology that, especially in the nineteenth century, argued for innate and complementary differences in the sexes, could, when cross-dressed, show themselves capable of the superior role even as they demonstrated that masculinity and its privileges was, in a sense, an act. As Alisa Solomon remarks in another context, "If men dressed as women often *parody* gender, women dressed as men tend to *perform* gender—that is, they can reveal the extent to which gender, as Judith Butler suggests [in *Gender Trouble*], is a 'regulatory fiction'" (145).

After seeing a performance of Gluck's opera in 1855, Eliot, in a letter to Sara Hennel, wondered at the use of women's voices in all the major roles and the opera's transformation, by way of Eurydice's resurrection, of mythic tragedy into operatic comedy (*Letters* 2:191). With this precedent of women singing the castrato version, Berlioz reworked the opera and the role of Orpheus for the famous diva Pauline Viardot. The Berlioz-Viardot production premiered in Paris to great acclaim and in 1860, ten years before the composition of *Armgart*, moved to Covent Garden. The opera quickly became a Viardot vehicle, and she sang it across Europe. Although her repertoire of roles was wide—too wide for the health of her voice—she was, and remains, best known for her Orpheus.

Eliot and Viardot were friends, and they moved in many of the same artistic and intellectual circles. Indeed, Viardot occupied in the world of music a place parallel to Eliot's in the realm of letters. No mindless bird of song or stereotypical diva was Viardot.[2] Daughter of the famous tenor and voice teacher Manuel Garcia and younger sister of the renowned prima donna Maria Malibran, Viardot became a singer only after the tragic early death of her sister. She was an accomplished pianist—Liszt was one of her teachers—and composer as well. She arranged for voice some of the piano music of her friend Chopin and after her retirement from the stage had planned to write an opera, alas never completed, based on a libretto by George Sand.

Accounts of Viardot stress her intelligence, musicianship, discipline, and devotion to her art. Chorley pronounced her a "consummate, devoted, and thoroughly-musical musician" and, after seeing her on stage, wrote that her performance had "fire, courage, and accomplishment, without limit" (2:46–47, 48). Commentators have seen her as a proto-Callas, a singer with a limited instrument who used it intelligently to achieve a striking depth of characterization. And she carried her passion for playing her roles with accuracy and depth to greater degrees than any singer before her: she did research to insure the historical accuracy of her costumes, and she was one of the first divas to prepare a role by studying an opera's literary sources as well as the music and libretto.

It is, though, for her connections with the major writers of the age that Viardot is best remembered in literary circles. Her sister Maria Malibran inspired some of George Sand's early work, but it is clearly Viardot who had the most profound effect on the writer: "She is the first woman since Alicia the nun whom I have loved with unmitigated enthusiasm," Sand confessed (Moers 506, 507). Viardot was Sand's closest female friend, and Sand's novel *Consuelo* (1842), an account of a brilliant singer dedicated to her art with a missionary zeal, is a tribute to her. Viardot herself thought the novel so captured her ideals and temperament that she once told an acquaintance to read *Consuelo* if he wished to know her better (FitzLyon 281).

But it is Viardot's connection with Eliot—they were close enough for Viardot to visit the writer at home when Eliot was too depressed to leave the house—that most interests us here. Rupert Christiansen writes that they socialized in Paris and London, which suggests that the two women had met before the Viardots, fleeing the Franco-Prussian War, took up residence in London in 1870, the year Eliot wrote *Armgart* ("George Eliot" 8–10). If Eliot did not personally know Viardot then, she would certainly have known her by reputation (part of that reputation being *Consuelo*), and George Henry Lewes's letters provide evidence that they knew each other by 1871: he describes a lunch party hosted by Eliot and himself—the guests included Trollope, Turgenev, and Viardot—at which Viardot "sang divinely and entranced everyone, some of them to positive tears" (Eliot, *Letters* 5:143–144).

Eliot knew Gluck's *Orpheus* before it became a vehicle for Viardot; she makes reference to it in her fiction as early as 1857, in "Mr. Gilfil's Love-Story."[3] But by 1870, when she wrote *Armgart*, Eliot could not have helped thinking of Viardot as she worked on this tale of a diva renowned for her Orpheus. As this and subsequent chapters show, many of the divas in texts by women are inspired by historical singers, and while we do not want to offer up Viardot as a transcendental signified here, we do want to begin the process of looking at the poem in its operatic context.[4]

Readers first meet Armgart on her return from a triumphant performance of *Orpheus*. Like Viardot, Armgart is not a conventional beauty; "The women whispered, 'Not a pretty face,'" she says scornfully (462).[5] Her triumph, then, is all the sweeter because it rests solely on the power and artistry of her singing and acting. As the scenes with her suitor emphasize, marriage defines the lives and identities of most women in her culture, but Armgart finds her life in her voice. "What is my soul to me without the voice / That gave it freedom?" she asks, and after losing her voice she laments, "Oh, I had meaning once" (508, 495).

Awaiting her return are Graf Dornberg and her cousin and companion Walpurga. In an exchange with Dornberg, whose repeated marriage proposals Armgart repeatedly rejects—they carry with them the expectation that she give up her career—the diva makes it clear that, for her, voice and gender are inseparable. "The great masters write / For *women's* voices, and great Music wants me!" she proclaims (480, our emphasis), and she notes proudly:

> Men did not say, when I had sung last night,
> "'Twas good, nay, wonderful, considering
> She is a woman"—and then turn to add
> "Tenor or baritone had sung her songs
> Better of course: she's but a woman spoiled." (478)

Armgart knows that she has a voice that, without the work of the knife, men cannot duplicate or displace. To have such a voice, she implies, frees her from the strictures and demands of the traditional gender code. Further, the voice is a way of addressing and redressing powers and institutions that would confine her, as Walpurga makes clear when she quotes her cousin to Dornberg:

> She often wonders what her life had been
> Without that voice for channel to her soul.
> She says, it must have leaped through all her limbs—
> Made her a Maenad—made her snatch a brand
> And fire some forest, that her rage might mount.
>
> . . .
>
> "Poor wretch!" she says of any murderess—
> "The world was cruel, and she could not sing:
> I carry my revenges in my throat." (457)

Armgart sees her voice as an empowering female difference in contention with traditional, oppressive powers. It is hardly surprising, then, that when she loses it after an illness, she blames not the illness but the cure: "You have murdered it / Murdered my voice," she tells the doctor (493). Later she laments, "He cured me of my voice," as if having a voice is, according to male medicine, a state of pathological deviance from which women must be saved (498).

This use of voice as a mode of female redress can take the form of a revision or supplement to the male-authored text. Armgart repeatedly describes her singing as a freewheeling flying and soaring, and one of the freedoms she appropriates for herself is the right to alter or supplement the text. In a moment that recalls Berlioz's complaints that in performance Viardot had altered words in the libretto and added roulades that he had not written, Armgart's singing teacher, Leo, complains that Armgart willfully sang notes that "Gluck had not written, nor I taught" (464).[6] Leo's insistence on fidelity to the score can be read as an attempt to keep the production—as opposed to the mere mimic performance—of art solely in male hands. His complaint "I hate my phrases to be smothered o'er / With sauce of paraphrase, my sober tune / Made bass to rambling trebles" suggests as much (463). Armgart's response to his complaint is more dismissal than denial; she *will* display her artistic vision and virtuosity. For Armgart, to have a voice is to have a say in production, to have the power to use the male text as, at least in part, a pretext for her own creative vision. "I gave that [the trill] up to you / To bite and growl at. Why, you said yourself, / Each time I sang it seemed new doors were oped" (466–467).

All this should make Dornberg uneasy, but he persists in his suit. He is unsuccessful, first and foremost, because of Armgart's single-minded dedication to her art: "I can live unmated, but not / Without the bliss of singing" (488). In this refusal to divide herself and her energies—"I will live alone and pour my pain / With passion into music," she declares (484)—Armgart recalls the dedication Sand so respected and admired in Viardot, who worked to extinguish all her passions save her passion for music because she believed that artistic achievement required the artist's indifference to all save her art (FitzLyon 321, 382). Thus Armgart declares, "I will not take for husband one who deems / The thing my soul acknowledges as good— / The thing I hold worth striving, suffering for, / To be a thing dispensed with easily" (484–485).

The exchanges with Dornberg suggest that Armgart has no intention of ever marrying. She never declares this outright, however, saying instead, "The man who marries me must wed my Art— / Honour and cherish it, not tolerate" (486). She knows full well that Dornberg, despite his sense of himself as liberal and progressive, is not that man. He too cavalierly and too patronizingly dismisses as "mere mood" Armgart's claim that she carries her revenges in her throat. He further declares that "too much ambition has unwomaned her," but even here he is smugly indulgent, confident that her "unwomanly" ambition is only a temporary state of deviance that marriage to him will cure (458).

In a culture in which gender roles are rigid and ambition and "womanliness" are supposed to be mutually exclusive, Dornberg's charge is heavy with implications. Armgart knows what Eliot's later and better-known diva, the Alcharisi in *Daniel Deronda*, openly articulates when she says, "Every woman is supposed to have the same set of motives [marriage and motherhood], or else to be a monster" (10:345). But the Alcharisi goes further than Armgart does when she defends her abandonment of Deronda: "You can never imagine what it is to have a man's force of genius in you, and yet to suffer the slavery of being a girl" (10:349). Significantly, especially since the role that crowns her career is the trouser role of Orpheus, Armgart never figures herself, her voice, or her career in the masculine terms that the Alcharisi uses, terms that, no doubt, underlie Dornberg's charge of "unwomanliness." Armgart resists reifying the binary oppositions the traditional gender code depends upon and uses to keep women secondary.

The singer, for example, repeatedly links her voice and her gender, as if to forestall charges that by putting her art before the prescriptions of the gender code she will be seen as "monstrous" and "masculine." In an argument that recalls the Wife of Bath's, she claims:

> Yes I know
> The oft-taught Gospel: "Woman, thy desire
> Shall be that all superlatives on earth
> Belong to men, save the one highest kind—
> To be a mother. Thou shalt not desire
> To do aught best save pure subservience:
> Nature has willed it so!" O blessed Nature!
> Let her be arbitress; she gave me a voice
> Such as she only gives a woman child,
> Best of its kind, gave me ambition too. (477–478)

Armgart is playing with Dornberg's own terms here; she later contends that appeals to nature and biology are really ideology: "I am an artist by my birth— / By the same warrant that I am a woman: / . . . I need not crush myself within a mould / Of theory called Nature" (480).

Within the context of these powerful assertions that to be a woman and to be an artist are not mutually exclusive, how then are we to read the fact that Armgart gives voice to Orpheus, the figure who for Western culture allies the artistic with the male? What is the status of the Orpheus role in this work, given that years earlier Eliot had figured bad women's art as "an absurd exaggeration of the masculine style, like the swaggering gate of a bad actress in male attire" (*Essays* 53)? Eliot's choice of genre, an unusual one for her, and the operatic setting are suggestive and critically helpful here. While the genre, verse drama, and theatrical setting both call up a thematics of "roles," and the operatic context suggests issues of gender, the performance history of Gluck's *Orpheus and Eurydice* calls up the issue of the relations between (gender) roles and biological sex. Thus we might be tempted to argue that because Armgart's identification with Orpheus is so complete—"Orpheus was Armgart, Armgart Orpheus," Leo marvels—she is, despite her rhetoric, masculinized (464). Or we might argue that by playing the manly part on stage Armgart experiences not some essentialized maleness but the freedom, power, independence, and artistic autonomy traditionally associated with the male role.

But the history of Gluck's *Orpheus* is one of gender reversal and slippage, and this, coupled with the poem's emphasis on the female voice, reminds us that Armgart consistently associates this very freedom, independence, and power not with the masculine role (it is significant that we never see her in male attire) but with her female voice. A woman acting the manly part suggests the extent to which gender is a role, a "performance." Eliot's two divas know that this is especially true for women. Speaking of her years as a wife, Deronda's mother says, "I acted that part" (10:362), and after losing her singing voice Armgart laments that she is "Prisoned now— / Prisoned in all the petty mimicries / Called women's knowledge, that will fit the world / As doll-clothes fit a man" (508–509). Gender roles are costumes for Armgart as well. Given the performance history of Gluck's opera, we can push even further. That here, in the opera, was a place where a female voice had a replaced a male's and where a male's could never again displace a female's—in the original register of composition, anyway—could not have been lost on Eliot. Perhaps she relished a further irony: according to legend, Orpheus outsang the Sirens to insure the Argonauts safe passage, and the Sirens, in despair at losing this vocal competition, threw themselves into the sea. The performance history of the opera reverses the gender politics of the original myth.[7] Moreover, thanks to Viardot and the other female Orpheuses before her, in Gluck's opera Eliot found as well a tradition that allied women with the most powerful and moving art, art so powerful that it could "force hell to grant what love did seek." When we trace back the series of gender bendings and reversals in the history of the operatic Orpheus, then, what may have appealed to Eliot is this: from the perspective of a nineteenth-century audience the figure of the first artist was always already in some sense female. (The image of Orpheus on the stage is, after all, a woman pretending to be a man who wears a tunic, a skirt.)

Like Viardot, who sang roles out of her range and thereby prematurely ruined her voice, Armgart loses her voice in her prime and at the close of the drama is reduced to the prospect of being an unwed voice teacher in a provincial town. Given Armgart's long confrontation with Walpurga, in which Walpurga accuses the singer of blind egoism, we may be tempted to read Armgart's illness as a punishment for her aspirations to renown and for her refusal to renounce the rages in her throat. Such a reading has the appeal of providing a thread with which to seam the drama into the fabric of Eliot's fiction. It neglects, however, a subtle difference between Armgart's fate and that of so many other Eliot heroines: the Armgart we see at the close is chastened, but she is neither dead nor dependent nor, as the Alcharisi is, desiccated and bitter. Unlike Dinah Morris, she is not completely silenced. Unlike Deronda's mother, she is not driven to marriage by the prospect of artistic failure or decline: "I will not be / A pensioner in marriage," Armgart declares (502). As a voice teacher, an occupation Viardot herself took up after she retired from the opera stage in the 1860s, Armgart still has a part, albeit a smaller and mediated one, in the production of art, and she still has the freedom and independence she has always associated with her female voice.

If we see this end as less punishing and/or tragic than other critics have, we appeal once again to Eliot's embedding of Gluck's *Orpheus and Eurydice*, especially its ending, for support. Monteverdi's *Orfeo* (1607) follows the traditional tale: the singer looks back and loses his Eurydice once again to the underworld. In Haydn's *Orfeo ed Euridice* (1791), Orpheus not only loses Eurydice but is torn to pieces by frenzied Maenads, the very figures Armgart herself offers as paradigms of angry women without voices, without outlets for their rage. But Eliot embeds Gluck's version of the Orpheus legend, and as the letter to Sara Hennel suggests, what Eliot found remarkable about Gluck's opera was its replacement of the traditional tragic ending, in which Eurydice remains in the land of the dead, with a happy one in which, despite Orpheus's looking back, Eurydice is given her freedom and reunited with Orpheus. What Gluck's opera presents, then, is the "resurrection" and return to the land of the living of the female character. Neither diva, whether singing Orpheus or Eurydice, dies. Eliot had misgivings about this innovation at the 1855 performance, but she was able to employ its resonances in 1870.

If we accept Armgart as the exception to the conventional Eliot heroine, we speculate that the writer was able to depart from her standard heroine in *Armgart* because she had before her the model of Pauline Viardot's achievement, devotion to her art, and, perhaps most important of all, survival. After finishing *Armgart* Eliot returned to the unfinished *Middlemarch* and began writing the "Miss Brooke" section. We might, then, read the verse drama as a therapeutic exercise in which Eliot, before settling down to the tale of another frustrated heroine whose life more closely reflected those of real Victorian women, satisfied a desire to explore the figure of an intellectual, achieving, and performing woman who survived.

Women at Work

Early in 1994, the Metropolitan Opera canceled its contract, on grounds of "unprofessional actions," with diva Kathleen Battle. The *Washington Post* noted that the cancellation "cemented yet another stone in that most durable of operatic stereotypes, the volcanic and impossible diva"

(Ringle 1). Among Battle's soprano sins, the writer lists "storming out of rehearsals, canceling performances, fighting with wigmakers." An earlier *Post* account recalled a 1993 incident in which "the temperamental Battle . . . walked off the stage after battling with conductor Christian Thielemann over tempo, refusing to appear as Sophie in Richard Strauss's 'Der Rosenkavalier'" ("Met" C).

Such autocratic behavior is, of course, a favorite motif of diva narratives, and along with promiscuity and professional jealously practically constitutes the diva stereotype. Opera histories chronicle much more extravagant and outrageous performances than Ms. Battle's and chronicle, as well, endless tales of divas' sexual misconduct and spiteful rivalry. The twentieth-century archetype for the difficult diva is perhaps Maria Callas. Her husband recounts an argument between Callas and a wealthy impresario who had given one of Callas's roles to a rival. After threatening to crown him with a twenty-pound bronze inkstand and paper holder, she "threw herself on [him], striking him in the stomach with her knee. It could have been a fatal blow. Maria . . . weighed more than two hundred pounds . . . and had the power of a young bull" (Menegheni 153). Recollecting in tranquility, Callas observed, "I only regret not having broken his head" (154). And Callas's legendary rivalry with Renata Tebaldi has inspired at least two novels, McCourt's *Mawrdew Czgowchwz* and Anne Edwards's *La Divina*. What revisionary narratives like *Armgart* provide, in part, is not a claim that such behavior doesn't happen—numerous examples are on historical record—but the personal, professional, and social contexts in which it occurs. Diva Margarethe Styr in Gertrude Atherton's *Tower of Ivory* (1910) suggests that "tantrums do not hurt a prima donna; in fact they are of use in inspiring the authorities with awe" (165). Diva Geraldine Farrar argues similarly in her autobiography, *Such Sweet Compulsion*: "It has been the accepted fact . . . that rival sopranos . . . must necessarily be at each other's throats and reputations. . . . I believe Mary Garden shared with me . . . the sporting instinct to profit from whatever value the credulous public drew from the headlines" (235).

In other words, such stereotypical off-stage activity is part of, or at least *in* part, a performance. Which is not to say, of course, that it is not "real," that, for example Battle's battle over tempo did not result from heartfelt indignation. But indignation is itself a performance, a cultural construct like walking out or stamping one's feet. What these divas call attention to is the performativity, the constructedness, of the roles we play, and they provide us, these texts claim, with the emotional satisfactions of modes of performance culturally denied to us. The point is not an obscure one, is, in fact, not only a given of current theories of performativity but a commonplace of everyday judgments of extravagant behavior—"Quite a show!"—or not-so-extravagant behavior. Henry Pleasants in *Great Singers*, for example, issues the following judgment on Jenny Lind's public persona: "The role of a[n] . . . 'Ugly Duckling,' the . . . plain, simply dressed, . . . unassuming poor-little-me . . . pure of heart and noble of thought, was the greatest of her roles" (198). We often make similar distinctions between the "real person" and the fabricated persona, the inauthentic and the authentic self—distinctions that vary according to whether the defendant is friend or foe. What we sometimes fail to acknowledge is the artful nature of the "real," the possibility that what we take for essence is, rather, construction. Pleasants makes a distinction between Jenny Lind's "facade" and the real woman behind it: "strong-willed, ambitious, dauntlessly competitive, capable of ruthlessness," as though the strong-willed, ambitious, competitive, and ruthless woman were not also a role that, to attain success, the diva must cultivate (198).

The literary diva who recognizes most clearly the coextension of roles and "real life" is perhaps Pellegrina Leoni in Isak Dinesen's story "The Dreamers" (1934), who "would never let herself become tied up in any of her roles" (347) and, after she loses her voice, resolves that she "will be always many persons. Never again will I have my . . . whole life bound up with one woman" (345). She appears in the story as the prostitute Olalla, the brilliant milliner and revolutionary Madame Lola, and the saintly Rosalba—all roles that she sustains for years and that rival her role as the great soprano. The dreamers of the title, all men, discover that the women they respectively knew as Olalla, Lola, and Rosalba are "really" the diva Pellegrina; they hound her to her death in pursuit of her "true" identity. But what the text suggests is that "great soprano," "diva," "prima donna," and "Pellegrina" are themselves public performances no more and no less "real" and authentic. The "essential" Olalla/Lola/Rosalba/Pellegrina is performance.

The variety of Pellegrina's roles may seem to replicate female stereotypes—the egomaniacal soprano whose self-love is "a zealous, a terribly jealous love"; the fallen woman; the terrorist; the saint (332). But that she is *all* of them suggests the limitations and even absurdity of such stereotypes and suggests as well the wide range of roles we are all capable of playing, do, in fact, play during the course of our lives. As a diva, she has perhaps special license to run the gamut of roles. As we have seen in

Armgart and *Daniel Deronda* and as we will see in many twentieth-century diva narratives, the diva is, par excellence and quite literally, the woman with a voice. Many writers, especially women writers, seem to choose the figure of the diva in order to explore what, for a woman, having a voice might mean.[8] And it seems to mean, first of all, that her range of roles spans more than one octave.

While Pellegrina Leoni may be the most chameleon of literary divas, the singing heroines in this chapter are, for the most part, systematic revisions of the diva stereotypes we discussed in the previous chapter. They are, that is, diverse women with voices of their own, voices that they worked hard to develop and hone, voices that they use to seduce both men and women not to death and degradation but to art, to what the texts often figure, despite their deconstructive energies, as something transcendent. A composer who becomes Pellegrina Leoni's friend and constant companion tries to describe what happened to him the first time he heard her sing: "Then I understood the meaning of heaven and earth, . . . life and death, and eternity. She took you out to walk in a rose garden, filled with nightingales, and then, the moment she wanted to, she rose and lifted you with her, higher than the moon" (331).[9]

In an amazing revision of Odysseus's encounter with the Sirens, diva Margarethe Styr herself comes to art when she is caught in a terrible storm off the Pacific Northwest coast. A companion ties her to the mast to keep her from the rising storm. "Alone in that raging waste of water, with death tugging at my feet . . . , I was born into the religion of art . . . [and] chosen . . . to be blest, to be lifted to its highest places—I—I—of all women!" (Atherton 90). Styr invokes Brünnhilde in her telling of this originary tale, but the Homeric allusion is unmistakable. Tied like Odysseus to the mast of the ship, she takes to herself the role of siren, here divine rather than demonic—or beyond that distinction altogether. The rhetoric of this passage recalls as well Mary's Magnificat, in which she sings "henceforth all generations shall call me blessed" (Luke 1.46). The title of the novel, *Tower of Ivory*, literally descriptive of Styr's throat, is one of Mary's titles. Styr, that is, has been chosen, like Mary, to be the vessel of the Most High, the bearer of the Word that is Art (rather than the divine man or the male artist). That the vessel is Styr's throat rather than her womb suggests the relocation of women's powers from reproductive organs to head and suggests as well the role of priest(ess) that, implicit in the verses of Luke, is only occasionally invoked in Christian worship—in, for example, the litany that addresses Mary as Tower of Ivory, House of Gold,

Ark of the Covenant. The blending in this passage of Homer, the New Testament, and the myths that inform Wagner's operas underscores the religious, the originary, the exalted place of art in the world of the text and the role that artists, specifically the diva, play.

The figuring of art as uplifting and of artists as—in imitation of the divine—lifters is a conventional one; what is significant in these diva narratives is the clear sense of the diva as a creative, originary artist (rather than merely a vehicle for the words and music of others) and of the diva's own power to lift—a priestly, godly, and therefore by convention masculine, power. Lena Geyer, for example, one night "boldly scaled the very heights of Olympus, carrying her captivated hearers in her wake" (Davenport, *LG* 136). And an admirer says that "every time I heard her sing she lifted me to a plane I could reach no other way" (3). The direct agency here and in the similar passage from "The Dreamers"—not "I was lifted" or even "her song lifted" but "she lifted me"—suggests that power, her power. An old man in Kate O'Brien's *As Music and Splendour* (1958) waxes eloquent about the voice of a young diva: "When you sing," he concludes, "you make a saint of a man" (298). The minister in Harriet Prescott Spofford's *A Master Spirit* (1896) experiences Domina's voice as "wings . . . and his thought soared with it into broad heaven-knowing heights" (57). In Nina Berberova's *The Accompanist* (1987), the female narrator describes hearing Travina sing: "When she took a breath and spread her large, beautiful lips and a pure, strong . . . sound suddenly rang out above me, I . . . realized that this was something immortal and indisputable, something which . . . gives reality to the human being's dream of having wings" (26). Large, strong, indisputable—all qualities associated with the masculine. Unlike the diffident, pliable, anxious divas of Moore, Meredith, and du Maurier or the cruel, careless divas of Cain, Merrill, and Gould, Travina is simply an artist who "walks, talks, sings" with confidence; "in her lurks a burning, a spark—divine or demonic—a distinct 'yes' and 'no'" (20). The "distinct 'yes' and 'no'" sets her apart from both the acquiescent and the imperious. Like a man, she can say yes and no appropriately, confidently. She can take care of herself. These traits prompt the narrator, a much more traditional woman—evidenced in part by her role as accompanist—to say, "Never in my life had I met a woman like that" (24).

John Ordham in *Tower of Ivory* has a similar if less exalted thought about Margarethe Styr. "It was the first time he had known a woman that worked for her living" (144), her room "not the room of a woman who lounged, but who worked, studied, thought. . . . It was its component of masculinity which had enveloped him" (144). In May Sarton's *Anger* (1982), diva Anna Lindstrom "astonishes" Ned Fraser: "How simply you can talk about yourself, your voice. . . . You appraise it quite coolly and give yourself full credit" (40). McCann in Willa Cather's "A Gold Slipper" (1920) is similarly taken aback when "Kitty Ayrshire's . . . bright, inquisitive glance roam[s] over his person" and when she confronts his disapproval (129). What so amazes Sonechka, Ordham, Fraser, and McCann is the "masculine" stance that these divas take toward power, toward the world, toward themselves. Most specifically, they think and they speak openly and confidently. They have, that is, a voice—"a distinct 'yes' and 'no'"—that seems a corollary of their singing voice. When the diva talks, as when the diva sings, people listen.

Lifting, in these narratives, is heavy work; and many of these texts stress the connection between hard and sustained work—so necessary to cultivate a singing voice—and this masculine stance. Work builds confidence, develops discipline, requires a moving out from home, self, and often country; it facilitates interaction and negotiation, thickens skin. One of the most striking differences between these revisionary texts and diva narratives like *Trilby* and *Sandra Belloni* is the *textual* presence of this work. Unlike Trilby or Christine Daaé, whose voices come, effortlessly, from outside themselves, or Veda Pierce, Sandra Belloni, and Evelyn Innes, who emerge as full-blown divas after a hiatus in the text, these singers are self-made women. Diva narratives like *Tower of Ivory*, *Of Lena Geyer*, and *The Song of the Lark* offer detailed descriptions of the diva at work—mastering an instrument, improving her breathing, acquiring language skills, repeating scales, poring over opera scores, expanding her range, studying performances of the past, perfecting gestures, memorizing parts. These singers work with composers, conductors, voice coaches, retired singers. They work alone. They work to earn the money to work some more. And they work not only to reach a goal but for love of the work itself. "I can't imagine not working," says Anna Lindstrom, " . . . work is . . . what I'm all about" (Sarton 22); Margarethe Styr, who in her life as Peggy Hill worked in the coal mines, "had no taste for love in an Italian villa, idle herself, with an idle man on her hands; she was a worker" (Atherton 282); Thea Kronborg teaches piano so she can work at her music, and she almost collapses from work before her respite in Panther Canyon; Lena Geyer's teacher describes her as "a tiger, so fierce in her work. Such a life she made for herself—*senza gioia, senza amore.* Nothing but work; all day, all night" (Davenport, *LG* 52). This hard work, then, offers the women alternatives to women's traditional work in the home. It is in large part the *kind* of work they do—work that involves both mind and body; work that expands their knowledge of other languages and other cultures; work that puts them in frequent contact with men, with ideas, with a large public; work that involves travel—that secures for them a voice in a wider world.

What is unusual here is not, of course, women working but the *narrative* of women working in a long tradition of narrative in which the role of women is so largely and so consistently a romantic one. And such a role is often explicitly rejected by the hardworking diva. For example, in O'Brien's *As Music and Splendor* a man asks aspiring diva Clare Halvey if she'd rather be an artist's model—recalling here Trilby's preferred profession—or one of "Rossini's light-headed ladies?" Clare responds without hesitation to what might seem no choice at all: "Oh, any of those gentleman's ladies! Because at least, however idiotic, I'd be doing the thing myself! Not just . . . having it done!" (73). This three-exclamation-point preference for the active over the passive is emblematic of the way these texts decenter the romantic. This is not to claim, however, that these narratives are either devoid of romance or impervious to the romantic imperatives of the genre; Styr kills herself for love at the end of *Tower of Ivory*. But, like so many plot developments in fictions based on myth, legend or other fiction,[10] her death is driven by forces outside the text, here, the narratives of Brünnhilde and Isolde. One knows, that is, from the beginning of this Wagnerian narrative that Styr must share the fate of the heroines she portrays. Such a fate, however, for the amazing, steel-willed, self-made Styr seems ludicrous. She kills herself to save the career of a weak, indolent, upper-class effete, many years her junior, whose only redemption is his witty conversation. Ordham becomes, during the course of the novel, increasingly odious; his very inferiority to his diva—and her acknowledgment of it[11]—emphasize the arbitrariness of her suicide.

Ordham has, predictably, awakened in Styr an erotic passion long dormant, and she vacillates at the end between the demands of such passion and the demands of her art. She suspects that if she gave up her career for him, as she would have to do—for reasons many, elaborate, and operatic—she would regret it and resent him for it, and she believes "profoundly" that "no born artist would sacrifice her career . . . for any man" (462). She deduces that since she might be willing to sacrifice her career to Ordham, she must not be a "born artist" and so not a real artist at all. The romantic narrative's assumption of a real—a natural—artist, however, works against the working woman narrative's allowance for, even insistence on, the possibility and the triumph of the constructed, the worked-for, "self." And this worked-for self is, as we have seen, consistently figured (how otherwise?) as masculine. The text's opposition between the woman and the artist ("the woman is sometimes stronger than the artist" [281]) must necessarily place the artist firmly on the side of the masculine in a culture that recognizes only two gender positions. To take these oppositions and distinctions to their logical conclusion would be to claim that a man can be a born artist, a woman only a manufactured one, only an artist-facade for the natural, man-centered, self-sacrificing woman beneath. The text does not, of course, go this far, but the sense of Styr's audience that the diva is a "terrifying creature, always an alien in their midst" suggests the text's own ambivalence toward that terrifying hybrid the woman artist, the working woman, the woman man (278).

Other texts find the hybrid less terrifying. It is perhaps the diva's status as hybrid that facilitates, in many diva narratives, her ability to slide so easily from one role to another, to blur boundaries, to reveal how oppositions inhabit one another. Diva Helena Buchan in Brigid Brophy's *The King of a Rainy Country* doesn't "set much store by all those distinctions any longer . . . all those ones we were brought up to think so important—class, colour, nationality, sex—even age. The only distinction I recognize now is between the quick and the dead" (217). Working as she does in an art that does not hold realism as its preeminent value, the diva is in a unique position here; the roles she plays force her to cross these boundaries. Aging divas are regularly cast as ingenues, for example, and, especially in literary texts, poverty-stricken immigrant girls eventually play operatic queens and goddesses. Divas cross national boundaries not only when they perform in important opera houses but when they take on roles in languages other than their own. Helen Buchan "can make love eloquently in four and die in four" (220), Lena Geyer in seven. But it remains the distinction between the sexes that most troubles these texts, as it most troubles the culture. And since, as we have seen, opera has from its beginnings troubled gender—with castrati, with cross-gender casting—such trouble stays center stage in the lives of fictional divas and, sometimes, the lives of the writers who create them.

Willa Cather: All Her Various Divas

Willa Cather is perhaps the writer most obsessed with the diva and her troubling roles; the sheer number, variety, and complexity of her divas necessitate a somewhat lengthy discussion: the figure appears in at least a dozen of her stories and novels, and Cather's *Kunstlerroman*, *The Song of the Lark*, is a portrait of the artist as a young diva. Cather critics and biographers have, of course, noted this: A. S. Byatt points out that the story of Thea Kronborg is both the story of the historical diva Olive Fremstad and "also . . . very closely related to the artistic ambitions and self-discovery of another great provincial woman artist, Willa Cather herself" (xiii); Richard Giannone claims that the singer's creative growth in *The Song of the Lark* is, for Cather, "an ideal analogy for the discovery and expression of all art" (85). Sharon O'Brien quotes Cather on the link between diva and novelist: they "have in common the unique and marvelous experience of entering into the very skin of another human being" (92).[12]

Cather was fascinated by singers and wrote dozens of reviews and commentaries on such contemporary divas as Nellie Melba, Emma Calvé, Clara Butt, Ernestine Schumann-Heink, and, of course, Olive Fremstad, her model for Thea Kronborg. Simultaneously, she created fictional divas, inspired both by these historical singers and by her own struggle to become a (woman) artist. Not all Cather's divas are models or figures for the great artist, however. Several, especially in the early stories, are, like the divas in the masculinist tradition, mere handmaids to a male artist. Katharine Gaylord in "A Death in the Desert" (1903) "used up [her] life" (74) for the great composer Adriance Hilgarde, the "real" artist, who exacts from Gaylord and several other divas their very lives—which they give willingly. As Gaylord says, "I fought my way to him, and I drank my doom greedily enough" (74). Singing women respond here to the male composer much as ordinary women in "The Garden Lodge," "from mansions and hotels, from typewriter desks, school-rooms, shops and filling rooms," women "young and old, however hideous, however fair," flock to hear singer Raymond d'Esquerre. They "hunger . . . for the mystic bread wherewith he fed them at this eucharist of sentiment" (53). The figure of the artist as priest, even with these small ironies, presupposes the artist as male—and the communicants as female.

In the early fiction, Cather's attitude toward the relationship between art and gender seems especially conflicted. On the one hand, male artists are exploitative and pretentious; on the other, they, unlike their female counterparts, are *real* artists. The women sometimes have aspirations, but, although they can reveal the egocentricity and pretentiousness of the male artists, they themselves are either outclassed or exploited—or both. The two divas in "The Count of Crow's Nest" (1896), for example, are simply substandard artists: one's "strength and salary were spent in endeavoring to force her voice up to a note which forever eluded her" (450); the other "had absolutely no musical sense" (461).[13] In "The Prodigies" (1897), about two singing children pushed unmercifully by their mother, the girl loses her voice, the boy "must be great enough for both" (423). Significantly, the real-life counterparts to the young singing siblings, whom Cather wrote about in 1894, were both girls, the Dovey sisters. For the young Cather, it would seem, the burden of art is quite clearly, on some level at least, a gendered one; the historical singers that Cather took as models for her characters are sometimes subordinated in her fiction to this assumption about the maleness of art.

When female artists aren't outclassed by their brothers, they are exploited, but they, and sometimes the texts themselves, seem to condone the exploitation. In 1896, for example, Cather praises Clara Schumann's sacrifice of her career—as "one of the most brilliant pianists in the world"—for her husband's (Slote 169). She concludes, "Clara Schumann was one of the few women since time began who loved an art and an artist unselfishly, and who have understood and cherished a genius. There is no higher wisdom, no holier tenderness. The women who have tortured and ruined musicians have been hundreds; the women who have helped them, how few. Perhaps . . . what Clara Schumann saved may balance what George Sand destroyed" (170).

No higher wisdom. No holier tenderness. Here, it seems, the male artist is not only a priest but a very god—and no sacrifice is too great to make for him.[14]

And none of these early divas regrets such sacrifice. When there *are* regretful divas, the regret is of another sort entirely. "No one ever went to the opera solely because her name was on the bill" (336), says the narrator of the diva in "A Singer's Romance" (1900). But Selma Schumman's real sadness is not the poignant contrast between her hard work (she was an "industrious and an indefatigable student" [336]) and the opera world's slight. Rather, the she regrets that her maid is in love while she, the diva, has never been; she "was a singer without a romance" (336), in obvious contrast to her namesake, Clara Schumann, whose romance, Cather argued, happily ruled her life.

A similar story from this period, "Nanette: An Aside" (1987), pretends to concentrate on the maid, Nanette, who loves a handsome Latin. But the story is, again, about the diva. Here, though, the diva is no overlooked or minor talent but the adored Tradutorri, the only woman "since

Malibran" who "sings with the soul" (408). But she, too, though she is thoroughly dedicated to her art and enjoys the adulation of the world, envies the love of her young companion: "Let nothing come between you and it; no desire, no ambition. It is not given to every one. There are women who wear crowns who would give them for an hour of it" (410). Katharine Gaylord and Clara Schumann use themselves up for male genius; these divas seem willing to use themselves up for a handsome face, an hour of love.

Significantly, however, they do not, although the high price they pay can be frightening. Tradutorri regrets her loveless life, but she sees clearly that such lovelessness is the result of her choices in the service of her voice. Holding in her hand "the score of the last great opera written in Europe," which had been sent her to originate the title role, she explains, "When I began life, between me and this lay everything dear in life—every love, every human hope. I have had to bury what lay between. . . . God is a very merciless artist, and when he works out his purposes in the flesh his chisel does not falter" (410). The diva must, that is, give up love for art, give up "everything" for art. The figuring of God as supreme artist suggests the significance of such renunciation. Only thus can the singer become like God, become divine, become diva. It is, then, perhaps the enormous price that most inhibits the female artist. Cather understands the necessity of the sacrifice but does not comment on or seem even to recognize the gender disparity in her representations of such renunciations. Clearly the high standards she sets for the artist—"complete self-abnegation," she says in one review—apply differently for male than for female aspirants. Robert Schumann and Adriance Hilgarde, for example, did not sacrifice love for art but had love in abundance. "Married nightingales," Cather wrote in 1895, "seldom sing" (Curtin 164), but it is only the female artists who must sacrifice marriage for their career—and they must do so fully conscious of the eventual cost.

The nightingale to which Cather refers is diva Helena von Doenhoff, who had announced her intent to marry. Though Cather's fiction of this period seems to suggest that women will regret the sacrifices they make for art—though not for the (male) artist—Cather castigates von Doenhoff for her choice and implies that von Doenhoff doesn't have what it takes to be a real artist if she could decide to marry at this crucial time in her career, her early thirties. The piece concludes with a direct scolding: "A little more patience, Doenhoff, a little more endurance, and you might have been one who should console us for Schalchi's age, but as it is, farewell, a long farewell" (Curtin 176). Some of the diva's admirers, among whom Cather clearly includes herself, "will not send her any flowers or wire her their congratulations" (175). The disappointment and scorn that color this interesting piece remind us of the difficult, double-bind position of Cather's divas. A choice for art—illustrated by the unnamed singer who has spent her savings and her self trying "to force her voice up to a note which forever eluded her"—is lonely at best, illusional at worst, most often both. A choice for domesticity like Helena von Doenhoff's, however, is an abdication of responsibility to both self and public and a sure sign that the woman didn't have the makings of an artist in the first place. It is not clear in Cather's early work that women ever do.

In *The Song of the Lark*, first published in 1915, and in the many diva stories in the 1920 collection *Youth and the Bright Medusa*, however, the prima donnas are much more obviously artists in their own right, and their choices, while requiring almost super-human discipline and self-sacrifice, are less fraught. Thea Kronborg, Eden Bower, Kitty Ayrshire, and even Cressida Garnet, who "was not musically intelligent" ("Diamond" 85), lead lives that, although often lonely and filled with compromise, are moderately happy, productive, and always rewarding—if not to the diva herself, at least to the public she serves.[15]

Cressida Garnet, the eponymous subject of "The Diamond Mine," is an acknowledged antidote to the stereotypical diva. "A charming exception to rules," she is good without being great, ambitious without being cruel, successful without being corrupted (7). As the story begins, she is marrying for the fourth time and still possessed of "unabated vitality" and "earning powers that were exceptional" (72, 88). The matter-of-fact way in which the narrator tells us all these things suggests the magnitude of the change in Cather's use of the diva figure. Cressida's marriages, for example, are not particularly successful (her husbands all "mine" her), but she maintains "her characteristic optimism" for the current match (72). The marriages have coexisted with the career; there's no question that after marriage this nightingale continues to sing.

Cressida Garnet is a deliberate revision not only of Cather's early divas but of at least one of the traditions of diva narrative as well. In the course of the story, the narrator—one of the few specifically female narrators of the Cather canon—remembers that when *Trilby* was published, Garnet "fell into a fright and said such books ought to be prohibited by law; which gave me an intuition of what their relationship had actually become" (85). The relationship at issue here is between Garnet and Miletus Poppas,

presumably her Svengali. But the differences between the Trilby-Svengali
and the Garnet-Poppas relationships seem as well the differences both between the Victorian and the twentieth-century worlds and between the
"masculinist" and "feminist" strands of diva narrative. Although the
Cressida Garnet who returned from Germany "was largely the work of
Miletus Poppas," this text, unlike *Trilby*, acknowledges that Poppas was
"quite as incomplete as his pupil" (85). Unlike the voiceless Trilby,
Cressida was, even before she met Poppas, "already a 'popular favorite' of
the concert stage" (85). She has from the beginning, that is, a voice of her
own, even though its professional training owes much to others. Though
Cressida marries several times, she, unlike La Svengali, never marries her
"maker"; Cressida and Poppas never, that is, become physically or legally
one. And, of course, there is no question of mesmerism or loss of self; in
fact, says the narrator, who has known her since childhood, "her actual self
was the least changed, the least modified by experience that it would be
possible to imagine" (85). Although, then, Cressida Garnet is a lucrative
"diamond mine" for friends, family, and professional associates, including,
of course, Miletus Poppas, she is fully conscious of, indeed a rather cheer-
ful accomplice to, the exploitation.[16]

Like the wasted, exploited Trilby, Cressida Garnet dies at the end of
the story. But this is a death with a difference, a death not at the hands of a
lover, not from a disease that results from her vaguely disreputable sex life
or even from the hard work and relentless training of her vaguely disreputable profession. Cressida Garnet dies on the *Titanic*, a kind of heroic, masculine fate, a Don Giovanni–ish fate for the woman who sings Donna
Anna. Garnet's fear—a fear exacerbated by her mediocrity as a singer—
that Trilby's story is her story is at every moment assuaged by a narrative
conscious of that story of the woman (or of Woman) without a voice of her
own, the diva as, by nature, artist manqué.

"A Gold Slipper" and "Scandal," the two stories that follow "The
Diamond Mine" in *Youth and the Bright Medusa*, introduce diva Kitty Ayrshire, a good musician, though without the voice for Wagner (Cather's notion of the voice consummate); she thaws her "hard-shelled public" with
"the beauty of her voice and the subtlety of her interpretation" (128). "A
Gold Slipper" also undermines stereotypical representations; the narrative
consistently undercuts the male character, McKann, whose judgments often
depend on prima donna stereotypes: "He comfortably classed all singers—
especially operatic singers—as 'fat Dutchwomen' or 'Shifty Sadies,' and
Kitty would not fit into clever generalization" (128); her wonderful recital,

"such . . . as cannot often be heard for money," seems not to move him (127). Kitty herself confronts his clever generalization and his evident disapproval. They argue. About art, artists, women. Kitty is smart and persuasive, but when she leaves, McKann concludes, "All that tall talk—! Probably got it from some man who hangs about; learned it off like a parrot" (147).

Here, of course, McKann repeats the *Trilby* premise: women do not have voices of their own. But readers, like Kitty herself, have no reason to collude in his remark. Kitty is not threatened by McKann but interested, amused, and challenged. She is the undisputed winner of all their arguments. To his "I have a natural distrust of your variety," for example, she responds, "I don't see why you should naturally dislike singers any more than I naturally dislike coal-men" (139–140). McKann's stereotypical notions of the prima donna are merely a screen for his stereotypical notions of women; all the while he is insisting on the truth of his own accepted and acceptable prejudices, Kitty's voices—both her singing voice and her independent, eccentric voice in the world—suggest something else to him, something vague but something that endures more persistently than his own body. In a nice reversal of narrative, and operatic, convention, it is the hard-headed businessman, not the worldly woman, who suffers here from a lingering illness. McKann fades away; the last we see of him is his "tired mind" (148). What remains is Kitty's gold slipper that has, all these years, meant life and youth to him, meant, that is, a different way of thinking from his own. McKann seems to be dying of his tired mind; Kitty and her eccentric voice—the voice, that is, that demands to be heard as a subject—live.

The story of the diva is necessarily a story about a female body that is both object and subject. In "Coming, Aphrodite!" (also in *Youth and the Bright Medusa*) Eden Bower very clearly consents to both positions. Readers of the story hear Eden Bower's voice before they meet her; it is a "young, fresh, unguarded, confident" (5) voice that appropriately represents the aspiring diva herself: "There was nothing shy or retreating about this unclad girl—a bold body, studying itself quite coolly and evidently well pleased with itself, doing all this for a purpose" (20). The bold voice, the bold body—both sing out, both are heard. Eden Bower, whose minor name change—she was Edna Bowers—reinforces her prelapsarian comfort with and connection to her own body,[17] has a clear purpose: "to be Eden Bower" (28). Eden Bower, that is, is both a person and a role, a young woman very much a physical presence and a famous diva whose fictive presence is announced via marquee. (Cather's first title for the story was "Coming, Eden Bower!" a title perhaps less elegant but still appropriate to the physical freedom, consistent ambition, and continuing artistic growth of the eponymous protagonist. On the other hand, the change from her own—fictive—name to the name of the operatic role she sings suggests again the collapse of boundaries between public and private inherent in these portraits of the artist as diva.)

In priming herself "to be Eden Bower," Eden succumbs to the romantic myths and stereotypes of the diva; at thirteen, she debated "whether she would or would not be the Czar's mistress when she played in his Capitol" (29). But she also knows that such a career demands hard work, represented in these early years by her religious and purposeful exercise and by the vocal training that she leaves love to pursue. Eden Bower, that is, recognizes, even before she becomes Eden Bower, that divahood demands her body be both object and agent/subject. While it is her voice and her body that make the sounds, that create the art, they are also the things heard and looked at. She casually accepts the voyeurism of her artist neighbor, Don Hedger, because she knows that her life will be a public one and her body her public instrument. Significantly, when Eden sets off for Europe she leaves behind for Hedger "a pale, flesh-tinted dressing gown he had liked to see her wear" (58). The gown, flesh-tinted, seems an intermediary or compromise between her naked body that has so fascinated the painter both as object of art and object of desire and the diva's gown that marks her public life as artist and only partly masks the bold body that is her instrument.

At age fourteen, according to biographer O'Brien, Willa Cather adopted a "masculine persona" that "she sustained for . . . four years": "Employing the transforming power of dress and disguise, she distinguished herself from other Red Cloud girls by cropping her hair, donning boyish clothes, and naming herself William Cather, Jr." (96). This masculine performance provides another link between Cather and her performing women, but it also provides Cather the author with firsthand knowledge of what it feels like to be male. Though Cather's divas seldom sing the trouser roles so common to the gender-bending singers of Eliot and Sand, they are often more like men than like "other Red Cloud girls." They are not, for example, like the divas of Moore, Meredith, and du Maurier, preoccupied with virtue or with the difference between bad women and good women. Nor are most of the narratives themselves so occupied. (An early exception makes clear the rule: in "The Count of Crow's Nest" [1896] the conscienceless diva Helena de Koch becomes the object of her father's horror on just these grounds. He seems less concerned, that is, that she is cruel, petty, and a thief than that she is an "adventuress"—"It will stare me in my grave! . . . Great God, it was true!" [470].) These divas and their narratives are preoccupied rather with the diva as artist, a role mainly occupied by men, a role impossible without the assumption of masculine prerogatives, without the acquisition of "masculine" traits, like ambition and "hardness," and "masculine" freedoms, like the freedom to leave one's family, to refuse marriage, to travel abroad, to make work the center of one's life. Willa/William Cather knew this as well. Most of Cather's divas, then, avoid both sets of diva stereotypes. Her singers are not whores, nor do they worry about becoming so; her singers are not puppets or parrots whose true voices belong to a man—unless that "man" is, like William Cather, part of the artist herself.

We have already noted that Cather wrote a defense (1894) of *Trilby* arguing that "in books at least, one cannot sin with impunity" and that du Maurier, therefore, must be acquitted of charges of immorality because he has, after all, "meted out punishment to his heroine" (Slote 364). While Cather's own diva-heroines may not become "perfectly happy and respected women," they do become famous, wealthy, and not unhappy, and they become so without bodily shame or sexual denial. They do, in other words, "sin" with relative impunity. But Cather's more significant dialogue with *Trilby*, in fact, takes place on other grounds, grounds not even mentioned in this piece. Cather's later diva fiction, that is, becomes increasingly critical of the *Trilby* scenario, of the notion of the diva as product of a male artist. We have seen the explicit mention of the issue in "A Diamond Mine," but it is most powerfully—in part because at such great length—refuted in Cather's *Kunstlerroman, The Song of the Lark*,[18] her most sustained antidote to the appropriated voice. Although Thea Kronborg, its protagonist, receives help and encouragement from a number of male mentors, including at least one "real" artist, there is never any doubt that Thea's voice is her own, never any doubt that, beneficent and inspiring as her singing is, the primary beneficiary is herself, never any doubt that the master she serves is her own desire.

Thea's teachers, even the best and most influential of them, Harsanyi, by any standards a "real" artist, only uncover in Thea what is already there. Neither the arrogant male artist of Cather's early fiction nor the informing genius of Svengali and the Phantom, Harsanyi is a great pianist and violinist who has himself had great teachers, who has allowed other great artists to influence his own work. The two "great artists" who "completely changed . . . his idea about strings" were, he says, Jenny Lind and Henrietta Sontag, both women, both singers. He listened to them "night after night," and "from that time . . . on his violin he tried always for the singing, vibrating tone" (260). There is no question here that these divas were artists in their own right—and no question that Thea herself will be one as well. But Thea has learned much earlier that women can be artists. A railroad man, Ray, with whom she is fast friends during childhood tells her tales about his adventures and discoveries. He admires the pottery of the Cliff Dwellers and acknowledges to Thea that "their women were their artists" (147). Thea, then, has in her formative years been surrounded by men who believe in women's talents and who take them seriously.

One of her early fans, physician Doctor Archie, once examines her head in search of something unusual, but "no, he couldn't say that it was different from any other child's head" (12); he doesn't try to locate her genius in her throat or her lungs. This is not to suggest that Thea doesn't depend on her healthy body. Doctor Archie is solicitous of it ("a girl who [sings] must always have plenty of fresh air" [71]), and Ray advises her to eschew corsets ("a girl with a voice like yours ought to have plenty of lung-action" [147]). But the text tries to complicate Thea's genius, to see it as closely allied to but not coextensive with her body and thus to make clear that Thea is an artist—dependent as are all artists on certain physical characteristics—but definitely not merely a conduit for someone else's art. Her name, Thea Kronborg, connoting both god and king, reinforces this.

Doctor Archie, in his refusal to identify female genius with the body, contrasts pointedly with a medical student later in the novel who prescribes for the singer when she is ill with a sore throat. Thea acknowledges the effectiveness of the young man's gargle and his sleep inducers, but she is angry with him nonetheless: "He had exceeded his rights. She had no soreness in her chest and had told him so clearly. All this thumping of her back and listening to her breathing, was done to satisfy personal curiosity" (356). Although the important men in Thea's life support and nurture her, the medical student reminds her—and readers—that such support and nurturance may be the exception rather than the rule. The incident calls up, in fact, an earlier incident when, after a concert, she is accosted and "tormented" by two men. Thea sees them as representative of a larger human force—"they were lined up against her, they were there to take something from her. Very well; they should never have it. As long as she lived that ecstasy was going to be hers. She would live for it, work for it, die for it; but she was going to have it, time after time, height after height" (254). The sexual language here—and in the encounter with the medical student—ac-knowledges the possibility of rape. They were there to take something from her, the "something" on one level her physical integrity. But that integrity at the same moment opens out to encompass emotional and artistic integ-rity as well. The "something," the "it," is simultaneously her virginity and her right to "ecstasy."

The connections between sexual fulfillment, artistic or aesthetic "ec-stasy," and a career are portrayed most thoroughly in Thea's relationship with Fred Ottenburg, the wealthy, energetic, devoted young man who loves Thea consistently and who fosters her art, not only with financial help but also with emotional support and sound advice. Although he and Thea are happily—we presume—married in the epilogue of the novel and, even more important, married without detriment to Thea's career, their early courtship is marked by the kinds of conflicts and ambivalences about love and marriage that pervade Cather's early work—married nightingales, after all, seldom sing. The difference is that the characters—and the text itself—while acknowledging common assumptions about marriage and about male-female relationships in general, begin to see that they can fashion something other for themselves.

At Panther Canyon, Fred sounds Thea out about traditional marriage: "Suppose I were to offer you what most of the young men I know would offer a girl they'd been sitting up nights about: a comfortable flat in Chi-cago, a summer camp in the woods, musical evenings, and a family to bring up. Would it look attractive to you?" The question clearly indicates that Fred can separate himself from "most of the young men" and that he assumes Thea is different from their "girls." Her response, immediate and emphatic—"Perfectly hideous!"—does not surprise him; she is not, Fred knows, "a nest-building bird" (394). What Fred does not tell Thea at this point is that he is in no position to offer her any of these things anyway: he is already married, a youthful indiscretion, a separation of many years. His circumstance calls into question his motive for putting himself and Thea into the category of the different. On the other hand, his own position has forced him to question marriage as an institution: "His own conduct looked crooked . . . but he asked himself whether, between men and women, all ways were not more or less crooked. He believed those which are called straight were the most dangerous of all. They seemed to him . . . to lie be-tween windowless stone walls, and their rectitude had been achieved at the expense of light and air. In their unquestioned regularity lurked every sort of human cruelty and meanness, and every kind of humiliation and suffering" (424). The "windowless stone walls" echo the images of confinement that many feminist critics have noted as characteristic of Anglo-American women's writing and echo as well Thea's own feelings of entrapment and the relief from them that her stay at Panther Canyon has afforded her. That she replies to Fred's quasi-proposal with "alarm" (394) suggests that she, too, envisions traditional marriage as a room of windowless stone walls.

It is, however, Fred who gives voice to the fears of Thea and to the text's fears for her. He sees an ordinary husband as "someone who would be a weight about her neck; who would hold her back and beat her down and divert her from the first plunge for which he felt she was gathering all her energies"; he sees his own role in her life as something quite different: "He meant to help her, and he could think of no other man who would" (423). Again, there are many men in this novel who help Thea, but given Fred's consistently commonsensical voice, we recognize the accuracy of his perceptions and conclude that Thea's men—Cather's men—are, indeed, exceptional and meant to be so, models rather than mirrors. They are, as much as Darcy, as much as Peter Wimsey, creations, fantasies, whimsies of a woman writer.

Fred explains the psychology, the ideology, behind his observations: "jolly fellows want to be the whole target. They would say you are all brain and muscle; that you have no feeling. . . . When they are not around, they want a girl to be—extinct" (393). Brain and muscle are, of course, the two things such fellows do not require or even desire in their women, but brain and muscle are precisely the requirements for a great singer. They are also attributes more commonly assigned to men than to women; Thea's brain and muscle emphasize again her "masculine" stance in the world. But even more significant in Fred's analysis is his claim that when women are not around, men want them to be extinct. The slow and careful buildup of the artist's character in this novel—assisted perhaps by the Scandinavian stereotype that Thea's heritage invokes—establishes a woman who is both physically and intellectually solid. And her presence has, by this time in the text, rooted itself in the ancient earth of Panther Canyon. The notion that Thea could be "extinct" in face of the absence of a male is ludicrous. And this very solidity makes her, to such "fellows," monstrous.

"Give one of 'em a big nature like that, and he'd be horrified. He wouldn't show his face in the clubs until he'd gone after her and combed her down to conform to some fool idea in his own head" (423). The woman here is figured as the object of a hunt—the hunt of a wild animal or monster that must be caught and, more important, tamed. The "fool idea" that becomes the pattern for such taming is, of course, a gender ideology that the text has argued against from the beginning. Fred recognizes the persistence, the history, and the ubiquitousness of such an ideology: the "fool idea," he says, in this fellow's head is "put there by some other woman, too, his first sweetheart or his grandmother or maiden aunt" (423). There is here, then, no escaping such a fool idea and no exoneration of women in its perpetuation and dissemination. Thus, if Fred, Doctor Archer, and Harsanyi are exceptions among men, Thea and her mother are exceptions among women. The "maiden aunt" who betrays her sex only throws into relief Thea's own maiden aunt, Tillie Kronborg, who, addlebrained though she is, refuses to accede to the traditional narrative about women and family. The town thinks at the end of the novel, for example, that Tillie, as the last surviving Kronborg, should be living with Thea, but Tillie herself is content living "alone in a little house with a green yard," supporting herself with "a fancy-work and millinery store" (576) and a little help from her niece.

Thea's mother, herself a woman who has all her life played a very traditional role, makes a similar refusal. She is very ill; Thea is abroad. Although Thea intends to return to Moonstone, she is at the last minute offered the opportunity to sing Elizabeth at the Dresden opera. She decides to stay and sing. Mrs. Kronborg defends Thea's choice: "When these things happen far away, they don't make such a mark, especially if your hands are full and you've duties of your own to think about. My own father died in Nebraska when Gunnar was born—we were living in Iowa then—and I was sorry, but the baby made it up to me" (492). What Mrs. Kronborg recognizes here is that even dutiful, family-oriented women like herself are often caught among their duties. She missed the death of her father; Thea will miss *her* death. But people have commitments and obligations elsewhere. She was having a baby; Thea is taking advantage of a "lucky chance" to make her career (485). "I guess," concludes Mrs. Kronborg, "I got about as much out of Thea's voice as anybody will ever get" (493), a judgment at once honest and generous—and significantly different from the judgment that Moonstone will pronounce, significantly subversive of it.

Fred's analysis of his own position as an exception, then, serves to highlight the other exceptional characters in the narrative, firmly reminding readers of their fictional status but insisting simultaneously on the possibility of new ways of seeing and ordering relations between men and women. The text itself illustrates this vision. Fred and Thea are at Panther Canyon climbing among the rocks when an old man sees them: "There on the promontory, against the cream-coloured cliff, were two figures nimbly moving in the light, both slender and agile, entirely absorbed in their game. They looked like two boys" (384). The old man—representative of the generation whose gender ideology both informs that of Fred and Thea and differs significantly from it—is fascinated by the apparition; he "forgot his pick-axe and followed" (384). What the man then sees is Fred's kiss, Thea's pushing him away, Fred's more hostile kiss, Thea's explanation that she pushed him because he "interrupted" her (387), and the quick resumption of their comradely companionship. Fred and Thea are here clearly trying to work out and work through the intersections of sex and friendship, of gender roles and personal needs, of traditional romance and their own vague visions of something other.

Thea's visions are, of course, like her sense of self, firmly rooted in her voice. "Her voice, more than any other part of her, had to do with that confidence, that sense of wholeness and inner well-being that she had felt at moments ever since she could remember" (272). And it is that confidence, that sense of her own autonomy which allows, even demands, her constant challenge to assumptions about sex and gender in general and about, more particularly, their intersection with art. Cather's original title for this novel was *Artist's Youth*, a title that, though less euphonious (and less misleading)[19] than the final one, emphasizes the collusion of the text in Thea's challenge. Its similarity to the title of Joyce's *Portrait of the Artist as a Young Man*, published the year after *The Song of the Lark*, reminds us of the assumptions Cather's culture had about the masculinity of the artist, assumptions that Cather's earlier work shared. That Fred and Thea's romp in the canyon looks like the play of "two boys" reminds us as well that for Cather, who for many years called herself William, the qualities and conditions needed to become an artist, needed for Thea to become a diva—ambition, freedom from home and family obligations, freedom to travel, physical solitude—are ordinarily figured as masculine.

What critics of *The Song of the Lark* attend to most thoroughly is Thea's visit to Panther Canyon, a respite that helps her to renew her voice, strength, and dedication to art and to her career. Less noted, however, are the material conditions of the episode. Fred provides her with a ranch to stay on, the Biltmers do the housekeeping, and Thea spends most of her days alone among the ruins. She makes a room for herself in one of the dwellings and does all her "work" there—for two months. What other heroine has spent so much time alone, has pitched her tent outdoors, has given her exclusive attention to theorizing about her art? The circumstances and process by which she comes to herself as an artist have more in common with initiation rites for men than for women.

When a young singer begins to reap the rewards of her hard work, however, those "masculine" qualities that have facilitated her career are, unless she is performing a trouser role, mostly at serious odds with the parts she plays. As we have seen, opera plots are mostly unkind, often fatal, to their heroines—mostly hyperfeminine, often victims. Although the first opera Thea learns is Gluck's *Orpheus*, she does not sing trouser roles—there is, for one thing, no possibility for them in the Wagnerian opera she sings. She does not have, then, the same opportunities for the expression of masculine power and privilege that Armgart and others do by virtue of the roles they play. But Thea subverts the operatic and social narrative nonetheless.

When Doctor Archie goes to hear Thea perform at the Met, he prepares by reading the libretto of *Lohengrin*. He knows, that is, that Elsa "sinks lifeless to the ground," according to the stage directions, and, of course, he sees this on the stage. He is taken aback, then, when Fred, commenting on the performance, says, "She becomes an abbess, that girl, after Lohengrin leaves her. She's made to live with ideas and enthusiasm, not with a husband" (512). Doctor Archie asks Fred "guardedly": "Doesn't she die, then, at the end?" (512). Fred's response suggests Thea's creative artistry and her refusal to be limited by the roles assigned her: "Some Elsas do; she didn't. She left me with the distinct impression that she was just beginning" (512). The end that Fred imagines for the independent and powerful woman whom Thea has made from Wagner's Elsa is "an abbess." Thea's artistic ability must be remarkable indeed to suggest such an end for the helpless woman who sings to Lohengrin: "My hope, my solace, hero mine, / Do thou protect me" and "As here I lowly bend before thee / There will I now and ever be" (act 1, scene 3).

Like the diva—but unlike the trembling Elsa—the abbess wields power in her own realm; like the diva—but unlike the subservient Elsa—her power exists independently of the power of men. In the medieval and Renaissance worlds the abbey was the only place where women could live "with ideas and enthusiasms" rather than "with a husband." But at least it was a place. In Moonstone, Colorado, in the early twentieth century or in Middlemarch, England, in the nineteenth, as George Eliot recognizes on behalf of Dorothea Brooke, there was no such place. By assigning Thea the role of abbess, Fred—and the text—make the connection between that role and the role of the diva, the only "real" artist role to which women can aspire, in large part because by this time (and at this time—before, that is, the resurgence of the high male voice, the drag queen scene, and the all-male opera companies of the late twentieth century),[20] as Eliot notes in *Armgart*, diva, like abbess, is a role that only a woman can play.

The title of this last section of the novel is "Kronborg"; appearing on a marquee, alone, it looks and sounds much different from the immigrant family name of young girl. It is a masculine name, connoting king rather than queen. It suggests, that is, that the "real" artist Thea has become has moved beyond the feminine endings of abbess, diva, goddess, Thea. For Cather, artist, like writer, has no feminine ending because what she does is the work of the Creator, or as Thea, playing Elsa, sings:

> As in my dream I dreamed it,
> As in my will it was. (512)

The Song of the Lark, though it romanticizes the role of the artist, does not ignore or downplay the difficulties of her life; Thea's aspiration to the transcendent is thoroughly grounded in material conditions. Thea works hard for her divahood. Readers are not spared the hours, weeks, months, and years that the young artist studies piano, voice, language, opera parts. Nor are they spared the emotional and psychological price of such a life: "There are many disappointments in my profession and bitter, bitter contempts" (549). But Thea understands that such disappointments and contempts—what other texts read as unacceptable sacrifices and petty jealousies—fuel her art. Contempt, for example, "drives you through fire, makes you risk everything and lose everything, makes you a long sight better than you ever knew you could be" (550).

What makes Thea, Eden Bower, Kitty Ayrshire, and Cressida Garnet, that is, so different from the divas of the previous chapter, from, indeed, Cather's own early divas, is that this "price" is only that—a price one pays for something wonderful and significant. If Thea is not a saint, if she has trouble with friends and lovers, if she has given up "normal" happinesses, if there is "but one way in which she could give herself to people largely and gladly, spontaneously" (533), so be it. If "a 'big' career takes its toll" ("Coming, Aphrodite!" 69), well then, it takes its toll. Eden Bower's search at the end of the story for news of her former lover's success seems motivated not by regret but by a desire for reassurance: "One doesn't like to have been an utter fool, even at twenty" (62). The point, the texts suggest, is that these divas *can* give themselves largely, gladly, and spontaneously—

through their singing—and their audiences are the beneficiaries, in a way different from but not inferior to the give-and-take of more personal intercourse. That this difference is, of course, a source of anxiety and ambivalence is not surprising in a culture that assigns the personal to women—and women to the personal. These texts insist that in spite of such anxiety and ambivalence women can move out of the personal sphere without mortal consequences and that women who aspire to art, like their male counterparts, must so move. Few do it with less anguish and more success than Thea Kronborg.

This is not, of course, to claim that Cather's later texts transcend ideology. They do not. The "hideous" Jew in "Scandal," the "vulture race" in "The Diamond Mine," the obvious preference for tall, blond singers and the Germanic goddesses they play illustrate well that trenchant critiques of gender ideology can exist with and quite mindlessly collude with reinscriptions of racial ideologies—and vice versa.[21] Or, more accurately, *some* racial ideologies, since *The Song of the Lark* decries prejudice against Moonstone's Mexican population and revalues Native Americans' contributions to Southwest culture, though it continues to stereotype these populations: "Mexican women of the poorer class," the narrative informs us, "do not sing like the men. Perhaps they are too indolent" (294).

What is most remarkable in these texts is not, of course, such stereotyping, which is ubiquitous in works of the period, but the original and varied representations of the diva, so often stereotyped in other texts. Cather's divas are variously brilliant, average, and mindless; musically gifted, musically adequate, and musically hopeless; possessed of mediocre, excellent, and extraordinary voices; kind, indifferent, and cruel; ambitious, lucky, and lethargic; wildly successful, moderately successful, and failures. They are, that is, suspiciously like not only their real-life singing sisters but artists in general and writers in particular. While many male writers understandably see the diva figure as the exemplar of the other, as a kind of Woman par excellence, with all the ideological baggage that figure carries (or has carried for her), many women writers, like Cather, see her as the exemplar of the woman artist, as—they hope, fear, and plot—themselves, the very selves who have had to take on "masculine" prerogatives—and sometimes even masculine dress and masculine names—to succeed. No wonder, then, that *The Song of the Lark* resembles more, as Susan Rosowski notes, a male than a female *Bildungsroman*; Thea, like Cather herself, has "talent, hardheadedness, egocentricity, and a certain ruthlessness" (Rosowski, "Writing" 69),[22] without which no artist survives but which have long been considered marks of masculinity. The female artist, that is—painter, potter, or prima donna; composer, sculptor, or writer—is always *en travesti*.

Playing the Manly Part

It is not only, then, those who are ambivalent about the diva's power, those who want her back in women's traditional place, who consistently construct the woman who so often performs hyperfemininity on stage as "masculine." And as we have suggested, when men are culturally constructed as the *opposite* of women, then "manly" is the only rhetorical alternative to "womanly," with its implications of silence, passivity, dependence, and dedication to men and their lives. It's not surprising, then, that writers friendly to the diva, writers who celebrate the diva, would find her "manly" as well.

Perhaps the most "manly" of literary divas however, is not Thea Kronborg but Lena Geyer, the eponymous singer of Marcia Davenport's 1936 novel *Of Lena Geyer*, a novel dedicated to Davenport's mother, diva Alma Gluck, but based most closely on Olive Fremstad. In many ways, *Of Lena Geyer* is the most radical of the diva novels we discuss in this study, the most daring in its presentation of a woman for whom art—and the work and habits that art necessitates—comes first.[23] Lena is "physically a big, broad-hipped, free-moving animal" (34) who "walked with a free stride that no ordinary woman could have copied" (201).[24] This turn-of-the-century woman has, that is, an appearance, a walk, a posture more "masculine" than feminine, underscored by her "handwriting bolder than a man's . . . at a time when most women were proud of their delicate spidery chirography" (88). The judgment is not left to the reader: "There was in her a virility," says Louis, Duc de Chartres, who becomes her lover (89).

Even more manly than her looks, handwriting, and general vigor are Lena's manner of eating and drinking and her voracious appetite. In the early days of his infatuation, Louis sees Geyer, playing Violetta, lift "her glass in toast to her lover with a gesture of complete authority! . . . Compared with the insipid wave that constituted most women's conception of the action, this struck me as a revelation" (90). In other words, Lena Geyer toasts—and presumably drinks—like a man. Louis begins sending her all manner of expensive and delicious food and wine, which she consumes always "with enormous relish," and on the basis of which she finally grants him an audience (103). The way to this woman's heart, that is, is through her stomach. Elsie deHaven, Lena's companion, says that "she reminded

me of a man when she ate" (203) and later describes Lena finishing break-
fast: "She was sitting with her feet stretched out in front of her like a man,
staring at the empty plates and licking a drop of maple syrup off the tip of
her finger" (279). Her unabashed sensuality is here clearly associated with
the manliness of her posture. Lena's manly and exuberant enjoyment of
food and wine is contagious. Elsie, who has always eaten like the lady she
is,[25] feels differently about her first meal with Lena: "Actually I think that
was the first meal I had ever eaten; all the others were just food I had con-
sumed in the routine of existence" (210). Lena's hardy appetite might as
easily be characterized as peasantlike—she chews on black bread, for example, while she studies—but the text chooses to oppose it to a ladylike
way of eating on the basis less of class than of gender, in part by insisting
on the "authority" with which Geyer eats and drinks as well as the "relish."
And her appetite for food is matched by an equally manly appetite for
work, both appetites closely associated with the fullness, the vitality and
the perfection of her voice.

Lena's capacity for work is, as we have seen, enormous. This motif,
too, is repeated throughout the text: she "works like a . . . fiend" (20); "she
had an absolute disregard of how much work she did" (51); she "seemed
aware of nothing on earth but her work" (77); "she practised her exercises,
scales, and arpeggios far more conscientiously at the end of her career than
she had the beginning" (447). To a significantly greater extent than any
other diva narrative we know, *Of Lena Geyer* is in large part not only a portrait of a working woman but one of a woman working. Again, however, the
woman working is here associated less with class—though peasant women
cannot indulge in ladylike idleness, as Sojourner Truth's famous speech so
graphically reminds us—than with gender.

When, as an already established and accomplished diva, she is offered the trouser role of Leonora in *Fidelio*, the text gives us a detailed account of how she goes about learning it, including her reduction of "the
tempo fully by half" and her "ten, fifteen, or twenty" repetitions of a "difficult interval" (156). Interestingly, the result of all this work is a "noble
Leonore," in her "severe breeches, boots and jerkin . . . with her own brown
hair dressed in a club in the eighteenth-century fashion" (165). Hard work
makes the man. Much later in the novel, the character most intimate with
Lena describes her current "way of working": Lena would "go to bed with
her score and sit there studying the dynamics. Though she already knew
every direction by heart, every *forte* and *piano* and *crescendo* and *diminu-
endo*, she would read them over and over . . . sometimes singing, sotto

voce. She was so intense about this . . . I was afraid she would become exhausted" (344). Lena, that is, no longer goes to bed with a lover—she has by this time dismissed the duke—but with her work. It is work that commands her loyalty and that is her chief duty. At one point she responds to the duke's complaints about her physical absence and mental preoccupation: "The moment you call my work intrusion, my ideals mere ambition, you release me from any duty I might feel toward you" (176). Eventually she sends him away for good because her passion for him interferes with her work.

Significantly, the text itself never suggests that such absorption in work is neurotic, unnatural, or bizarre. Although Lena has clearly sacrificed sexual love for work, and although a scene near the end of the novel assures us that Lena loves Louis still, there is no sense that such sacrifice was too great or that Lena did not lead a happy and fulfilling life. The text is, in fact, careful to wean the reader away from the charming duke, in spite of the sympathy generated by his first-person interpolated narrative. In other words, it is the duke's own text that betrays him. His class prejudices, for example, become more pronounced in the latter part of his narrative; he gradually becomes more possessive of Lena and resentful of the time she spends away from him. When she tells him that out of loyalty to her teacher, Lilli Lehmann, she must spend the summer in Salzburg instead of with him, he rebels. "Lena, I do not wish you to go," he says (175), assuming that his "wish" will be her command. Lena's response is immediate and unequivocal. "She puckered her brows and bent her head slightly as if she had not heard right. *'You* do not *wish* me to go? . . . But I have already said that I must. I am going'" (175). By the time the duke pronounces upon the "really unfeminine element" in Lena—"that she was singularly devoid of feeling toward a home" (184)—the reader realizes that his admiration of her "masculinity" has definite, and selfish, limits.

The assurance and relative unambivalence of the novel's "feminist" stance here makes *Of Lena Geyer* an unusually progressive text, not only for its time but even for our—presumably more egalitarian—own. Even more surprising is its almost candid exploration of homoeroticism,[26] an exploration that is, again, linked to the diva's gender bending: Lena Geyer, in true manly fashion, takes to herself a wife.

The novel repeatedly insists that the relationship between Lena Geyer and the adoring Elsie deHaven is not an "unnatural" one. Louis's "detestation of her [Lena's] American worshipper emanated not so much from jealousy as from actual fear of the nature of her attachment" (197); he boils "with fiery determination never to allow the two to meet" (193). But even he, quite early in the "attachment," decides that it was not *that* but "was more a case . . . of a wealthy, solitary . . . , suppressed woman who was finding the outlet for her entire emotional existence in worship of her ideal" (197). Another character explains that Geyer clings "to Miss deHaven knowing that the mild, worshipping little woman could not exact any affection from her that would obstruct her work" and that Lena has "no compensation for the relationships of a normal existence" (387). In other words, however one characterizes the relationship between deHaven and Geyer, it is, officially, definitely not sexual, whereas the relationship between Louis and Geyer definitely was. Elsie deHaven herself simultaneously recognizes and refutes the possibility that her relationship with Lena could be interpreted as a sexual one: "Although the world has since said many cruel things about this strange, almost passionate friendship between Madame Geyer and myself . . . not one word of the essential accusation is true. Call me a freak if you like—the fact remains that my feeling for Lena Geyer was childlike in its simplicity, and yet more powerful than any other emotion in my life" (208). The reader has no reason to doubt the straightforward and honest deHaven—"the essential accusation," the accusation of sexual intimacy, is false.

The details of the relationship, however, clearly build a case for a "passionate friendship" that is highly erotic and obviously an alternative for Lena to the liaison with Louis and for Elsie to marriage and family. At their first meeting, Elsie offers Lena her hand when she leaves. Lena, however, "put both her hands on my shoulders and stood a moment looking into my eyes. Then she bent down and kissed me on both cheeks" (204). At their next meeting, Lena undresses in front of her. On another occasion, Elsie weeps with regret after having spoken to the diva with, she fears, "impudence"; in response, Geyer "strode across to me and put her arms around me. . . . She was strong and warm. . . . For the first time in my life I was freely and utterly giving way to deep feeling" (208). Perhaps the most erotic scene between the two occurs one night after a performance, when Elsie "slipped behind Lena and put over her shoulders a new cloak of mink, lined with crimson velvet. . . . When she felt it in place of her own cloak she whirled round and seized me . . . and flinging out one side of the cloak she caught me inside it" (256). The gift of fur and scarlet velvet suggests the sensuousness of Elsie's feelings for Lena, a sensuousness closely connected to Lena's voice, the sound of which is, for Elsie, at first "like electricity," something that "rushed through" her, "poured into" her, "melted"

her (225); it becomes "a physical sensation, almost like a taste" (226). And
we recall that when she shares her first meal with Lena, Elsie feels that she
has eaten for the first time. Lena opens up for Elsie a whole world of sensuality—"I did not even know I was repressed . . . yet once I felt freed, I
knew that I had never lived before" (225).

Besides this general awakening of her senses, Elsie spends a great
deal of time enveloped in Lena's strong, warm embrace, her "deep feeling"
on these occasions certainly both passionate and erotic: "I felt as if I should
die for love of her" (208). Other characters opine that the feelings, the sen-
suous ones at least, are fairly one-sided, but it is Lena who initiates the
kissing and embracing, Lena who assumes, as is her wont, the "masculine"
role in this courtship dance. And it is, quite literally, a courtship dance, led
by Lena Geyer, culminating in a scene in which Lena gives Elsie a new
name—Elsa, after the wifely Wagnerian role that Thea Kronborg so transforms. Then, "breaking into the Wedding March, she seized Elsa by the el-
bows and marched her smartly around the room" (245). That Lena takes
this "marriage" very seriously is clear in her response to Henry Loeffler's
proposal late in the novel: let Elsa decide. She says to deHaven, "You are
the main question now. Elsa, I won't marry Henry if you leave me," and to
Loeffler, "you're marrying both of us" (416, 417).

While Lena plays the husband role at the beginning of the relationship, there are many indications of role reversal as well. These reversals
might at first seem surprising given Geyer's masculine stance in the world,
but with them the text puts more distance between the women's relationship
and the traditional model of heterosexual coupling, with its rigid complementary roles. Geyer and deHaven construct a place of greater freedom.
Elsie, for example, gradually takes the place of the duke in Lena's life. Like
Louis, Elsie paves the way for the relationship by attending every performance and sending wonderful flowers to the beloved diva, and it is upon
Elsie's flowers that Lena grows dependent. Late in the novel, when Elsie is
in the hospital and is unable to send them, Lena loses her voice in the
middle of a performance, something that has never happened previously.
Like Lena's relationship with Louis, her relationship with Elsie quickly
takes on daily companionship as one of its characteristics: "Within two
weeks of our first evening together," Elsie says, "I was seeing Lena Geyer
every day" (211), and it is Elsie's daily companionship on which Lena depends for the rest of her life. Elsie, that is, functions as "husband" as well
as "wife." Perhaps the most dramatic example of this flexibility and
reversibility of roles is Elsie's conscious refusal to support Lena finan-

cially. Lena has taken for granted the duke's paying for their household, their entertainment, their food. Elsie, however, refuses to be either husband or wife. She does the household accounts, pays her own full share, and charges Lena for hers, risking, she knows, Lena's disapproval and possible dismissal of her and their relationship.

This shift from a glamorous heterosexual coupling between the diva and a duke/prince/king/male genius (the usual partners in traditional diva narrative and fantasy) to a homoerotic coupling between a diva and a plain—though financially independent—sensible, unglamorous woman is striking and dramatic. It also encourages further transformations. As the narrator describes it, "Lena Geyer's new menage in the summer of 1907 was the greatest possible contrast to the romantic one of the five preceding years. Instead of the duke to watch over her she had Elsie deHaven. Instead of the ubiquitous Pierre as major-domo to superintend traveling and domestic arrangements, she had Elsie's prim and correct Mademoiselle. Instead of the French and Austrian retinue provided by the duke, the household consisted of her own Dora, somewhat less surly in this gynaecium . . . ; Elsie deHaven's New York–Irish maid, Nellie; and a cook from Brienn . . . Anna" (236). Lena Geyer's "menage" has become a "gynaecium," a world of women that remains a constant, like Anna the cook, "for twenty-seven years" (236). This almost systematic replacement of men by women becomes the base on which Lena Geyer builds her brilliant career.[27]

The duke makes light of the relationship with Elsie, decides, as we have seen, that the "passion" is all on Elsie's side (197), a judgment echoed by other men in the novel (the mild, worshiping little woman could not exact any affection from her), including perhaps the narrator, a young devotee of the great singer, for whom the term "gynaecium" can hardly be a happy one. But when he lets Elsie speak for herself or when he quotes her letters, a much different picture emerges. Her own assessment of the relationship of Lena with the duke, for example, is quite different from that of the male "sources": although "she was intrigued by his good looks, his money, and the fact that if she were his mistress she would be the envy of Europe," Elsie says, "her taste for the pleasures he provided faded. His conversation bored her" (214). The duke himself practically acknowledges this. When Mahler tells Lena that she is ready to learn Leonora in *Fidelio*, "Lena's face," the duke mourns, "lighted with a radiance that caused me to feel . . . a twinge of envy; few of my suggestions for her pleasure had ever evoked such delight" (155). In spite, then, of the occasional rhetoric suggesting that Lena's life is truncated by her sacrifice of heterosexual passion, other passages describe another kind of passion—for music, for food, for her "household," for life itself—that diminishes and calls into doubt the notion of sacrifice.

Two incidents—both, significantly, narrated by Elsie—illustrate clearly that this ambivalence has become a motif in the text. In the first incident, Lena herself repeats the platitudes of heterosexual romance. When Elsie assures her that she has never "had a man," Lena shakes her head:

> "I don't understand it. . . . You're living a whole life without the most important thing in it. What do you do with your emotions?"
>
> "You know what I do."
>
> "You sublimate them, you idiot. . . . Do you mean to say it's enough for you to get everything you want out of me? Out of . . . the noises I make?"
>
> "Certainly. . . . And it's enough for you, too, if you are realistic about it. What would you do with a man, actually, Lena? What would you do if you had one hanging around this summer?"
>
> "Kill him. . . . I have to learn *Tristan*." (342)

This passage moves, like the novel itself, from the central assumption of the heterosexual romance plot—that a relationship with a man is "the most important thing"—to the more practical, "realistic" admission that both women are doing quite well without such a relationship, that, in fact, a man "hanging around" would detract from their work and their general contentedness. What seems to us of special interest here is that this admission is a significant variation of the frequently heard assertion that good companionship and satisfying work are more enduring than sexual passion. What Lena's life illustrates so vividly is the *passion* of good companionship and satisfying work. Neither she nor Elsie, that is, lives without passion; on the contrary, it is passion that most obviously characterizes the life they have chosen to lead.

The second incident occurs some months later and clearly underscores the lesson of the first. Elsie, in fact, recalls to Lena in some detail the previous conversation:

> "What about that man you were craving last summer?"
>
> She looked at me as if I had spoken Chinese. "Man?" she repeated blankly. "What man?"
>
> "Any man," I said. "Don't you remember, you told me what was

the most important thing in life and said I was an idiot to go without it?"

"You'll be worse than an idiot if you don't stop talking drivel," Lena said, burying her face in her score again. "You'll be a corpse." (344–345).

Although several months have passed between the two exchanges, they are separated by only a couple of pages. The reader, that is, needs no reminder of the previous words. That the text repeats them anyway suggests both the pervasiveness of their sentiment—a relationship with a man is "the most important thing" in a woman's life—and its own departure from it. Lena would kill a man who distracted her from her work and her gynaecium; Lena will kill Elsie if she doesn't stop "talking drivel"—that is, reproducing her own repetition of the cultural cliché.

Lena does, as we have seen, eventually marry—after a serious breakdown during which she loses her voice entirely—but her relationship with Henry Loeffler hardly qualifies as a grand passion,[28] and Elsie's interpretation of the marriage implies a radical reversal of the sublimation cliché voiced and then denied by Lena herself. Elsie says that "when we all actually believed that she would never sing again I had to realize how natural it would be for her to accept some substitute for the broken mainspring in her life" (414). A relationship with a man, that is, could serve as a substitute for her work rather than her work as a substitute for a relationship.

Lena does, however, sing again, and the circumstances remind readers of the difference between the heterosexual romance, at its most and least romantic, and the homoerotic bond. Once again, it is Elsie whose words and actions illuminate this difference, though it is Henry who relates the conversation. When Lena begins to regain her physical strength after the breakdown, Elsie asks Henry whether he, in his "heart of hearts," wanted Lena to sing again." He answers this honest, straightforward woman honestly, "The answer would be no" (422). He would prefer to make her happy as his wife. The answer reminds readers of occasions when the duke urged Lena to settle down, to make a home. He loves her voice, but he would prefer that she spend her time with him rather than in constant practice and in pursuit of the best roles and the best opera houses. Elsie, on the other hand, makes her home wherever Lena is, never demands more attention than Lena gives, and responds with unalloyed happiness when Lena's voice returns: "Elsa rushed to Lena and threw her arms around her. 'Thank God,' she choked" (424). In fact, Lena knows that "her voice meant more to Elsa than to anybody in the world—even herself" (448). The women are, then, united in their passion and dedicated to it without reserve. Lena's voice, Elsie says at one point, means "as much to me as parents, a husband, children, or anything most women attach themselves to" (203), not, the text implies, as a substitute, but as a perfectly "natural" if unusual object of desire.

Lena Geyer's career comes to an end fairly early in her life. Unwilling, like many divas, to sing until listeners begin to make remarks about her failing voice, she stages a farewell performance and leaves the profession. She becomes, in fact, "Mrs. Loeffler," just what Henry most wants, and seems happy in her domesticated ménage à trois. But neither she nor the text can long survive her domestication.[29] Lena begins to look "sallow," "drawn" (459), "tired," and "rundown" (460); the diagnosis is cervical cancer, caused by "ragged tears . . . after the difficult delivery of a child" (469). Henry and Elsie thus discover what the reader has known since the beginning of the "biography"—that Lena Geyer started her life in the United States young, unmarried, and pregnant. (The child, conveniently, does not survive.) Though Elsie faints at the news, it does nothing to change their relationship—they turn gray together—and Lena dies listening to *Tristan*. Like many diva narratives, then, *Of Lena Geyer* ends with the death of the diva. But there is no sense of death as punishment or even death as interruption. Once Lena retires from the stage, what she lives for is gone, but she has lived and triumphed and led a life of excitement and variety and accomplishment that few people—and fewer women—could even dream of. While "ragged tears" of childbirth suggest the difficulties of birthing the female artist, they may be read, at a more literal level, not as a judgment on promiscuous sexual behavior, never a concern of the novel, but as one of the distressing and fatal consequences, long known to Lena, of heterosexual romance. Or at least of the woman's role in it. In other words, there is little sense here that Lena's death is tragic—she has, after all, achieved what she most desired and has, besides, died surrounded by devoted friends. If her death suggests anything at all beyond the need to bring the narrative to satisfying closure (the novel presents itself as a "biography," and as such the only proper closure is death of the subject), it is that a woman's best shot at happiness is resistance. Using her well-trained voice. Playing the trouser role.

If Lena Geyer is the most "mannish" of our divas, the aspiring and eventually accomplished singers of Kate O'Brien's *As Music and Splend-*

our (1958) are the most "boyish" and the most surprising. The protagonists of this novel of apprenticeship are Clare, Luisa, and Rose, all intelligent, gifted, hardworking young singers. This is the story of their exhaustive and exhausting training. And in this novel—and in no other we have found—the "masculinity" of this training and the sexual ambiguity of opera itself are taken to their logical, if to conventional eyes uncomfortable and unacceptable, conclusion. When convent-school friends Luisa and Clare begin to perform professionally, their signature opera is, like Armgart's, Gluck's *Orpheus*, with mezzo-soprano Luisa in the trouser role. At the conclusion of a performance, "their brilliantly made-up eyes swept for each the other's face, as if to insist that this disguise of myth in which they stood was their mutual reality, their one true dress wherein they recognized each other, and were free of that full recognition and could sing it as if their very singing was a kind of Greek, immortal light, not singing at all" (113). In other words, what these roles presage is the enduring and obviously physical love between the two singers, a love affair unusual only in that they are both women. For the first time, that is, a diva narrative clearly—Luisa is "Clare's sworn lover" (334)—acknowledges the happy potential for cross-loving in cross-dressing, for a literal blurring of "disguise" and "reality," for the seizing of the quintessential masculine privilege, making love to a woman: potential that, as we have seen in this and previous chapters and as we shall see in following chapters, haunts almost every diva text.

CHAPTER 4

Diva Truths, Diva Lies,
Diva Lives

I . . . always made fun of the autobiographies of opera
singers. If you've ever had one of those pompous,
gilded volumes . . . you know what they are like.
—Frances Alda

$\mathcal{L}$ena Geyer refuses to write her auto-
biography because, she says, "I would not tell the truth" (Davenport, *LG* 3).
She assumes that proper autobiography is a telling of the truth, the whole
truth. Instead of writing her own life, then, she lets a young opera fan,
David Freeman, write it for her. She talks to him more and more freely; she
gives him permission to extract the truth from her friends and associates.
This is to be a truthful biography. Except, of course, that it isn't a biography at all, it's a novel; Lena Geyer is a fictional diva, and the biographer a
fictional character.

Late in the novel, one of the characters claims that "there's never
been a sensible book about an opera singer and the reason is it can't be
done. You'll get bogged down in sinking sentimentality, and the first thing
you know you'll make a movie queen out of Lena" (260). But, of course,
Of Lena Geyer is a book about an opera singer that purports to be a biography. To avoid getting bogged down in sinking sentimentality, the biographer compiles documents, conducts interviews, goads the aging Geyer
herself into revealing secrets. And then he lets his texts speak for themselves, tell the truth. Except, of course, that the documents, the interviews,
the revelations are all fictions—fictions because they are the paraphernalia
of a novel, fictions because artifice is the condition of possibility of all narrative, even narratives we call "true stories."

The condition of the biography is Lena Geyer's death; only when she
is no longer alive can the truth be told. The book opens, then, with
Freeman's eyewitness account of her funeral. The truth. Out of the truth of

death comes the fictional text of this true biography in which, of course, the biographer himself, seeker of truth, is a fiction. He is, further, the fiction of a biographer. Marcia Davenport, the author of *Of Lena Geyer*, wrote a biography of Mozart before she wrote this novel. Her biography makes use of documents, letters, memoirs, manuscripts, paintings, prints, papers—and other biographies. "I have tried," she concludes in her foreword, "to tell the truth" (xi). Davenport is, besides, the daughter of diva Alma Gluck; *Of Lena Geyer* is dedicated to her. Who better then "to tell the truth" than someone who has lived the life? We know, however, that a life is itself a kind of fiction—of continuity, of coherent and consistent identity, of beginnings and endings. A life becomes a life only in the telling of it. A life is a narrative. The autobiographer's "I," like the biographer's "he" and "she," is always—unavoidably, necessarily—a character.

A fictional biography like *Of Lena Geyer*, then, reminds that all (auto)biographical writing is a kind of fiction. The autobiographer, the biographer shapes the life tale to conform to the genres of autobiography, biography—here, even more specifically, to the subgenre of diva lives, which Frances Alda describes in the epigraph. The tale is thus bound again—by other beginnings and other endings, beginnings and endings being always arbitrary and conventional. It is bound, too, as is any "true" narrative, by memory. It is bound by the arbitrary survival of this or that document, by the fictionality of the documentation itself, dependent as is any document on individual perception and memory. Memories contradict other memories, perceptions contradict other perceptions, documents contradict other documents, memories contradict perceptions contradict documents. In this morass of misremembering, misperceiving, misreading, misrecording, telling the truth becomes a more and more elusive aim and impossible task. But, of course, *Of Lena Geyer* is a fiction, less dependent, then, on the vagaries of memories, perceptions, documents. Some would say fiction is therefore more true or possibly more true—whatever that means, whatever Truth might be—than genres like history, autobiography, biography that pretend, or at least once pretended, to Truth.

David Freeman records for his readers his own truths about Lena Geyer, others' truths about her, her truths about herself. Whatever *his* readers see, Davenport's readers understand by the end of the novel a simple fact about these narratives that promise the truth of Lena Geyer—they are, if not contradictory, at least different.[1] All these truths don't add up to the Truth; all we have are varied versions. *Of Lena Geyer* is a long novel, a detailed novel, a novel that covers, in good biographical fashion, birth and death, ancestors and survivors. But readers may wonder, in the end, what the novel covers *over*; what, that is, are the truths that Lena herself won't tell? More to the point, perhaps, what are the truths that the text won't tell?

The biographer discovers, with Lena's permission and aid, the usual scandalous material, her sexual "sins"—the four-year affair with the duke, even the early affair and subsequent pregnancy, the revelation of which sends Elsie into a swoon. And Lena claims—in dramatic, Edith Piaf fashion—that "I never have regrets for anything" (186). Why, then, can't she write her autobiography? What is the "truth" she cannot tell? A hint might be the "truth" that gets told too often. As we have seen, Elsie and everyone else in the biographical circle insist—perhaps, we might say, protest too much—that the relationship between Elsie and Lena is an "innocent" one. Why? Because it is? Or because lesbianism is the unspeakable truth of the narrative? The truth that Lena Geyer cannot tell, that David Freeman cannot uncover, that the text itself cannot allow to surface?

What Terry Castle attempts to establish in her essay "In Praise of Brigitte Fassbaender" is a homoerotic history of the diva world from Gerry-Flappers and other gangs of diva-adoring young females to the diva worship of Willa Cather, George Sand, Anne Lister, Ethyl Smyth, and Queen Victoria to the years-long attachments of Mary Watkins Cushing and Olive Fremstad, Margaret Anderson and Georgette Leblanc, Radclyffe Hall and Mabel Batten. Before the (sometimes/someplaces) contemporary acceptance of female homoeroticism, the opera house, Castle suggests, "was one of only a few public spaces in which a woman could openly admire another woman's body . . . all in an atmosphere of heightened emotion and powerful sensual arousal" (203). The opera, in Castle's view, becomes a hothouse of lesbian outpourings, the safe and respectable location for a mighty return of the repressed.

Elizabeth Wood tries in her notion of the "sapphonics" of the female singing voice to describe "a space of lesbian possibility, for a range of erotic and emotional relationships among women who sing and women who listen" (27). She, too, uncovers a history and a literature of this "lesbian" phenomenon. Both Castle and Wood illustrate their histories with the story of Lena Geyer and Elsie deHaven, whose fictional relationship is based loosely on the relationship of Olive Fremstad and Mary Watkins Cushing, that connection, too, a purportedly intimate but "innocent" one between a diva and her greatest fan. That is, the Geyer-deHaven and the Fremstad-Watkins alliances are read—at least by Castle and Wood, lesbian readers—as homoerotic, sapphic, lesbian, a reading specifically warned against in the text itself.

With the exception of *As Music and Splendour*, none of the diva narratives we discussed in the previous chapter give any overt sign of the lesbian or sapphonic history of opera that Castle and Wood document; yes, Margarethe Styr "hates men" (Atherton 18), a frequent code for lesbian, but the narrator makes clear that she is "essentially a man's woman. If her brain accepted a mate at all, it must be a man's" (178).[2] Thea Kronborg rejects marriage but pointedly enjoys sex with Fred—and marries him eventually. Of course, the "masculinization" of the divas carries with it the constant possibility of the "masculinization" of desire, of, that is, desire for a woman. But this possibility is, as we have seen, fairly consistently denied, countered, and ignored. It is all the more remarkable, then, that the possibility should so openly pervade *Of Lena Geyer*, a novel in which the truth of biography is marked out as patently allusive—and illusive.

Castle's and Wood's histories lend support to the suggestion that lesbianism is a suppressed "truth" of this multileveled and enigmatic text. And if, as Castle and Wood argue, female homoeroticism does permeate the history of opera, then lesbianism may be a suppressed "truth" of less fictional diva lives as well, of diva autobiography and biography in which female homoeroticism is conspicuously absent. If, in other words, female eroticism is an inextricable component of the opera world, its absence in diva "lives" seems suspicious, especially when that absence is accompanied by pointed, even gratuitous emphases on heterosexuality and "normality." And, as we will show, the more contemporary the life story is, the more it emphasizes the "ordinariness" of the diva's life, perhaps because the specter of lesbianism has in the last few decades so explicitly haunted the rich and famous. We are not, of course, suggesting that this or that diva is really or truly a lesbian (we hope we have complicated those terms— real, true, lesbian—enough for readers to trust that we would never argue for such a claim) or consciously attempting to answer charges of lesbianism. Rather we suggest that lesbianism becomes a matrix in diva life stories for a whole series of closely related issues and accusations that plague the woman on stage, the woman exposed, the woman who moves from the private sphere to which she is traditionally relegated to the public sphere traditionally reserved for men—accusations that include a loss of femininity, an inability to mother, usurpation of masculine prerogatives, ruthless and therefore unwomanly ambition, rampant and therefore unwomanly selfishness, immorality, idiocy, and uncontrollable jealousy, as well as lesbianism itself.[3] The diva autobiography and biography, then, become spaces in which these accusations can be answered, and, it seems, these answers

must—in response to increasing public demand—be more specific and explicit as those issues become the subject of more widespread public debate.

In 1993, on the verge of spectacular success as a diva, Cecilia Bartoli
dismissed an interviewer's questions about her love life. "I have never had a
serious relationship. When do I have time for boyfriends? Look at my
schedule" (Price 46). A couple of years later, the answers have changed. It
may well be, of course, that having achieved a certain status in the world of
opera, Bartoli can now afford to turn some attention to her private life. But
it may also be that handlers and publicists and Bartoli herself recognize the
danger in not having time for boyfriends. Such a dismissal threatens to
make an exception of Bartoli, to put her outside the category of the ordinary woman and so to question her womanhood. If her career is more important to her than marriage and family, she might belong to that dread
category the career woman, that ball-breaking, ice-queen-ish, self-sufficient creature only an epithet away from the man-hating lesbian.

A more recent interview with the young diva lays these concerns to
rest. "Bartoli isn't devoting all of her energies to her career," the writer
says. He quotes her: "'I like to go to the beach, and the mountains, to ski,
swim and cook, and go to the movies . . . . I have no particular man in
mind, but I would like to be married while I am still young enough to start
a family. What is life without men? Like a desert without water,' she says
emphatically" (McLellan). The writer reassures us. She is *not* just a career
woman. She *emphatically* likes men. She wants marriage; she wants children. (The wonderful ambiguity of her question and answer escapes him—
and perhaps her—entirely. A desert without water is—a desert.) Without
for a moment doubting the sincerity of her desires, we note that the contemporary diva would have little popular success without such desires,
without such reassurances, as contemporary diva life stories illustrate.

Comparing male and female singers, Helena Matheopoulos in her
Diva: Great Sopranos and Mezzos Discuss Their Art (1991) observes that
"female singers attach far greater importance to their personal lives. Unlike
their male counterparts, all artists in this book spontaneously brought up
this factor" (9). Most proclaim the importance of husband and children.
Matheopoulos, in fact, concludes that "the role of that often maligned
breed—the diva-husband—should . . . not be underestimated" (9). What
she fails to consider is why, in contrast to the lesser role of the divo-wife in
Bravo, her book about male singers, the diva-husband emerges as hero in
this text, why the women attach far greater importance to their personal
lives. While the reasons are complicated and of a piece with similar and

much-studied differences between the discourse of men and women, for our purposes and from our own limited "survey" of diva literature, we can suggest the simplest explanation: that it is not acceptable for women to succeed without men or for women to be happy without heterosexual love. Women who value their careers know this. Consciously or unconsciously, ingenuously or disingenuously, sincerely or cynically, they conform, or present themselves as conforming. While few of the divas in this volume go as far as Katia Ricciarelli, whose "dream had always been to find a man to whom I could voluntarily submit and who could dominate me" (170), most of the twenty-six singers interviewed emphasize the importance of their roles as wives and mothers. It is, of course, the exceptions to this discursive convention that are most interesting and revealing.

Two of the exceptions are the two African-American divas featured in the book, Leontyne Price and Grace Bumbry, both of whom have had to overcome the enormous prejudice of the white opera world.[4] Neither places much importance on her "personal life"; both explicitly reject traditional female roles for themselves. Both stress the "responsibilities" of their respective voices. "As a person who breaks tradition," Price says, "you have this extra responsibility. You *must* speak for more than just yourself. If you fail, more than just you fails" (159). It is perhaps this sense of political responsibility that takes precedence over concern about womanliness, this sense of being outsiders that renders insignificant—as well as useless—attempts to conform. Far from conforming, both Price and Bumbry rebel against implicit suggestions that they are missing out on something important. Price says that "no single human being could have given me what my audiences . . . gave me" (165). And Bumbry emphatically claims that she would not think of interfering with her career to become a mother. "Absolutely not. You see, anybody can have children but it is not everybody who has been given this wonderful gift and I do think that such a gift carries a certain responsibility" (269).

Price and Bumbry are, along with Teresa Berganza ("My husband always says we live in a ménage-à-trois: he, myself, and the Voice. As far as priorities go, the Voice wins hands down!" [252]), the most adamant of these twenty-six divas about their own voices. We used Price's eulogy to her own voice as epigraph for this book: "I think I've had one of the most beautiful lyric soprano voices I've ever heard. I'm *mad* about my voice. It was *gorgeous*" (164). Bumbry admits that "from time to time I am so overcome by a beautiful sound that I just sit back and think 'Oh God, how is it possible for *that* to come out of *this* throat?' It gives me goose-flesh" (269).

No false feminine modesty here, no submissive pose, no suggestion of attractive feminine weakness.

Price and Bumbry acknowledge and revel in the power of their voices in ways that recall the declarations of earlier divas rather than their own contemporaries.[5] Like the autobiographical fragments Matheopoulos's interviews of them provide, diva life stories from the early part of the century could, as we have suggested, still allow for dedicating oneself to art or work alone, for eschewing marriage and sometimes sexual relationships altogether. Divas who did marry could relegate the acquisition of a husband to a footnote. Lilli Lehmann in *My Path through Life* (1914), for example, introduces her husband in a parenthesis on page 357 of her five-hundred-page tome. Thereafter he appears perhaps a dozen times when he sings with her or when he, seemingly rarely, accompanies her on a trip. She says early and matter-of-factly that she "became unsuited to every kind of society out of love for my art" (141). And she makes clear that her marriage is not a romantic one but an alliance closely linked to her work and her career. The relationship, she says, is one "of strong co-operation in the development of ourselves and of our art, that should lead our united lives to a single lofty goal" (372). The rhetoric recalls the "lives" of saints like Francis and Clare, celibate in their joint undertakings. While Lehmann makes no claims to celibacy, it is her mother with whom she ordinarily sleeps, her mother's arms that she longs for when she is unhappy or hurt.[6]

Olive Fremstad was married twice, but, according to Mary Watkins Cushing, "a favorite theme" of the diva's was that "marriage is not for serious artists!" (34). In *The Rainbow Bridge*, Fremstad claims that her first one was "only a side show!" (34). Like her fictional incarnation Lena Geyer, she responds to rumors of affairs with "I have no lovers—they interfere too much with work" (86). Not surprisingly, both of Fremstad's marriages are short-lived. Only a few weeks into her second, she announces to Cushing that the two of them are going away: "I am suffocating . . . I must breathe!" (292). Geraldine Farrar's autobiography, *Such Sweet Compulsion* (1938), has Farrar's mother commenting thus on her daughter's marriage: "I had . . . never thought she would consider matrimony. She was not brought up to be good material for tandem going" (146). A mother's almost boasting admission that she raised her daughter *not* to be a good wife would be much less acceptable in later decades. The admission is complicated by the fact that it is Farrar herself who is writing the comment, using her mother as a partial narrator of her autobiography (the text alternates between sections written in the two voices). In other words, a strategy of narrative ventriloquism allows Farrar to boast of her unsuitability "for tandem going" and to imply that to be so is to be an obedient daughter. Farrar does marry, but while her mother's role in the narrative is enormous, is indeed structural, her husband's is minuscule.

Lotte Lehmann's autobiography, *Midway in My Song*, published the same year as Farrar's, decries the effects of marriage on her mother's voice: "The deep cello tone of that heavenly organ was swallowed up by the four walls of our 'best room,' the red plush furniture and the stupid bunch of dried grasses" (8). This antagonism toward "home" is unusual and unusually aggressive; it expresses the constriction of throat consequent upon the constriction of women's lives. Lehmann finds the details of her own everyday life, *her* equivalent of red plush furniture and bunches of dried grasses, "entirely unimportant to me" (218), and she is "terribly" annoyed by an article that dwells on them (written, interestingly enough, by Marcia Davenport). She unselfconsciously admits that even before she thought of becoming an opera singer and so dedicating herself entirely to art, she determined to avoid the four walls of marriage and become a nun (21).

According to Emma Calvé's 1922 autobiography, *My Life*, she too was, at one point in her life, "fully determined to become a nun,"[7] which she attributes to a sense "of religion and mysticism" common in singers; she cites with pride a couple who send flowers to "you who are the bearer of the Fire Divine" (77). Her voice, she says, "is a mysterious, a heavenly visitor . . . an angel from another world" (249). Of her successful performances, she rhapsodizes, "In these moments, it is as though I became a supernormal being. . . . I become multiple. The power and strength of many is mine" (255). The diva becomes in these passages more than nun—goddess, priest, "bearer of the Fire Divine."

Another bearer of the Fire Divine who talks about her vocation in equally Romantic rhetoric is Luisa Tetrazzini, whose autobiography, *My Life of Song*, appeared the same year as Calvé's. Tetrazzini, too, sees her "calling" as a sacred one; singers, she says, are "the media through whom our fellow-creatures touch the celestial plane while yet on earth" (222). Unlike many later divas, Calvé and Tetrazzini seem unconflicted by such aspirations and claim them proudly. Tetrazzini enjoys, she says, "being 'lionized'" (109); advised not to be too ambitious about her Covent Garden debut, she replies, matter-of-factly, "But I am ambitious" (177). She brags several times about the fabulous fees she commands and takes pleasure and pride in their being higher than those of her male counterparts: "This ($2500) was the highest salary which had ever been paid in New York to a prima donna for a season in grand opera. Caruso at that time was earning, I believe, $2000 a performance" (241). She is proud as well that the fabulous fees are well deserved; she refers to herself as "a woman . . . earning her living with her voice" (254).

There is no sense in her text that the ambition or the desire for fame and money ought to be downplayed, that womanliness is a goal, or that she must assert heterosexual credentials: "As a girl looks forward to her wedding day had I looked forward to my professional debut" (61). What "a girl" does is of no particular concern to Luisa Tetrazzini, aspiring artist, singer, diva. If, by setting herself off from the world of "a girl," she risks the accusation of masculinity, she takes pleasure in that, too. She recounts with pride and pleasure the sort of exploits usually associated with male life stories,[8] many of the exploits, in fact, carried off in male drag. As an adolescent, for example, she dresses as a young swain and courts—with obvious delight and admirable success—the neighborhood girls. "One of my dearest friends," she brags, "allowed me to walk by her side for a long distance while pouring out my love-sick soul—until she discovered that I was none other than her little friend, Luisa Tetrazzini" (20). Dressed as Napoleon, she is also a success at a masked ball. On a more practical level, she dons the garb of a sailor boy in order to escape from Argentina when an official tries to detain her; she narrates the tale with such relish and such a clear sense of herself as hero that it reads like a boy's adventure story (112).

A journalist asking for a pithy version of her life story tells her that "it is your failures that I want to hear about, signora, not your successes. . . . I want a kind of a Cinderella story about you; one night a beggar maid, and the next night the belle of the ball, betrothed to the prince" (208). He wants, that is, a female *Bildungsroman*, the sort of story that Lena Geyer, too, refuses to tell. But Tetrazzini will not oblige him. She doesn't recount failures; she doesn't see betrothal as the climax of her story. Being belle of the ball or betrothed to a prince is aspiration far below that of a woman whose calling is "majestic" (222), who "chortle[s] at her foes" (294), who "secures [a] man's liberty with the magic key of song" (107), who keeps a pet leopard—but never a diary (140).[9] And, besides, there is no prince. The only man she mentions in a romantic context is an obsessed and wealthy suitor in Argentina who threatens suicide if she refuses to kiss him. She calmly cajoles him into giving her the knife—which she then appropriates for subsequent performances: "For fifteen years, in all parts of the world, I used this same dagger when singing 'Lucia'" (123).

She thus emasculates the only "lover" who is part of her life story by appropriating his phallic weapon and turning it into a fictional one, into a prop for her performance. She never does kiss him.

The "greatest day of my life" is not the occasion of her wedding or the birth of a baby but of lunch with Adelina Patti, the woman whose story and song inspired her as young child. When Patti comes to one of her performances, Tetrazzini, in the midst of a "storm of applause," has "eyes only for her" (225). Tetrazzini, then, ignores the heterosexual romance in favor of a homosocial bond that permeates the narrative—"Patti's Death and My Birth" is the title of the first chapter. Patti was the Queen of Song; Tetrazzini, who has no desire to marry a king, is heir to the throne.[10] *My Life of Song* is an amazing narrative—unselfconscious, vigorous, proud, and not so much defiant of traditional assumptions about women and art as oblivious to them.

Of this group of diva autobiographies, written in the first half of the century, Frances Alda's *Men, Women, and Tenors* (1937) insists most emphatically and explicitly on her femininity. Alda claims, for example, that "I am not writing as a singer. . . . I am writing as a woman" (4). Her husband of many years, Giulio Gatti-Casazza, director of the Metropolitan, is mentioned early and often. Her favorite role "of all the forty . . . I have sung" is Mimi, because she "is all feminine" (37). She proudly states that she is *not* a feminist.

It is tempting, then, to read Alda as an exception among these forceful, "masculine" divas. But the claims for femininity have little to do with traditional associations of femininity with weakness, femininity with subordination, femininity with passivity. Her world, she announces, is an "active" and "exciting" one (4). She is ambitious. She takes pleasure in her diva perks. "Why should I lead anyone to suppose that I haven't always enjoyed immensely being a prima donna? On the stage and off it" (100). She eschews the label "feminist" because "You couldn't make a feminist out of a woman who knows, and doesn't care if the world knows it, too, that in some things she's as elemental as Eve, and as unashamed" (92).[11] By "some things" she seems to mean liking sex, liking men's attention, enjoying clothes; she emphatically does not mean subservience or even wifely devotion. Like Eve, she rebels against such strictures and scorns women who obey them: "I'm not the kind of dear little woman who runs away from her career the minute the curtain is down, and hurries home to cook supper for her husband and darn his socks and listen to him read . . . from the evening paper. . . . I'd rather ride a surf-board on Long Island Sound"

(100–101). She hates the role of Anna in Puccini's *Le Villi* because she has "a deep-seated contempt for any girl who let her lover walk off and leave her, and then died of it" (119). Her commonsense and egalitarian attitude toward relations between women and men extends to her own marriage. She refuses, even in private life, to be called Madame Gatti-Casazza (137); and she acknowledges unapologetically that "I knew I was not, and never had been, in love with my husband. . . . I admired his genius" (162).

Like the divas who prefer roles that are less "little grisette" than Mimi (37), Alda claims for herself many "masculine" traits and prerogatives. She brags that she "can't remember a time when I couldn't beat my boy playmates at tennis, or swim as far and as fast as they could" (26). The implication is that she can still. She doesn't hesitate to criticize men. "I was beginning to understand something that I know now to be true of men—of bank directors no less than tenors. They are the real prima donnas" (121). She here uses the epithet "prima donna," of course, to denote the stereotype of the woman on stage—self-indulgent, irrationally demanding, and egocentric. By referring to men as prima donnas, she makes clear that such behavior and traits are no more acceptable in men than in women and that no behavior or trait is the exclusive provenance of one sex. She refers to herself as a "peacock" (137), proudly claims to be a "worker" (46). In spite, then, of her sense of herself as intensely feminine, or perhaps because of it, she pushes at the limits of the feminine to challenge its very definition, to demand that it include a life—free, sexual, ambitious, unashamed—traditionally outside its pale.

The diva life that is perhaps most consciously defiant, least willing to entertain traditional mores while entirely cognizant of them, and most adamant about art and career first is *Mary Garden's Story* (1951). Indeed, defiance is actually the predominant motif of the text. Like Lehmann and Calvé, Garden admits to "thinking seriously of taking the veil" (133) but ultimately defies expectations of marriage or other heterosexual romantic couplings in more dramatic and more "masculine" ways.

As Garden writes the autobiography—or dictates it—someone advises her that "she needs to put 'romance' into the book" (292); otherwise readers will not be interested. But "romance," Garden thinks, is no one's business but her own. Governor James Cox of Ohio, an admirer, argues against Garden's desire for privacy, urges her to suppress it for a higher good: "But if your love helped a great man, I think that's a very interesting thing to tell the world" (294). If, that is, Garden is writing an autobiography to reinforce the culture's gender code, to assure her readers of her womanliness, present herself as happily subordinating herself to "a great man," then she should tell all. "Romance" becomes, in this view, what romance usually is, a guardian of the status quo.

Garden acquiesces in the demand for romance, but she uses that conventional theme for a much different end from the one Governor Cox advocates: "I'm glad I was persuaded to put 'romance' into it, if only to show as forcefully and frankly as I know how that my music always came first. . . . My passion was opera, and that was the only real 'romance' of my life" (294). Garden thus acknowledges at the end of her story the thesis of the whole, a thesis she states in various ways from the very beginning: "I'm perfectly reconciled to what I'm going to miss, and I know there will never be room in my life for marriage" (11); "I can truthfully say I have never felt that way about any man" (43); "I must confess that as his [her first lover's] brother spoke to me I couldn't even remember Pete's face" (130); "Sometimes I wonder why I've never been crazy about men like so many other women. . . . I like to do my own thinking, not their thinking—*mine*" (144); "My career never gave me pain. It never gave me anything but joy, and what man could give that?" (155); "I never let any man kiss me on the stage—not once" (164); "Nobody ever took me from my work, not a man who lived. That was my life and my passion, my work" (229). This selection of quotes, from the first chapter to the last, illustrates the determination and the single-mindedness with which Garden pursues her thesis, the acknowledged theme of her story, the perceived motif of her life.

Garden's declaration of independence from men and marriage facilitates the "masculine" stance she, like Tetrazzini, assumes in the world and on the stage. She is, for example, quite proud of her performance as Le Jongleur de Notre-Dame, usually a tenor role: "I was to be the first woman ever to sing the role of the boy juggler" (131). She assesses her voice with bravado: "It was a brilliant voice and it cut through an orchestra like steel. It was both big and piercing. . . . I was always its master and never its slave. It obeyed me, and not I it. And I used it as freely as a painter uses his brush" (154). The rhetoric here is remarkable. Women's voices are, as we have seen, often described in rhapsodic terms—they are frequently heavenly, for example. And they are strong, full, glorious, uplifting, pure. But a voice that cuts through an orchestra like steel is a voice that leaves behind any vestige of traditional femininity, a voice that many would find unattractive and unwomanly. And, in fact, Garden acknowledges that many critics did not like it and were "baffled" by it (154).

The voice is "big and piercing," again words that suggest masculinity.

And in control of this powerful, steel-like, piercing instrument is its *master*, Mary Garden herself. She chooses the masculine, not the feminine form of the word; Mary Garden is never, in any sense of the term, "mistress." She is the "artist" who uses her voice, here claiming her rightful place among the brotherhood of artists. Such confidence, such claims, such masterful control were, not surprisingly, threatening. At one point, a man tried to kill her; asked why, he replied only, "She talks too much." Granted, the assailant seems to have been as mentally unstable as the madly infatuated girl who killed herself for love of Garden, but his reason has a certain awful and predictable logic. The voice that Garden used to such effect on the opera stage became a voice-in-the-world. Mary Garden was a woman who, on stage and off, commanded an audience, who spoke her mind, who publicly proclaimed her independence from men. In other words, she talked too much.

For a year Mary Garden was director of the Chicago Opera Company.[12] Again, men were threatened. "The women singers were charming and co-operative, but the males were just a pack of jealous boys. I've never seen such jealousy in my life, and I was told that some of them began plotting to take my place" (175). At this time, too, she started receiving death threats in the mail—anonymous letters, knives, revolvers, bullets. A box of bullets was accompanied by a letter: "Remember that there should be twelve bullets in this box. Count them. There are only eleven. The twelfth bullet is for you" (173). She does not speculate about the sender(s), but it seems clear that her anomalous position as female director, the voice of authority, the voice that "properly" belonged to a man, occasioned the missives.

Boy, master, artist, director—masculine roles that Garden plays, juggles, not only with confidence but with pleasure both on stage and off. Her easy familiarity with these roles makes it seem unsurprising that she often takes a "masculine" stance toward other women as well, their bodies, their voices, their company. When, for example, she looks at Lily Debussy's body stripped for surgery, she reflects that "in my life I have never seen anything so beautiful as Lily Debussy from the waist up . . . too divine for words!" (84). Garden's tribute to Melba's voice is, like Tetrazzini's to Patti, as erotically charged as a lover's: "It left Melba's throat, it left Melba's body, it left everything, and came over like a star and passed us in our box, and went out into the infinite. . . . My God, how beautiful it was!" (93).

Garden rhapsodizes not only about women's bodies and voices but about their demeanor as well. "During one of my lectures in 1949 I was asked what I liked most about America. Without a moment's hesitation I replied 'its people.' I might have said, 'Its women!' My God, are the women of American strong!" (259). It is, of course, the strength of them that she admires, their "masculine" qualities, the qualities she nurtures and announces in herself. One has only to read these passages to realize how unusual such appreciation for women is from the voice or pen of another woman. Praise of women itself tends to be, except in feminist circles, a masculine prerogative. It is women's role to praise men, a role that, for the most part, Garden refuses to play.

Criticism of men and praise of women are two acts that almost inevitably invite the charge of lesbianism—at least in post-Freudian times. And, as we have been arguing, women with loud, strong voices attract the charge as well. Opera itself—a world that embraces artifice, pushes the human voice and body to their limits and beyond, flirts with gender reversals, offers an acceptable space for same-sex voyeurism and desire—has served as a homosexual underground, most notoriously male but clearly, as lesbian historical research indicates, female as well. Above the ground, however, the subject is seemingly ignored but carefully defended against, a strategy we isolated in many of the fictional narratives as well. Autobiographical narratives, for the most part, repeat the strategy, but with an important difference. Cather's divas, for example, may be fantasized alter egos, but they are not read as "Cather." This is not the case with diva autobiographers, as fantasized as the "selves" they construct may be. The fearlessness and defiance of Mary Garden are thus remarkable when she allows the L-word to surface in her own text. She describes a scene in the office of M. Carré, director of the Paris Opera (and one of Garden's many suitors). He considers staging a new opera called *Aphrodite*, but hesitates because "it's very Lesbian" (97). Scolding M. Carré ("I had no idea you were such a prude"), Garden eagerly agrees to listen to it and seems entirely unconcerned about its controversial content, unconcerned that playing a lesbian might tempt her audience to conclude that she is a lesbian. The opera is produced, Garden loves her role in it, and she proclaims it "one of the most spectacular successes the Opéra-Comique had ever enjoyed" (98). The point is not, of course, to suggest that Garden was a lesbian but to argue that her *Story* is exceptional in its casual treatment of and acceptance of lesbian eroticism as well as in its enthusiastic embrace of her own unfeminine positions and even her less than womanly (according to her) body: "There was a certain dash and exuberance to the role [Massenet's Cherubin], and, again, thanks to that body of mine, I was the perfect boy" (138).

Like Lena Geyer, Olive Fremstad, as she is portrayed in Mary Watkins Cushing's *The Rainbow Bridge*, is a perfect boy as well. She has, for example, a famous "windblown stride, both on the stage and off," that is "inimitable and challenging" (123). During a vacation in Maine, she "caught half a dozen perch before supper and fell on them with true Scandinavian appetite" (203). Her attitude toward work is, like her many fictional sisters, a "masculine" one—"As usual, only work mattered" (203). Even as she is dying, she pronounces that "it is not against the pain and the infirmity that I rebel. . . . No, it is because I cannot work that I fret and grieve" (315).

The Rainbow Bridge, we noted, represents Fremstad as, like Garden, determined to eschew romance in favor of art and work, though Fremstad, unlike Garden, briefly stumbles on occasion. And what she concludes from those few weeks or months that she lives with a man is that "a serious artist can't have lovers and still *think!*" (184). While Cushing refuses to mention or discuss the homoeroticism implicit in Fremstad's woman-centered existence, *The Rainbow Bridge* is, unlike later diva life narratives, unapologetic about the importance of homosocial bonds and unselfconscious about describing those bonds in homoerotic language. Of Fremstad's effect on her, for example, Cushing says, "Witchery of this kind is high-voltage and irresistible. . . . My enslavement became absolute" (120). When she meets Geraldine Farrar, Cushing describes her response as temptation to adultery: "Even I, dedicated heart and hands to another singer, felt my pulses quicken and the fatuous smile of the 'Gerry-flapper' spread across my face when, in a drift of delicious perfume, trailing furs, plumage, and the sparkle of jewels, she [Farrar] brightened my exile" (173).

Although Cushing does not attempt to articulate Fremstad's feelings about *her*, the diva, according to Cushing, realizes again and again that she can't get along without her. "You hold in your hand the success of my married life," she tells Cushing just before the second wedding (285). And while, as we have seen, Fremstad finds life with a husband suffocating, she welcomes Cushing's presence in her country retreat. Not surprisingly, however, in *The Rainbow Bridge* Fremstad struggles, it seems, to find language to describe her relationship to Cushing, a girl of only seventeen when she first begins to live with the already famous diva. Secretary, buffer, even mother are terms Fremstad uses, then seems to discard. Eventually they become just "friends"; only once does the text use the word "love" of their relationship.

1. " 'Himmel! The roof of your mouth . . .' " One of George du Maurier's illustrations to his *Trilby* (1894).

2. Jenny Lind, P. T. Barnum's nightingale, America's anti-diva. An engraving by Mote after Hayter. *(Courtesy of the Library of Congress.)*

3. Emma Calvé, "Bearer of the Fire Divine," c. 1907. *(Photo courtesy of the Library of Congress.)*

4. Mary Garden as Thaïs c. 1907. The diva as nun. *(Photo courtesy of the Library of Congress.)*

5. Defiant Mary Garden: "I never let any man kiss me on stage—not once."
c. 1909. *(Photo courtesy of the Library of Congress.)*

6. Luisa Tetrazzini c. 1908: "As a girl looks forward to her wedding day had I looked forward to my professional debut." *(Photo courtesy of the Library of Congress.)*

7. Diva rivalry as popular entertainment. Cartoon from *Puck*, 1910.

8. Olive Fremstad c. 1911. Dreaming of Mary? *(Photo courtesy of the Library of Congress.)*

9. Geraldine Farrar as Joan of Arc c. 1916—"not a tandem-goer," says "Mother." *(Photo courtesy of the Library of Congress.)*

10. Carmen, of course. Geraldine Farrar c. 1915. *(Photo courtesy of the Library of Congress.)*

11. Farrar's tiger tactics. *(Photo courtesy of the Library of Congress.)*

12. Divas formidable and toothsome. Caruso's caricatures of Tetrazzini *(above)*, Farrar *(left and opposite, top)*, and Destinn *(opposite, bottom)*. *(Photo courtesy of the Library of Congress.)*

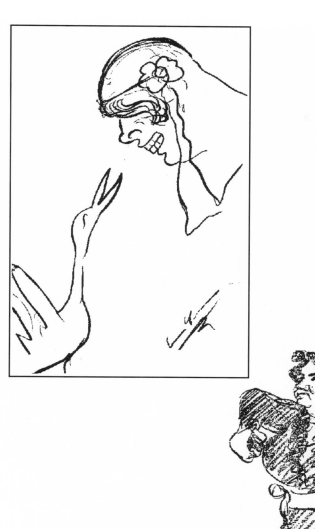

13. Frances "not-a-feminist" Alda on a butch day, not a "little grisette." c. late 1920s. *(Photo courtesy of the Library of Congress.)*

14. The Derivative Duo, Susan Nivert and Barb Glenn, reveal the source of the Queen of the Night's irritability in "P.M.S. Aria," sung to "Der Holle Rache." *(Photo by Barb Penoyar.)*

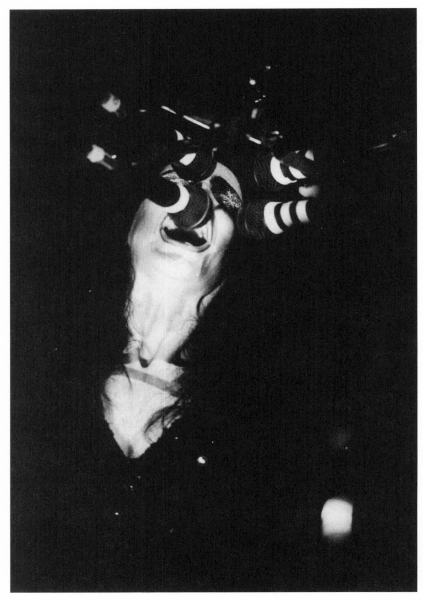

15. Diamanda Galas. A Medusa for the electronic age. *(Photo courtesy of Paula Court.)*

But whatever the bond between these women, sexual or not (probably not), homoerotic on one side or both, the narrative clearly works to present a Fremstad whose life is centered on music rather than on personal relationships, on career rather than family, on present success rather than past history. Her first marriage is "a side show"; her second, too, Cushing describes as performance: "She could hardly have looked more beautiful, but I felt that she really should have been in costume, wig, crown, and all, for the whole scene was pure theater and only the footlights were missing" (288). Marriage, wedding days, these putative "most important" or "happiest" days in a woman's life, are here acknowledged as "show," and what takes place on the stage as life: "I spring into life when the curtain rises, and when it falls I might well die" (119). Almost every diva says something similar: for many hours a week, many months a year, she *is* Tosca, Lucia, Carmen, Orpheus.[13] She is many. To speculate about her personal history, to recount her romances is a small part of her story, and for many of these early twentieth-century divas the least important part.

Diva lives from the early twentieth century that center on art and career to the exclusion of the personal offer a marked contrast in both content and rhetoric to more contemporary life narratives that—like the Cecilia Bartoli interviews quoted earlier—systematically defend against charges of careerism, masculinity, lesbianism. David Fingleton's 1982 biography of Kiri Te Kanawa, for example, announces that, "Singing for Kiri is emphatically not her 'life,' not even her 'career,' but simply her job. . . . When she is away from the job and back at home with her family, opera and singing tend to be put aside; opera is not a fact of family life." In fact, he claims, even when she is supposed to be working, she is easily sidetracked "by her children and the normal daily life of a healthily extrovert young woman" (34). The phrasing here is curious and implies that a life dedicated to music would be somehow abnormal, unhealthy, self-centered, perhaps even unwomanly, un-young-womanly, at least, though Te Kanawa is thirty-eight at the time of publication. Gone are the borrowings from the rhetorical traditions of religion and Romanticism. We see here a different kind of construction, the construction of the "natural woman" who just happens to be a diva. Instead of the suspect life of the overinvested diva, Kiri (he calls her Kiri, too) lives, he (re)assures us, a perfectly normal life, far removed from the music-centered existence of a Calvé, a Garden, or a Lotte Lehmann— the details of whose everyday life are, as we have seen, "entirely unimportant" to her.

Although Kirsten Flagstad's autobiographical writings were first published as *The Flagstad Manuscript* just a year after Mary Garden's autobiography, Flagstad was twenty years younger than Garden; the twenty years
have dramatically altered the rhetoric of the diva narrative. If her life story
has a theme, it is that she is a very ordinary person, a very ordinary woman
who, "before all else . . . wanted a simple and tranquil home life, and a husband to love and respect me" (Biancolli vi). When she has a child, "the
baby occupied all my thought. I wasn't interested in anything else" (26).
When she marries for the second time, she intends "to give up singing as a
profession. I didn't have to earn my own money anymore. . . . Besides, my
husband didn't want me to sing. . . . He preferred me . . . being plain Mrs.
Henry Johansen" (49). Why, then, does she go back to the opera stage?
"The truth is I am womanly enough, weak enough, to yield to the insistence
of friends" (89). When she goes to Bayreuth, she wants to assure her readers that "I had my husband's approval" (54). She is happy about her
daughter's early marriage: "My daughter's ambition, as it had been mine,
was to be a good wife and nothing more. She never showed any inclination
toward an artistic career, and I must confess I was extremely happy she
didn't" (92). Her attitude contrasts with that of her own mother, a woman
of Garden's generation, who regularly became "frantic" over her daughter's
"lack of interest" (26) in her operatic career and who, like Geraldine
Farrar's mother, raised her for work and public achievement.

Flagstad—because she returned to Norway during its occupation by
the Nazis and because her husband was arrested for collaboration after the
war—was accused of having Nazi sympathies and picketed (like some of
our fictional divas) when she later performed in the United States. Her interviews emphatically deny any sympathy whatever with Nazi ideology,
but, of course, she, along with even the most anti-Nazi Americans, sub-
scribed to Nazi ideology about women. The equation of "womanly enough"
and "weak enough" suggests women's dependence on men, on, specifically,
husbands—to "lean on" and to make the decisions for them. In fact, she
says that when "you are suddenly left" without a husband, the "worst" thing
is that "you find you must learn all over again to make your own decisions"
(159). Her emphasis on her husband's approval of her return to the stage,
her repeated claims that she *really* wanted only wife- and motherhood, her
repeated denials that her career meant anything to her assure readers of her
adherence to the code of womanliness that permeated the period after the
Second World War.

The interviewer and compiler of Flagstad's autobiographical writings,

Louis Biancolli, notes and then questions Flagstad's insistence: "The craving for husband, home, and homeland had become an obsession. Yet behind it I suspected a professional restlessness. . . . An artistic compulsion was in her blood to stay, all avowals to the contrary" (xiv). Flagstad herself occasionally acknowledges that opera seemed to be her destiny (50) and that "I have always been happiest when working" (198). She even admits that "now that my loss [of her husband] is far behind me, I have grown more confident and independent. I decide things for myself, and rather enjoy it." But she immediately retreats from such personal and social heresy: "Sometimes it frightens me to realize how changed, how self-sufficient, I have become" (159). The ambivalence is palpable. Though opera is her "destiny," she submits to it rather than embraces it: "I never really returned to music. It sort of came to me. . . . I slowly slid into it again" (53). Self-sufficiency is the first step down the slippery slope to the unnatural. Her fear, then, seems to be of independence, of any sort of ambition, of any hint of unwomanly or masculine behavior—or at least of being perceived (perceiving herself?) as independent, ambitious, unwomanly. Her own preface to *The Flagstad Manuscript* insists that "I am just the average person who walks the earth, not at all the sort of person that anyone could possibly think capable of doing the queer things good, ordinary people refrain from doing" (v). It is not at all clear to what she is referring here, perhaps to the accusations of Nazi sympathies. But "queer things" suggests as well, perhaps unconsciously, the association of the exceptional with the unwomanly, the unaverage or unordinary with the perverse, the ambitious or aggressive or active woman with the queer woman.

While Flagstad's expressions of fear may be exceptional among diva life stories, and while *The Flagstad Manuscript* may be very much of its historical moment and geographical location, that moment persists in surprising ways. Beverly Sills, for example, opines in her 1987 autobiography that "when you don't need the money and you have a very satisfactory marriage, it's difficult to muster the drive necessary to establish a great career" (168). She claims repeatedly that her marriage and her children are much more important to her than the opera stage. And she makes clear that she believes in womanly behavior and feminine roles. When she sings in Buenos Aires, for example, and cannot take her earnings out of the country, she buys a ten-karat diamond ring that she plans to sell. In transit, she falls in love with it but finds herself in a dilemma, because, in the words of her mother, "Your husband has to buy you your jewelry. Women do not buy their own jewelry" (242). Sills's solution is to sweet-talk her rich husband into paying her for it so she can assure herself that she didn't commit the gender sin of buying herself not just "jewelry" but, specifically, a ring, that ubiquitous sign, as Virginia Woolf's *Orlando* so vividly notes, of yoked coupledom.

In this context of heterosexual normality, it is safe for Sills to rhapsodize about a TV special with Carol Burnett, during which Sills "stood there with my arm around Carol [and] thought: *I'm never going to be any happier than I am at this moment. . . . And I love this woman Carol Burnett*" (271, emphasis in the text). That night the two stars "cried and cried . . . because we knew we'd have nobody to play with the next day. After that, we telephoned each other three times a day" (272). Safely secured to heterosexuality by happy marriages and dedication to family, their intense female intimacy is acceptable and even cute. It is not, of course, to be taken seriously, since all the two women are doing is playing, like children, or telephoning each other constantly, like giggling—or weeping—adolescents. The adult relationships in Sills's life, with husband and children, remain safely untouched by the homoerotic—not, of course, a term she uses or would even accept—flirtation.[14]

Sills vigorously asserts not only her own normality but that of other women as well, defends them, too, against charges of careerism and masculinity. She expresses astonishment, for example, at "the difference between Barbara's [Walters] public image and her private reality. Barbara's a great romantic" (273). Walters, that is, is not *really* "the tough news correspondent I see on television" (273) but a real woman, a believer in the heterosexual romance. Sills explains that the "passion" of diva Rosa Ponselle, one of Sills's earliest mentors, for the Baltimore Civic Opera was a result of Ponselle's loneliness and depression after her husband divorced her to marry another woman (67). In other words, Ponselle's work is a substitute for heterosexual romance, which must be the most important thing in a real woman's life.

This ideology seems at odds, of course, with Beverly Sills, renowned diva, whose career "spanned more than thirty years" and took her "to the world's greatest opera houses" (vii). At odds, too, with Beverly Sills, director of the New York City Opera, the person who, according to this narrative, saved said opera from financial ruin and established it as the progressive partner to the Met. Even when she retires, she writes, she "won't completely sever my ties," nor will she "retire from the workplace. As dotty as it might seem, the idea of unemployment still scares the daylights out of me" (347). The passage is an interesting one. It expresses a real need to work, a need that the narrative has previously denied to women who have sufficient income and a happy marriage. At the same time, it trivializes that need as the "dotty" notion of an aging female star, the adjective suggesting "dotage," whim, silliness, frivolity. Sills is thus, at the narrative's conclusion, still playing out the dilemma of the woman artist: How can one be both woman and artist? Would a real woman take her art/work seriously? Would a real artist take time off—some of the most productive years of a professional life—for marriage and parenthood?

Renata Scotto insists that "I am a better singer for having become a mother" and that "I cannot say that I live for music. . . . Life itself is what is important, my family" (105). Marilyn Horne, a contemporary of Scotto and Sills, quotes in her autobiography the dancer Alexandra Danilova: "I am not a successful *woman*. A woman's success is in marriage and children. I wasn't successful in marriage and I have no children. I am a successful 'creature,' not a successful woman" (149). Danilova's claim points out that "woman" is a social construction; the term refers not to an adult female person but to a role that the adult female is expected to, but sometimes does not, play. The context does not tell us whether Danilova's remark is a boast or a sad admission of failure, a dismissal of the cultural definition of woman or a thorough internalization of it. But Horne uses it to establish her own success at womanhood. On the same page as the Danilova quote, Horne downplays her disappointment at not getting a good role at the Met: "I didn't mind that much . . . because I was awaiting something else, something more wonderful than my Metropolitan debut," a child, whose birth "was the most important moment of my life" (149). Horne, that is, *is* a successful woman. Her marriage does not work out, but she has a child; she "really" believes that "we're here to procreate" (155), and she continues to be a practicing heterosexual.

Like Mary Garden, Horne directly confronts the issue of lesbianism, but unlike Garden, she is defensive against this threat to her womanhood. "At one interview, I was asked by an inquiring idiot if there was any truth to the rumor that we [she and Joan Sutherland] were lesbians! . . . Such rumors pop up now and again, but I don't think anybody believes them. In our case, the evidence against it is too overwhelming" (189). That the inquirer is an "idiot" suggests the idiocy of the question itself, the exclamation point its unthinkability. There was, after all, a husband. There is a lover, a daughter. "Lesbian" has no place in this heterosexual scheme. No one believes "such rumors" anyway. "In our case" implies that "such rumors" are operative in other "cases" as well, that "such rumors" abound.

But no one believes them, Horne claims. There are, that is, no lesbians in the opera world, only the anomalous homoerotic moment like Sills's with Carol Burnett, and like Horne's with Judy Garland. "Putting our arms around each other, Judy Garland and Marilyn Horne belted out medley after medley of popular songs for no audience but ourselves. . . . After Judy and I swore eternal friendship, Henry took me home" (147). Horne has already established that she had had too many drinks at the time; she further distances herself from the scene by referring to herself in the third person. Whatever happens, then, between singing women is childlike (we had no one to play with) or adolescent (we swore eternal friendship) and has nothing to do with adult sexuality because it has nothing to do with heterosexuality.

Giovanni Battista Meneghini in his biography *My Wife, Maria Callas* goes to even greater lengths to defend Callas against "such rumors." First of all, when Visconti admits to Callas his "sexual preference"—the words "homosexual" and "lesbian" are studiously avoided throughout the narrative—she develops, Meneghini claims, an "aversion" to Visconti that "was obvious, extreme, and at times almost maniacal. She said that she did not want him near her, that even his scent and breath annoyed her" (185). Small wonder, then, that when she herself is the object of a "crush," an "onerous courtship" (231), she is "nauseated" (232). Thus he dismisses the "serious and unfair insinuations about my wife and Elsa Maxwell" (231), the American journalist who, according to Meneghini, pursued his wife "with sad, oppressive letters . . . full of the most grotesque inanities" (232). Although he does not actually claim to be quoting from the letters, he asserts that Maxwell used "phrases such as" these: "Maria, the only thing that sends me into ecstasy is your face and your smile"; "I want to contribute as much as I can to your joy in life, so that you continue to create new and stupendous interpretations"; and "I do not dare write all that I felt, or you would consider me mad. But . . . I am only a person different from others" (232). The only reason, of course, that these are "grotesque inanities" is that they are written from one woman to another. Meneghini quotes at length Callas's own letters to him, which might be seen as much more grotesquely inane: "When I think that I must sing my first *Forza* alone, without you here, I cry, not only in my heart but with my whole being" (60); "I ask that if you love me just a third as much as I love you, I will be happy" (62); "We must be proud of having a love so pure, so extraordinary, and rare. . . . If I lost you . . . I would lose all my faith in life" (99); "I've lost more than seven pounds. . . . I would die without you, who represent . . . all of the ideal attributes!" (129). In the service of heterosexual romance, dramatic, hyperbolic, and conventionally formulaic declarations of love are read as moving evidence of true feeling; Meneghini uses them to refute accusations that Callas never really loved him. The more modest declarations of homoerotic love, however, he relegates to "grotesque inanities" that "nauseated" the true-womanly Callas.

Meneghini's narrative is, in fact, a paean to Callas's true-womanhood. Its theme is that the marriage—until, of course, Aristotle Onassis "robbed me of Maria" (282)—was the center of her existence, far more important than her art or her career: "It is not true that her art was the most important thing in her life, as people have always maintained. . . . What mattered more to her . . . was our love and mutual happiness" (29). He treats the notion that "her art was the most important thing in her life" not as the proud and lofty claim of divas like Lilli Lehmann and Mary Garden but as an attack on Maria Callas's femininity, of which he is the defender. He quotes Callas's letters and statements in support of his thesis: "If Battista had asked it of me, I would even have given up my career for him" (29); "Do not forget that a woman thinks of and lives for her husband" (40); "Battista is the master of the house and one must show him great respect" (215). The last quote is Callas's explanation of why she never sat down at the table before Meneghini was seated, a dramatic—stagy—gesture of subordination that suggests that Callas saw wifehood as a role. Meneghini's praise can thus be read as enthusiastic applause for her performance.

In addition to his catalogue of Callas's conjugal affection and adherence to a "traditional concept of family life" (215), Meneghini takes pains to refute charges that Callas did not want children. False, claims the outraged husband; "the truth is . . . that we both ardently desired to have children" (111), but Maria could not conceive. His evidence here seems considerably weaker than his evidence for her great love. She does at one point write, "I want so much for us to have a baby," but the "confession" is immediately followed by the speculation that "a baby would be good for my voice and my bad skin" (131). The hope that a child would benefit the voice might suggest to a more cynical reader a minor subordination of family to career. But Meneghini is not a cynical reader and takes pride in this further evidence of his wife's perfect conformity to and performance of traditional womanhood.

We are not, however, suggesting that Callas herself did not participate fully in this narrative of wifely devotion. Her own memoirs, from 1957, sing the same song—with embellishments. "If Battista had wished, I would have abandoned my career without any regrets, because in a woman's life (I mean a real woman) love is more important, beyond compare, than any artistic triumph" (Lowe 127); "I have said that in spite of my growing success, I wasn't content. I wanted, in fact, the warmth of my own home and the tranquillity that every woman derives from a happy marriage" (Lowe 132); of the small and hurried wedding ceremony, "Once again, I had been deprived of the joys and fantasies dearest to the female heart: the wedding preparations, the gifts, the flowers" (Lowe 133). "A real woman," "every woman," "the female heart"—all suggest Callas's understanding of and concurrence with Danilova's distinction between the "creature" and the socially constructed "woman"; the latter's "success" has nothing to do with art, music, or career and everything to do with marriage and family. Even the wedding ceremony itself and its cultural trappings become the locus of female joy, sign of feminine success and admission ticket to the association of Everywoman. To dedicate oneself to art in the tradition of Thea Kronborg, Lena Geyer, Emma Calvé, and Mary Garden is to lose the ticket, to risk failure as a woman. And if one is a failure as a woman, what is one? A creature? A man? A lesbian? The possibilities seem especially frightening to these mid-century divas and their biographers, caught as they are in an atmosphere of Freudian orthodoxy and postwar cultural pressure on women to return to home and hearth.

To Meneghini, Elsa Maxwell, the woman with "proclivities" and "tendencies," is a "witch." Although he is sure that "Maria was never influenced by [Maxwell's] ambiguous feelings," he is equally convinced that "the change in Maria which caused her to leave me . . . started after her introduction to that witch, who was even then an extremely intelligent woman and, for that reason, fascinating" (236). The convergence here of witch, lesbian, and extremely intelligent woman illustrates well the matrix of fear that surrounds and often envelops the diva herself. Like Elsa Maxwell, she is "fascinating" in her perceived difference; like the siren, her ability to fascinate can be fatal to happy marriage. To speculate that the narrative's lesbian has so fascinated Maria Callas as to change her permanently (without, however, influencing her sexual orientation in any way) is perhaps Meneghini's own reflection—in a not very reflective narrative—on the effects of his fascination with that intelligent and powerful woman Maria Callas. Their mutual insistence on portraying her as a properly submissive wife masks the towering and frightening achievements of the woman who, in the opinion of many music critics, revolutionized opera. Meneghini's fear and loathing of Elsa Maxwell, then, may mask on some level a fear and loathing of Maria Callas, a fear and loathing that Callas herself perhaps shared. Toward the end of Anne Edwards's novel *La Divina*, about a Greek diva and her loves, the Callas figure, Athena Varos, explains why her love affair with a Greek shipping magnate has silenced her voice. "The reason I haven't sung for so long is simple . . . Mano [the Onassis figure] makes me feel like a woman. I mean a *woman*—defenseless, with all her weakness. And he protects that woman. I've had this fear that if I went back on the stage to become a diva again—well, you know, it hardens you" (354). Married nightingales seldom sing because true women don't sing. While the conversation is a fiction, the sentiments seem of a piece with some Callas herself spouted, especially in the identification of woman with defenselessness and weakness. If such is the nature of woman, then the hardened, strong, powerful figure of the diva is a constant challenge to it. "Diva" and "woman" coexist only with great tension and ambiguity, if they can be said to coexist at all. The question, then, recurs: if the diva is not a woman, what is she?

La Divina is a biographical fiction that begins and ends with Mano's defection to a widowed American heiress. Athena, of course, is devastated, since "for eleven years she had loved [him] more than herself or her music" (10). But she rallies. Her disappointment in love is opera's gain; she goes back to work. Callas's own rhetoric in the early 1970s, after Onassis's marriage to Jacqueline Kennedy, changes significantly from that of her fifties memoirs. "What is there in life if you do not work? . . . You can only live on work, by work, through work. . . . I *work*: therefore I am" (Lowe 160). This is a rhetoric that seems to correspond more closely to colleagues' observations and professional assessments. She "was a workhorse" (Lowe 7). According to Visconti, "Maria is possibly the most disciplined and professional material I have ever had occasion to handle. Not only does she never ask for rehearsals to be cut down; she actually asks for more, and works at them with the same intensity from beginning to end" (Lowe 220). The disciplined and professional workhorse seems far distant from the submissive wife, the intense and thoroughly engaged singer/actor from the happy homemaker. While she may, at the height of her career, have portrayed herself as weak and defenseless, even perhaps as Galatea to Meneghini's Pygmalion, she seemed to others the zenith of daring and control.

Sergio Segalini claims that "In order to make her revolution even more true . . . , Callas would even dare to do what no one until then had done. In the space of a few months she lost sixty-five pounds,[15] and the awkward and clumsy actress became a woman of astonishing beauty, with a

royal bearing and perfectly controlled gestures. For Callas thought . . . that
in order to save opera she also had to make it credible to an entire generation that . . . demanded a much more coherent, much closer vision of the
desires of the contemporary world" (Lowe 177). In other words, Callas not
only reinvented opera, according to Segalini, she reinvented herself, carved
a new body out of the old, made herself astonishingly beautiful, all in the
service of her vision for opera. This version of Callas—in perfect control
of every aspect of her body, her life, and her work—is markedly at odds
with Callas the submissive wife or Callas the creation of Meneghini. This
is Callas the perfectionist, who put work and career first, not the Callas
who claimed that she often "loathed my career because [it] forced me to be
apart from him, and I dreamed of abandoning it" (Lowe 131).

Callas's rhetoric, as we have seen, varies considerably over the course
of her career. A more dramatic illustration of the divided self, or from another point of view the protean performance, is Janet Baker's 1982 "autobiographical journal," *Full Circle*, which covers only one year of Baker's
life, her last year on the opera stage. In it, Baker movingly—but seemingly
unaware of its presence—expresses the modern ambivalence about career
and womanhood; she is caught between two constructions and rhetorical
traditions. The book is, first of all, dedicated to her husband and to her parents, thus establishing immediately her familial concern. In the first para-
graph of the introduction, she claims "a long and very happy marriage to
the kindest man in the world" (xi). And to be happily married, we have
seen, means renouncing ambition for divahood: "I have never longed for
the bright lights, fame, or the drug of audience acclaim. Although these are
part and parcel of the job, they have no reality for me" (xii). In other
words, Baker claims for herself complete "normality," utter simplicity of
desire, a self-presentation quite different from, for example, that of Lotte
Lehmann, who, like most pre–World War II divas, "would ten times prefer
such a life to the contentment of the unambitious" (*My Many Lives* 4).

For Baker, "the sole reason for being a performer" is "that I believe
my voice [was] given to me by God, to be shared with others" (xii). This
early confirmation of womanhood—she gets the voice only to give it—
seems perhaps reassuring to a diva who was once asked by the director of
the opera to stop wearing trousers to her rehearsals for Alceste, to, that is,
"lose my trouser image and concentrate on being feminine and vulnerable."
The director claims that she "will move and walk differently without my
trousers." And, indeed, he is right. With a caftan on, "Alceste is already
feeling so much softer" (17). In the volume's nearly sixty photos, almost all

the "at home" portraits feature Baker in trousers, and in the final set she is trousered even in the opera photos—her last and perhaps best known role is Orfeo. The written protestations of marital happiness and the written refusals of unwomanly ambition, then, serve as the text's caftan. By the end of the introduction, the diva is already feeling so much softer, feminine, and vulnerable.

Most stunning perhaps is what seems to be Baker's final assessment of her distinguished career as an opera singer. "If someone asked if my career has been 'worth it,' in other words worth the sacrifices made by me and members of my family, worth the separations, the agony of performing . . . the strains and pitfalls of being a public figure, my honest answer would have to be 'No'" (52). No? Is the message to readers, then, to young women with voices, to young women with ambition, that it's not worth it? Give it up? Stop now before you make too many sacrifices? Before you decide not to have children? The reader can already see where this will lead. Women are private beings, whose real desires are, as Te Kanawa, Sills, and Callas suggest, home, children, perfect husbands, and domestic tranquillity.

But this praise of traditional marriage is not the text's last word. The figure of the diva always reveals the fissures of a culture's gender ideology, and the discourse of these post–World War II divas often seems equally divided. Later in the text, she claims that women singers "who begin a career and then opt out to concentrate on a family, never feel completely fulfilled by family life if it is at the total expense of their ambitions. . . . The natural performer must, somewhere along the line, perform!" (240); she knows with certainty "that to have disobeyed my instincts to sing would have ruined my life in some deep way, and I would have been far happier unmarried but performing, than married and not performing" (240). She then reiterates the theme in a more specific context: "Someone asked me what I would have done if Keith had wanted me to give up my career. . . . I replied without hesitation that I would not have found it possible to give up my career for anyone or anything" (246).

These passages, when juxtaposed with the opening passages, create a kind of dizziness. Husbands are essential, but she could have done without. Bright lights, audiences mean nothing, but a performer must perform. Her career has not been worth all the sacrifices, but without it her life would have been ruined. *Full Circle* is a journal rather than an autobiography, Baker claims. Perhaps this means that *Full Circle* is thus free to keep circling back on itself, to let obvious inconsistencies stand unexamined. But more likely, Baker does not even see as inconsistencies the demanding contradictions that construct the diva—between the public and the private, ambition and humility, manhood and womanhood, art and passivity, artifice and honesty. Baker thinks, for example, that it is "fitting that the last role I shall ever play on a stage is Orfeo.... Usually, characters one plays contain facets of one's own personality, but ... Orfeo is on every level myself" (223). The photographs confirm this; it is in the *Orfeo* photos that Baker looks most "natural," most comfortable, most energetic. Eliot's Armgart, too, was Orpheus and Orpheus was Armgart, but what Eliot explores Baker would rather pass over in silence. To claim that Orfeo is "on every level" herself misses the most basic contradiction of all: Orfeo is a man, and the role of Orfeo a trouser role, a male played by a female, a male with a woman's voice, a woman in drag.

We are all, of course, many different selves; contradictions abound. We spill out of our categories. Our actions don't quite correspond with our explanations of them. We fail to live up to our own standards of behavior. We fall short of our ideals. We often desire and act in ways that contradict the social roles our culture demands we perform. We as critics are not, then, expecting consistency, suggesting hypocrisy, or accusing either auto- biographers or biographers of misrepresentation or willful ignorance. We are simply looking at the narratives themselves and reflecting on their own demands and discontinuities. Geraldine Farrar recognizes part of the prob- lem in her own autobiography: "Biographies of famous prima donnas often have a distressing and monotonous similarity.... The Cinderella legend has a perennial appeal to ... imagination. The early wonder-child invari- ably overcomes poverty, the ugly duckling period of awkwardness ... to find herself an alluring magnet of temperamental display, after the indis- pensable European sojourn has been heralded in the home gazettes, and one's home people are brought to a prostrate chorus of admiring approval and love" (17). Farrar has given these words to her mother, the narrator, we pointed out, of sections of *Such Sweet Compulsion*, dead at the time of the writing. The mother thus becomes fictional biographer in the daughter's au- tobiography. And the tale the mother tells is not very different from the prototype she disparages. Her daughter overcomes many hardships and "ju- venile plainness of feature" to become a world-famous diva. Much later, Farrar describes a film in which she starred, *Temptation*, "a special story, the type that has since served anybody who can lay claim to a vocal chirp—how the little home-town girl makes good in grand opera, upon merit and virtue" (144).

There is a sense, then, in which diva life narratives write themselves.

They have a form, a trajectory, a preordained outcome, a resonance with the era's ideology. In other words, they have conventions. They must be what readers expect them to be. Fictional diva Olga Bracely in E. F. Benson's *Queen Lucia* tells another character that she was taken "out of the gutter." She quickly amends this to a "truer" version: "Well, out of an orphan school." She recognizes here that the Cinderella motif is an important one for a diva, one that she fully intends to exploit. "That's all about my early life just now, because I am keeping it for my memoirs, which I shall write when my voice becomes a little more like a steam whistle" (53). In other words, the sad, mysterious past belongs not really to her present life but to the diva narrative, to the memoirs. When her voice goes, she will fuel fame and fortune by telling stories, stories that are, in fact, already written.

Farrar and Bracely refer specifically, of course, to the basic plot, the Cinderella plot. What we have been suggesting in these pages is that the conformity of the diva life story doesn't end with conformity to this plot; it provides an ideology of womanhood that, in turn, dictates the rhetoric and content of these narratives, narratives that must address certain concerns and keep certain secrets, especially the concern about femininity and the secret of sexuality. This concern is teasingly but firmly expressed in Scotto's autobiography, titled appropriately enough *More than a Diva*, when she and her husband "insisted on a tenor Romeo, which would be the first time for the opera, because it would work better for my approach to the role" (73). In other words, Scotto is willing to flout operatic convention—in which Romeo is a trouser role, played by a woman—to adhere to social convention. She and her husband will not allow a woman to make love to her, even on the stage. Her "approach to the role" of both Juliet and Woman demands heterosexuality.

These issues come together in an interesting way in a contemporary biography of an early nineteenth-century diva, April FitzLyon's biography of Maria Malibran, published in 1987. FitzLyon, a modern, literary biographer, is, of course, aware of the pitfalls of biography and discusses them in terms similar to those of *Of Lena Geyer* and *Such Sweet Compulsion*. "In most of these works [about Malibran], and in biographies . . . the principal characters in La Malibran's story have become stereotypes: La Malibran and Beriot are romantic lovers; Eugene Malibran [Malibran's first husband] is the villain. . . . Sontag is the wicked rival. . . . Malibran has now herself become the heroine of innumerable soap operas" (268). FitzLyon deplores the attempts at saint making that followed Malibran's death and the suppression of facts that those attempts required, facts like Malibran's many pregnancies, at least one of which resulted in a child, quickly abandoned.

Neither saints nor idols of the popular imagination—if they are women—can afford abortions or abandoned children. But there are times in history when they can as little afford a nonsexual existence. Before the scandal of Malibran's affair with the violinist Beriot, the singer tried to explain to her husband why she did not want him around: "I think a theatrical life demands a great deal of calm and the life of a virgin which is what suits me perfectly" (FitzLyon 89). But apparently, in the age of Romanticism, as in our own, such virtue was excessive. Her reputation for refusing men caused rumors "that she was not a completely formed woman physically." She had, besides, a "boyish figure" and the "habit of wearing men's clothes" that "added to the androgynous effect she sometimes produced" (91). The suggestion is that her running off with another man, becoming pregnant by him, and having a child with him, scandalous as they were, were more easily forgiven and forgotten than her earlier deviations from the Romantic ideal. Scandal in the service of love is, of course, a part of the Romantic ethos and as such more acceptable in the Romantic age than not having time for men. Much more acceptable even to a modern biographer: FitzLyon glosses over Malibran's "habit of wearing men's clothes" and dismisses as well her "adolescent crush on Guiditta Pasta," a crush caused, according to FitzLyon, by Malibran's deprivation "of companions of her own age" (39). The crush seems to have been an explicitly erotic one; Malibran referred "to Pasta as her 'bride'" and declared that she wanted "to 'eat' her" (39), but FitzLyon does not suggest homoeroticism or speculate further on any of Malibran's "masculine" tendencies, including her appropriation of male roles originally written for uncastrated men. FitzLyon comments at length, for example, on Malibran's role as Desdemona in Rossini's opera but only mentions that, in imitation of her idol Pasta (and her father, Manuel Garcia, who was famous for the role), she also played Otello (115).

A clue to FitzLyon's puzzling omissions might be an odd statement she makes about Malibran's difference from contemporary singers. "In La Malibran's day . . . the star did exactly as she felt like doing and everyone else had to fit in with her. La Malibran's temperament was such that she would have found it very difficult to submit to the discipline of a modern director or conductor" (73). In other words, FitzLyon portrays Malibran as a fixed personality, with no suggestion that Malibran's "temperament" was a culturally constructed one: it was acceptable in Malibran's time for a diva to do "exactly as she felt like doing"; she was thus free to be as "idiosyncratic" and "exaggerated"—FitzLyon's adjectives—as she liked. Modern divas do not have such luxuries; they may get bounced from the Met for much lesser sins than those of their older sisters, but they adapt "to the discipline of a modern director," because they must. Likewise, Malibran's romantic adulterous affair with Beriot seems to confirm for FitzLyon the diva's heterosexual credentials, but as the subtitle of the biography announces, Maria Malibran was a diva of the Romantic Age. We might then speculate that Malibran's sudden burst of heterosexual fervor (she had earlier written to her husband, "I never feel the slightest desire, and even if people talk about anything connected with what you appear to like so much, I feel disgust! . . . Ah! I don't even want to think about it" [85]) was as inspired by the Romantic ethos as her adolescent homosexual fervor was by her "isolation."[16] We are not, of course, claiming here that Malibran was a lesbian, only that to dismiss her homoeroticism while exploring at great length her heterosexuality is to erase again the homoerotic history—ever rumored, always denied—of the diva world.

CHAPTER 5

Divas, Death, and Detectives

She is a singer, and therefore capable of anything.
—Bellini, trans. John Rosselli

"*To* Sherlock Holmes she was always *the* woman." So, surprisingly, opens one of Conan Doyle's early stories, "A Scandal in Bohemia." The tale is rather simple. (And we briefly retell it here for those whose memory of childhood reading is as bad as ours): Holmes's client, the king of Bohemia, arrives at Holmes's door in a transparent disguise and is quickly unmasked by the great detective. He wants Holmes to recover a compromising photograph of himself with an opera singer, or, in his words, "the well-known adventuress, Irene Adler," who has possession of the photograph (165). He has tried everything to retrieve it, including two burglaries. According to the king, Adler threatens to make the photograph public on the day of his betrothal to a mate more suitable than Adler, more suitable than an opera singer, a Scandinavian princess. Holmes dons two disguises to solve the problem. First, as an out-of-work, unkempt groom, he follows the singer and inadvertently becomes a witness to her secret marriage to Godfrey Norton, a London barrister. Later, Holmes impersonates a clergyman, wounded in a fight that he himself has staged with others acting the parts of ruffians. He relies on Adler's kindness to tend to him and thus give him access to her sitting room. Watson, having been carefully coached by Holmes to provide the special effects in this little bit of street theater, throws a harmless smoke bomb through the window of the sitting room, and Holmes watches Adler rush to a secret hiding place to save her most valuable possession—the photograph—from fire. When Holmes, now knowing where the photo is hidden, returns to his Baker Street address, he hears a voice that he frustratingly cannot place and that seems to be coming from a "slim youth in an ulster" say to him, "Good night, Mr. Holmes."

Early the next morning Holmes returns to Irene Adler's home with Watson and the king. They plan to ask for her and, while they are waiting in the sitting room, take the photograph from its hiding place. To Holmes's astonishment, the maid announces that Adler and Godfrey Norton have left for the Continent. Holmes rushes to the hiding place and finds there a letter addressed to him from Adler, announcing that the impertinent youth of the night before had been she and that she has no intention of blackmailing the king. Included in the missive, in place of the incriminating photograph, is a photo of herself alone, which Holmes requests in lieu of an offered ring, as part payment for bringing the case to a satisfactory, if partial, conclusion. "And that," concludes Watson, "was how a great scandal threatened to affect the King of Bohemia, and how the best plans of Mr. Sherlock Holmes were beaten by a woman's wit. He used to make merry over the cleverness of women, but I have not heard him do it of late. And when he speaks of Irene Adler . . . it is always under the honourable title of *the* woman" (175).

Irene Adler is "*the* woman" not only for Holmes but also, it seems, for Holmes commentators. One confesses that Adler is "the erotic fantasy of most male Sherlockians" (Schweikert 99), and at least one Sherlockian paper, taking its lead from the king's claim that she is an "adventuress," is devoted to speculations about her sexual prowess and insatiability. Irene Adler is certainly the Sherlockians' choice for Holmes's erotic fantasy (perhaps they are as happy and relieved as Watson to find so glamorous a bit of evidence with which to establish the lifelong bachelor's heterosexual credentials). Trevor Hall speaks, extravagantly, of Holmes's "hopeless passion" for Irene Adler (140), and a number of Sherlockians speculate that the detective and the diva later reunite, either for a clandestine affair or for marriage, "a spiritual marriage," according to one critic (Atkinson 67). The issue of this union, one Sherlockian has argued in a nice bit of Sherlockian fantasy, is Nero Wolf.[1]

Of course the Sherlockians are but a small part of what might be called the "Holmes industry," which ranges from their mock scholarly exegesis of the Conan Doyle canon in publications like *The Baker Street Journal* to the film and video versions of Holmes stories to the many revisions and extrapolations of the characters and cases, varyingly parodic, like *The Seven Per Cent Solution* and, most recently, the wonderful, revisionary detective novel by Laurie King, *The Beekeeper's Apprentice*.[2] One of the most recent and significant of these revisionary expansions—one that shows, as well, that it's not just men who find Irene Adler fascinating—is a series of detective novels by American writer Carole Nelson Douglas. Her

Good Night, Mr. Holmes (1990), *Good Morning, Irene* (1990), *Irene at Large* (1992), and *Irene's Last Waltz* (1994) all feature diva Irene Adler as the detective-heroine. In a structural doubling of the Conan Doyle stories, Penelope Huxleigh, a conventionally minded clergyman's daughter and unemployed governess whom Adler rescues in the first novel from a life on the streets, acts as Adler's Watson in all the novels and in *Good Night, Mr. Holmes* tells a long and intricate tale that culminates in the events of Conan Doyle's "A Scandal in Bohemia." Holmes and Watson are minor characters in the Douglas novels, and other characters from the Conan Doyle canon, like Jefferson Hope from *A Study in Scarlet*, make guest appearances, as do such turn-of-the-century historical luminaries as Oscar Wilde, Lillie Langtry, Bram Stoker, Charles and Louis Tiffany, and Sarah Bernhardt. The novels thus use the Irene Adler figure to link the closed and obviously fictional world of Holmes and Watson to the "real" literary and artistic world of late-nineteenth-century London.

Irene Adler is American by birth, opera singer by profession. Both her origins and her profession contribute to her marginal position in Victorian society; both lead to her "dubious and questionable" reputation and the epithet "adventuress" in Conan Doyle's story. In Douglas's texts, however, Adler's Americanness allows her a freedom from the class and cultural constraints so evident and so repressive in Holmes's late-nineteenth-century London. For example, while Penelope Huxleigh, clearly Adler's foil, believes her mild infatuation with her former charges' uncle is inappropriate because he is above her social station, Adler sees nothing inappropriate in aspiring to be the wife of the crown prince, later king, of Bohemia. (Adler's American disdain for keeping to one's place here is supported by historical precedent; a number of historical singers married aristocrats, although to do so they usually had to wait until retirement or give up the stage.) Adler's American past is ever mysterious in both the Doyle story and the Douglas series, and readers' desire for her history clashes with Adler's own apparent desire to be free of history and the social confinements it constructs. As one of the characters in *Irene at Large* explains, "She invents herself and has no need of antecedents" (36). As an American, she is linked to a country short on history and hierarchy and a country, as well, where the line between murderer and hero—as in the case of another of Doyle's Americans, Jefferson Hope—is thin indeed. Much can be made, we think, of the relationship between her seemingly lawless homeland and the detective enterprise itself, located as it is both outside and inside law and criminality, a point Conan Doyle's Holmes is himself fond of making. But Irene Adler's status as diva as well as detective puts her on the margins of society and links her to transgression and criminality, and her divahood as much as her American origin emphasizes her capacity for self-invention.

When Doyle's Holmes dons his clerical disguise, Watson remarks, "His expression, his manner, his very soul seemed to vary with every fresh part he assumed" (170). Irene Adler has a similar talent, linked in Doyle's story to her profession: her letter to Holmes explains that "male costume is nothing new to me. I often take advantage of the freedom which it gives" (174–175). Conan Doyle's story tells us that Adler is a contralto. As such her repertoire would have included trouser roles, including first man heroic parts formerly sung by castrati. Douglas's novels expand the cross-dressing theme and, like the story, link it to issues of performance and freedom. Gender, the novels suggest, is a function of performance and costume, or, as Judith Butler so convincingly argues, cross-dressing "implies that all gendering is a kind of impersonation and approximation" ("Imitation" 21). As we have seen, cross-dressing, is, on a more practical level, especially perhaps for women, a means of escaping confinement within the gender code's crippling constrictions. For example, the singer dismisses Huxleigh's disapproval of her plan to walk out in male dress with Sarah Bernhardt: "This will be a petite adventure, that is all. Sarah has never gone out '*en homme*' in public; it is quite a necessary exercise for her acting. Besides, respectable women are not commonly welcome in the great cafes of Paris, and I am eager to see these boulevard wits in action" (*Good Morning, Irene* 12).[3] Douglas's revision of "A Scandal in Bohemia" repeats the scene in which Irene Adler dons an ulster to observe Holmes—and to tease him— without herself being detected. In both texts Adler's cross-dressing functions as a way to escape the detecting, controlling, and confining—the disciplinary—male gaze and as a way to detect in turn. Douglas's novel emphasizes this by presenting Adler's male dress as a means of gaining not only freedom from observation and confinement in convention but also literal physical freedom. To escape from the king and his plans to end her career by keeping her as his imprisoned mistress in an isolated country castle, she dresses as a man and makes her way to England.

Whatever the nature of Holmes's attraction to Irene Adler, Conan Doyle's story makes clear that the detective admires her because he considers her his equal. Disguising himself as persons of a different class and/or gender is a favorite Holmesian mode of detection, and his success implies that he is, as critic Rosemary Jann argues, a master reader of social codes (685–687). Adler's theatrical training and her place on the social margins enable her to become a master reader and user of class and gender codes as well. Generally, Holmes manipulates and exploits those codes in the service of restoring bourgeois values and traditional class hierarchies, and in Conan Doyle's story, Holmes's failure to see through Irene Adler's masculine disguise suggests that despite his celebrated powers of observation the detective's perceptions are still, sometimes at least, compromised by adherence to the conventions his work reaffirms. It just doesn't cross his mind that a woman might have the invention or the skill to use costume and performance to disguise herself as a man, that a woman might be able to play the manly part so convincingly as to fool even him.

Conan Doyle's Irene Adler, Jann argues, is like Holmes in that her transcendence of social codes ends up reasserting them: "She successfully usurps both the appearance and the prerogatives of a man by disguising herself and later escaping the country with the incriminating photograph . . . [but] she voluntarily polices herself so that her potential subversion of social order is muted. By choosing not to use the photograph, she ultimately abets the more pervasive pattern in Holmes's stories, whereby the upper classes are almost always enabled to escape social and legal punishments for their crimes" (699–700). Cross-dressing may always simultaneously unsettle and reinforce binary gender distinctions, but Douglas's Irene Adler is less easily read as an unwitting collaborator with the status quo, in part because her Irene Adler never intends to play the role of rejected romance heroine and blackmail the king. Douglas's Adler keeps the photograph for the same reason that she cross-dresses, to protect herself from outraged patriarchal power.

Although one can argue that cross-dressing for protection is an almost legitimate and socially sanctioned excuse, an excuse hardly threatening either to gender codes or to compulsory heterosexuality, Adler's enthusiasm at the prospect of mixing with the Parisian wits suggests an additional, and more subversive, motivation—pleasure. In fact, according to Douglas's text, Irene Adler convinces Sarah Bernhardt not only to explore Paris *en homme* but also to abandon her role as Ophelia and take on Hamlet, a role for which the historical Bernhardt was famous. Such pleasure taking, only implicit in Conan Doyle's Adler, is the signature trait of Douglas's Adler, and she enthusiastically encourages her female companions—even the ever-proper Huxleigh—to take pleasure as well.

Finally, although Huxleigh finds Adler's penchant for male clothing scandalous because unconventional, the real scandal is that Adler doesn't see her behavior as a scandal. While Huxleigh often asserts that her friend's masculine performance doesn't compromise her *intrinsic* femininity, Adler herself never speaks of her behavior in essentializing and binary terms, a rhetorical absence that perhaps bespeaks a philosophical rejection. And significantly, Huxleigh pays tribute to her friend's cross-dressing talent in spite of her disapproval of the practice: "Godfrey Norton was the most strikingly handsome man I had ever seen, save upon the stage, when I went to see Irene perform" (*Good Night, Mr. Holmes* 121). Not only is this language extravagant for the usually discreet and reserved Huxleigh, but it is erotically charged as well, as are many of Huxleigh's descriptions of the singer. To unsettle gender oppositions, recent theorists have pointed out, tends to destabilize as well the compulsory heterosexuality those oppositions support. The erotically charged rhetoric of the novel's figure for conventional authority (Huxleigh is a former "governess," a disciplinarian) thus positions the diva as a figure who, in her consummate ability to pass and in her obvious enjoyment of cross-dressing, unsettles the sex-gender-sexuality system.

Huxleigh claims that with the donning of male clothing, Adler takes on conventionally masculine characteristics beyond those expected of a good actor: "Male guise even seemed to increase her strength" (*Good Night, Mr. Holmes* 275–276). But to further weaken Huxleigh's attempts to essentialize manly characteristics like strength, the diva gives such characteristics an obvious material base: "No great trick to being the strong sex," she says. "It's easy when not wearing a constricting whalebone fence and seams that split at any gesture larger than a drawing-room flutter" (276).

Irene Adler's profession not only encourages her cross-dressing, performance, and self-invention but also entangles her and the texts in which she appears in issues of female voice. "I've heard that voice before," Holmes puzzles when he hears the "Good night, Mr. Holmes" in front of 221B Baker Street (173). His failure to recognize that voice is, as well, his failure to give credit to the intellectual powers of women in general and Irene Adler in particular. And it was presumably Adler's voice that proved the undoing of the king of Bohemia; where would he have met her except in her role as "Prima donna Imperial Opera of Warsaw"? Their meeting and subsequent relationship, he says to Holmes, made him "mad—insane" (166).

In *Good Night, Mr. Holmes*, Adler informs Huxleigh in a letter from Warsaw that the symbol of Poland is a "siren . . . said to lure men to a watery death with their unearthly voices" (197). The king, unlike Douglas's text, wants to link Adler to the creatures who lure men to infidelity and madness, if not literal death. Little wonder, then, that in "A Scandal in Bohemia" the king himself identifies Irene Adler not as diva but as "adventuress," a word that, as Douglas's Holmes notes, "two centuries ago . . . designated a woman who lived by her wits, [but] today . . . has been debased to describe a woman who lives by her willingness" (*Good Night, Mr. Holmes* 7). Douglas's text argues that "adventuress" may mean only "adventurous"—that is, that there's a familiar double standard at work here: when a woman is adventurous, she's labeled an adventuress. "A Scandal in Bohemia," of course, participates in the masculinist tradition of diva narratives, which portrays the female opera star as the consummate adventuress. Like the siren-singers of that tradition, Conan Doyle's Irene Adler is certainly presented as a male-centered woman—her romantic rejection is motivation for blackmail. Douglas's *Good Night, Mr. Holmes* tries to rewrite both a particular story and an entire representational tradition. Her Adler, like so many of the divas in women's writing, lives by her wits, not her willingness. Her identification is with other women; her voice is not the seductive lure of the siren seeking the destruction of men but, in Penelope Huxleigh's words in *Irene at Large*, "a goad or a lure" to bring a voice to women previously voiceless.

Like Armgart's Walpurga, Thea Kronberg's Aunt Tillie, and Lena Geyer's Elsie deHaven, Penelope Huxleigh is transformed and emboldened by contact with her diva. At their first meeting, she is "mesmerized by her voice alone" (16). Further association with Irene empowers her writing ("Before those halcyon days with Irene, my notations were scant and . . . dull beyond imagining" [*Good Night, Mr. Holmes* 169]), widens her experience, encourages her not to view the world from the judgmental perspective of bourgeois propriety ("Thanks to Irene, I had seen much more of life than a Shropshire parsonage would have ever allowed. I could drink tea with a woman who admitted to liaisons with two men to whom she had never been married, and I winced only mildly [*Good Morning, Irene* 191–192]), and empowers her life ("Inspired by Irene's intrepid ways, I began working with the Salvation Army in Whitechapel" [*Good Night, Mr. Holmes* 170]). Solving part of a mystery, Huxleigh realizes "I had duplicated [Irene's] methods without knowing it" (191). A homeless waif when the series opens, during the course of it Huxleigh becomes a typist (money earned through Adler's detecting pays her tuition), gets a job, travels alone to Bohemia to help rescue Adler from the king, and by the time of *Irene at Large* becomes herself a heroine.

Adler explicitly uses her voice as opera singer and detective—that is, as a woman who lives by her wits—to improve the lot of other women. An exception to the stereotypical Victorian woman, she does not abandon their cause. In *Good Night, Mr. Holmes,* for example, Charles Lewis Tiffany employs her to search for Marie Antoinette's diamond belt, known as the Zone of Diamonds. He mistrusts her because she is a woman but is eventually convinced to hire her. "You are quick, Miss Adler," he says. "I'll say that for you." She responds, "Then perhaps my wit will persuade you to reconsider hiring women clerks in your New York establishment, Mr. Tiffany" (67).

Good Morning, Irene, the second novel, finds the unconventional Adler—somewhat to her surprise and against her principles—happily and faithfully married to Godfrey Norton. But she continues to defend other choices. When Huxleigh objects to Sarah Bernhardt's "immorality," for example, the singer praises Bernhardt's accomplishments and says approvingly that "perhaps she finds the concentrated attentions of a single man debilitating to her career and shares herself among many in order to devote to none" (11).

The diva's expressive voice thus translates easily from stage to life: "Even when speaking she could imbue her words with all the emotional command of a coloratura soprano" (*Irene at Large* 78). More accurately, though, we might suggest that the voice underscores the series' sense of the interchangeability of stage and life or the performativity of life itself. Related to the use of disguise, this notion nonetheless goes further. Holmes recognizes the relationship between stage and his profession as detective explicitly in "The Valley of Fear" when he claims that "some touch of the artist wells up within me and calls insistently for a well-staged performance . . . the blunt accusation, the brutal tap upon the shoulder—what can one make of such a denouement?" These sorts of references to the stage, especially operatic performance, are ubiquitous in the Adler series and extend the notion of "performance" to everyday activity. In *Good Morning, Irene*, Holmes describes "foreign crimes" as "the stuff of opera" (116), and in *Irene at Large*, the singer admits to "concocting plots on an operatic scale" (47). Adler exclaims in *Good Night, Mr. Holmes*, "Alas, I feel like a character adrift in the wrong opera. I do not know my part and must improvise" (163); later in that novel Huxleigh accuses the singer of talking "as though you were caught in the plot of a grand opera" (212). Adler herself recognizes the melodrama of her suspicion that the king's family may have conspired in the death of his father: "Not," she says to Huxleigh, "good light opera at all" (*Good Night, Mr. Holmes* 238).

In Douglas's novels, the performative is not limited to the realm of the professional, whether detective or operatic. As they escape from Bohemia, Adler tells Huxleigh: "We must appear normal; in short, we must render a performance worthy of the great Ellen Terry" (285). The comment suggests that the situation in which they find themselves is far from normal but also calls up the Wildean insight that normality itself is a kind of performance. It is not an accident that the two historical figures who feature most prominently and repeatedly in the Douglas novels are those notorious drama queens Sarah Bernhardt and Oscar Wilde.

Of course, in making the parallel between opera and life, Adler refers to *her* life, which is, we know, fiction. Specifically it is genre fiction—historical and detective—both of them highly conventional genres with a penchant for the dramatic, even melodramatic, plot. When Adler complains that her life imitates opera, readers recognize the irony: it, unlike "real life," *is* carefully and melodramatically plotted. Indeed, the central mystery around which Douglas recasts Doyle's story takes genre fiction as one of its central concerns. Irene *reads* genre fiction, specifically a romance novel written by Godfrey Norton's mother titled *Clovis of the Crossroads*, in order to find clues to the whereabouts of the Zone of Diamonds, which Tiffany has hired her and, separately, Holmes to find. *Clovis of the Crossroads*, she comments, "would make a grand opera—tragedy both political and personal with room for tender arias among the heather" (346). What is remarkable about this comment is that the kind of writing that has been dismissed even by Norton, the sympathetic and proto-feminist son, as women's fiction—"her books were considered suitable for a female audience. . . . It never occurred to me to actually read one" (334)—is here, like crime and detection, elevated to the status of serious art. Of course, as we have seen, the "serious" or "high" art of opera is treated in this novel with irony and revealed to be the rich cousin of that "popular" and "low" entertainment, melodrama. The joke is on the skeptical, snobbish listener/reader, who would make much of these distinctions, here represented by Godfrey Norton, who has no time for the feminine, the frivolous, and the "low." In refusing to read his mother's romantic fiction, Godfrey has colluded with his hated father, Black Jack Norton, who, assuming that his wife's work would be neglected and forgotten, buried his treasure—Marie Antoinette's Zone of Diamonds—at the crossroads described in Mrs. Norton's novel. Only when Irene Adler resurrects the book and takes it seriously is the mystery solved. She wins the detection competition with Holmes because, in part, Holmes once again fails to take women and women's interests seriously enough.[4] Holmes's indexes, filled with facts of Victorian life, apparently do not include plot summaries of "women's fiction." No Henry Tilney is Holmes.

Thus is gender allied with genre in the text, genre fiction seen as the (enforced) provenance of women writers. Since the solution to the central mystery depends on *Clovis of the Crossroads*, a work of genre fiction hitherto rejected and ignored, the text suggests the social and financial cost of ignoring (or, as Holmes learns, failing to recognize) women's voices and the popular genres in which women often speak—of which *Good Night, Mr. Holmes* and its successors are, of course, examples.

As we have suggested, performance, for both Conan Doyle and Douglas, functions to blur the oppositions constructed between masculinity and femininity and between art and life. Douglas's additions to the Conan Doyle tale blur the boundaries between "serious" and "popular," "high" and "low," "art" and "entertainment." She further links gender, genre, and class by reminding readers of the traditional discursive hierarchy that places masculinist discourses like Holmes's fact file, Godfrey Norton's legal writing, and, one assumes, "serious literature" above women's writing, represented as popular fiction. But where does this leave us, academics who take seriously popular genres? What does it mean to take these genres seriously?

Good Night, Mr. Holmes closes with "A Scholarly Afterword" in which one Fiona Witherspoon, Ph.D., claims that the narrative we have just read is a compilation of Penelope Huxleigh's diaries and previously undiscovered fragments by John Watson, M.D. Witherspoon, president of the Friends of Irene Adler (an organization parodic of the Baker Street fan clubs), takes the material, as Sherlockians sometimes do, not just seriously but literally. The Huxleigh diaries, she argues, "prove that Irene Adler, at least, was no fiction and thus lend credence to the actual existence of Sherlock Holmes" (404). And so in a wonderfully absurd "she is, therefore he is" syllogism, the text calls into question the truth claims of Watson's narratives in particular, of realist fiction in general, and, more broadly, of the enterprise of literary criticism.

Witherspoon further uses the Huxleigh diaries and the newly discovered Watson fragments to "correct" details of the Doyle narratives. But the so-called fragments themselves hint that, on the contrary, the Douglas narratives might be further fictionalizations of the Doyle narratives. In *Irene at Large*, Holmes asks Watson if he doesn't think that "the naval-treaty affair had a rather lukewarm ending." Watson replies in the affirmative: "I must say that if I had any desire to turn it to fiction, I would find the ending rather inconclusive and unsatisfactory" (334). The situation is remedied in *Irene at Large*: the solution to "The Naval Treaty" mystery that Adler discovers there is less inconclusive and unsatisfactory, and more explicitly critical of British imperialism. In this Douglas takes the advice of Conan Doyle's Watson, who freely admits in "His Last Bow" that Holmes's own recounting of his cases "needs some little editing to soften it into the terms of real life" (991). That Watson does more than a little editing is confirmed by Holmes himself in a story that the detective narrates, "The Adventure of the Blanched Soldier," in which Holmes admits that he has in the past accused Watson "of pandering to popular taste instead of confining himself rigidly to facts and figures" (1000).

The Irene Adler series does of course "pander to popular taste" in its blend of historical romance and mystery. But as *Good Night, Mr. Holmes* illustrates so graphically, to sneer at and ignore popular taste is to close one's ear to the voices of women and other historically oppressed people who could speak, write, and sing only in the few modes and genres available to them. In "A Scandal in Bohemia," Irene Adler's voice escapes the disciplinary gaze of Holmes's inquiry. In Douglas's text it is Adler's voice that refuses the discipline of Victorian gender codes only to be subjected to Fiona Witherspoon's academic gaze and machinery, which at once mocks Sherlockians and, finally perhaps, the academic enterprise in which we are here engaged. That is, we want to take seriously popular genres and women's writing, and yet we recognize that in doing so we, like Doctor Witherspoon, subject their voices to our disciplinary gaze and confine them in our jail of jargon.

*M*indful, then, of the pitfalls of academic appropriation of popular genres, we do nonetheless need, as Irene Adler warns us, to work in, and on, those genres. Several of the novels we discuss in other chapters straddle the always tenuous line between serious and popular fiction, but the texts we look at here, by virtue of their obvious adherence to the conventions of the detective novel, fall clearly into the category of genre literature. The Holmes canon has, of course, gained status as "classic" detective literature, a status that, again, challenges the validity of these distinctions. However questionable the differences, however flexible the category, critics have widely acknowledged both the conservative tendencies and the revisionary possibilities of detective fiction, both of which we have seen in the juxtaposition of the Holmes and Douglas texts, both of which we will see in several other detective novels that feature the diva—as victim, as villain, as detective.

The diva stereotypes that we laid out and laid open in our earlier discussions of more "serious" texts are taken for granted in these works of popular fiction. The divas of detective fiction are often, and often unambiguously, either sirens or ciphers; in Kay Nolte Smith's *Elegy for a Soprano*, for example, the diva "brings people under the spell of her personality . . . and turns them into blind worshippers who stop living for themselves" (80). In some texts, however, the stereotypes are assumed in order to be examined and rejected, as in Barbara Paul's *A Chorus of Detectives* and *Prima Donna at Large*. Not surprisingly, most diva detective novels, whether British or American in origin, adhere to the conventions of the formal or British school of detective writing, the school most often concerned with the worlds of middle- and upper-class social elites, the same elites who, these days anyway, can afford to frequent the opera. Opera is, after all, even more obviously than the theater, which Marilyn Stasio is describing here, "an elite industry that produces an esoteric form of art for limited public consumption" (44).

Dennis Porter reminds us that, unlike the urban, hard-boiled, American tradition, in which crime is simply a part of the chaos of its surroundings, "the formal detective novel is founded on the central irony of the surprise of crime" and that "to the endlessly repeated irony of the most unlikely suspect, the formal detective novel added those of the most unlikely detective and the most unlikely place" (86). That triumph of civilization and temple of civility the opera house—with its high domed ceiling, its elaborate chandeliers, its opulent curtains, its reserved boxes where nobility cavorts, its high-priced tickets that effectively keep out the crime-prone masses—is, of course, as unlikely a place as any for serious crime. Yet there are passions and violence inherent in opera itself that make murder an appropriate accompaniment. Stasio, speaking here again of the relationship of theater to mystery fiction, makes a point that applies equally to opera: it is "steeped in the same kind of criminal behavior that thrills readers and inspires authors of genre fiction" with its "knives, swords, rapiers, spears, guns, battle-axes, vials of poison, vats of malmsey, [and] fluffy pillows" (44).

In opera, the diva is most often the victim of this violence—and this is the case as well in most detective novels. From the death of the diva on the opera stage, it is a small step to the "real" death of a diva. "It seems," says a mystery subject guide in summary of hundreds of music mysteries, "that temperamental sopranos are more likely to be killed than conductors or other personnel" (Menendez 145). And more likely as well to be, if not murderers, then very serious suspects and villains of another sort, guilty at the very least of the diva sins we have been discussing—overweening ambition and uncontrolled sexuality.

A quick look at some of the "typical" novels in which a temperamental prima donna is the victim and/or villain reveals the tradition against which the novels we are most interested in—mysteries that revise these roles and provide for the diva, as in *Good-Night, Mr. Holmes*, other, more surprising ones—position themselves.[5] We make no attempt here to be exhaustive. Hundreds of these mysteries have been written, though most are out of print, and we discover new ones every time we check out the new releases at our local bookstores.

Kay Nolte Smith's *Elegy for a Soprano*, Ngaio Marsh's *Photo Finish*, Robert Barnard's *Death on the High C's*, and Fred Jarvis's *Murder at the Met*—to mention some of the more easily available and well-known texts—are good examples of what we might call the "temperamental-soprano-as-corpse" novel. They present the future corpse in similar—and by now familiar—ways, as, for example, a volatile combination of unsanctioned sexuality and egoism. The main character in *Elegy for a Soprano*, Vardis Wolf's daughter Dinah Mitchell, is testament to both: illegitimate and abandoned—in a trash can—for Wolf's career. What so enthralls the diva's audiences is "the sight and sound of the dark eroticism" of her voice (3), and Mitchell herself describes the physical, even sexual effect of hearing her mother (though she is unaware at the time of her relationship to Wolf) sing: "The voice seemed to go right through me. No, into me, almost as if my own body was helping to produce the sound" (21). Vardis's followers, who call themselves the Wolfpack, are bound to her with passion—their "association with her was one of the most intense in their lives" (7). The eroticism, explicit and implied, of both Vardis's voice and its effect on others is thus "dark," incestuous, seductive. This power, combined with Vardis's ambition, make her on the one hand "a great artist, a brilliant woman" and on the other "a terrible human being. Quite monstrous actually" (58). She abandons her own child to her death, ruins the career—and life—of the man she marries, and tries to take over the life of her niece, Jenny, her most outspoken defender.

Vardis's father was a Jew; she hid from the Nazis as a child. She is a passionate anti-war demonstrator. She is a genius who "could speak them all . . . all the languages" (51). She is, as Jenny says to her mother Merle's chagrin, alive (185). Until, that is, she is dead. Poisoned. Murdered. Punished, everyone seems to agree, for crimes against the nature of womanhood. Her bearing, that "air of confident authority one was used to seeing only in soldiers," is the outward sign of her profound abandonment of the role of woman (40). The chief witness against her and, it turns out, her murderer is a more womanly woman, her longtime friend and sister-in-law. "For almost thirty years," Merle says, "I watched her destroy my brother Conrad, who was a magnificent pianist, but she kept him from having the career he should have, always making sure he did what she wanted instead" (77). What the text does not recognize is the gendered nature of this pronouncement. Who objects to the male genius who appropriates the career of his wife? Indeed, the text seems to endorse the proposition that a woman's appropriation of another's life in the service of her own—monstrous inversion—is grounds for murder: although she is working with the police, the detective-heroine, Dinah Mitchell, refuses to reveal her knowledge of the murderer to them, and the text appears to sanction this decision. Vardis Wolf, bad mother, bad wife, bad aunt, deserved to die for her sins against gender.

In *Photo Finish* sexuality and ambition are similarly—and less subtly—linked. Troy Alleyn, famous artist and wife of Ngaio Marsh's series detective, Inspector Alleyn, is eager to paint La Sommita's portrait. "I do want to have a go at her: a great, big flamboyant rather vulgar splotch of a thing. Her arms . . . are indecent. . . . She's so shockingly sumptuous" (8). A hostile photographer portrays her as "an infuriated gargoyle" (1). Gaylene Ffrench in Robert Barnard's *Death on the High C's* is also a "gargoyle" (38) and is described in terms equally repulsive: "her eyes bulging, her face shining with sweat and with anger, jealousy, and contempt oozing out of every pore" (70). She oozes sexuality as well with her "brawny shoulders and fleshy arms" in a "very low-cut" bright pink dress, "leaving to the imagination only the question of how it was kept up" (71); she is, her associates agree, "a nymphomaniac" (89). The conventional responses to the stereotypical diva's combination of imperious behavior, threatening sexuality, and glorious voice, fascination and fear, motivate descriptions of her physical presence that mark her as simultaneously disgusting and enthralling. Millicent Millions, diva-victim in Fred Jarvis's *Murder at the Met*, "exuded an incendiary power, a suffocating presence" (15) and has, in common with other divas, "a kind of awesome beauty and deadly efficiency—and . . . so do coral snakes" (153).[6]

Gargoyle, snake, spider (a young composer in Marsh's novel "walked into La Sommita's bedroom like a fly . . . into a one-way web" [5]), divas elicit little sympathy when they die. La Sommita has, by the time she is stabbed, been proclaimed (like Vardis Wolf) "a monster" by Troy Alleyn (43). In death she is as repulsive and sex-infused as she was in life: "The Sommita lay spread-eagled on her back . . . her biblical dress . . . torn down to the waist. . . . She might have been posed for the jacket on an all-too-predictable shocker" (77). One of the suspects tries to explain his horror at her "awful face" rushing at him: "It might as well be one of Dracula's ladies after the full treatment" (120). Gaylene Ffrench of the bulging eyes, shining sweat, and oozing pores is, appropriately enough, electrocuted. Not only is no one sorry that she's dead, one of the investigators senses that "no murderer had enjoyed such universal public sympathy since the gentleman who robbed the Russian Imperial family of the counsels of Gregory Rasputin" (149). When an opera house security guard is killed as well, one of the singers says, "It's not like with Gaylene—no one could ever say that he asked for it" (114). La Sommita and Gaylene Ffrench—seducers, nymphomaniacs, monsters—asked for it.

The death of the somewhat sympathetic Millicent Millions does elicit minor sorrows. But at least one character feels that "she deserved it. She had it coming" (113) and the inspector assigned to the case, Todd, addresses the dead diva as he wonders who killed her: "Look around you, Fisherman's Wife.[7] You are back in your hut in rags. Somewhere, someone draws the line against the limits of ambition" (224). By this time he suspects that Millions was "as bloodless as a computer" (191), "a subtle, vicious avenging angel" (236), and he soon realizes that she was more manipulative than even her colleagues could have imagined: The murder "was . . . preposterous . . . brilliant, ingenious, and malevolent. It was devilish, fascinating, and hugely theatrical. And only one person could have manipulated it" (231).

Like Wagner's Isolde, her final role, Millicent Millions poisoned herself; in fact, "she plotted her death perfectly so that all of you, who had in some way or another betrayed her, would fall under suspicion" (233). Here, then, the diva is both victim and villain, awesome beauty and deadly efficiency, in face of which no further sympathy could be sustained, especially after the testimony of her own mother (from whom she had completely cut herself off for no discernible reason) that she "was a ruthless little tyke" with "no love in her, not one scrap" (220).

When Inspector Todd proclaims that only one person could have plotted a death in such a calculatingly clever way, Million's chief rival, Amelita Dawson-Da Guerra, cries out, "She killed herself!" and the inspector remarks, "Only another diva could have guessed" (232). Amelita is, of course, one of the main suspects—the two women hated "with that special venom which great divas save for one another" (167)—and the inspector here links the two divas in the crime; there is no doubt that Amelita *could* have killed Millicent, as she herself admits: "It's a role I've played often enough before, Tosca, Medea, Turandot.... I'm sure I'm quite capable of it" (197). That she did not is no evidence of her innocence. Divahood being, to conventional eyes, a crime against womanhood, just being a diva taints Amelita Dawson-Da Guerra, associates her with the murderous women she plays.

Mr. Aldrich, chairman of the Met board, guesses that the "murder" is the result of "some sort of intramural rivalry.... Opera singers are a breed apart ... they are bigger than life, and their passions are magnified correspondingly" (127). Opera itself is, of course, bigger than life, and the very passion, violence, and excess of the characters on the stage transfer easily to the "real" world. As the inspector senses in his frustration at being unable to find Millions's murderer, "Everywhere . . . there was too much. Too much motive. Too much opportunity. Too many people. Too much interaction" (148). "That special venom," likewise, moves smoothly from the metaphoric to the literal. Whether Millicent is poisoned by Amelita's hatred or by her own hand seems of little consequence to the novel's tale of diva rivalry and diva deadliness.

Gaylene's rivals in *Death on the High C's* are more complexly drawn and less villainous. Bridget Lander, in fact, is a sympathetic character throughout, a first-rate talent and very much in control of herself. She is, besides, engaged to be married, her sexuality therefore, the text implies, firmly disciplined, unlike that of the nymphomaniac Gaylene. By the end of the novel, however, Gaylene's egoism seems to have contaminated her. And the second-rate Guilia, who has been quite sweet and generous for most of the novel, seems at the end contaminated as well—by Gaylene's sexuality. She throws over her Italian bass boyfriend (one of Gaylene's former conquests) and begins "thinking something very physical" about Gaylene's Aussie hunk (252). Even the nicest sort of diva, then, is corrupted by the power and sex that permeate the opera, power and sex that seem not altogether indigenous either to the British or the American stage but are, like many of the divas, Italian imports. The foreign virus.

In these three novels the stereotype of the diva seems of a piece with the stereotype of the Italian. We have seen that American Millicent Millions is "highly uncharacteristic of the soprano breed," as opposed to her spiteful Italian rival, Amelita, a "silk-draped Dracula" (27) who has an "astronomical income" but is so greedy that she refuses "to send her mother money for a cataract operation" (27). When the inspector visits the home of Rita Quercia, Millions's ex-protégée, he takes one look at her parents' "embarrassing" Italianate house and concludes that her father "must be a construction millionaire with solid Mafia connections" (161). Though Millions is not herself Italian, even she is contaminated by association. When she threatens to withdraw the directorship of a foundation from her old singing coach, the woman accuses, "The foundation was a loaded pistol, and she aimed it at me with all the heartless concern of a Mafia gunman" (191).

While Gaylene Ffrench is an Australian (and so, like an Italian, much less civilized than the British Bridget), her lover is Italian and has, the narrative informs us, an "oily Mediterranean head" (24). Although he wonders that Galene, "who spent much of her professional life singing in the works of Italian composers, should regard his ancestry as a matter for crude racial abuse" (27)—she calls him a "pommie-wop"—he is as unpleasant a character as she; and it is the narrator, not one of the characters, who comments that moving gracefully "is something Italian sopranos can always do, at least until the pasta takes its toll" (46).

The anti-Italian sentiment in Ngaio Marsh's *Photo Finish* is part of the very fabric of the novel. Alleyn deduces that La Sommita, the diva, is "of the purest Italian—perhaps Sicilian—peasant stock and utterly uninhibited" (40). (Significantly, her "American Sicilian" lover is described—by detective Alleyn—as "like something out of *Trilby*" [13].) Troy knows even before she meets La Sommita that the diva's behavior will be "High operatic with tantrums between sittings" (9), and Troy's final drawing of La Sommita has her "in full cry, mouth wide open, triumphant," which prompts the judgment: "This is the portrait of a Voice" (75). In other words, the most famous diva in the world is all body, all Italian passion, her voice a mere freak of nature. Like her, also given to histrionic and irrational behavior are the Italian servants, Marco and Maria, who attend her; they are, another character claims, "straight out of grand opera," Italian opera, of course (122). Given the text's pervasive antipathy toward everything and everyone Italian and Anglo-American culture's conventional linkage, in constructions of "Italianness," of all Italians with the mafia and thus with crime, the solution to the murder is hardly surprising. La Sommita's lover and her maid actually belong to a mafiosi family that has for generations been feuding with La Sommita's family. They kill her as an act of (Sicilian) revenge. While the Italian diva is victim, then, the characters most closely associated with her, fellow Sicilians, are the villains.

The close association here of Italians not only with crime but also with uninhibited, excessive, and destructive passion suggests, again, the text's distrust of passion itself, of (that Italian invention) opera itself. Early in the novel La Sommita refuses to attend a party "because the host's money came from South Africa" (37). This decision is regarded as one more instance of the diva's ridiculous and brainless behavior. The implication, of course, is that La Sommita feels common cause with South African blacks, associated, like Italians, with all that is primitive and irrational, akin also to the wild, unpredictable, "primordial" New Zealand island where the violence of the novel occurs (22). In contrast to this is the civilized behavior of the British. The trip to the island is harrowing; Alleyn praises his wife's "intrepidity." She replies: "What did you expect me to do? Howl like a banshee?" (22). Howling is, of course, just what the text does expect from the diva and her Italian cohorts, and howling is, of course, not so far removed from the full-bodied singing, the all-encompassing Voice of La Sommita, the best, the highest of her kind.[8]

Divas (and Italians) are, of course, not merely passionate. They serve as figures for a kind of all-encompassing and transgressive excess. Their punishment in these novels has to do not only with their uncontrolled sensuality but with their uncontrolled ambition and greed as well, excessive traits suggested by Millicent Millions's name and nickname, "the Solid-Gold Diva" (12). As the epitomizing image La Sommita's wide-open mouth suggests, divas "consume" in every sense of the word. Millions's rival, Amelita, who once ate "forty chicken legs at a sitting" (27), has a "hideous smile" that expresses her "naked, ruthless, pitiless ambition and self-esteem" (30), and the other diva in the novel, Italian Rita Quercia, once Millions's protégée, is "all fortissimo and ambition" (128). In conformity to the diva stereotype, the women use sex for career advancement; Amelita, for example, has "an agate-hard eye for acquiring . . . superrich lovers" (32); Millicent Millions wants more than anything to marry the rich and influential Mr. Aldrich, whose mistress she has been for many years.

As we have seen, many diva narratives link uncontrolled sensuality with uncontrolled ambition. In Dorothy Dunnett's *Dolly and the Singing Bird*, one of the most structurally interesting diva mysteries, the diva is not only villain and victim but narrator as well. Tina Rossi, Polish-Italian diva, foreign spy, narrator, establishes the link between sensuality and ambition with clarity and candor. Of her relationship to the rich and powerful Stanley Hennessy, she says, "I do not antagonize people like Stanley. . . . But I make them pay highly for what they buy" (100). Rossi denies that she is promiscuous—"with the work I have to do, this would be impossible" (3)—but she uses her sexuality to get what she wants: "I cannot be forced. If I choose to sleep with them, they have been lucky, this throw. If I do not . . . then they must act the good loser. . . . For the jewels I keep, always" (104). That she makes them pay highly, however, does not imply that the sex is only a business transaction; it brings pleasure as well. With a villain hiding in the closet, Tina makes love with the owner—a duke—of a famous steam yacht. Afterwards she realizes that the closet had a keyhole: "So Goldtooth must have enjoyed what came next. Even I did, and I'd a lot on my mind" (145). The men she couples with are similarly clear about the mercenary nature of their exchanges with the diva: "You know what I paid this little singing bird for the privilege of having my ear shot off?" asks one disgruntled "suitor" (209).

Her ambition is, of course, of a piece with her greed. While she describes in great detail her bank account, jewels, and wardrobe—her yachting outfits include a "little gold alpaca coat" (128), "a cire rainsuit lined with lynx fur" (156), and a "Ricci suit and sheared beaver jacket" (304), among many others—she makes clear that she "learned to sing for fame, as well as for fortune: for that moment when the thunder of the orchestra is suspended, the choirs stop, and my voice is revealed, single, pure, and celestial. . . . I do not want to lose that elation, that power, that applause" (135). Tina Rossi's excess mounts almost to megalomania as she announces in the midst of a dangerous storm: "I could have lifted up my voice then and quelled the sea and the wind: I could have sung Brünnhilde and Isolde" (263). In an interesting inversion of the siren myth—too simple to capture Rossi and her motives—Rossi is instrumental in saving the yacht and the people on it, thanks in part to the "supple and strong" chest muscles that she has developed from singing opera and that she uses to pump water out of the floundering boat (263).

What makes this text so fascinating is the alternating and interweaving of the diva as female hero (the woman with strength, drive, genius, beauty, self-earned wealth, and an undisputed voice) and diva as female villain (the woman with exactly the same qualities). For example, Rossi refuses to marry a man she seems genuinely to love because, as she has explained earlier, she has seen "what happens when one meddles with men. Children happen, and a room and kitchen in Pollokshaws, and hard work where there is no point in smiling, for most people you meet are worse off than yourself" (90). Feminist hero or unnatural woman, unbearable cynic?

What the feminist reader is likely to admire about this "obstinate woman," who dislikes "being pushed. By anyone, anywhere," is precisely what more traditional readers of detective fiction are likely to deplore (81). Such readers, schooled in the conventions of the genre, are more likely to catch the clues in the diva's excesses (to read traits like obstinacy as excess) and recognize more quickly the novel's conservative trajectory. It is the feminist reader who may be taken in by the charming narrator, the feminist reader who more easily overlooks the warnings of Rossi's excess: the ninety thousand pounds in her bank account, the wanton wardrobe, the unabashed sexuality. Like the Fisherman's Wife, she aims too high, wanting, with her voice, to quell the winds and the seas.

Tina Rossi's is a story of the rewards that come from hard work and ambition—or it would be such a story but for gender. She has humble origins: her mother, who dies giving her birth, was a potato picker. Raised in institutions and foster homes, the orphan "worked hard . . . and . . . is not ashamed of [her] past" (86). In other words, like many literary and folk heroes', hers is a rags-to-riches story. And, also like many such heroes, she tells this story herself. She "like[s] to remember" the story, in fact; she likes to tell it—"how I, from nothing and less than nothing, have become Tina Rossi," world-renowned diva (86).

The story that Tina tells, while "true," is, however, only part of the truth, as she admits late in her narrative. She has stolen military secrets from one of her lovers, a good, honest man, a brilliant scientist, who doesn't want to believe in the betrayal. "He was not seeing me," she says. "He was seeing probably his precious, world-famous *diva* with the candid heart, who rose, unspoiled from her humble beginnings. . . . That was me, too" (292). In other words, the-unspoiled-diva-with-the-candid-heart is a role like the roles she plays on the opera stage, part of her but only part. The storybook word here is "unspoiled." Tina Rossi *is* spoiled, as her extravagant clothes and unabashed egoism, when read through the conventions of the genre, should have warned us. And, of course, the extravagant clothes and unabashed egoism are inextricably associated with her divahood. Millicent Millions advises her protégée, Rita Quercia, that "when you walk out on that stage, you must know in your heart you are a queen. You must know for absolute fact that you are the greatest singer alive. Then, and only then, will you be able to give a performance" (173). In other words, the diva is in a position impossible to a woman; in order to *be* a diva, she must take on the roles that can by definition never be hers— ruler, pope, god. It is important that the Fisherman's Wife is a wife. While aspiring to be ruler, pope, even god might be intolerable ambition in the fisherman himself, in his wife it is much worse than intolerable: it is unnatural.

As we have seen, literary divas frequently suffer the fate of the Fisherman's Wife they so obviously resemble. Tina Rossi wants too much. To get it, she turns traitor, and even her voice, which includes at this point not only her singing voice but her narrative voice as well, cannot save her. That is, *as* narrator both of this story and of her story, she seduces, but only until "the truth" emerges. The counterspy scolds the brilliant scientist: "The risks moral and ethical you were running made tonight's big thrills look pretty small beer—what got into you? Oh, no need to answer. Tina Rossi got into you" (299). The scientist here is seduced by Tina's story just as readers are. Like readers, he sees what he wants to see, trusts in the intrinsically untrustworthy. In order to end the narrative, however, Tina Rossi must confess her duplicity—on both levels. She is not the unspoiled diva with the candid heart whom trusting Kenneth thought she was; she is not the reliable narrator whom trusting readers thought she was. The sympathetic identification often evoked by the first-person narrator, the persuasive storyteller, erodes with the excess of Rossi's ambition, an excess presaged by an act of musical hubris: "Every coloratura from the beginning of time has recorded the Bell Song from Lakmé: I did it in Rome. That was when I first caused a sensation by altering the top cadenza from E to G sharp in alt" (289).

Sensation, of course, is what she's after, but sensation demands everescalating satisfaction. She succumbs, apparently without remorse, to the highs of greater risk taking and greater wealth. She becomes a spy and is responsible for blowing up a submarine, a situation about which readers are, until the last pages of the novel, unaware; the revelation is especially painful given Rossi's heroic behavior during the near-fatal storm, but that, too, can be read as mere self-preservation. Accustomed as we are, that is, to at least minimal modesty in female narrators, we are encouraged to misread Rossi's motives. Thus, there is a real sense in which betrayal of her country (the "her" here needs examination—born in Scotland of Polish-Irish parents, in what way is Britain hers?) is paralleled in the text by betrayal of her audience—both the fans of her singing voice and the readers of her narrative voice. And her punishment fits the crime.

"Don't hope, Tina," advises the counterspy. "There's too much piled up against you. Between us, I'm afraid we have silenced your voice" (307). To silence Tina Rossi's voice is, of course, to end her life. And the "us" consists of the counterspy, his associate, and Tina's lover Kenneth—all men who admire the voice, who have, to one extent or another been, like the readers, seduced by the voice, but who cannot, in the end, let it be heard. It is explosive; it wreaks destruction. Men's tools of war aren't safe as long as it sings. And this quite literally—the detonator of the bomb on the submarine was set to Tina Rossi's G sharp in alt.

Rossi does not go quietly. "I shall still have my voice," she asserts. "Other people won't be able to hear it, that's all" (307). It's a brave claim, not entirely believable given what we know of her ambition. But she seems almost to enjoy the unraveling of the plot, the intelligence of the counterspy—and she rejects his pity: "If I've made a mistake, I can pay" (309). Again, Tina Rossi remains an unreadable character, eliciting from readers both disdain and admiration. The counterspy lured Rossi onto his yacht with the promise of a portrait—he, like Troy Alleyn, is a well-known painter—which he presents to Rossi at the end, a portrait that has changed significantly from his early sketches. Rossi enumerates some of the changes: "The eyes were not misty, but liquid and cool; the mouth, beautifully drawn, was the trained mouth of a singer" (310). She concludes, "It was my own face, the face I was born with. The face I cannot escape" (310). But, of course, this is not the face she was born with. It is rather a face that has been stripped of the romanticism of diva worship ("not misty"), a face that acknowledges the construction of the diva ("trained mouth"). Rossi's claiming it as her own acquiesces both in the deconstruction of the diva and in the circumstances that have now framed her. The novel concludes with Rossi calling to memory—both hers and ours—the endless succession of foster homes in her past, as she "set off downstairs as I had done, over and over in childhood. To the nameless persons waiting below" (311). From Tina Rossi, the name known all over the world, to namelessness, from Voice to voicelessness, from freedom to frame, from adult success to the humiliations of childhood, Rossi's fate is the gendered fate of the Fisherman's Wife.

Several other writers of detective fiction have attempted to reverse or rewrite this fate. In *False Notes*, by Chelsea Quinn Yarbro, for example, it is a mean and temperamental *tenor*, Gui-Adam Feuier, who is murdered and whose death elicits little sympathy. Especially infuriating to one of the sopranos was his treatment of a fellow musician and wife of a baritone: "Linnett was a beautiful woman, inside and out, and Gui-Adam ruined her" (79). Although the women are suspects—especially "all the women he was chasing"—none is especially villainous or even temperamental (72). And the murderer turns out to be Linnett's husband. The thoroughness of this revision is emphasized by the detective team—a native American lawyer, Charlie Moon (a series detective), and his associate, Morgan Studevant. It is Morgan who is the opera buff and who saves Charlie's life with her aikido skills. All the traditional roles and rules of diva detective fiction are reversed here, with the result that the diva herself drops out or is at least decentered, the power of her voice shared among several characters in the text, but most notably Charlie Moon, whose voice as "a dumb Indian" is sometimes not heard, and Morgan Studevant, whose voice is often inappropriate, strident, awkward, clumsy ("I hope she can keep that tongue of hers under control," says an officer from the hostage-bargaining squad, [153]) but who, threatened with two knives and a thirty-eight, outtalks a crazed killer.

Donna Leon's *Death at La Fenice* also decenters the diva. The victim here is a world-class conductor, in his seventies, poisoned between the acts of *La Traviata*. The diva, Flavia Petrelli, "one of the leading opera singers of the day," is one of the prime suspects (25). Although she is once called "arrogant" (190) and "something of a bitch" (217), there are no tales of imperious (an adjective saved for the dead conductor) prima donna behavior, no anecdotes of jealous rages. Though she has had a husband and several lovers, no one suggests that she used sex to further her ambitions. An intelligent woman and superb musician, La Petrelli—"a simple little country girl" (212) whose ex-husband "beat her, quite regularly and quite severely" (215)—elicits general sympathy and admiration. The source of the friction between her and the conductor, and between her and several other important figures in her world, is her lesbian relationship with an American archeologist. While, one of the characters explains, "there are a great number of lesbian singers," (he adds parenthetically that they are "strangely enough, most of them . . . mezzo-sopranos"), they "are far less tolerated than their male colleagues who also happen to be gay" (217). The friction is severe: the conductor has threatened to expose her to her ex-husband, who will undoubtedly then seek custody of her two children and undoubtedly get it, even though he once beat his wife so severely that she was hospitalized. The diva, that is, has a motive.

In a genre in which homosexuality and crime are linked with great frequency, a suggestion or revelation of a character's homosexuality is often a clue to his or her guilt. Lesbians, especially, turn out, with great regularity, to be perpetrators of crime—usually murder—in mainstream detective fiction, especially if they're attractive and talented, as "the divine Flavia" certainly is, and as is her lover, Brett Lynch.[9] That neither of these women is the villain thus thwarts reader expectations of the guilt of both divas and lesbians. Brett Lynch, who "seems always to have been of this persuasion," (220) and to whom the detective initially takes a strong dislike (another conventional clue to guilt), becomes, by the end, a friend of the detective and one of the most interesting and sympathetic—if prickly—characters in the novel.

Death at La Fenice, taking place as it does in Venice, also revises the anti-Italian sentiment of much diva detective fiction. Most of the main characters are Italian, including the detective, Brunetti; most of the Italians are sympathetic. It is not an Italian man, for example, who is "incapable of believing that he was unattractive to any woman," but the victim, a German (121). It is not the Italians seriously wronged by the maestro who act out their vengeance, but a Hungarian. Italians are by no means all good or heroic, of course. It is the Italian ambassador who "was a lickspittle and tried to send [Flavia] back to her husband," one of the characters reveals. His wife, however, intervenes; she is "a Sicilian—and let not a word be said against them," the storyteller, another Italian, insists (215). Thus does the novel rehabilitate even Sicilians, the most maligned—being the most southern and the most poverty-stricken—of Italians.

The consistent revisionary tactics of the text are made explicit in a comic scene in which Brunetti's young daughter watches a television broadcast of *La Traviata*. She has no sympathy for the hero ("I still think he's a jerk" [190]) and is indignant about the opera's treatment of Violetta ("As long as she's supporting him, then she's got the right to do whatever she wants" [186]). Even the superb performance of La Petrelli, the world's leading Verdi singer, cannot overcome for her the impracticality of the plot: "Even if she lived, how would they support themselves?" (190). By calling into question, albeit comically, the conventional gender ideology that opera so often reinscribes, that opera so often makes romantic and glamorous, the text reminds us that it is calling into question the conventions of opera fiction as well.

Although the diva here is a more developed character than the singer in *False Notes*, the focus of the novel eventually moves away from her since she turns out to be neither victim nor villain. Another diva who is neither victim nor villain does, however, manage to maintain center stage: in Barbara Paul's *A Chorus of Detectives* and *Prima Donna at Large*, the diva, Geraldine Farrar, is also the detective. Although in the former the diva is only one of a "chorus" of detectives, the text refers to the group as "the Geraldine Farrar team of detectives" (147). In *Prima Donna at Large*, Farrar is not only detective but narrator as well. In using a whole cast of historical singers—Geraldine Farrar, Rosa Ponselle, Emmy Destinn, Caruso, and Antonio Scotti are only a few of the historical stars who have significant roles in these texts—Paul rewrites the clichés of opera anecdote and history as well as of the diva detective novel. While there are fights and feuds among the principals, they respect and defend one another and acknowledge their musical debts. When Emmy Destinn, for example, tells Farrar that she's the best Carmen she's ever heard, Farrar remarks that "prima donnas just don't *say* things like that to each other"—but in Paul's books, they do (*Prima Donna* 44).

Farrar herself exhibits a number of "prima donna" tendencies in *Prima Donna at Large* (when one of the men is ill and cannot sing, she resents the attention he's getting: "Everyone seemed to have forgotten that I had created a new role only the night before. . . . They should have been talking about *me*" [12]), but she also counters them. Hearing about the current work of former diva Calvé, she exclaims, "Emma Calvé, my inspiration and my idol! Now I was the one who was singing *Carmen* while she was playing the Palace along with the jugglers . . . and the trained-dog acts. . . . The thought gave me no pleasure, no pleasure at all" (*Prima Donna* 184–185). Displaying, that is, the requisite amount of egoism, she also cares deeply about her colleagues and her predecessors. Prima donnas are, of course, supposed to be jealous of the younger generation of singers, but in this, too, Farrar breaks the stereotype; she takes on the role of mentor and protector of the young Rosa Ponselle and scolds the chorus for their unfair treatment of her.

In *A Chorus of Detectives* Emmy Destinn at first appears as a somewhat stereotypical diva figure, aloof and prickly, but Farrar defends her behavior: "Try spending a war virtually locked up in your own house with armed Austrians watching every move you make and see how *simpatico* you are when it's over" (59). Emmy, despite her prickliness and despite the rivalry between herself and Farrar, also supports and defends her colleagues; the narrative forcefully informs us: "Whatever Emmy Destinn thought of Rosa Ponselle personally, the older soprano was still a musician before everything else; she responded wholeheartedly to the younger woman's performance" (79). The young Ponselle is unpopular, especially with the chorus, because of her vaudeville roots, and given the chorus's resentment of her, she becomes one of the suspects when a number of chorus members are murdered. The choristers especially suspect her: "Every one of them would swear to having seen Rosa . . . lurking backstage when she had no business being there, a knife in one hand and a vial of poison in the other" (155). But in this determinedly revisionary text, it is not the diva who kills.

For much of the novel, however, the prime suspect is another woman, a woman with almost no voice at all, Mrs. Bukaitis, a scrublady in the opera house. Her lowly position in the opera hierarchy allies her thematically with Ponselle, the ex-vaudeville performer, and her status as immigrant—she's Lithuanian and is, in fact, working with a Lithuanian terrorist group—recalls the anti-foreigner rhetoric of much diva literature. But, like Rosa Ponselle, Mrs. Bukaitis, too, turns out to be innocent of the serial chorus killings, and although she does try twice to plant a bomb backstage, she is given, in the end, a somewhat sympathetic and persuasive voice. "You squander money on luxuries like opera while men and women in my country are being enslaved," she argues in defense of her ethnic group, and "You assume I am ignorant because I scrub floors," in defense of her class (*Chorus* 175). Farrar herself is linked to both Bukaitis and Ponselle at the end of the novel when she sings the leading role in *Zazà*, the role of a "cafe singer who abandoned her career for her lover, only to learn he was already married to someone else" (173). The text thus makes a clear effort to address, even if only tangentially, issues of class and makes the case for questioning the difference between "high" and "low" culture. The cafe singer, the vaudeville singer, the scrublady: what separates them, the text inquires, from the stars of the opera stage? *"Scotti and Gatti,"* Farrar muses at one point (referring to famous baritone Antonio Scotti and opera manager Gatti-Casazza), "sounded like a Vaudeville team" (196). *Prima Donna at Large* takes place just before World War I, and *A Chorus of Detectives* is set just after the war, before, in other words, opera had lost its popular base. But both novels were written in the eighties and so written with keen awareness of the widening gap that was to grow between "high" and "low" culture, between elite entertainment like opera and the medium that replaced vaudeville as popular entertainment, film.

Farrar is especially aware of the "ordinary" opera fan, working- and middle-class fans who haven't the wealth or social position to be powerful patrons of the diva, and she is eloquent on their importance. In both *A Chorus of Detectives* and *Prima Donna at Large*, the Gerry-Flappers, "fresh-faced young girls eager to join the army of females who worshipped the ground Geraldine Farrar walked on," are treated by Farrar with affection and respect (*Chorus* 37).[10] In *A Chorus of Detectives* they facilitate the performances, for example, by knowing "just when to start the chanting—not too early, not too late" (37), and in *Prima Donna at Large* Farrar sends them off to find Uncle Hummy, "an elderly Italian" who frequents the opera house, lives "mostly on handouts," and is a great favorite with Farrar and Caruso (36). He is suspected of the murder in this text—in part because he is ill-dressed and odd—but Farrar refuses to believe that he had anything to do with it. She respects him, that is, in much the same way she respects her female adorers, and by sending them to look for him, she acknowledges their commonality.

The Gerry-Flappers prove themselves competent and successful detectives, under the direction of their leaders, Mildred and Phoebe, whom Farrar affectionately refers to as "MildredandPhoebe"—"since you never saw one without the other" (47)—suggesting, of course, that they are a lesbian couple. Farrar looks on admiringly ("What unexpected talents these girls had" [*Prima Donna* 230]) when Phoebe effortlessly picks a lock. Gerry-Flappers remain lifelong fans, Farrar explains, and she, in turn, remains loyal to them, refuses, that is, to condescend to opera fans, finding her greatest support among the very old and very young, among the ordinary, the eccentric, and the gay people who walk the streets of New York.

The crime in *Prima Donna at Large* is the disabling of Philippe Duchon, a baritone, hated by everyone for his autocratic ways; he is, that is, the stereotypical prima donna, imperiously issuing orders even to Toscanini—"You will have a door put in the set, and you will do so before the next performance!" (57). He tries to upstage Farrar and Destinn, he clearly wants Gatti-Cassaza's position, he calls Uncle Hummy a tramp, he refuses to rehearse. He behaves, that is, in the same explosive, unpredictable, cruel ways that divas behave in many of the texts we have looked at. When, however, someone puts ammonia in his throat spray, thus permanently ruining his voice, even his enemies are indignant. Farrar herself says that *"going for the voice . . .* was simply unimaginable" (138). There is a clear sense among the singers that no matter how much they all hated the obnoxious and infuriating baritone, no matter how often they themselves had thought of some operatic weapon of revenge—"guns, poison, knives, nooses, heavy clubs for banging people over the head" (138)—Duchon did not deserve what he got. The novel thus continues to rewrite the diva narrative not only by substituting a prima donna–ish baritone and emphasizing the divas' loyalty rather than rivalry but also by asserting that even the most despicable victim did not "ask for it."

In addition to rewriting the diva narrative, *Prima Donna at Large* also attempts to revise the gendered narrative of opera itself. We have seen that this narrative too often depends on, in Catherine Clément's phrase, "the undoing of women"; even the most adamant defenders of opera must acknowledge that women are overwhelmingly the victims of operatic violence. It is perhaps *Carmen* that illustrates this most pointedly—the independent, confident, sexually active, rebellious woman cannot be allowed to live. And it is *Carmen* that the Metropolitan Opera is performing at the end of *Prima Donna at Large* with Geraldine Farrar in the title role and Caruso as Don José, her killer. The two singers, generally friends, have been angry with one another and have been acting out that anger during the performance. Finally, enraged by Caruso's attempt to upstage her, Farrar does the unthinkable. Although, as Farrar remarks, "the outcome is ordained. . . . Carmen's death marks the end of the opera," when she sees Caruso coming at her with the knife she rebels: "I snatched the knife out of his hand and thrust it *hard* at his stomach." Caruso/Don Jose has no choice at this point but to "die." And, Farrar continues, "a tenor who has been unexpectedly 'killed' is in no condition to sing his final lines. . . . So I sang them. *'C'est moi qui lui ai tue!'* I sang, changing the French to fit the circumstances. *'Ah! José, mon José, adore!'"* (215).

Farrar's revisionary act here might be read as the culmination of the liberties that divas have taken with the operas they sing. Mostly, as we have seen, they change a note, like Tina Rossi's G sharp in the "Bell Song." Here the diva changes, by one thrust of the knife, the entire opera. Not only does Carmen for the first time in opera history survive, but her voice—the voice that has teased, the voice that has seduced, the voice that has demanded, rejected, asserted—triumphs over the voice of Don José. "It is I who have killed *him*." And it is she who finishes the opera, Don José at her feet silenced, Caruso at her feet enraged, his voice constrained by the dramatic demands of the opera stage.

Toscanini, speechless for the first time in the novel, and Gatti ("Disgraceful, perfectly disgraceful!" he roars [216]) are horrified by Farrar's desecration of Bizet's opera; Toscanini even refuses to take a curtain call. Abandoned also by the rest of the cast, Geraldine Farrar must go out to the audience alone—"rumpled, sleeveless, battered and bruised—but *the winner*," she gloats (216). She is, then, like the Carmen she has just played, both triumphant and unrepentant. And, like the new Carmen, she survives. "The people in the audience were actually stamping their feet while they cheered," and a famous director effuses that it was the "most exciting theatre I've seen in ten years!" (217). Engaging narrator, triumphant performer, relentless sleuth—the diva here reverses her status as victim and villain and projects her voice from the stage into "real life."

While revising the diva detective narrative, Paul's texts, with their playful incorporation of historical singers and opera history, seek to revise conventional assumptions of opera history as well. As we have seen, diva biographies and autobiographies as well as behind-the-scenes tales of opera performances frequently model their narratives on stereotypes of women on the stage. While both *A Chorus of Detectives* and *Prima Donna at Large* repeat some of these narratives (the rivalry between Emmy Destinn and Geraldine Farrar, the resentment of the upstart Rosa Ponselle, the upstaging that occurs during performances), they also attempt to explain them. For example, to talk about the vulnerability of the diva's voice—to overwork, to age, to illness, to enemies, to fashions of singing style—undercuts the essentialism that underlies such narratives. Rivalry and resentment—or ambition, bitchiness, arrogance, egoism, aloofness, promiscuity—are not constitutive of divahood, they are not "just how divas are," as many texts imply. Rather they are possible and comprehensible and even predictable results of the historical and social conditions that determine and, at times, facilitate the precariousness of a diva's existence *as* diva. By emphasizing these conditions and presenting historical singers as characters who both succumb to such conditions and fight against them, Paul's novels ask readers to look again at the assumptions of diva lore.[11]

These novels are, then, with Douglas's Irene Adler series, part of the larger body of feminist detective fiction that both revises the genre itself and asks readers to look again at the assumptions about gender that most texts, even historical texts, make. When women characters move from the positions, as victims and villains, that are so prominently theirs in traditional detective fiction as well as in opera to positions as detectives and narrators (not exclusively, of course; there are many women victims and villains in feminist detective fiction), something changes in the world. While, as many critics argue, detective fiction as a genre is conservative of a very traditional order (a racist, classist, sexist, homophobic order), and while no doubt much feminist detective fiction reinscribes traditional values, it simultaneously demands new vision, at the very least a literal vision of a woman at center stage refusing the exclusive role of victim/villain and using her voice to demand both power and justice. That this voice has been effective, at least within the genre, seems beyond doubt: the new detective fiction proliferates, its detective-heroes no longer only the white, heterosexual women who replaced white, heterosexual men but black, Hispanic, Asian, openly gay men and women of a wide range of class and age, whose voices we ignore at our peril.

CHAPTER 6

Divas Do the Movies

A serious artist can't have lovers and still think.
—Olive Fremstad

*T*here were divas in motion pictures even before there was sound. Producer Jesse Lasky recruited Geraldine Farrar for a series of silent films after he saw her in a Met performance of *Madame Butterfly* and observed the Gerry-Flappers' adulation. Farrar made a number of films between 1915 and 1919, first with the Lasky Company and later with Samuel Goldwyn's company. Best known are her *Joan the Woman*, in which Farrar plays the cross-dressing saint, and her 1915 *Carmen*, one of many silent film treatments of the narrative and a film that affected later performances of Bizet's opera at the Met. According to Farrar's autobiography, the offer to star in the film was an attempt to capitalize on her previous success on stage: "The real object of my engagement in Hollywood was to film *Carmen*, this having been my triumph of a previous season. Whether or not I would prove screen material was an undertaking of small risk, for the Metropolitan prestige and my personal réclame would guarantee one feature picture, while curiosity would do the rest" (166). As a warm up, she filmed "a melodramatic Spanish play called *Maria Rosa*" and was especially pleased at the way director Cecil B. DeMille "understood my enthusiasm and left me free to express natural impulses wherever my feeling prompted them" (166, 169). Farrar took full advantage of this freedom: "My biggest fighting moment was not the traditional third opera act where the two women claim the bewildered Don José, but a vigorous quarrel in the tobacco factory where the amiable Jeannie Macpherson . . . loaned herself to my assault in a battle that made screen history" (170).

On her return to New York, Farrar imported this freedom and violence into a production of the opera: "As in the movies, . . . in the opera version I fell upon a chorus girl in the provocative first act, seized and kicked her, and bowled her over in an exciting tussle. . . . Much was made about this violent innovation by the music critics, . . . Caruso is said to have given me a sharp reprimand about such tiger-like tactics in my scenes with him, with special emphasis on the unfortunate importation of movie technique! He may have done so, I can't recall in the excitement of the uproar, but I do know that he never sang better in his life—nor did I—and we shall let it go at that. For he too, knew good box-office. . . . The public continued to flock, hoping for gore and, I think, even murder" (170).[1]

Here lies, we suspect, the germ of Barbara Paul's *A Chorus of Detectives*, but what interests us at this juncture are the themes of violence and a kind of leveling of (aesthetic) hierarchies in the complaint about Farrar's "unfortunate importation of movie technique" into the high art of opera. The complaint is linked to another: when she slapped Caruso during a 1916 performance of *Carmen* (no doubt an example of her "tiger-like tactics"), a critic complained of "disillusioning vulgarity" (quoted in Dizikes 404). Complaints about Farrar's coarsening of aesthetic standards mask another source of unease. Her performance is also an aggressive leveling of gender hierarchies, as Paul's novel implies and as John Dizikes argues: "To the young women who adored her, it was a feminist slap, the diva fighting back" (404).

In *Opera, Ideology, and Film*, Jeremy Tambling shows how the nascent film industry "made operatic material into part of its own discourse, and used operatic glamour to sanction its own ideologies" (17). Farrar was not the only singer of her era to make the jump to film; Caruso and Mary Garden also tried but were less successful in the medium than Farrar. Hollywood's importation of singers like Farrar, Tambling argues, was designed to "advance the dignity of the motion picture"—to raise the status of cinema by associating it with the glamor, wealth, and elite status of the "high" art of opera (25).[2] Of course this practice of middle-brow and popular entertainment "borrowing," by appropriating and domesticating, opera's prestige (even at times by satirizing opera), has a long history and continues today. We read, for example, that Disney plans to follow *Pocahontas* with an animated *Aida* arranged by Elton John. Opera's prestige will help to sell the cartoon but no doubt will also be used to sell Aida tee-shirts, backpacks, and fast-food kiddie meals.[3]

The use of opera singers in the silents also served, according to Tambling, to coalesce "life and the ideological representation of life." His model is Farrar's *Carmen*. "Farrar moves from illusion to illusion: from singing *Carmen* to acting it in another version: the effect of this is to 'naturalise' the idea of a woman as a Carmen—or at any rate, either a virgin or a whore" (25). Given Farrar's reputation (at least among the Gerry-Flappers Lasky sought to entice into the moviehouse) as an icon of independent and adventurous womanhood, we wonder whether Tambling's attempt to cast her solely as the instrument of a repressive gender ideology is too easy. Tambling neglects, as well, the professional benefits singers may have gotten from their filmmaking. Farrar writes, "I remember Mr. Gatti asking pointedly, before Caruso signed his [film] contract, if I thought the movies would react unfavorably on his opera prestige? . . . I assured him solemnly that I had experienced no lack of enthusiasm in my opera and concert audiences, and that an artist should consider every legitimate domain that would encourage his popularity and emolument" (171). The greater the number of venues, the less a singer had to depend on one, whether opera or concerts, for a living; the greater the popularity, the higher the fee; the greater the income, the greater the control over one's career. Making films provided freedom and creative autonomy in this very practical sense as well.

But singers in silent films? Voiceless or de-voiced divas? Film theorists have long characterized classic sound film as a form that functions to silence women as it frames them as objects of male desire and pleasure, and certainly the importing of female performers from stage and opera into film helped to reinforce the construction of women in film as silenced objects of a masculine gaze and as archetypal players of roles.[4] At the very beginnings of film is the spectacular silencing of the very women known to have voices, of women whose professional lives and authority were grounded in their voices. Yet here, too, there are complications to a reading that would see only repression here. Farrar was quite literally without a voice during a later period of filmmaking with DeMille (she made films for a twelve-week period after the opera and concert seasons were over). Troubled with severe vocal problems and unable to convince Gatti to let her spend a year in silence rather than have surgery, she had an operation at the close of the spring season and was ordered not to speak or sing for the summer. In a "mother" section of *Such Sweet Compulsion* (in the corresponding "daughter" narrative, Farrar speaks only of vocal problems, not of the specifics of surgery and silence; she has a reputation to uphold), we learn that "the movies were a godsend. Her mind was kept busy, her body active, that summer of imposed silence" (150). In other words, while on one level silent films rendered and represented as voiceless the very women known for their voices—a silenced Carmen, like a silenced diva, must have had considerable appeal to conservatives—on another level making films provided the periods of vocal rest necessary for maintaining the voice while still allowing the diva's career to progress. To be silent in one medium, as Farrar reasoned to Gatti, helped to increase the numbers who wanted to hear her voice in another. Here again, Farrar's circumstances provide an epitomizing extreme, as "mother" continues: "A fall concert season was to precede the opera season and, aside from several intimates, we had tried to keep news of Geraldine's vocal condition out of public and press domain. This was fairly easy in Hollywood, since the super-subject of all subjects there was exclusively the movies" (150).

Like the silent film industry, the phonograph industry had also tapped "high art" as a way to construct itself as respectable and hence desirable to middle-class consumers. The industry's production and promotion of classical discs helped to make the practice of listening to classical music, especially vocal music, a feature of domestic entertainment for an aspiring American middle class.[5] By the time sound was added to film in the late twenties, the middle-class public had already been primed, as it were, for sound pictures that, like the silents before them, sought to appropriate the prestige of classical music. Looking back on her career, Farrar calls the last of the films she made during her first year with Lasky and DeMille "a special story, the type that has since served anybody who can lay claim to a good chirp—how the little home-town girl makes good in grand opera, upon merit and virtue; it was called *Temptation*" (144). Opera themes and plots along the lines of Farrar's *Temptation* were frequent in films of the thirties. Early in the decade, Jeanette MacDonald played opera singers in *Oh for a Man* (1930) and *Children of Dreams* (1931) and Met soprano Grace Moore starred in a 1930 bio-pic about Jenny Lind called *A Lady's Morals*, but it was not until 1934, with the enormous popularity of Moore's *One Night of Love*, that film studios began to recruit singers in earnest and Met stars began to follow in the footsteps of Farrar. Columbia had Moore; Paramount signed her colleague Gladys Swarthout, and RKO signed Lily Pons, a French soprano who was also making a career at the Met.[6]

Directed by Victor Schertzinger, *One Night of Love*, which follows the "small-town girl makes it big in opera" scenario, was both a popular and critical success (six Oscar nominations, including Best Picture and Best Actress). The film rewrites *Trilby* as comic romance. American singer Mary Barrett travels to Italy for voice lessons and is there "discovered" (men are always "discovering" women and their voices in these films) by a famous teacher and impresario, the suave Giulio Monteverdi, who will take

Barrett as a student only if she agrees to turn over to him complete control of her life; he must monitor every breath she takes, every morsel she eats. He likens himself to a sculptor, but Barrett soon finds him to be more po- liceman than Pygmalion. "I've been in jail for two years," she later com- plains as she escapes from Monteverdi to "go out and go crazy," to "be human just once." Despite this rebellion against the rigors of her training, she is in love with Monteverdi, and he, although he had previously learned not to mix business with love, is in love with her. When a former pupil re- turns and tries to win Monteverdi back, Barrett, at this point a rising star, fears she has lost him. She weeps, acts out, threatens to break engagements, and runs off. Tambling, who reads the film as a Jamesian study of a young American abroad, sees Barrett's temperamental star behavior as evidence that Europe has corrupted her New World innocence (44). We, rather, see her fits of temper as stereotypical diva behavior; the erotic rival is, after all, a former pupil of Monteverdi's who is now, as well, a professional rival.

We have argued that divahood is the sign of female excess in masculinist narratives about female singers, and female excess is contained best, *One Night of Love* implies, when jailer and beloved are one. When Barrett decides that she has lost Monteverdi, she doesn't run off to marry someone else, although someone else, a rich young American, is available. Instead, she decides to manage her own career. She leaves Monteverdi in Europe—"I can sing without you," she declares—and goes to the Metro- politan, a venue for which, Monteverdi had decided, she wasn't yet ready. Not surprisingly, performing the tale of Cio-Cio-San's suicide over the loss of Pinkerton is near professional suicide for Barrett. Rehearsals for her de- but, in *Butterfly*, go badly. She is nervous; she can't sing well; she walks out on rehearsals. "So this is the great prima donna," comments the dis- gusted Met manager ironically, walkouts being consummate prima donna behavior. On opening night she can't bring herself to go on until she sees Monteverdi in the prompt box. She then takes the stage and sings her part beautifully while he mouths to her "I love you," a declaration that, accord- ing to the logic of the prompt box, she will echo.

Here the film ends, with a comic revision of *Butterfly*'s tragic ending. The lovers are reunited and looking to marriage. Endings like this prompt Tambling to conclude, correctly, we think, that *One Night of Love* and other thirties diva films work to convince viewers (especially female viewers, we would argue) that the romantic ideal is operatic (41). To love is to live in operatic glamor and passion. The heterosexual couple is figured as harmo- nious duet. And although it's not clear what will become of Barrett's career, it's difficult, given all the effort Monteverdi has invested in her voice, to imagine that she will give up performing or that he, like so many husbands we have seen in other diva narratives, will demand she leave the stage. But this utopian promise of the harmonious blending of love and work is less progressive than it may first appear: it is grounded in renunciation. Barrett doesn't have to renounce her career because she has finally done what Monteverdi first demanded, renounce herself. She has already been suitably tamed and domesticated by the realization that she can't sing without the pedagogue/policeman/husband. Sculptor and prompter, Monteverdi is in complete control, and Barrett is his greatest work.

With their performance scenes, their backstage looks at the process of putting on a show, and their stress on the suppression of wayward individualism, opera-themed musical films share many of the conventions and values of classic Hollywood musicals. But the wayward individuals contained in these films are women with voices, voices good enough to allow them to survive successfully, even opulently, on their own. From this vantage point, diva films of the thirties can be linked to another genre popular during the years of the studio system, the "woman's picture," films that, from the career comedies of Rosalind Russell to the noir *Mildred Pierce*, centered on a woman's life and her choices.[7] Despite the conservative closure of women's films—heroines choose love over career and thereby suggest that a woman's real career is marriage and motherhood—the narratives leading up to that choice reveal other possibilities and, further, represent women as strong, smart, capable, and ambitious. Despite their official enforcement of traditional gender relations, these films, like many masculinist diva narratives, provided women viewers with representations of female strength and autonomy and thus points of possible identification.[8] Jeanine Basinger describes this "paradox" of the woman's film: "If it is true, as many suggest, that Hollywood films repressed women and sought to teach them what they ought to do, then it is equally clear that . . . the movies first had to bring to life the opposite of their own morality. . . . In asking the question, What should a woman do with her life? they created the possibility of an answer different from the one they intended to provide at the end of the movie" (6–7).

Most of the opera-themed films of the thirties are versions of a masculinist "diva domesticated" narrative, but in them conservative closure conflicts with depictions of divahood's obvious attractions—wealth, glamor, independence, power. The Jeanette MacDonald–Nelson Eddy romance *Rose Marie* (1936, directed by W. S. Van Dyke from a Rodgers and

Hammerstein musical), for example, recounts the taming of diva Marie De Flor by Canadian mountie Sergeant Bruce. The opening scenes quickly establish that De Flor has everything—money, fame, power over her own life—except, according to her maid, love. (We have not seen her pining, however.) Already an outlaw by her divahood—she is ambitious, imperious, temperamental, manipulative, cruel, self-absorbed—she identifies only with her outlaw brother, who has just escaped from prison. Showing a misguided (brother Jack is a rotter) but commendable family loyalty, she jeopardizes her career by running out on her engagements and secretly making her way to the Canadian backwoods to find her brother and help him escape the country.

Stuck in a country town and robbed by the "half-breed" her brother has sent to guide her to him, the diva tries to get a job singing in a saloon. Upstaged and unsettled by the sexual suggestiveness of Belle, the saloon's regular singer, De Flor withdraws from the competition Belle has forced on her (thus winning the status of "good girl" and assuring the audience that despite her years on the stage she has not lost all of her feminine modesty) and begins to talk to the suave and cultured mountie who is after her brother. Her voice has, of course, given her identity away. "I'd know your voice in a million," Bruce later acknowledges, and it doesn't take him much longer to recognize that diva Marie De Flor must be the sister of murderer Jack Flowers. Despite their mutual attraction, De Flor knows that she must shake Bruce and find her brother. Bruce, once he knows who De Flor is, sees her as a way to track Flowers. At one point, the diva does manage to get away from the mountie, but once again her voice gives her away. Riding through the wooded mountains, she sings and enjoys the echo; he tracks the sound. The echo figures the diva's singing as a solitary and narcissistic pleasure, an excessive self-doubling that marks her for the policing forces. In popular narratives about police and villains, of course, to implicate oneself, to confess to transgression, is to "sing."

Tracking the sister finally leads Bruce to the brother. After Jack's capture, a depressed Marie returns to her career. She returns not to Juliet, the first role we see her perform, but to Tosca. The film opens with a performance of *Romeo and Juliet*—calling up, in order to duplicate, Shakespeare's themes of star-crossed love and clan feud. Warring Montagues and Capulets epitomize the distance between those other two clans, divas and police. Warring families are also doubled in the backwoods scenes by Bruce's narrative about warring Indian tribes and a pair of cross-tribal lovers who communicate through the "Indian Love Song" that the mountie and diva appropriate, during friendly times, to represent/express their love for each other. The embedding of *Tosca* adds a further gloss on De Flor's circumstances. Her depression leads to total collapse, a climactic breakdown during a performance of the third act of Puccini's opera, the execution scene. De Flor thinks she hears Bruce's singing voice, becomes disoriented, falls out of character, and finally faints just before Tosca's suicide.

The pans of the camera across the audience show that only the diva and the film viewer hear Bruce. De Flor has so internalized his voice that she hallucinates it, an apt image for her reinscription in the patriarchal order. Tosca is a diva, of course, a diva who helps an "outlaw" lover help an escaped prisoner and who, in self-defense, kills an evil policeman. Divahood, the displacement of *Romeo and Juliet* by *Tosca* implies, is suicidal. By falling quite literally out of character just before Tosca is to make her famous fall to her death, the diva De Flor avoids self-destruction. The difference signals that *Rose Marie* is a romance, not a tragedy. The parallels between the film's narrative and the opera's emphasize significant differences as well, like the difference between Bruce's good cop and Scarpia's bad cop. Godlike in its disembodiment, Bruce's voice, not De Flor's, is the transporting and saving singing voice. While Tosca rightly rejects the advances of the evil Scarpia, head of the Roman police, De Flor saves herself by loving the good policeman Bruce. He, not brother Jack, is the man worth sacrificing her career for.

The next scene finds De Flor much changed—not merely depressed but completely passive. She hasn't sung in six months and, rejecting a proposal for a tour, declares: "I don't care if I ever sing again." Her manager is distraught; he misses the imperious ambitious diva and complains that she hasn't fired him in six months. "I was so sure you'd be yourself again, that I'd hear your voice echoing through the hills," he laments and in so doing ironically figures De Flor not as diva but as the wood nymph Echo. After he leaves, however, she does break into song, into the "Indian Love Song" that she and Bruce had agreed to use when one needed the other. Her desire is rewarded; the mountie walks in and they sing the song together. No more solitary self-doubling: the diva's voice joins in a harmonious duet with the good policeman, a duet that promises happy coupling and the end of her career. The film is titled after the diva's birth name, Rose Marie Flowers; by loving Bruce and internalizing his voice, diva Marie De Flor returns to herself, Rose Marie.

As attractive as the wealth, power, and glamor of divahood may be, then, these films present it as a detour on the road to a woman's "natural" destiny, heterosexual coupling and domesticity. Few of these thirties opera films make this ideological trajectory more clear than *I Dream Too Much* (1935, directed by John Cromwell), a comedy starring soprano Lily Pons as a reluctant opera star and Henry Fonda as an unsuccessful American opera composer who lives in Paris. In the opening scene, Annette throws a tantrum during her singing lesson, but this spectacle of female anger and diva temperament reduces Annette to the status of a child in need of discipline—the singer is rebelling against singing—while confirming that divahood is not her natural bent but something imposed on her. Her singing master declares that he will make her a singer in spite of herself; she asserts that she doesn't want to sing, that she wants something more—at the moment, to go to the village festival and to dance. Again she is figured as childish, but also as commendably girlish. As she runs away her teacher threatens to send her to a convent. Nunhood and divahood—we have seen the connection before—are linked here as equally imprisoning (her escape entails climbing a wall, literally "going over the wall") and as similarly misguided channelings of healthy heterosexual erotic energy.

She falls from the top of the wall onto Jonathan, the composer, whom she will marry within a few hours. They go to the festival together; she wins a bride doll; they dance and they drink too much. The scene shifts to the next morning; they share a bedroom (but not a bed), and Annette informs Jonathan that they were married the night before. She has, it appears, fallen into his life permanently. We are meant to see Annette's actions in marrying the drunken Jonathan as less manipulative than single-minded; the ambition her singing teacher wants her to channel toward her voice is channeled instead toward traditional womanhood, toward the step beyond parties and dances.[9] For all her singing talent, she is not by "nature" a prima donna.

Jonathan is nevertheless distraught. Marriage and family will interrupt his work: "Who ever heard of a composer with a baby?" he asks and suggests that in his frustration he will "probably beat you." "I wouldn't care," she responds lightly. The film reminds that we are in the realm of comic fantasy by gesturing toward the extremes it refuses. Men can be wife-beaters; women can be masochists. But as Jonathan will not be a wife-beater, so Annette will not be a man-eater, despite the fact that she is always eating (she even steals and consumes a small boy's macaroons). Her nonstop consumption is less a figure for female dissatisfaction and hunger than a comic reference to male fears of the vagina dentata, fears that the singing mouth is always the devouring mouth. The petite Annette remains just that; she never grows large or fat or monstrous. Indeed, she manages to soothe Jonathan's mock brutality and convince him that marriage won't hinder his work only when she assures him that she can cook, that she provides rather than takes. For Annette marriage doesn't conflict with career; it becomes the way to make sure she won't have one. We never, after all, see her *choose* to be a diva; she only takes up singing opera at the direction or in the service of men.

On their return to Jonathan's Parisian garret, Annette proves herself a model of domestic and culinary efficiency, even if the vacuum cleaner does disturb Jonathan's concentration and even though they fight when Annette announces that she wants to start a family. ("I want a baby, not ideas"— again, the ambition and assertive directness of the stereotypical prima donna is placed in the service of conventional duties.) One of their neighbors is a veteran vaudevillian whose act includes a trained female seal. When he calls the seal a "lazy hussy," we recall the singing teacher's similar complaint about Annette. No wonder the sensible and pragmatic Annette would rather be a wife than a diva: female performers are little more than a variety of trained seal.

Happy homemakers sing in the kitchen, of course. Hitherto ignorant of Annette's talent and training, Jonathan appropriates her voice as soon as he hears it: "I've discovered your voice. . . . I'm going to make you an opera star. . . . You can sing my opera." Putting his own work aside, he takes a job as a tour guide in order to pay for her lessons. What might at first appear to be a role reversal that departs from the conservatism of the narrative is, in the end, merely a different route to his primary goal of getting his opera heard. Annette, after all, has no ambition to be a diva—although she does enjoy singing popular songs at a restaurant to supplement their income. When Jonathan finds out, he admires her performance but forbids the repertoire: "Such songs will ruin your voice." She counters, "We should forget about my voice. . . . I don't want to be an opera singer, I just want to be your wife."

Their marriage deteriorating, Annette takes Jonathan's opera, *Echo and Narcissus*, to impresario Paul Darcy without Jonathan's knowledge. She sings portions for him, including "I am the Echo, you're the song." *I Dream Too Much* uses the myth in a different way than *Rose Marie*; here the reference is, of course, a comment on Jonathan's self-absorption and Annette's self-effacing loyalty, but the reference also serves to further diminish the diva by figuring her as the woman fated never to express herself, destined always to repeat the discourse of another. Echo and Trilby have much in common. Predictably, Darcy is more impressed with Annette's voice than Jonathan's opera, and like Jonathan before him, he declares that he has "discovered" Annette's voice and will make her a star. Again the *Trilby* narrative appears; he promises to "change [her] completely into a perfect creation." Significantly, Darcy is taken with Annette not only because she has a great voice but because she is petite and attractive, a departure from the conventional singer, who is, he says, "supposed to be large and homely." That Annette is more exemplar of True Womanhood than stereotypical monstrous prima donna is, for Darcy, a marketing advantage, but it is also a reassurance to the audience that Annette is not "by nature" a diva, a reminder, at the moment of her big break, that she prefers conventional womanhood to divahood.

His prerogatives usurped, feeling increasingly powerless and marginal, Jonathan protests that he doesn't want another man to remake his wife. Annette tries to soothe him—"If I succeed maybe I can help you"—but this appeal to Jonathan's self-interest doesn't save him from self-pity, envy, and resentment. Diva narratives, we have argued, are about the possibility that women might speak authoritatively, that "objects" might become speaking subjects; despite Annette's (and the film's) attempts to diminish herself, Jonathan knows that her voice gives her status and authority. At a party after her Paris debut in *Lakmé*, a drunk and angry Jonathan declares, "Even if you become the greatest singer in the world, you will still be just a silly little girl." The attack is a symptom of Jonathan's envy and his own fear that her success has unmanned him, turned him into a girl, but it also brings together the two positions, diva and little girl, that the film has all along worked to conflate—divahood is immature, potentially regressive, merely a stage on the way to wifehood.

When Jonathan later overhears that she plans secretly to finance a production of his opera, he leaves her, declaring, "I'm tired of being a lap dog to an opera singer." Failed composer and usurped Svengali, Jonathan sees himself in the feminine position, as a pet. Without irony, she promises to give up her career for him and laments, "I wish I had never sung a note." There is little here to suggest that this offer of retirement is, as it was for Grace Moore the year before in *One Night of Love*, a manipulative ruse, a bit of prima donna duplicity. When Jonathan scoffs and tells her that she really does want a career, we see this less as a direct hit than as a projection of Jonathan's own ambition. Indeed, Jonathan's ambition, self-absorption, competitiveness, and temper make him the real prima donna in the scene, as the film's embedding of *Lakmé*'s narrative of female devotion and martyrdom emphasizes.

The deserted wife goes on with her career, eventually becoming rich, famous, glamorous and influential. This seems abundant recompense for the loss of any man, let alone the weak and whiny Jonathan, but Annette, of course, is unhappy and collapses during a performance of *Rigoletto*. "I lost everything I really wanted," she declares and tells Darcy that she plans to retire. "Have you gone mad?" he, and we, ask. "Yes, and I like it," she answers. Loss of her domestic life makes this diva demented (a development that constructs desire for conventional womanhood as "sanity"), and in a scene that parallels her opening escape from the singing master, Annette runs away from Darcy and her commitments. "I want some fun; I'm tired of being cooped up like a canary." To sing is to be caged; professional, not domestic, space is the realm of confinement.

During this rebellious escape from professional commitments she again runs into Jonathan, this time into the cab he now drives to earn a living. After a few icy moments, they enjoy driving around Paris and end up jailed for wading in a public pond. Confinement as a couple reinforces Annette's desire for confinement in the couple: when Darcy comes to bail her out, she declares, "I'm going to be a taxi driver's wife and have a baby." The impresario is upset, but a policeman smiles approvingly. Yet happy domesticity finally depends, the film makes clear and Annette sees, on a husband's professional success, even if it takes a savvy and well-connected wife to insure it. Convinced that "Jonathan needs a little success," she again goes behind his back and reworks his opera into a musical, titled *I Dream Too Much*, that Darcy produces to great success. The repetitions in the action stress the absolute necessity of the major difference, Jonathan's success. "She sings my songs just as I write them," says a happy and now celebrated Jonathan. As she promised, as she has all along desired, Annette places her career and talents in the service of his. Annette is finally fully Echo, and Jonathan can finally stop resenting her.

And Jonathan can remain Narcissus. His forced detour through feminine dependence and powerlessness has taught him little. In the final scene, they are rich, Jonathan is successful, and Annette is retired. "Some people are born to greatness," he declares. "And some people are born to have babies," responds Annette, echoing his sentence structure while dotingly playing with their child.[10] The echo of Malvolio, of course, is another bit of gentle fun at Jonathan's expense, an indulgent, and finally accepting, recognition of his vanity and his willingness to forget that his big break depended on his wife's money and power. Jonathan's convenient lapse of memory functions to reinforce our recognition that all his success depends on his wife's success. By having Annette desire domesticity more than divahood from the start, and by constructing Jonathan's success as both a derivative of hers and a vehicle by which she achieves her desire of full-time wife- and motherhood, the film constructs a rough, semiegalitarian reciprocity within its undeniable conservatism.

The transformation of *Echo and Narcissus* from opera to musical comedy, Tambling observes, enacts the "triumph of American music over Europe" (45). It also serves as a model for a shift in musical films during the thirties. By the forties, the young woman who goes to New York is headed for Broadway rather than the Metropolitan Opera. While the early film industry tried to borrow the prestige of opera, of European "high culture," it soon shifted its attention to American music. As film domesticated the diva, so it domesticated the musical genres it privileged. Plots structured by a conflict between classical music and jazz or swing allowed the musical to "[affirm] itself while applauding popular forms" (Feuer 55–56). A number of diva films in the mid- and late thirties anticipate this shift. *San Francisco*, starring Jeanette MacDonald as an opera singer and Clark Gable as a saloon owner named Blackie, shows the diva romantically caught between an attentive, gentlemanly, rich, and bloodless opera patron and the self-absorbed and rough-hewn Blackie (we know he is salvageable because a priest, played by Spencer Tracy, has faith in him). After choosing the opera patron, and thus her career, she runs to the bankrupt Blackie's aid and wins a performance contest so that he can use the prize money to save his bar. She wins by singing the title song, "San Francisco," not in operatic but in dance-hall style. The victory of popular over elite vocal styles is a pyrrhic one in this rather heavy-handed film, however. The diva-cum-dance-hall-belter no sooner walks off with the prize than the 1915 San Francisco earthquake occurs and levels saloon and opera house alike. In the final scene, the opera patron is dead, a penitent Blackie is on his knees, and the diva joins the rest of the homeless survivors in singing hymns.

This sort of generic/aesthetic leveling might not be surprising in MacDonald's work; she made it to the opera stage only after making it big in film. Met diva Lily Pons, however, seems to have made her film career playing women who reject the very operatic career that Pons herself depended on and cultivated. Like *I Dream Too Much*, her 1937 *That Girl from Paris* (directed by Leigh Jason) features a French opera singer who rejects opera as imprisoning. The diva walks out on her wedding to a rich opera patron who has the power to make her career, falls in love with an American dance-band musician named Windy (her rival for his affections is

Lucille Ball), follows him to America, and, after many plot machinations that have her back on the opera stage and once again about to marry the patron—behavior that is clearly presented as prostitution—she ends up with her American man and his American music.

The representation of the opera/popular music conflict as a competition of vocal styles in *Rose Marie* and *San Francisco* reappears in Busby Berkeley's 1939 *Babes in Arms*, in which Judy Garland represents swing and clearly gets the better of Betty Jaynes and her operatic voice.[11] Given the dearth of opera-themed films in the forties, we might say that *Babes in Arms* confirms the triumph of popular over elite culture, of America over Europe, of film over stage as mass entertainment. The classic Hollywood musical strives for the status of folk art; it works to construct an illusion that we are watching amateur performers whose singing and dancing are figured as the spontaneous overflow of powerful emotions rather than the performance of composed and choreographed work (Feuer 3–15). The diva narrative, with its stress on rigorous training, hard work, and money—even in its conservative versions like *One Night of Love*—had progressively less to offer a genre that increasingly celebrated American forms and cast professionals as amateur singers. Finally, the fading of the diva from Hollywood film might also be a function of classic film's tendency in the forties to reinforce the construction of women as figures to be seen and not heard. Working women who have a say in their destiny and the wider world cause more anxiety in an era when, as in the forties, women increasingly occupied the jobs vacated by men who were drafted. Noting this shift to more anxious and repressive representations of women with (speaking) voices in forties film, Amy Lawrence points out that "films produced in the mid 1940s . . . return obsessively to the issue or, more accurately, the *problem* of woman's speech" (107). For example, in *Sorry, Wrong Number* (1948) bedridden Barbara Stanwyck's voice is the only thing that keeps her from total passivity; talking on the phone, her sole compensation for her immobility, gets her killed. At the other extreme is another film released in 1948, *Johnny Belinda*, which stars Jane Wyman as a mute.[12]

*I*f it is not surprising to find so many divas and opera plots in early Hollywood musical films, the many diva plots in another film genre, horror, are predictable as well. Basinger notes that when the impresario, usually an asexual helper-figure in the woman's picture, "goes mad with his desire to control and/or love the woman, the genre moves . . . toward the horror category" (317). The first film of *The Phantom of the Opera* is a silent version released in 1925; at least three others, plus a musical, followed. *Trilby* has spawned three *Svengali* films, including one starring a young Jodie Foster. Mad impresarios are not the only figures of excess in diva narratives, of course. Masculinist diva narratives, as we have suggested, conventionally represent the diva as a monster, or at least potentially monstrous. Italian director Dario Argento's 1991 *Terror at the Opera*, something of a slasher *Phantom of the Opera* in which a young singer named Betty is terrorized during a production of Verdi's *Macbeth*, tries to combine these two strains of diva horror. The protector turns predator, but the singer's potential for monstrous—phallic—excess is consistently emphasized.

The opening credits roll over a rehearsal scene in which prima donna Mara Chekova, singing Lady Macbeth, throws a temper tantrum. The production's live ravens, which fly around the opera house, are driving her crazy. Accusing one bird of never taking its eye off her, she storms out of the opera house and is hit by a car. The stereotypical bad diva dispatched, her young, attractive, modest, and sweet-tempered understudy, Betty, gets the call. Neither as ambitious nor as competitive as Chekova, Betty is reluctant to step in. She is too young for the part and her voice isn't right for it, she tells the director; she doesn't want to make her debut in a work so famous for bringing bad luck. As we have seen, the film diva worth saving is always the reluctant diva. Betty works hard to set herself off not only from Chekova but also from that monstrously unsexed, dagger-bearing, but finally self-destructive female Lady Macbeth.

Opening night is a triumph for Betty, but bad luck for the usher who finds the phantom slasher in a closed box and is murdered when he tries to evict him. Murder and mayhem occur on stage and off. A private, off-stage murder becomes a public spectacle within a spectacle when it interrupts the performance. The slasher is as much a master of spectacular murder as the production's director, who made horror films before moving to opera and the murder-filled *Macbeth*, and by extension, as Argento himself, known for his highly aestheticized murder scenes.[13] Opera seems ever the elite art of choice for filmmakers intent on leveling aesthetic hierarchies. Murder is a fine art; diva and murder are linked as objects of specular fascination; diva and murderer are linked as artists.

The scene of Betty's debut performance emphasizes the thematics of voyeurism and spectatorship that the film stresses from the first few frames (when we see nearly the entire opera house reflected in a raven's eye) and continues to stress in the scenes leading up to Betty's debut (from a ventilation duct in her flat we see her in bed and assume we are caught in the point of view of the slasher). The film also keeps blurring the boundaries between private viewing and public spectacle. The film shifts, for example, from a view of Betty on stage through the slasher's binoculars to the view of a young girl, obviously a fan, watching Betty's debut on a television simulcast. The young girl, it turns out, is the person who watches Betty's bedroom through the vent. Even when she isn't singing this diva is subject to the gaze of others, under constant surveillance. Her voice is not powerful enough to overcome the forces and apparatus that would confine her in the objectifying gaze, in the small box of the television screen, in technology. The issue is whether she submits to these disciplines because she is a "good" diva or whether they are imposed upon her, by fans, by the film, because she has the potential to become a monstrous diva.

Among those who flock backstage to congratulate Betty after her performance is a policeman, Alan Santini. We assume he is there to investigate the murder and are, with Betty, surprised that he comes to her in the role of fan, or, as he says, her "first fan." Betty assumes that being a cop and being a fan of opera (divas) are incompatible, a version of the lesson of *Rose Marie*. Neither Santini nor his men find the slasher, of course, and later, after the opera house has emptied, the phantom breaks into a costume cabinet and slashes at Betty's costume with a knife. The shredded costume makes clear that the slasher's ultimate target is the new diva *as* diva—and all the Lady Macbeth-like traits that stereotype implies.

But first there are other murders to stage for Betty's benefit. The scene shifts to Betty and the young stage manager in bed; she apologizes for being a "disaster" as a lover, and he points out, with some disappointment, that her reticence and discomfort set her off from the usual prima donna. Tradition has it that singers are "incredibly horny," he tells her, that they make love before a performance to relax the voice. He leaves the room for a moment, and the slasher grabs Betty from behind. He gags her, binds her to a pillar, and tapes needles to the top of her cheeks so that she must keep her eyes open as he repeatedly stabs the stage manager on his return. We see the murder through Betty's eyes; the image resembles a view from behind prison bars. Immobilized and silenced, she is forced here, and later when the slasher murders the costume mistress in front of her, into the position of the voyeur. Before he cuts her loose, he fondles her chest from behind and says in a low, growling voice, "It's not true, Betty. You're a bitch in heat." To the slasher, she's a siren. Is she or isn't she a "true" diva?

Steven Shaviro argues that these scenes of forced voyeurism and aestheticized murder make the diva complicit in the murders by making her watch: "The cop in *Blue Steel* and the opera singer in *Terror at the Opera* are overtly appalled by the violence they are compelled to see, yet there's a latent—secretly desirable—erotic thrill in the way these gory spectacles are produced for *them*. They do not 'identify' with the murderers, but they are transformed, and even energized, by their involuntary participation. It is precisely to the extent that these scenarios are so blatantly prurient and por-nographic that they resist being classified according to the conventional bi-nary of sadistic male violence and helpless female passivity" (49).

Shaviro is correct in arguing that the film refuses to model spectatorship on a simple gender opposition—males, females, and ravens are all watchers; we even see the diva peer through a peephole (at us). But does watching the violence and excess make Betty complicit in it, or are the violence and excess produced to make her recognize a complicity that by the slasher's logic, and perhaps the film's, already exists and to reconfine the diva in another role, traditional womanhood? Betty is immo-bilized; the needles create the illusion that she is viewing the scene through prison bars. The murders are as much about confinement as complicity. Moreover, we didn't find the energizing thrill that Shaviro attributes to Betty, in part because Betty's escape after the murder of the stage manager has her wandering the night streets in hysterical fear until she is finally res-cued by the director. Viewing the murder has the effect of transforming her into a stereotypical female who needs a man to rescue her (here the "direc-tor" himself), a hysterical woman who weeps and screams rather than a privileged and powerful diva who sings.[14]

Shaviro's reading also leads us to expect that the "transforming en-ergy" will somehow affect the diva's performance, that the eroticized visual will somehow make the vocal more erotic, but the film doesn't offer a scene that clearly sets up such a link. In other words, by attending only to the visual and not to the vocal, by, that is, neglecting the fact that Betty is a diva, or has the potential to be a diva, Shaviro's reading misses the fact that Betty is already connected with excess and with violence to traditional gen-der categories. He wants to see the scene operating to break down gender binaries, but as a diva Betty has already done so. The diva is always the site where gender and related binary oppositions break down and, in mascu-linist narratives, the place where those traditional oppositions need to be reasserted. The slasher wants to make Betty see erotic violence because he already attributes to her an unfeminine violence and desire that he wants to punish.

The slasher turns out to be the policeman. As protector becomes predator, so the objectifying voyeuristic gaze, this turn makes clear, is also a monitoring gaze of surveillance. Santini had earlier murdered Betty's mother, also a diva. Betty's "first fan" had wanted to be her mother's "first man," but, according to Santini, she was a withholding siren. "You are just like your mother; she tortured me; I was her slave." Divas must be confined in victimhood before they victimize others. They are sirens who drive the forces of order to madness; they are as well, given that slashing is generally a symptom of impotence in horror films, Medusas who castrate. Like mother, like daughter is the raging policeman's worry; thus Betty must die. Divahood, as the policeman's use of a logic dependent on heredity implies, is by nature a potential in all women.

We don't know if Betty's mother was the siren Santini paints her, but we do know that questions about the extent to which Betty is a diva, or has the potential to become one, have haunted the film from its start—from Betty's attempts to separate herself from Mara Chekova's temper and competitiveness to the ambiguous scenario of the opera singer who has sex with the stage manager while claiming incompetence. During the final chase, Betty convinces Santini not to stab her by saying, "I realize it now, I am like my mother." After he is captured, she reverses herself and declares, "It's not true. I'm not like my mother." Was mother a siren or a Mara Chekova? Santini, in his madness, thinks he is killing off another dangerous diva who refuses to submit to male desire and authority. Although the film doesn't extract so final a punishment for Betty's having a voice, it doesn't reward her for it either.

While recent American slasher films, Carol Clover observes, tend to show the "Final Girl" assuming the masculine role and becoming her own rescuer (35–64), in this Italian film Betty must be rescued by a squad of policemen. Nor is there after Santini's arrest a triumphant return to the stage, which would solidify Betty's position as terrorized innocent and Santini's as vanquished evil. Rather, the final scene follows Betty's eyes as she looks at the natural landscape around her (Santini's capture has taken place in a mountain valley) and says, "I no longer want to be with anyone, I'm not like anybody. . . . I like the rain, the clouds, the insects." Joining the side of "nature," she takes up women's traditional place. Using her voice to pronounce her own exile and powerlessness, that voice is now a childlike monotone, catatonic. Her condition recalls the sleepwalking/mad scene of Verdi's opera and further suggests the diva Betty's diminishment, paralysis, and reinscription into traditional womanhood. This is, of course, rather like the state in which Santini confined her during the murder scenes—her voiced quelled and her power to move restricted. Announcing her otherness, "I'm not like anybody," she also announces her withdrawal and renunciation, her voluntary marginalization. She seeks not the urban cultural centers where she can become rich and famous, not the powers and pleasures that divahood can provide, but the simplicity of nature. As in so many of the musical films we discussed earlier, the potential diva, potential horror, is tamed as she renounces stage and ambition. But this is, finally, a horror film and not a musical; just as the film closes, we see Betty's hand free a lizard. The gesture can be read as confirmation that she has renounced "phallic" divahood, but it can also suggest that she still has "phallic" powers to let loose on the world. The final horror might be that the diva as phallicized woman, as unsexed as Lady Macbeth, might always return, that Betty is the uncanny return of the siren mother.

As *Terror at the Opera* suggests, more recent films about divas—a theme more interesting now to European than American directors—depart from the model of Hollywood films of the thirties, which concentrated on the diva's life and choices. Films like Istvan Szabo's *Meeting Venus* (1990) tend to focus on male responses to the diva and the consequences for men when they desire a diva.[15] We want to close this truncated tour through diva films by looking at what is perhaps the best-known of recent films about divas, Jean-Jacques Beineix's *Diva* (1981), based on Delacorta's thriller novel of the same title. As critics have pointed out, Beineix's film is a postmodern tale about the myth of self-presence and about the separability of women and their voices.[16] Despite the courtship of eager record companies, African-American singer Cynthia Hawkins (soprano Wilhelminia Fernandez) refuses to allow her exquisite voice to be recorded. A young delivery man with a hidden tape recorder, Jules, does manage to tape her during a Paris concert. When word of this high-quality bootleg recording leaks out, a Taiwanese company (Taiwan does not recognize international copyright—in the novel the company is Japanese) seeks to get the tape from Jules any way it can. Meanwhile, Nadia, a former prostitute and current mistress of crime boss and Paris police official Saporta, makes a tape implicating him in an international drug and prostitution ring and, while running from Saporta's henchmen, drops it into the saddlebags of Jules's moped just before they murder her in order to silence her. Through most of the film, then, Jules is chased—by the recording company's men, Saporta's thugs, and the police investigating (under Saporta's direction) Nadia's murder—for one or the other of the tapes.

The taping links the glamorous diva with the ex-prostitute and emphasizes the conventional linkage of divas and actresses with prostitutes as women who place their bodies on public display. Jules, enthralled by the diva, is in thrall to this equation. After stealing the diva's voice with his recorder, he goes backstage for an autograph and steals the diva's dress as well. He later hires a black prostitute to wear it for him as a prelude to sex. The scene is certainly about, as critics have noted, desire, displacement, and substitution, but it is also about a particular kind of narrative of desire, what we might call the private pleasures of fan fantasy, and its dependence on and reinforcement of stereotypical images of the diva. The stereotype of the diva who is erotically, exotically, available, who is easy, the scene suggests, is a fan fantasy. When Jules finally does get to sleep in the diva's hotel suite, he sleeps on the couch. Cynthia Hawkins, unlike most representations of the diva, is African-American; here the film refuses the traditional linkage of divas and black women with hypersexuality even as it emphasizes white male desire to colonize the black female body.

On one level, however, the diva is as much a commodity in circulation as the prostitute. Nadia—who as an ex-prostitute is, as one cop puts it, "out of circulation"—wants her taped voice to circulate after her death so that Saporta will be unmasked; Cynthia Hawkins, on the other hand, wants to keep her voice from circulating in her absence.[17] Only presence, she argues, gives voice authority; only presence insures plenitude; technology always distorts. A Romantic purist in a postmodern world. Of course to record a voice is to make it infinitely reproducible, and Hawkins refuses as well the commercial advantages of her mass circulation: there should be no business in art, she argues at a press conference (apparently oblivious of the fact that it is the business of art that allows her to save her voice by singing only twice a month). "Do you often act out of caprice?" one of the reporters asks of her refusal to cash in, an ironic reworking of the stereotype of the diva as both capricious and greedily ambitious. Later, her manager, who understands that the bootleg tape threatens an infinity of unauthorized Cynthia Hawkinses who don't pay royalties, sums up the situation: "You can go on acting like a diva, or you can be a responsible artist." He offers another argument: "No voice is eternal." Voices age; presence will not always hold out the promise of perfection. In other words, he wants her to learn the lesson of Natalie, that recorded voices remain after the body producing them is gone.

The diva of postmodern, postindustrial capitalism (Jules lives in a garage filled with junked luxury cars; juxtaposed to his extensive recording equipment and this detritus of heavy industry is his shrine to Cynthia Hawkins, a poster over which he drapes her dress) is not the woman who has control of her fate by virtue of having a voice. The film and book are both titled *Diva*. The lack of a definite article gives Cynthia Hawkins's story exemplary status; we might say that the narrative is a study of postmodern *divahood*. Accompanying the film's deconstruction of the diva as privileged, empowered, and unconventionally autonomous (if still exoticized) other is a study of the diva as a construction of her (male) fans. The narrative line of the film follows the trajectory of fan fantasy: Jules appropriates the diva's dress and fantasizes about her in and out of it; she doesn't report him to the police when he returns it, however. She goes out with him instead. ("So you are a real fan," the diva says when a penitent Jules brings back the missing dress and tells her that he once traveled on his moped from Paris to Munich in order to hear her). Take from the "good" diva and she gives you more. Suffer for the diva (Jules's home is trashed and he is nearly killed), and she rewards you with her notice and affection. The fan fantasy of the heterosexual male is nostalgic for chivalry.

For all her claims of artistic autonomy and her essentialist faith that her presence insures an originary aesthetic plentitude, the diva understands herself as the construction of her fans. "I need an audience," she tells reporters demanding to know why she won't record. She tells Jules, "If you didn't exist it would be necessary to invent you." Significantly, she says this just after she has accused him of confusing her with Tosca. Jules is in love with the role of the diva (as the scene with the prostitute implies, any [black] woman can, for Jules, occupy it). As suicide, Tosca is an emblem of self-loss, "self-loss" here in the sense that the "selfhood" of the diva is always performative. We never see Cynthia Hawkins in an opera, only on the concert stage—her role is the diva. Moreover, the diva must invent the ideal fan as the fan invents, and technology repeatedly "reinvents," the diva. The circularity of this collaborative invention of diva and fan is emphasized by parallels between ideal diva and ideal fan. Denying commercial ambition, the diva declares, "I sing because I like it." Denying commercial motivation for his taping, Jules says, "I do it because I dig it." Riding his moped around Paris, Jules wears the diva's dress wrapped around his neck like a scarf; her costume becomes his.

Separable from her body, circulated in a masculine economy, the diva's voice, most critics agree, is reduced to the status of fetish. In the narrative of fan fantasy, by which desire constructs scenarios of presence and perfection, the fetish/supplement is transformed into endowment. In the fan fantasy, the fan gives the diva her voice, as the film's close makes clear. Tired of being chased, feeling guilty for having taped her voice, Jules returns to the opera house in order to bring his diva the tape. Taking her leave of Paris, the diva has walked onto the empty stage. Jules sneaks in, puts the tape on the sound system, and then meets her on stage as it plays. "It's the only tape," he assures her, and he calls it "my gift to you." Thief is transformed into patron, into source. Fantasy reigns; she is not angry, merely surprised and relieved. Listening, she says, "I've never heard myself sing." To listen to oneself is to recognize one's own division and alienation, to participate in one's own objectification, to recognize one's own lack of power and mastery over one's voice. For Koestenbaum, "it appears that the voice singing Catalani's aria is the fan's, not the diva's—as if Jules has truly appropriated her sound" (49). For us, the film implies that the diva's voice has always in a sense been the fan's, that he didn't have to "appropriate" it because it was never fully hers. Fan fantasy in a masculine economy posits the male as the source of the diva's voice. The male fan gives the diva her voice, and gives her, as well, fan's pleasure. The two positions open to the diva are commodity and debtor. Getting the tape back reinforces the lessons of having the voice taped, stolen. For all its postmodern moves, then, *Diva* tells an old story. Cynthia Hawkins is really the Solitary Reaper.

•

The Diva's Mouth

A Comic Interlude

Opera is funny. And its female star is the funniest thing about it. Witness the ease with which she is parodied by people, including young children who have never seen an opera, who know of opera only that they don't like it. And what they especially don't like is that kind of singing, that kind of voice, you know, the kind that vibrates and goes very high and seems to scream at you and pretends to ridiculous emotions and keeps at it even when it's coming out of the mouth of a woman who's supposed to be dead and who looks more like a beached whale than the helpless young beauty she's supposed to have been.

Even the most ardent fans of opera admit the charges. Opera is crazy, melodramatic, unrealistic, unnatural (that soprano Orpheus, that fifty-year-old Carmen, that two-hundred-pound Mimi), politically incorrect, and over the top. The very same qualities in the diva's voice, for instance, that lift you off the earth, can, on a bad voice day, induce a severe case of the giggles. A high-voiced Romeo can disconcert for several uncomfortable moments before the willing suspension of disbelief kicks in. The singing of mundane exchanges—"Who is it?" "Time to go." "What was I saying?"— seems sometimes forced to the point of hilarity. And the very physical gymnastics that singing (sustained, high, low, loud, dramatic) requires can seem comic. Try turning off the sound during a TV opera broadcast. Those mouths!

"Georgie was very busily engaged . . . on a water-color sketch of Olga sitting at her piano and singing. The difficulty of it was such that at times he almost despaired of accomplishing it, for the problem of how to draw her face and her mouth wide open and yet retain the likeness seemed almost insoluble" (Benson, *QL* 123). Georgie, the diva worshiper in E. F. Benson's comic Lucia novels,[1] understates or evades—as he always does—

"the problem." Not so much, that is, a problem of retaining the likeness, it is a problem of making Olga Bracely, the great diva, object of his devotion, look ridiculous, a figure of fun, all mouth. Or, worst of all, object of the sarcastic barbs of the sharp-tongued inhabitants of Riseholme and Tilling, especially Lucia.

The problem exists not only for the portrait painter but for other portraitists, the writer and the actor, as well. The large-scale work that a larger-than-life woman with a larger-than-life voice necessitates threatens always to slip from the heights of drama to the depths of unintended comedy. If, however, the comedy is intended—the hyperbolic narratives of both opera and diva *Bildungsroman* are easily exploited—then the huge mouth that threatens to envelop the diva's face, and her listener altogether, becomes a cavity of the comic. Several groups regularly both perform and parody the diva. La Gran Scena Opera, perhaps the best known, is all male, reversing the cross-dressed opera roles to campy—or more campy—effect. One of the stars of their 1985 video is the "world's oldest living diva," Gabriella Tonnoziti Casseruola. Madame Tuna (or ton of ziti) Casserole parodies the diva's size, Italianness, association with food, and tendency to sing beyond her prime. The chatty emcee, retired diva Sylvia Bills, is, of course, a campy Beverly Sills. The exaggerated performances as well as the soprano voices emerging from these manly bodies remind us of the hyperbolic nature of opera itself and of the diva role it has constructed. In late 1995 the company staged, in the manner of Adelina Patti, its Tenth Annual Farewell Concert.

Recently, two singers who perform and record as the Derivative Duo have appropriated such parody for women, often excluded from the camp scene. And like Castle's and Wood's more serious work to recover opera history for female homoeroticism, Susan Nivert and Barb Glenn's performances boldly claim opera as "part of our heritage." Opera, one of them jokes, is "sung in a foreign language so straights won't tumble to the fact that it's all about gay and lesbian relationships" (Edmonson 54). Their CD, *Opera for the Masses*, takes this supposed hidden subtext and makes it text, sung in English, leaving thereby no possibility of their audience not "tumbling" to the lesbian content. *The Magic Flute*'s ostensibly heterosexual "Thy high purpose shines right clear / Nothing's nobler than a man and wife" becomes, for example, "Feels so good to do what I like / Think I'll grow up to be a dyke." Their costumes, too, turn the heterosexual finery of the opera performance to lesbian parody—"thrift-shop cocktail dresses and red high-top tennis shoes." And the full-page photograph of them that appeared in *The Advocate* shows them open-mouthed—comically distorted, that is, in just the way that Georgie feared his portrait of Olga might be. Nivert wears glasses—have you ever seen a diva with glasses?—with her brocade dress, elaborate jewelry, and feathers. "Dime Store Divas," one critic calls them (Fillipenko). Such parody does, indeed, democratize—*Opera for the Masses*—an art that has become in the last century an art of the elite. It strips opera and its divas of their pretensions, real and imagined, and it gives back to the performers themselves control over the production. It gives back, as well, an imaginary "heritage" to a group of women traditionally invisible and almost entirely without a voice.

Not all opera or diva comedy, of course, has this overt and subversive political agenda. But the generally subversive nature of comedy itself facilitates the bursting of every bubble, and even the gentlest of comedies, like Benson's Lucia novels, play in complicated and subversively ironic ways with the diva narrative. Like Georgie, the narrative itself seems to puzzle over ways to portray the diva without the distorting effect of her open mouth, an effect that reinforces the stereotype of the dangerous diva, the autocratic, the calculating, the devouring diva, the diva dentata. She can eat you up and swallow you down. What Benson has brilliantly done is expand and exploit the diva stereotype—such expansion and exploitation quite easily comedic—by displacing it onto two "divas" who have nothing to do with opera, most notably Lucia herself, a respectable, idle, country matron, and prima donna of first Riseholme and then Tilling. The "real" diva in the series, Olga Bracely, is explicitly distanced from the stereotype, and the character called "Diva" (short for Godiva) is as well one of the benevolent figures in the narrative(s).

Olga herself is set up as a "masculine" woman—"she looked like some slim beardless boy" (QL 33)—and is almost universally admired and loved: a friendly, lively neighbor, entirely dedicated to her art. When she practices a new part for hours a day, Georgie begins "to perceive what sort of work it implied to produce the spontaneous ease with which Brünnhilde hailed the sun" (QL 124). When she sings, an "air of intense concentrated seriousness" overcomes "her gaiety, her lightness" (QL 65). In this seriousness, in this dedication to work, neither of which is ever compromised by her personal life, Olga follows the diva pattern set up by the (heretofore) women writers who, as we have seen, systematically dismantle the stereotypical diva narrative loosely associated with male writers. Like other revisionary literary divas, Olga raises, lifts, ennobles all who hear her. "The great new star sailing into the heavens had just picked him [Georgie] up by force of its superior power of attraction," even as it raised Lucia "to a magnitude she had never possessed before" (*QL* 68). Unlike the divas of more realist narratives, however, Olga is—a most surprising position for a diva—too good to be true. When, for example, she "unwittingly" exposes Lucia's musical ignorance, she quickly allies herself with Lucia's mistake; "she had made a guest of hers uncomfortable, and must at once do all she could to remedy that" (*QL* 104). When she realizes that Lucia is beginning to feel usurped, she urges Georgie to renew his allegiance: "Just attend to her, Georgie, and buck her up. Promise you will. And do it as if your heart was in it; otherwise it's no good" (*QL* 126). Lucia interprets Olga's influence as "malevolent" (*QL* 107) and her own schemes as "benevolent" (*QL* 108), but readers—and the other characters—see the situation reversed. Olga is wholly benevolent and Lucia often malevolent—especially toward Olga herself.

The title of the first Lucia novel, *Queen Lucia*, suggests the motive for this tension. It is Lucia who in her efforts to rule Riseholme has become the stereotypical diva figure; her musical pretensions and ineptitude both associate her with and distance her from the real diva, who does not at all correspond to the stereotype. For example, far from seducing men away from other women, Olga, when she realizes the extent of Georgie's adoration, gives him back to Lucia. When Georgie and Lucia marry midway through the series, it is Olga who provides the honeymoon house for their sexless idyll (WL 758). Far from indulging in petty rivalries, Olga makes sure that Lucia "wins" whenever possible. Olga "enjoys herself simply by giving to other people" (*TL* 892). Lucia, on the other hand, indulges constantly in "prima donna" behavior. It was her "habit," for example, "to arrive last at any party, as befitted the Queen of Riseholme, and to make her gracious round of the guests" (*LL* 170). She flaunts her connections to princesses and duchesses; she becomes mayor of Tilling. She sees Olga as a threatening rival ("it was . . . obvious to her mind that Olga was a pretender to the throne she had occupied for so long" [*QL* 110]) and treats her accordingly; she also sees, more accurately, Elizabeth Mapp as a rival and sets out to put her firmly in her (inferior) place, making that place official by appointing Mapp "mayoress" to her mayor. Mapp, then, in the novels after *Queen Lucia* becomes the rival diva, and Mapp, unlike Olga, is perfect for the part—spiteful, mean, and ambitious.

The parallels that the narrative sets up between Olga and Lucia and between Lucia and the diva figure are numerous and pointed. In addition to her title, "Queen of Riseholme," parallel to Olga's "Queen of Song" (*TL*

875), Lucia has a group of ardent fans—the Luciaphiles—modeled after such groups as the Gerry-Flappers. Wherever she is, Lucia also has a special, adoring, queer admirer, Georgie in Riseholme, Stephen Merriall in London, Irene Coles in Tilling. Georgie, as we have noted, temporarily switches his allegiance to the real diva, Olga, but the text takes pains to establish the parallels between him and Merriall, Olga even suggesting that Merriall is Georgie's "double" (*LL* 216) and Lucia acknowledging that they perform similar functions as her devotees (*LL* 237).

Both men are fashion-conscious. They wear identically cut trousers—that resemble "long frocks" (*LL* 168)—and similar little capes, clothes that link them to one another and suggest their joint effeminacy. There are, as well, more significant indications of their effeminacy, sign in these camp, coy texts of a latent but palpable homosexuality. Georgie's most consistent occupation, for example, is embroidery, for which the more "masculine" characters, like "the Colonel," despise him (*QL* 80); Stephen Merriall is a gossip columnist who writes under the name Hermione. Major Benjy refers to Georgie as "Miss Milliner Michael Angelo" (*ML* 564); another character asks of Stephen, "And who was the man who looked as if he had been labelled 'Man' by mistake when he was born, and ought to have been labeled 'Lady'?" (233).

When we meet them, both Olga and Lucia are married women, a fact that both Georgie and Stephen take comfort in. The men court their divas, but they make clear that their gestures of adoration have limits. Although Georgie tells Olga that he cannot go to America with her "because I adore you" (*QL* 141)—thus implying that the temptation to be her lover would be impossible to overcome—"he really wanted to dress up as a lover rather than to be one" (*QL* 109). Stephen is happy to play the part of Lucia's lover once he understands that the long looks and lingering fingers are for public consumption only; he is, he knows, "no hand . . . at amorous adventures" (*LL* 240). In the course of the novels, Lucia's husband dies. When she and Georgie think about marriage, he is adamant about one thing—"the question of connubialities . . . : it must be a *sine qua non* of matrimony, the first clause in the marriage treaty, that they should be considered absolutely illicit" (*WL* 755). Lucia and Georgie do marry, after agreeing "that no ardent tokens of affection were to mar their union. Marriage, in fact, with Lucia might be regarded as a vow of celibacy" (*TL* 855). When Olga's husband dies, Georgie is relieved to be already a married man: "It had thrilled him with daring joy to imagine that had Olga been free, he would have asked her to marry him, but even in those flights of fancy he knew that her acceptance of him would have put him in a panic" (*TL* 855). For both Georgie and Stephen, as for numerous gay diva devotees, playing consort to a diva is play par excellence, important play, emotionally and aesthetically satisfying play, daring play, but firmly and definitely play.

When Lucia takes up residence in Tilling, artist Irene Coles takes up the role of diva worshiper—and more: "Poor Irene seems to be under a sort of spell. . . . She can think about nothing except that woman" (*ML* 350); she "burst[s] into tears" when she hears the news that Lucia and Georgie are getting married (*WL* 758). Just as Georgie and Stephen are characterized as feminine and therefore homosexual, Irene is characterized as masculine and therefore lesbian. "The Disgrace of Tilling and her sex," according to Miss Mapp, Irene smokes cigarettes, wears knickerbockers, and has a "handsome, boyish face" with "closely cropped" hair (*MM* 304). Another character calls Irene "that rude *unsexed* girl in shorts" (*TL* 891, emphasis added). Her Tilling epithet, "Quaint Irene," comes close to calling her queer, and Tilling society acknowledges that she lives "in a very queer way": "with one gigantic maid, who, but for her sex, might have been in the Guards" (305). Though Irene is quaint and masculine, a "suffragette" and a "socialist" (*MM* 304), qualities that would in other texts mark her as unattractive, she, like Lucia herself, has her admirers. At one Tilling affair, she finds herself "surrounded by both sexes of the enraptured youth of Tilling, for the boys knew she was a girl, and the girls thought she looked so like a boy" (*ML* 523). Her paintings are as sexually ambiguous as she is; a chronic reviser of her work, she turns, for example, "her women wrestlers into men" (*ML* 526).

Like Georgie's uncritical worship of Olga Bracely, Irene's worship of her diva is boundless and blind. "In a sort of ecstasy," she says to Lucia, "You can do everything. . . . You play like an angel, and you can knock out Mapp with your little finger, and you can skip and play bridge, and you've got such a lovely nature that you don't bear Mapp the slightest grudge for her foul plots. You are adorable!" (*ML* 542). If we substitute Lucia for Mapp in this encomium, it could easily be a tribute from Georgie to Olga. The difference, though, is that Olga really can "play [and sing] like an angel"; she really does have "a lovely nature" that doesn't bear Lucia the slightest grudge for her foul plots. The real diva, that is, with her "air of joyous and unrepentant paganism" (*TL* 875) and her masculine mode of being in the world, has none of the faults or pretensions associated with divahood, faults and pretensions that are here played out with other characters altogether.

The result is diva comedy that suggests that prima donna behavior—with all its gay trappings—far from being the territory of the always suspect woman-on-stage is much more likely to belong to her entirely respectable and womanly detractor. The Lucia texts, then, have managed to portray the singing woman without the comic caricature, like the caricature Georgie fears to make of his portrait, like the exhibited caricature of Olga in *Lucia in London*—the caricature, that is, in which the diva consists "entirely of a large open mouth" ready to devour (242). In similar generous, gentle, and gender-bending fashion, the Lucia novels both use and reject caricatures of women, gays, and lesbians. For all her diva pretensions, Lucia remains for the reader as for Georgie and Irene the source of life, interest, and change in Riseholme and Tilling. For all their quaint mannerisms, Georgie and Irene are appealing characters, lined up with Lucia against mean Mapp and macho Major Benjy. Irene is, as well, a serious and accomplished artist, attested to by the fact that critics find in her pictures "a lot she didn't intend to put there" (*TL* 847). Irene's art, that is, becomes, like Olga's performance, an analog to the text itself and an invitation to textual interpretation.

Benson's diva texts are, first of all, about art and interpretation. Olga Bracely acknowledges this about her own life story when she refuses to disclose details of her early life "because I am keeping it for my memoirs, which I shall write when my voice becomes a little more like a steam whistle" (QL 53). The diva's life, on stage and off, shapes itself into a narrative for an audience, an audience of detractors and admirers, of gossipmongers and music lovers. But her narrative, larger than life as a diva's must be, comes to stand for the narratives of all the characters in these comedies, all of whom are performers on small-town stages. The diva's own performance, that is, is displaced onto the performative lives of more ordinary "divas," of other performers on the local stage, and the part of diva worshiper becomes here as much a performance as the part of Carmen or Queen of Tilling.

Erotic desire is also aligned with the performative in these novels, even as sexual activity is never performed. There is no "real" sexual passion in Riseholme or Tilling, signaled not only by the many celibate marriages and chaste flirtations but by the total absence of children as well. The emotional and/or social attachments—between Georgie and Olga, Stephen and Lucia, Georgie and Lucia, Irene and Lucia, for example—are sanctioned by acknowledged models like marriage, like extramarital affairs, like diva worship, models that themselves constitute, according to these texts, accepted and acceptable performances. And that is all we see. What readers know, of course, is that there is always and everywhere sexual activity and sexual passion. The campy genius of these texts is that the text-repressed sexuality is wholly fluid and ambiguous. Georgie is obviously not sexually attracted to Lucia, whom he marries, or even Olga, whom he adores. His treasured photograph of Olga shows her "in her cuirass and helmet" (QL 34). To whom, then, *is* he sexually attracted? Irene's obsession with Lucia fuels her paintings and her wicked tongue; when she asks Lucia, "Won't you ask me to come and stay with you at Riseholme some-time?" (*ML* 542), what is she asking for? And what is her relationship with her gigantic maid? Why are Olga and Lucia so utterly indifferent to their respective husbands' lengthy absences? What sexless relationship is sig-nified by the Mapp-Flint's too obvious affection ("those little tweaks and dabs . . . —that shows there must be something real and heartfelt, don't you think?" asks Lucia wickedly [*WL* 632]) and Elizabeth Mapp's false pregnancy?

Sex, that is, is nowhere and everywhere and impossible to describe or pin down. Sex is the unperformed in these texts of performances, as it is the unperformable in the mannered society of Tilling and Riseholme. And the very fictionality of the towns suggests that sex is unperformable as well in mannered fictions. The ambiguous gender positions of characters like Georgie and Stephen and Irene—so consistently cross-dressed by the text—compound its allusiveness. And illusiveness. Like the operas that Queen Olga sings, like the *tableaux* that are Queen Lucia's favorite enter-tainment, the lives of the Tillingites and Riseholmites are pure perfor-mance, performance imbued with a pervasive and fluid sexuality—the sexuality, perhaps, of the diva herself. Its consciously thorough repression not only highlights it but makes it the subject of embarrassed comedy, of uneasy laughter, like the diva's open mouth with its simultaneous hilarity, dangerous sensuality, and transporting ecstasy. These texts dismantle the stereotype of the diva and her sexuality by comically multiplying and dis-placing her; in doing so, they simultaneously dismantle, by comically mul-tiplying and displacing sex itself, the notion of a monolithic sexuality. In other words, a world of divas and diva worshipers is a world of change and unpredictability, a world of unstable gender relations and chaotic sexual-ities, but a world always interesting and, like Queen Lucia, Worshipful Lucia herself, "the picture of vigor and vitality" (*ML* 541).

CHAPTER 7

Express Yourselves

DIVAS POP AND POMO

Never miss an opportunity to theatricalize.
—Callas in Terrence McNally's *Master Class*

*I*n his conclusion to *The Great Singers* (1966), Henry Pleasants laments the "police escort" that, in the contemporary opera world, supervises "the singers' every utterance" (348). He bemoans the "Germanic philosophy of the sanctity of composition and the immutability of the written note" that informs the training of contemporary opera singers and informs as well, we might add, the expectations of contemporary listeners. The Western operatic voice is now restricted, controlled, and policed in ways unthinkable in pre-Mozartian times. Pleasants further suggests that the difficulty of contemporary serious music—difficult to sing, difficult to listen to—and the incompatibility of popular music with classical voice training contribute to the stagnation of the standard repertoire, a repertoire itself adhering to the conventions of the sanctity of composition and the immutability of the written note. Confined and stagnant, young singers, Pleasants argues, should continue the accomplishments of Callas and Sutherland in reviving an older tradition in which the musical line "must be shaped, varied and embellished" (352).

Since the publication of *The Great Singers*, opera singers have, of course, done just that. Along with the increased popularity of early music, especially early music performed on original instruments, singers like Julianne Baird—whose voice, Will Crutchfield writes, "might be called an 'authentic instrument' for Handel, Monteverdi and Purcell" (H23)—have helped restore an early opera tradition that many major houses work to represent in their schedules. Even more amazing, perhaps, is the proliferation of small ensembles that specialize in such performance. What singers gain is not only a more expansive repertoire but the archeological satisfaction of digging in and re-creating the past, the artistic satisfaction of embellishing what they find, and the creative satisfaction of improvising. Though the early music and authentic instrument movements have, as does any musical tradition, their own set of policing procedures, there is for singers an excitement, freedom, and even danger about such performance rare in twentieth-century opera culture. "Improvising and embellishing," Julianne Baird remarks, "is like going out on a limb: You can go out a certain distance safely and still get back. But you don't know how far that is unless you test it" (Crutchfield H38). Like Armgart—who, her teacher complains, performs notes that "Gluck had not written, nor I taught"—Baird and other singers of early opera specialize in and experiment with the not-written and the not-taught as, in part perhaps, a way of evading the opera police and courting danger while still remaining within an operatic tradition.

Much more obviously and more frequently, young persons who want to sing and to perform reject—if they even consider—that tradition and choose another idiom altogether in which to express themselves freely, stake out their territory, and court danger, an idiom that, Pleasants says, very few "serious" singers can master (349). Popular music is not only a less policed but a more democratic idiom. It does not require the extensive, expensive training of the opera singer, nor does it require the same vocal equipment. The popular singing voice is most often cyborgian—enhanced, that is, by an array of electronics unimaginable to composers of early opera. Unimaginable, in fact, to most of us. This is not to suggest, of course, that many popular singers are not highly trained musicians with powerful and interesting voices. Many are, and are as well their own composers and librettists. Victorian diva Pauline Viardot wrote music, but most of what she sang came from an established repertoire, composed by men. Many opera singers have had music written *for* them and have been instrumental in creating operatic roles. But most of the roles opera singers perform and almost all the music they sing are created and written by others, again almost always men.

Popular artists of both (or all) sexes, on the other hand, often write and arrange their own music and lyrics, create or direct their own videos, accompany themselves on instruments, manipulate their own equipment, distribute under their own recording labels. This control—though itself limited and policed by access to equipment and airwaves, producers, spin doctors, and the fluctuations of the music marketplace—over the production of their often elaborate performances exceeds the control of even the most demanding and demanded prima donna of the opera world. Until very recently, such control was largely limited to male performers, who dominated—with notable exceptions—the rock, pop, jazz, blues, and country scenes. But the last ten years has seen a remarkable proliferation of female performers who do much more than sing, many of whom have come to be called "diva" and who exhibit more similarities to than differences from their sisters in opera.

We have chosen to discuss three of these women, Madonna and Annie Lennox from the pop/rock tradition and Diamanda Galas, whose work is a hybrid of "serious" music and the most extreme fringes of rock. Left out of this discussion are numerous fascinating performers—like Liz Phair, Yo Yo, Kate Bush, k. d. lang, Julianna Hatfield, Ferron, PJ Harvey, Queen Latifah, Melissa Etheridge, Me'Shell NdgegeOcello, as well as groups, both Grrrl and otherwise, like L7, Bikini Kill, Shakespear's Sister, Salt 'n Pepa, disappear fear, Zap Mama, Well-Oiled Sisters, Tiger Trap, Bratmobile, Ikue Mori & Tenko, Sweet Honey in the Rock. ("Everyone's a diva these days," complains a writer for the pop music magazine *Spin*. "You can't move for girl singers—solitary or roaming in packs—with multiple octave ranges, superhuman breath control, and the ability to coax gospel soul out of the most innocuous jingle. And I'm sick of it" [Bernstein].) But they are, at this point, less studiable, less commented upon, less media-constructed cultural phenomena in the diva tradition than our two pop queens of the eighties, picked out of numerous other pop queens for their self-conscious appropriation of the diva mode. Diamanda Galas, too, explicitly sees herself in that tradition and revels in the epithets—scream diva, diva of death, diva of disease—assigned to her.

Probably the most popular, and certainly the most written about, pop diva during the late eighties and early nineties was Madonna.[1] Her influence has extended well beyond the music scene; we've heard numerous claims that she's the most widely known woman in the world. Most of her critics of the late eighties and early nineties are not music critics at all but culture critics eager to assess her influence, to see her as representative of "today's youth" (though she's hardly a youth), to speculate on (hope for, long for?) her waning popularity, to deplore her materialism, to enshrine her as a postmodern heroine. A recent critic claimed that in the past decade "virtually all the roots of every major fashion trend—and many minor ones, too—can be traced back to her. And not just here in the U.S.; like the skies her presence is global" (Oldham). Like the divine, she's omnipresent.

Her name itself—though it's her "real" name—suggests this extraordinary status and is, besides, a sort of play on the meaning of "diva." It's a name that inspires her own plays on and associations with the divine, including the titles of her albums *Like a Virgin*, *Like a Prayer*, and *The*

Immaculate Collection, an obvious pun on the Immaculate Conception. It is not, of course, only the titles that suggest Madonna's religious connections and aspirations. The song "Like a Prayer" (lyrics with Patrick Leonard), for example, begins with the tentative invocation "God?" and proceeds to collapse the madonna and the whore: "When you call my name / It's like a little prayer / I'm down on my knees / I want to take you there." *The Immaculate Collection*, which also includes "Like a Prayer," is dedicated to the pope, "my divine inspiration." Religious imagery, ritual, and diction permeate her videos, her rhetoric, and Alek Keshishian's film documentary of her work, *Truth or Dare*. In the *Like a Prayer* video, for example, we see "a miraculously weeping statue, the stigmata, the Saint Teresa–like union between the saint and the believer, and the highly physical musical performance by the Andrae Crouch choir" (McClary 165). *Truth or Dare* adds another layer of religious imagery and ritual to the stage performances it documents by showing Madonna gathering her dancers and others for a backstage prayer before starting a show. In a *Rolling Stone* interview, Madonna makes clear that such ritual is integral to her own religious history: "Oh, I believe in everything. That's what Catholicism teaches you" (Fisher 1:40). That the madonna is the diva of Catholicism has not escaped her notice; her career has been a systematic attempt to become the diva—or the (pri)madonna—of a pop subculture that has for millions replaced traditional religion.[2]

Madonna also capitalizes on, plays with, and reverses the relationship between homosexuality and the diva. Most of her dancers, for example, are gay, and in *Truth or Dare* she must soothe a young straight dancer who feels left out. She clearly relishes the gay ambience and uses it to enhance her flirtatious and maternal (one might argue "maternalistic") exchanges with the dancers. She is here the young diva, gathering to herself the even younger gay devotees. Madonna is, of course, actually as old as many opera divas, but the style she cultivates, much to the annoyance of some of her critics,[3] is a very youthful one, and this youth suggests that she sees herself and her admirers as inheritors of the diva–gay-devotee tradition. Irate critics who deplore her remark (which we read ironically) that the gay dancers are "emotional cripples," whom Madonna must mother, miss this tableau; madness and emotional instability, as we have seen, characterize, perhaps constitute, the fan. At the same time that she cultivates this scene, she refers to herself unselfconsciously (if anything she says or does can be called unselfconscious) as a "fag hag" (Fisher 1:36), thus positioning the diva as fan of gay men as well as gay men as fans of the diva.[4]

Unlike divas of the past, however, and unlike most opera divas, her links are primarily to black and Latin male homosexual traditions, established in part by her popularization of "voguing" in her videos and songs. (Madonna has been much more popular with young black audiences in general than most white pop/rock icons.)[5] In "Strike-a-Pose," voguing, whose star practitioners are commonly referred to as "divas," collapses difference—"It makes no difference if you're black or white / If you're a boy or a girl," if, one infers, you're gay or you're straight. Though some critics have accused Madonna of "appropriating" voguing, of stripping it of its gay, racial, ethnic, and political content and advocating naive and ultimately destructive color-blindness, others counter that she has not only given enormous visibility to issues of race and sexuality but has given us as well a way to act out those issues. As queer theorist-activist Cindy Patton puts it, "Madonna's dismissal of the 'deep' truth of gender and racial difference is less a pluralistic nostalgia in the service of oppressive color- or gender-blindness than it is an attempt to enlist us in a performance that, in its kinetics, deconstructs gender and race despite its dancer" (96). In other words, the very gender-mocking gestures and movements of voguing enact a queer sensibility even when it's white, yuppie, heterosexual males who are dancing.

Madonna's gay appeal, however, is certainly not limited to males. Her broadest fan base, at least in the late eighties and early nineties, has been teenage girls, the maddest of these dubbed "wannabes," a term that has come to suggest any girl who adopts Madonna dress but that described, at one time at least, the fan(atical) groups of girls who followed her in much the manner of the Gerry-Flappers.[6] "When Madonna arrived in New York for her Virgin Tour, the news was full of reports of young fans, 'wannabes,' dressing up like Madonna and hanging around Madison Square Garden, where she was scheduled to perform" (Tippens 267). That these young women are perceived as wanting to be Madonna takes the process of the female fan's identification with her diva, which we discussed earlier, a step further. Earlier divas are represented, or represent themselves, as giving voice to the anger and desire of silenced women; to want to be Madonna implies that Madonna motivates a desire in these women to be their own agents, to use their own voices and bodies. Not all of these hangers-on are lesbians, of course, but it is widely acknowledged in lesbian lore—and publications—that Madonna's lesbian fandom can be intense. Lesbians who "adore" Madonna, Deb Schwartz writes, "wear black bras and rosaries as they bump and grind in lesbian clubs, they paint her on triptychs, they erect altars to her in their bedrooms" (214). The concrete forms this "ado-ration" takes repeat Madonna's play on her name; her admirers "adore" her as she presents herself—the madonna of Catholicism. That the adoration is so thoroughly imbued with camp suggests a consciously constructed con-nection between lesbian wannabes and gay diva worshipers of an earlier era, a connection that illustrates the new alliance between lesbians and gay men precipitated in the eighties by the AIDS crisis and strengthened by (mostly younger) gay men's and lesbians' development of queer sensibility and theory.

It is not difficult to see Madonna's appeal for lesbians, especially younger ones in revolt against the "vanilla sex" that some older lesbians and some older lesbian writing have seemed to advocate. Madonna's frank sexiness and public celebration of a wide variety of sexual practices offer support, exposure, and a possibility of widespread acceptance for the "sex radicals" in the ongoing lesbian sex debates. But the appeal is more com-plex than that. In her piece on Brigitte Fassbaender, Terry Castle makes much of what she calls Fassbaender's "homovocality," that is, her un-abashed ability to express passion for and passionate interest in women and her ability to convey the sense that she's singing to women. "She is unsur-passed," Castle writes, "at conveying adoration: of female voices, bodies, and dreams" (33). Though the content of Madonna's songs and videos is for the most part quite heterosexual, her primary interest and passion *is* the female body—that the body in question belongs to Madonna herself only adds an interesting twist to the notion of homovocality—and it is her fe-male voice and body that is the object of female fans' adoration.

An early Madonna biography quotes her contemplation of her navel, which she regards as the "most erogenous part of my body. . . . I have the most perfect belly button. . . . When I stick a finger in my belly button I feel a nerve in the center of my body shoot up my spine. If 100 belly but-tons were lined up against a wall I would definitely pick out which one was mine" (Fiske 62). Fiske notes that this "sexual-physical pleasure . . . has nothing to do with men" and that "she is choosing a part of the female body that patriarchy has not conventionally sexualized for the benefit of the male" (62). Lesbian writers—Monique Wittig in *The Lesbian Body* and Jeanette Winterson in her *Written on the Body* the most obvious ex-amples—have for years, of course, been exploring the erotic possibilities of the female body in very similar ways. Madonna moves such explorations from lesbian and literary enclaves to the screens and stages of the world. Even aside from the matter of the belly button, Madonna's fascination with her own body and her uninhibited expressions of her sexuality are quite clearly not male-dependent, a situation that might account in part for the fact that her popularity is lowest among white heterosexual males.[7]

Many male critics have, in fact, taken umbrage at Madonna's apparent lack of concern about men's sexual response. John Simon, for example, dismisses her as not at all sexy in real life (he saw her at a party) and "small" besides (240–241); rather than dismissing her, Milo Miles exaggerates her anti-male potential: she is "the kind of woman who comes into your room at three A.M. and sucks your life out" (quoted in D. Marsh 33). Simon's scorn only underscores Madonna's appeal to women, most of us not raving beauties or statuesque models. Miles puts Madonna in the long tradition of devouring-woman images; she is sister to the siren and the lesbian vampire. The unwarranted viciousness of these attacks is endearing to lesbians, often objects of the same kinds of criticism.

Lesbian fans and commentators have been especially interested in what we might call Madonna's "lesbian moments": her "confession" in *Truth or Dare* of youthful "fingerfucking" with a high school girlfriend, the female-to-female sex scenes in *Sex*, and her open flirtation with Sandra Bernhard. Madonna has denied that she's a lesbian, but she implies that she does not hesitate to engage in lesbian activity. Though some lesbians find this ambiguity irritating, the position is certainly congruent with Madonna's strategy of shifting selves and multiple identification and may be, Deb Schwartz suggests, more helpful to lesbians in the long run: "Instead of investing in the concept of a stable identity (that is, sitting with hands folded in laps, dimes between knees, and calmly stating 'That's right Mr. Letterman, we're lesbians'), they [Madonna and Bernhard] made lesbian sexual practice visible. They engaged in a more radical form of visibility that underscored their interest in the practice of sex rather than the formation of identity" (217). Madonna repeats this strategy of making "lesbian sexual practice visible" in *Sex*, though some lesbians have objected to the specific content of the practice in those works.

Madonna thus illustrates—in her songs, in her videos, in her interviews and live appearances, in *Sex*—like her operatic counterparts, that the diva world, in both its traditional and its vogue/rock/pop incarnations, can accommodate, enjoy, privilege, and occasionally even "translate" homosexuality, cross-dressing, transgender and cross-racial connections; they are, indeed, constitutive of that world.

But perhaps Madonna's most comprehensive appropriation of the diva role is her insistence on performance and her chameleon ability to change not just her part in the opera but her part in her own narrative.[8] The difference between her blond and brunette incarnations, for example, is dramatic. Is this the same woman? In a fascinating interview with Carrie Fisher that appeared in two parts in *Rolling Stone*, Madonna talks about the tatoo that Sean Penn got on his toe after they were married, a tatoo of her nickname, "Daisy." She goes on to explain that "No one calls me Daisy now. . . . After Daisy there was Lulu because I was worshiping Louise Brooks. . . . The next name was Kit Moresby from *The Sheltering Sky*." By the time of the interview, however, "it's Dita, from Dita Parlo, an actress from the Thirties."[9] Fisher asks who gave her the current nickname. "I gave it to myself," she responds, taking on the div(a)ine and masculine privilege of naming. And Dita (with its obvious similarity to "diva"), she continues, is a name she intends to hold on to until "I find somebody else to be enamored of" (1:36).

The enamored-of ones are all performers of one sort or another and all dead, as are the subjects of the films she wants to star in—Frida Kahlo, Martha Graham, maybe Marilyn. They are also all female. But part of Madonna's attraction to Kahlo, for example, seems to be her, to Madonna's mind, masculinization—in both her art ("she overemphasized that [the dark hair on her upper lip] in her paintings, which made her masculine and hard looking") and her physical presence ("she had almost a beard; she had to shave practically") (Fisher 1:39).

Madonna is, then, both "enamored" of high-achieving (and so "masculinized") women and—by taking on their names, either in her "real" life or by playing them on screen—desirous of "becoming" them. She is, that is, a lover of divas—a position traditionally labeled masculine, often gay—and an aspiring diva, a woman who herself can, through roles and costuming, appropriate masculinity. In her 1990 Blond Ambition tour, Madonna wore a monocle, sign, as Marjorie Garber points out, "of a fantasized and dated patriarchy assumed and transumed by the pansexual material girl" (155). But while wearing a monocle is a clear parody of an identifiable male stance, it also calls up a certain set of early twentieth-century lesbians, like Radclyffe Hall, Una Troubridge, and Romaine Brookes, who wore both monocles and tuxedos to, as Garber notes, "assert sexual difference within" (155). Even when Madonna dresses in a Michael Jackson outfit and imitates his dance steps (and his crotch grabs), she does something more complicated than take on a male persona, since Jackson's own masculinity and sexuality are constant objects of question and comment.

In spite of the complex fluidity of both gender and sexuality that characterizes her performances, Madonna does insist on both her femininity and her heterosexuality, her public flirtation with Sandra Bernhard ("She ran off with another girl," Bernhard claims in the September 1993 *People*) and her occasional admissions like "I'd like to know what it feels like to go in and out of somebody" (Fisher 1:40) notwithstanding. This insistence, whether strategic or simply a product of cultural biases, suggests, we think, her performative overreach. That is, the limits, whatever their source, continue to haunt her. Or as Douglas Crimp remarks, "She can be as queer as she wants to, but only because we know she's not" (Crimp and Warner 95). She can strike as many masculine poses as she wants to, but only because we know she's a material girl.

In a much-discussed segment of *Truth or Dare* Warren Beatty accuses Madonna of being interested in nothing that isn't for an audience. The context is a medical examination of her ailing throat, and the question is whether the examination should be done on or off camera. "Turn the camera off?" Beatty says sarcastically. "She doesn't want to *live* off camera, much less talk." What Beatty objects to here is Madonna's recognition of her selves, all of them, as performers and, by extension, other selves (including his) as performers. This recognition is one of the most compelling things about Madonna and one of the reasons that so many postmodern theorists have written about her.[10] Although she sometimes seems to hold on to distinctions between a conventional, "real," or private self and an observed or public self, at times recognizably distinct from it, this "real" self is clearly also a constructed self.

In the Fisher interview, for example, she pretends to spontaneous, and therefore "real," responses and revelations and at the same time points out some of the limits to revealing your "real" self under any circumstances. "Everything I do is measured by what I think her [her shrink's] reactions will be" (Fisher 1:36). First, of course, this comment recognizes that her shrink (a shrink she "shares" with Carrie Fisher) might read the interview, which means—to Madonna—that she must monitor her performance in the interview, in every interview, because she understands that such performances will, in good Foucauldian fashion, be monitored. She recognizes, exploits, turns back on itself the subtle surveillance of modern disciplinary power.

But the comment suggests further that even in the privacy of therapy, as opposed to the pseudo-privacy of the "intimate" interview with Fisher, the performance is maintained. Madonna's remarks also point out the performative nature of therapy itself. Despite its highly defined roles, clear therapist-client boundaries, and dependence on transference, we tend to think, misguidedly, that therapy is a process that strips away all artificiality and artifice. In another interview at about the same time, Madonna uses visits to a psychiatrist to illustrate the indistinguishability of acting and "truth": "It's like when you go into a psychiatrist's office and you don't really tell what you did. You lie, but even the lie you've chosen to tell is revealing" (Hirschberg 198). To Madonna, lying to a therapist is what one does, what everyone does. Therapy is, after all, a performance.

Her word choice here suggests another truth-telling site and implies that it, too, is more accurately a performance site. You also "go into a" confessional to "tell what you did." And in the Fisher interview, Madonna uses almost the same words: "When I did go to confession, I never told the priest what I thought I'd really done wrong. I'd made up other, smaller crimes" (1:40). Confession, then, whether in a confessional, a psychiatrist's office, a documentary, or an interview, is one more opportunity for performance. And the burden of interpretation is on the priest, shrink, reader: "Even the lie you've chosen to tell is revealing." What is revealed, however, is a *mise-en-abyme* of the ever-elusive "really."

Thomas Allen Harris, in a piece on Madonna's *Sex*, quotes his own therapist's response to that book: "her / public persona is so strong, so embedded, that / therapy could be difficult if not impossible" (39). What the therapist fails to recognize, represses for the sake of her/his profession, is that Madonna illustrates the possibility that there is no life beneath the "public persona," only lives with enormously complicated relationships to many personae. What the therapist mourns is perhaps one of Madonna's contributions to the postmodern aesthetic—she is immune to therapy. That is, she is evidence that therapy, too, is a performance and that even our most well-therapized selves are performative. And since, like most Madonna critics, we are all but ignoring the music itself—easy to do with such an iconic figure—we might note that some critics,[11] at least, illustrate ways in which the music underlines the singer's motifs, here the elusive and illusory selves that we have been discussing and that lead so many commentators to call her "chameleon." In "Express Yourself," Melanie Morton explains, "*self* is first sung on G, then on F sharp, moving to F natural, then on G, moving back to F sharp, and lastly . . . , *self* is sung on F sharp to F" (228). The selves, that is, that the song urges us to express are as sliding and unstable as Madonna's own. (Confronted with a similar analysis by Susan McClary, Madonna apparently dismissed it, but, as Robert Christgau notes, "that Madonna professes to have no idea what McClary is talking about doesn't diminish its truth value" [205].)

As we noted, Madonna does try to construct a gap between the "private" and public selves, usually to assure readers/fans that she is, in this circumstance, telling us the Truth about herself. One instance of this strategy, of particular relevance to our interest in Madonna-as-diva, is her admission in the Fisher interview that "I don't like blow jobs" (1:40), an admission that she later repeats: "They don't tell me I give good head, believe me, because I don't give it" (1:120). This in spite of numerous lyrics that imply otherwise ("I'm on my knees / I want to take you there")[12] and in spite of the drawn-out scene in *Truth or Dare* in which she enthusiastically—and punctuated with appropriate noises—illustrates with a bottle how she "gives head." (This, by the way, is a response to a Dare, and so perhaps a hint that it was *not* Truth?)

Fisher seems taken aback by the claim that "I don't give it," and Madonna explains, "Who wants to choke? That's the bottom line. I contend that that's part of the whole humiliation thing of men with women. Women cannot choke a guy." Fisher interjects, "Some would argue." (The implication here being, we presume, that some men say they choke on women's fluids and/or smells.) Madonna continues, "Yeah, but still, it doesn't go down into their throat and move their epiglottis around" (1:120).

Both women seem to agree that a blow job is "the thing men really enjoy" (1:40), yet Madonna refuses to oblige, because she finds it humiliating and because it constricts her throat and disturbs her epiglottis, sources of her own power and voice. Divas, as we have seen, often identify themselves with their throats or are so identified by others. And as Madonna sees her self, or selves, as public territory, so does she see her throat. In the *Truth or Dare* sequence mentioned above, a sequence that seems almost unbearably intrusive, it is Madonna's throat that is the site of contention between her and Warren Beatty. He wants it examined off camera; she doesn't mind the exposure. "Why should I stop here?" she asks.

The analogy between throat and vagina, conventional in diva discourse, reappears. "Why should I stop here?" is, of course, Madonna's position not only on the exposure of her throat but on the exposure of her sexual parts as well. Wayne Koestenbaum notes that "voice commentators describe the larynx as labial—based on visual analogy and on the association between women and invisible things" (*QT* 160).[13] Beatty seems to agree. The throat is to him not a proper object of public display, perhaps because it so closely resembles the vagina, perhaps because both are "naturally" hidden. But Madonna directly questions this assumption in a later interview, where she asks, in a discussion of this scene, "What's so intimate about my throat?" (Pribram 201). "What's so intimate about my vagina?" she might as easily have asked. Nothing, in fact, is intimate to a performing self, as Madonna has consistently illustrated in her videos and live performances. The difference between vagina and throat, however, is crucial: a penis in her vagina does not obstruct her voice, a penis in her throat gags her. Again, we see the self-sufficiency of Madonna's stance: neither her sexuality nor her voice is primarily for the pleasure of anyone but herself. Her audience is welcome to look, but the untouchable territory, the protected territory, is the source of her ability to express herself(selves)—and to make her empowering millions.

Whether, of course, Madonna *really* refuses to give head is beside the point. There is no *really* in Madonnaland.

Carrie Fisher introduces her interview with some of her own perceptions of Madonna, many of which we've heard before ("Madonna has no equal at getting attention" [1:35]). But one comment seems particularly relevant here—"she will answer any question because she is genuinely interested in her own reply" (1:36). Again, we see Madonna as great talker and consummate performer, here the improviser who, like divas before her, takes liberties with her voice, the impromptu actor who can hardly wait to watch her own performance. In this one (the interview itself), by her elaboration of the numerous women she becomes, by her dismissal of men's desires, by her insistence upon the primacy and integrity of her organs (the sexual ones that deserve pleasure, the vocal ones that need unrestricted access to air), she places herself clearly in the tradition of the literary divas we have been discussing.

But she doesn't stop there. In a 1991 MTV special Madonna summarizes public perceptions of Madonna: "She's a freak. She's a man in drag. Just kidding. I'm a woman in drag—I'm a man and a woman. I'm your worst nightmare" (Lentz 155). The religious right and the Catholic Church have for a long time seen Madonna as one of their worst nightmares. Her bad-girl image has offended audiences all over the world. But the context of her comment here is not Madonna the bad girl but Madonna the sexually ambiguous, Madonna the I-don't-know-who-or-what-I-am-and-I-don't-care. In other words, she's also the nightmare of identity politics, the nightmare of the therapist, the nightmare, perhaps, of us all. In a nightmarish sequence on *Saturday Night Live*, right after the inauguration of Bill

Clinton, Madonna, in her most obvious Marilyn Monroe mode—sweet little girl seductive—sings "Happy Inauguration, Mr. President." At the end of her song, she makes even more seductive moves, which the audience assumes are meant for Bill Clinton (as Lentz correctly points out, the scene alludes to Monroe's seductive, sirenic, performance of "Happy Birthday" for/to/at John F. Kennedy [155]). The camera, though, following the lines of Madonna/Marilyn's gaze, moves on to Hillary Clinton; no, Madonna indicates, not her either. Finally we realize that it's Chelsea she wants.

Lentz perceptively notes that "we witness the transformation of a woman, popularly constructed as desperately heterosexual, into a woman constructed as shamelessly queer" and sees this as comic evidence that Madonna performs not only for "straight male titillation, but also for the benefit of queer women" (155). But our own queer woman response was much more ambiguous (hence our labeling the sequence "nightmarish") than Lentz suggests. Our point here is that Madonna/Marilyn was *not* seducing Hillary Clinton—about whom we have all heard numerous rumors of lesbian affairs, whom we perceive as tough, powerful, and able to take care of herself—but Chelsea, the fragile, the innocent, the young, the inexperienced, the awkward, the cultural vision of the early adolescent girl. And the adolescent girl is the dominant culture's fantasy of the object of predatory lesbian desire. We could barely watch it. Enough, we wanted to say, this is over the top.

What we're suggesting here is that over the top, or to borrow Julianne Baird's phrase, going out on the limb until it breaks off, is what Madonna is all about. She uses her status as diva to exploit that stereotype, and in this she has been wildly successful, witness the endless critical comments about her prima donna sins: greed, endless manipulations, hunger for power, megalomania, need to control, self-absorption, narcissism, and exhibitionism. And once she has established herself as a diva par excellence, she makes two additional moves. First, she boldly assures us that all these horrible things she's accused of are really all right, a point usually missed by her critics. As Carol A. Queen (a "sexuality activist") emphasizes, "Madonna is called an exhibitionist as if that were a problem and not an inspiration, a pathology rather than a source of pleasure" (143). And Madonna herself speaks persuasively about women and power: "While it might have seemed like I was behaving in a stereotypical way, at the same time, I was also masterminding it. I was in control of everything I was doing" (Gilmore). In control and proud of it. After MTV refused to air the *Justify My Love* video, Forrest Sawyer on *Nightline* commented to Madonna, "In the end, you're going to wind up making more money than you would have." Madonna's response: "Yeah, lucky me" ("Madonna Interview" 280). Instead of apologizing or explaining or justifying, Madonna simply accepts that good things come to those who manipulate.

Susan McClary illustrates this crucial difference between Madonna and the opera heroines she so often resembles: "Like Carmen or Lulu, she invokes the body and feminine sexuality, but unlike them she refuses to be framed by a structure that will push her back into submission or annihilation" (*Feminine Endings* 152). As we have seen, divas, both historical and literary, do not allow themselves to suffer the same fates as the characters they represent. But Madonna, in control as she is of her musical world,[14] incorporates her refusal "to be framed" into the characters or personae themselves. McClary discusses this in terms of the end of "Live to Tell": "It sounds as though the piece has ended in a foreordained defeat of the victim—she who is offered only the second-position slot in the narrative schema. In her live performance, at this point Madonna sinks to the floor and lies motionless for what seems an interminable length of time. . . . But then she rises from the floor, bearing with her the ghosts of all those victims—Marilyn most explicitly, but also Carmen . . . and all the others who were purged for the sake of social order and narrative closure—and begins singing again" (159). Significantly, Madonna calls her film company Siren Films.

This enthusiastic claiming of what have been devastating criticisms of women (controlling, egocentric, exhibitionist) and this self-conscious enactment and revision of female stereotypes, strategies Madonna shares with Diamanda Galas, lead directly to the second of Madonna's post-diva moves, embarrassment. Madonna embarrasses us. She has embarrassed us from the beginning, and every time we think we've come to terms with it, managed to explain it away as postmodernism or postfeminism or queer positivity, she embarrasses us again. This time, we say, critics say, she has gone too far, she has sold out, she has become a parody of herself, she has demonstrated definitively her lack of talent. We thought she was a (sort of) feminist and then she played a sex kitten for *Vanity Fair* (or whatever her latest retro performance); we thought she was queer positive and then she made that awful remark at the end of *Sex*; we thought she was iconoclastic and then she castigated Sinead O'Connor for ripping up a picture of the pope.

We mention these particular incidents not at all because they are themselves the most dramatic or outrageous or politically incorrect things

Madonna has done but because they are illustrative of things she does all the time. "I keep trying to like her," Merrill Markoe writes, "but she keeps pissing me off" (Sexton, "Intro" 14). It's very difficult to write about her because the day the manuscript goes to print she will probably do something to necessitate rethinking everything we have written. We hesitate to quote critics because we know that some of them have already changed their minds about Madonna. At least for today. Cindy Patton neatly summarizes one of the "switches" that constantly force reevaluation: "The Blond Ambition tour abandoned the carefully constructed 'womanist' promotion of women strong enough to cope with men, and it unleashed the queen of gender disorder and racial deconstruction who is so disturbing to white feminists and white heterosexual men" (93).

With the publication of *Sex*, she "disturbs" a whole new set of critics, including black feminist bell hooks, who used to defend her, and lesbian critic Sonya Andermahr, who begins an essay "an ardent Madonna fan" and ends it "bored" (39).[15] We draft this as Madonna begins her Girlie tour, which last night's television news predicted will fail, even though seventy-two thousand came to the opening performance. This time, the newscasters pronounced, Madonna has gone too far. "Her goal, I think," one critic writes, "is to do things that will sooner or later make you very uncomfortable and me very uncomfortable, even though as we sit here today we could both agree that we are the two biggest Madonna fans in the world" (Sexton, "Intro" 16). Madonna thus uses her status as diva to confuse, disturb, and embarrass both fans and critics in an attempt, we suggest, systematically to stake out and claim a territory-without-limits for the female voice.

*O*ften mentioned with Madonna and other gender-bending pop figures like Boy George, David Bowie, the ex-"Prince," k. d. lang, and Michael Jackson, Scottish singer Annie Lennox has startled audiences for ten years with her varied and often androgynous personas, including her much-commented-on appearance in full drag as Elvis Presley at the 1984 Grammy awards. Her most famous costume/persona is her "perfect, pin-stripe tailored male drag," which Dave Marsh sees as of a piece with the eighties trend toward "more independent, harder-rocking female performers" (32). But drag is by no means Lennox's only costume. A critic calls her the "chameleon queen of rock video" (Morse); "chameleon" is the adjective that appears in almost everything written about her. Though she often appears in a man's business suit or a tuxedo, at other times she's in fancy dresses, made up "with drag queen excess—a woman imitating a man imitating a woman"

(Robins 15). "Carrot-topped androgyne, platinum-blonde chanteuse, trussed-up tart—she has played them all," says Ong Soh Chin, including a "Tammy Faye Bakkeresque televangelist" (Alleman 264). Each new video, another critic claims, "presented a new Annie"— the vamp, the gigolo, the ambassadress from another planet" (Corliss 70).

Although the similarities between these incarnations and those of Madonna, between these descriptions and the common critical vocabulary about Madonna, are obvious, Lennox critics are less hostile, even when they don't like her music, and they write much more consistently about the music itself. Part of the reason is perhaps the general consensus that she has an interesting and eloquent voice, "a throaty, dexterous instrument," according to one critic, "that throbs with pathos" (T. White 3). A more important and perhaps more revealing reason, however, is that, in spite of her numerous and exaggerated poses, her voice is perceived as "authentic" or "real" and Lennox herself as "really" someone quite ordinary. There is, that is, a woman (and quite a "good" one) behind the diva.

"Indeed, no matter how exotic Lennox's stage pose has become," writes Timothy White, "her vocals have never *felt* performed. . . . It's this curious combination of visual artifice and *complete emotional authenticity* that has made Lennox a singularly compelling artist" (3, emphasis ours). White attributes Lennox's success, in part, to her "urgent sense of creative candor." Other critics concur: "A soulful singer" (Cromelin 57); "a soulfully voluptuous voice" (Joyce); "soulful singing . . . more personal than before" ("Recent Releases"); "mature and expressive singing" (Kot); "Lennox spills it all on the opening cut" (Riccio); "When she talks about following her instincts, she means it" (Morse); "Lennox's elastic voice . . . hinted at deep emotional wounds beneath the chilly surfaces" (Kot); "Lennox shares her deepest self with impeccable generosity" (Agassi). This rhetoric is motivated and maintained not just by the writers' lack of rhetorical imagination but by Lennox herself, who talks about her music as "representing my sensibilities as truly as possible" (T. White 3); as the lyrics themselves pronounce, "This is the fear / This is the dread / These are the contents of my head." Lennox, in other words has a soul, a self, a "beneath," that gets expressed by, but is not defined by, both her songs and the fantastical creatures of her performances.

It's difficult to imagine Madonna critics, whether fans or detractors, discussing her soul, her candor, her expressiveness, her wounds beneath the surface, her deepest self, her emotional authenticity. In fact, Lennox critics and Lennox herself constantly—sometimes explicitly, sometimes not—

contrast the two singers. "Unlike some of her image-obsessed peers, notably Madonna, Lennox is above all an exceptional singer," Brian Johnson
writes, who expresses "shivering depths of emotion" (57). If there's a contest, Lennox clearly wins. She is, after all, unlike Madonna, a real person.
"Offstage, she's just a pale, angular—and beautiful—woman . . . who . . .
smiles at the places in the conversation where a regular person would"
(Gates 82) and who, "in her private life, which she chooses to keep *very*
private . . . wears little makeup" (Alleman 264). Even more significantly
perhaps, Lennox "has turned her workroom into a nursery" and once decided not to follow a new release with the customary tour because "it
would interfere with her *real* life as the mother of a toddler daughter"
(Michael, emphasis ours). In another interview, she assures us that "while
my work is important to me, if I felt that I was doing it to the disadvantage
of my child, I'd have to stop" (Agassi).[16] Not only, then, is Annie Lennox a
real person with real "depths" (in fact, she claims that between 1990 and
1992, she "reclaimed a person from an artifice" [Alleman 264]), but she is
a real woman, a real mother, as well. Madonna, on the other hand, "doesn't
have a maternal bone in her body" according to her "closest advisors"
(Andersen 179). (Like Lennox, and like some of the mid-century divas we
looked at in our discussion of diva life narratives, however, Madonna
sometimes presents herself as a "real woman": she repeatedly claims that
she wants to have children, for example, and her "motherly" stance in *Truth
or Dare* reinforces the motherly connotations of her name. But then she admits that to keep up people's fantasies, "you need to get married, have a lot
of children" [Mailer 48]. Motherhood as PR. As this book leaves our
hands, we learn that Madonna is with Child.)

    Lennox is, then, despite the gender-role play that made her famous,
offered up as the essentializing counter to Madonna's postmodern role
player. Critics set her up this way—in an updated version, perhaps, of the
diva wars of old—and she seems willing to occupy this position, to perform that role. As "not Madonna" and "not the Diva" her self-presentation
recalls that earlier anti-diva diva, Jenny Lind. Like Lind, she longs for
home; like Lind, she allies herself with the values, conventional and traditional, of her listeners. "I'm not the ambitious blonde," Lennox declares in
a 1992 interview, obviously referring to Madonna's 1990 Blond Ambition
tour (Johnson 54). That she loves to see "sexuality" but doesn't "always
want it thrust into my face" (Alleman 266) can be read as another critique
of Madonna. Lennox mentions Madonna directly, as well, and in the same
distancing vein: "The thing that makes me go tense when I see certain

things she's done is I don't see an end to it. It's a kind of power craving. . . . It concerns me from a human standpoint, because I think, to what point is all of this advancement, where is it taking us?" (Robins). As is her wont, Lennox is annoyingly vague here: What "certain things" is she talking about? What does "all of this advancement" signify? But the slide from "she" to "us" seems revealing. It signals that she is "one of us" and implies that she is less concerned about Madonna herself than with the effect she has on "us," as though Madonna's "power craving" and "advancement" somehow incite the rest of us to "admire power for its own sake." The quote concludes, "I find it somewhat dehumanizing that someone can go that far with fame and live with it." It's not clear who is "dehumanized" here: Lennox, Madonna, all of us? But what is clear is that, to Lennox, Madonna has gone too far, has crossed some unnamed boundary, and that this crossing is so threatening that it makes her "go tense," a common reaction, we have speculated, to Madonna's insistent going-too-far.[17]

What Lennox finally offers, we want to suggest, as an antidote to Madonna, a much more interesting and powerful antidote than these vague diatribes, is her first solo release, album and video, *Diva*.

Annie Lennox, as lead singer, and composer Dave Stewart, for many years her lover, were the enormously popular British duo the Eurythmics, whose first album appeared over ten years ago. In 1992 Lennox ended a three-year silence with the release of *Diva,* which in its first week reached the top of the British music charts. Of its hit single "Why" one critic wrote, "Last week, all of London seemed in thrall to a bittersweet Scottish lament" (T. White 3). The album has enjoyed considerable popularity in the United States as well. While some critics lament the absence of Stewart and the "energy" of the Eurythmics, others see the album as Lennox's finest work, "beyond the flashy sound bites of her former band" (Evans 41). "It turns out," one critic writes, "that one Eurythmic was all we ever needed" ("Recent Releases").

The title has been the subject of much critical speculation: To what extent does Lennox see herself as a diva? Is the diva a persona that distances Lennox from the sometimes clichéd lyrics of the songs? Lennox herself minimizes the significance of the title and further distances herself from the stereotype of the calculating, never spontaneous diva when she claims that the title just "came to me" when she saw, in a London costume shop, the extravagant feathered headdress she wears in the video and in the cover photo of the CD (Morse). The headdress sighting was, she says, an event that occurred after the album was already completed. But the title seems, this narrative of accidental origins notwithstanding, accurately to evoke the meditations on power and fame that pervade the lyrics as well as Lennox's interviews from the period of the album's release. In a *Vogue* interview, Lennox says that the title-inspiring headdress seemed to her "the strongest kind of image: a sense of decay . . . very beautiful—but . . . very artificial" (Alleman 266). Decay, beauty, and artifice are certainly recurrent motifs in the album and video and strongly suggest the ambivalence of the singer's relationship to the diva figure.

Lennox repeatedly claimed that "the album's title is completely ironic" (quoted in Corliss 70). She knows, that is, from her "experience as a female singer . . . something of what it's like to be that sort of grande dame" (Riches). Her word choice here is important: "that sort" suggests a definite distance between herself and the diva, and "grande dame" implies a certain dismissive attitude toward that figure. "I'm not a diva," she explicitly asserts in an interview, "and if I were, I'd be far too busy being one to ever have time to consider the implications of that role" (Riches). Unlike the diva, then, Lennox eschews the limelight for a more private life that provides time for thought, thought that, in turn, informs her music and performance. One infers, then, that the diva, as Lennox understands her, does not think, does not have time for self-reflection. At every turn, it seems, Lennox's notion of the diva recalls the stereotypes of the masculinist tradition of diva discourse.

Yet a diva is, of course, a female singer who has attained a certain level of stardom, and Lennox is undoubtedly that. Thus: "I have this funny relationship to that persona that is a diva, and I'm fond of it. Obviously, it's meant a lot to my life, but at the same time I realize it could be very destructive" (Michael). The word choice here is awkwardly careful. Lennox doesn't admit to being a diva; she only admits to having a diva persona to which she—the private, the real Annie Lennox—has a "funny relationship." Again, she seems here to distance herself quite firmly from that persona. Other singers, she asserts, confuse the persona and "the real person" and "try to . . . live the diva life in private . . . a very destructive thing" (Michael). The singer who most obviously lives the diva life in private is, of course, Madonna. Lennox's assertion that she is not "the ambitious blond" is made in the context of the release of *Diva*, and it is as not-a-Madonna-album-and-video that we'd like to explore *Diva*.

The most obvious difference between *Diva* and a Madonna album and video is the simplicity of production. Lennox's friend Sophie Muller directed the video, and, aside from the tourists in St. Mark's Square,

Lennox is the only character in it. The Venetian setting epitomizes Lennox's diva themes of beauty and decay, and two of the segments can be read as direct references to and revisions of Madonna's *Like a Virgin* video. The Venetian palace interiors of that video reappear in Lennox's "Money Can't Buy It"; instead of Madonna's miniskirted wedding dress and white veil, Lennox wears a red dress and white towel styled like a turban (a parodic deconstruction of Madonna's veil and her "play" with the "exotic," perhaps?) as she looks in a mirror and sings, "I believe in love alone." The "Primitive" segment reproduces the canal scenes of *Like a Virgin* and is shot in the same way, with the camera in the front of the boat directed at the singer sitting in the back. Gone are the bouncy rhythms and elaborate costumes of *Like a Virgin*. Dressed somberly in a tightly buttoned and nondescript black overcoat, Lennox sings, "Ashes to ashes, dust to dust, this is what becomes of all of us. . . . Let it all go by." Madonna's spectacle of glamor and sensuality is displaced by a sister of the grim reaper, an effect enhanced by the occasional superimposition on Lennox's makeupless face of another face, Lennox wearing deep red lipstick and a veil with stars on it, that fades almost as quickly as it appears.

Except for the last cut on both video and album, a song from the thirties, and two songs on which she collaborated with Peter-John Vettese and P. Buchanan respectively, Lennox wrote all *Diva*'s lyrics. On the recording, Lennox does some of the keyboards and all the voices. Nothing, that is, could be further from the work of Madonna with her huge array of singers and dancers and songwriters and bizarre costumes and high-tech production. Lennox's diva, Lennox *as* diva, is very much alone. It is, of course, ironic that *Diva*, more than her work as half of the Eurythmics, establishes Lennox as a diva, a solo singer, a solo performer. While, that is, Lennox seems both to counter and to mock by her solitude and simplicity Madonna's status as diva surrounded by adoring supporters and fans, she also reinstates the stereotype of the diva as a woman so far above the crowd that she's ultimately alone, as the scene in St. Mark's Square—in which the elaborately dressed singer is surrounded by photo-snapping tourists—suggests. When she sets up the diva figure as a singer past her prime, caught up in fame and fortune, unable to distinguish between the diva life and "real" life ("a legend in my living room"), then, she fears not only the fate of Madonna but her own fate as well.

One of the album's songs, "Money Can't Buy It," which Lennox also performs on the video, expresses best, we think, some of the ambiguities and uneasinesses with which Lennox seems to wrestle here and in her interviews. What money—and, the lyrics continue, sex and drugs—can't buy is, of course, love. And several critics read this song as an assertion of those values, like love, that they and Lennox find lacking in the world: the song "finds Lennox championing love over a cushy lifestyle" (Joyce); "Lennox still believes in love as the ultimate goal" as she "flaunts the shallow benefits of success" (Riccio). "Cushy" and "shallow" suggest, of course, the critics' agreement with what they perceive as Lennox's sentiments. For the most part the lyrics support that reading; the chorus, for example, says over and over again, "I believe in love alone yea yea." One critic calls the song "convincing" (Agassi); another comments on the "great conviction" with which she here repeats a "familiar theme" (Robins). And the verses as well reinforce the familiar themes of Lennox's interviews: "Won't somebody tell me what we're coming to . . . / All the money in the world won't buy you peace of mind." These are, of course, themes familiar not only to Lennox herself but to pop music in general. Even Madonna believes in love.

But the real interest in this song lies in a rap section that occurs just before the final chorus of the creed: "Pay attention to me / 'Cause I'm a rich white girl . . . / I got DIAMONDS . . . / I got so many that I can't close my safe at night." Critics see this section as self-reflection, "self-mocking" (Evans 41), part of the "stylized self-portrait" (Gates 82) that is Diva. Lennox herself concurs, "I say this from my perspective, I'm one of those materialistic people that has a lot of things . . . [which] . . . has made it difficult for me to have the thing that perhaps I needed most" (Robins). Lennox's reading here underlines the portrait of herself that she has constructed since the release of the solo album—a repentant ("Have mercy on me," she sings in "Legend in My Living Room") materialist who has now discovered her real person and her real values, "reclaimed a real person from an artifice." But this reading seems too simple. For one thing, it's difficult not to see the rap voice as the voice not simply of the diva figure, the diva persona, but of a particular diva whose most famous song proclaims, "I am a Material Girl."

The opening of the rap section strongly suggests this: "Now/ Hear this/ Pay attention to me." It is, of course, the attention that Madonna not only demands but gets (we recall here Fisher's comment that "Madonna has no equal at getting attention") that is so irksome to her critics. And although "pay attention" is a common enough idiom, the economic metaphor echoes Madonna's own such use in "Material Girl": "If they don't give me proper credit, I just walk away." Even Lennox's use of the epithet "white"

("I'm a rich white girl") seems a comment both on Madonna's popularity among blacks and on accusations that Madonna has exploited race for profit. Further, the excess expressed in having so many diamonds that she can't close her safe echoes Lennox's remark about Madonna's having "gone that far." It is the excess of Madonna that makes Lennox (and us) "tense," and excess that is so clearly the subject of the rap.[18]

In the video version of "Money Can't Buy It," Lennox poses in front of a mirror with a towel wrapped turban-like on her head, implying that the turban, with its suggestion of exoticism and royalty, and the elaborate jeweled and feathered headdress she wears on some of the other cuts, are nothing but pretension-deflating towels. She sings cheek-to-cheek with her mirror image, sometimes smiling at it, a pose that reinforces accusations of narcissism so frequently made against divas in general and Madonna in particular. Koestenbaum comments on the diva as "never alone; her solitude is peopled with reflections of herself" (*QT* 114), as Lennox's diva is here quite literally; to him, though, a diva's narcissism has the advantage, unlike more ordinary forms of narcissism, of not seeming "silly" (86). But there is something silly, quite deliberately silly, about Lennox's diva, perhaps the flirtatious smiles at her reflection, perhaps the demythologizing towel on her head.

The opening cut of the video, "Why," also has the diva in front of a mirror. At first she is unadorned and seemingly unhappy about the way she looks. With makeup and costume, including the feathered headdress, she constructs an elaborate figure who tries on various poses, first in front of the mirror, then in front of a photographer-less camera. The poses she strikes are sensual and languorous, reminiscent of photographs of famous divas from an earlier era. The difference between the plain woman who opens the scene and the plumed diva who emerges is striking and emphasizes the artifice necessary to the diva life, artifice that becomes the subject of the other cut featuring the diva costume, "The Gift." Just before the music begins, we see the diva blindfolded; the blindfold quickly becomes a mask, which she wears through most of the segment. She is in St. Mark's Square, sometimes alone, sometimes with hundreds of pigeons, sometimes with passers-by and fans, who shower her with confetti and requests for photos. She is, quite literally, statuesque, towering—in her very high heels—first above buildings, then above the people who are photographed next to her. She sings, "Take this gilded cage and set me free" and "I can't go on living in this same sick joke."

The diva becomes here the artificial woman, painted beyond recognition, bejeweled (diamonds . . . you heard about those), blindfolded (and so, of course, metaphorically blind), masked, sculpted, and caged. The only other use of "sick" in the *Diva* lyrics is the "sick dream" of "Money Can't Buy It." Its use here links this elaborately constructed diva to the rich white girl of that song and so comments again on the artificiality, shallowness, and ultimate destructiveness of divahood. If, then, we see *Diva* as a "stylized self-portrait," it is the portrait of a self from which Annie Lennox has clearly distanced her "real" self: I'm just me. I'm a simple girl from Aberdeen, daughter of a boilermaker.

What we're suggesting here is that Annie Lennox has more in common with the diva than she is sometimes willing to admit. Beyond her own history (if we read "Legend in My Living Room" as autobiographical) as a self-crowned "Queen of doom,"[19] Lennox's presentation of herself as a simple and real person, as opposed to the wily, slippery chameleon she appears to be, is itself a construction. And compared to Madonna's consistent and tradition-defying refusal to be either simple or real, Lennox's construction of the anti-diva, the anti-Madonna, is a fairly conservative one, conservative in its dependence on the stereotypes of the masculinist tradition to define divahood and conservative in its celebration of conventional and traditional values—simplicity, motherhood, ambitionlessness—for women. Lennox's role as gender bender is itself a kind of drag that hides, in order to reveal, the traditional woman she has constructed underneath. It's tempting to call her the "backlash diva" given how much her self-presentations recall the postwar divas before her who worked so hard to present themselves in their autobiographies as simply "real" woman. It's the gesture of Kiri Te Kanawa as she bows deeply after a performance and blows kisses to the audience. It's just me. I'm a simple Maori girl from New Zealand. Cecilia Bartoli. It's just me. I'm a simple girl from the Italian countryside. Cinderella. The fairy-tale diva narrative lives on.

CHAPTER 8

Diamanda Galas

CALLAS WITH AN ATTITUDE

*I don't think that I could survive if the work I
was doing was detached from the time in which I
was living, and that time includes AIDS. That's
why I'm not going on stage and singing Tosca or
Norma, with all due respect to those works and as
much as I love them. . . . They don't really explore the
nature of the time we are living in—the very visceral
nature of it.*
—Diamanda Galas

*B*efore Lorena Bobbitt cut her husband John and incited a national debate over the boundary between anger and insanity, rage and pathology, so neatly tied together in notions of female "madness," there was Diamanda Galas and her vocal composition *Wild Women with Steak Knives*, what she calls a "Homicidal Love Song for Solo Scream."[1] "Solo" is somewhat misleading; as in most of the pieces Galas writes and performs, her voice in *Wild Women* takes on a multitude of parts/roles—here the voices of the fragmented "selves" of a schizophrenic woman. Anger and insanity combine; female insanity is figured as a symptom of anger. The roles/voices are distinguished through varied timbres, textures, registers, and vocal styles that exploit to the full Galas's extraordinary range of three and one-half octaves. Screams, wails, whispers, keening, glossolalia, and cries of "listen" bespeak rage, terror, isolation. The effect is amplified, in all senses of the word, by Galas's use of multiple microphones and other technological aids that multiply and fracture one voice into multitudes.[2] The voices are the frenzied Maenads'—Eliot's Armgart, remember, claims them as sisters when she declares that she carries her revenge in her throat. The politics are Medusa's: she who is the object of the gaze gazes back; Galas's performances often work to disrupt the objectifying gaze of masculinist power and lay bare the politics of spectatorship. We have pointed out that the revisionist tradition describes the diva's voice as a point of identification for other women, as a vehicle for their anger and desire and a site for female community. So, too, with Galas's narrative of her own vocal history, although, as ever with Galas, in the extreme: "Some of my earliest performances were in mental institutions. . . . The response I got was very positive; it was very much a shared kind of community expression. A lot of women were interested in the way I was using my voice—extroversion of the soul, so to speak" (Avena 180).

Predictably, reviews in the mainstream press of Galas's performances often employ rhetorical strategies that, Perseus-like, try to cut her down to size, try to domesticate her and reinscribe her in traditional women's roles. In his *New York Times* review of *Insekta*, Edward Rothstein calls up the conventional figure of the demented diva—the diva "leaves behind rationality, emulating madness"; her voice "is always on the edge, touching on the forbidden, breaking the boundaries of earthly melody"—and enrolls Galas among their numbers. By the close of this very mixed review, however, he decides that Galas is somehow beyond divahood, that she "has redefined the diva: She is already over the edge, already beyond madness. She is neither noble nor heroic nor tragic. She is merely a victim"—as if victimhood doesn't always haunt the diva; she plays victims; she sings to avoid becoming a victim herself. Galas's threat to the system of binary oppositions on which cultural constructions of gender and sexuality depend leads another critic to engage in a massively defensive but finally incoherent remarshaling of other oppositions: "That operatically trained instrument is a force of nature, climbing from an ashen whisper to Callas-like brilliance, and beyond that to a harsh mechanical purity, like a tea-kettle whistle" (Brown, "Galas's Screams"). Joe Brown's use of the nature/culture opposition fails to stabilize the system and inadvertently deconstructs it (how can a trained voice be a force of "nature"?), but he can still close with a triumphant image of "nature" domesticated. The female voice that aspires to climb, to rise, is punished through ironic reversal. To be beyond Callas— who despite her own rages and other nontraditional gender behaviors still tried to perform traditional femininity—is to be beyond divahood and beyond womanhood. Galas as Callas is transformed into Olympia, a singing mechanical doll.

Wild Women, an early composition, which, in its use of a variety of vocal techniques and electronics is typical of much of Galas's work, privileges themes we have stressed throughout this study—excess, transgression, female "madness" in its multiple senses. Galas is a diva who not only sings mad scenes but writes them, and her revisionary political impulse works here on the stereotypes of both the female malady and the demented diva. Rothstein's attempt to read Galas as an over-the-top Lucia notwithstanding, Galas's mad protagonists are not Lucias or Elviras. As Susan McClary points out: "Like other performance artists, she enacts her pieces upon her own body. This is politically very different from the tradition of male composers projecting their own fantasies of transgression as well as their own fears on to women characters. Galas is not interested in the narrative of raising the specter of the monstrous, flirting with madness, and then reimposing control. . . . She enacts the rage of the madwoman for purposes of protesting genuine atrocities" (*Feminine Endings* 110). The works Galas has composed and performed take up a number of tragedies and horrors— imprisonment, political torture and murder, mental illness—but the atrocity she is most associated with is AIDS. Her trilogy *The Masque of The Red Death*, which Galas has described as a "one-woman opera," is one of the first serious musical responses to the epidemic (Hilferty).[3] Sections of *The Masque* reappear in the *Plague Mass*, a shorter performance version of *The Masque*. A portion of the *Plague Mass* served as the germ of the more recent *Vena Cava*, one long "mad scene" that seeks to articulate the fractured voices of someone suffering from AIDS dementia.[4] Heteroglossia, both *Wild Women* and *Vena Cava* suggest, is the essence, as it were, of subjectivity. Screams, pleas, and obscenities mix in *Vena Cava* with spirituals, snatches of Purcell, and a powerfully sung rendition of "Porgi Amor" from Mozart's *The Marriage of Figaro*. In its new context, the Countess's plaintive and painful "Grant, O love, some sweet elixir to heal my pain, to soothe my sighs! To my arms restore my loved one or vouchsafe that I may die" becomes a militant, political anthem. By quoting one of the most beautiful musical (if politically retrograde) expressions of desire that Western culture has to offer, *Vena Cava* recoups desire and beauty for the HIV-infected body, the very body that the dominant culture has argued should renounce its desire and has figured as having been, through illness, punished for its desire.

The coupling of mourning and militancy achieved in *Vena Cava*'s quotation of Mozart is the defining strategy of the *Plague Mass*. As many commentators have pointed out, Galas's most important operatic model is Maria Callas; "the vocal and visual resemblances are remarkable," notes Thomas Avena (177). Galas herself lists Callas among her idols, and photographs of Galas wearing large dark glasses or heavy eye makeup—"no diva performs without her *full* eye makeup," Galas insists—pose her as more Callas than Callas herself (Juno and Vale 9). But Callas is not the only female singer from Greece with whom Galas identifies; she also places herself and her work in the tradition of women singers of *moirológia*, dirges and lamentations for the dead, which sometimes call for vengeance. Since antiquity, death has been an occasion for female vocal performance in Greece. Women not only prepare the corpse for burial but also sing dirges, their formulae passed down through an oral tradition. Often the women pull their hair, beat their breasts, and rend their clothing as they sing, cry, and wail.[5] Thus the disruption of death becomes, as well, the occasion for the disruption of women's traditional silence and eruption of women's voices; the women sing and lament with, according to Galas, "the violence of somebody who's been in a hole for a really long time" (Gehr 118).

Galas has called *moirológi* singing "a radical performance tradition" (Carr 190), and a number of features of that tradition are important for understanding Galas and her *Plague Mass*. Some of the more accomplished singers of *moirológia* became, in effect, some of the first professional female singers in Greece. Tradition required that kinswomen be the primary dirge singers, but particularly skillful singers were sometimes asked to join them and were compensated in some way for their participation (Alexiou 10, 40–41). Not surprisingly, we have seen the pattern before—civil and religious authorities during both the classical and Christian periods tried to control, at times silence, these women's voices: in the *Laws* Plato forbids "hired songs," and Church father John Chrysostum condemns dirges as "blasphemies" (Alexiou 10, 28). Historians have offered a number of possible reasons, some of them unrelated to gender, for official attempts to limit and control funeral rites and practices, but the terms with which the early Church tried to condemn and curtail these popular and pagan practices, so as to appropriate them in the service of its own patriarchal power, are highly gendered.[6] Chrysostum, for example, lists dirge singing and breast beating as symptoms of "this disease of females" (Alexiou 28) and argues against female performance by calling for female modesty. The terms are similar to other Church arguments about women "displaying" themselves on stage. Women who perform are ever pathological and/or corrupt:

> What are you doing, woman? Tell me, would you shamelessly strip
> yourself naked in the middle of the market-place, you, who are a part
> of Christ, in the presence of men and in the very market-place? And

> would you tear your hair, rend your garments and wail loudly, danc-
> ing and preserving the image of Bacchic women, without regard for
> your offence to God?
>
> (Alexiou 29)

Again the Maenads—also known as Bacchae—are called up, here to link
female voice and performance to transgressive sexuality, madness, disorder, and disease in order to foreclose the possibility of linking them to politics, art, and anger.[7]

As Margaret Alexiou shows, patriarchal complaints about female
dirge singers inaccurately and unfairly figured their performances as art-
less, as spontaneous and disordered exercises in excess and self-indulgence
(28, 34). Galas's work has been characterized similarly, as mere screaming,
a charge she rejects: "People have also called my work 'primal screaming,'
but I have problems with a word like 'primal.' . . . Although my work is
very emotional and concerned with things that are larger than life, it is also
very disciplined. I prefer to call it 'intravenal electroacoustic voice work'"
(Holden). Other listeners have tried to place the *Plague Mass*, and thus by
extension Galas herself, on the side of the "good" feminine, the sentimental. She rejects this reading as well: "In 1986 my brother was diagnosed
with AIDS. It is bizarre that I was working on this two years before Philip
was diagnosed, but that is how things are. Unfortunately, people tend to
want to sentimentalize the work, to see it as a reaction to my brother's illness . . . : 'Oh, she's mourning the death of her brother from AIDS!' This is
seen as sufficient explanation. It is also used by idiots and misogynists as a
deprecation of the work, as if it is some pathetic sentimentality" (Avena
187–188).

Galas herself connects the emotional intensity of her work with her
heritage: "The intensity of my work has a lot to do with my being of Greek
descent. . . . Greeks pretty much scream about everything—it's part of the
family. What I do is commandeer and control these emotional forces and
propel them in different directions in order to take the audience on an emotional voyage" (Holden). The military rhetoric—commandeer, propel—is
important. In a number of interviews Galas traces both her ancestry and her
dirge singing to the Spartan Maniots, whose lamentation tradition was well
developed and stressed not just grief but militancy (see, for example, Juno
and Vale 11). The voice of militancy in Maniot culture is a woman's voice;
when men died in wars or blood feuds, Maniot women called for revenge.
According to Alexiou, "Although the act itself rested with the men . . . the
women maintained the consciousness for the need to take revenge by con-

stant lamentation and invocation at the tomb. . . . The dirge is always the strongest where the law of vendetta flourishes, as in Sicily or Mani today" (22). In other words, Maniot women transformed lamentation into political discourse and grief into political action. "Patronizing sympathy is revolting," Galas contends; "it has nothing to do with Greek tragedy or Middle Eastern . . . mourning, which not only expresses the mourning of the family, but—more importantly—the *anger* of the dead" (Juno and Vale 12). As call to action and cultural critique, Galas's work exemplifies what critic Douglas Crimp has argued is the most necessary kind of art about AIDS: "a critical, theoretical, activist alternative to the personal elegiac expressions that [have] appeared to dominate the art-world response to AIDS. . . . AIDS . . . requires a critical rethinking of all of culture: of language and representation, of science and medicine, of health and illness, of sex and death, of the public and private realms" (15).

From this vantage point we see why critics have linked the *Plague Mass* to Haydn's *Mass in Time of War* and Britten's *War Requiem* and why Galas herself is careful to separate her work from traditional requiem masses. "It's a plague mass, as opposed to more traditionally a requiem mass, in the sense that it's very active mourning," Galas observed in an interview. "It's a political discussion. It's for the dead, but it's for people living with AIDS, for the AIDS community, for the families. It deals with a geography of the plague mentality, a slow death in a hostile environment. It discusses how to stay alive in this kind of place" (Brown, "With Songs"). For Galas, requiems induce political quiescence; as a "plague mass," her work emphasizes that epidemic diseases have long been the occasion for the division and policing of persons and groups: "'Plague' refers specifically to a quarantine mentality as represented in Leviticus, by the way in which the disease is received within the community, the way people with it are isolated as 'unclean,' much as lepers used to be," she argues. "A requiem mass helps to pacify the living so they can feel the dead are resting in peace. . . . The dead from this disease, I don't think of them as resting in peace" (Polkow). Mourning is transformed into a call for action. The final section of *The Masque*, "You Must Be Certain of the Devil," is an angry and aggressive call to act up and fight back, against the Roman Catholic Church and evangelical preachers who are quick to condemn and slow to show compassion, against skinhead gay-bashers, and against everyone who ignores or merely watches the spectacle of suffering and disease. Using gospel idioms and reworking such well-known spirituals as "Swing Low, Sweet Chariot" and "Let My People Go" (a setting that closes the *Plague*

Mass recording), Galas taps a musical tradition that, she claims, is about survival and resistance and appropriates it for a new fight against the forces of marginalization and bigotry.

Galas borrows her title, *The Masque of the Red Death*, from Poe, of course, and the trilogy includes settings of passages from Lamentations, Leviticus, and the Psalms, settings of poems by Corbiere, Nerval, and Baudelaire, reworkings of gospel music and spirituals, and settings of her own lyrics as well. As Richard Gehr notes, in "confronting the historically determined residue of 2,000 years of Judeo-Christian ethics [and some of its critics], Galas sorts through the preexisting structures of feeling and thought that the culture has provided as tools, sometimes inappropriate or actually destructive ones, with which to face the disease" (117). Not just to "face" the disease, we would argue, but to know/represent it, as Gehr's sense of *The Masque* as a Foucauldian "genealogy of the idea" of a plague's capacity to generate social division and oppression implies (117). *The Masque*'s strategy of quoting many and varied discourses reminds listeners that the new is always read through epistemological frames provided by earlier discourses, discourses that always have ideological investments. There was, in other words, a set of representations of disease and (homo)sexuality that was already, as it were, waiting for AIDS to appear, representations (that disease is punishment for sin, that homosexuality is a disease, for example) through which AIDS was read and which were used to construct the "meaning" of AIDS.

"The most dangerous thing about the AIDS epidemic is the way we are conditioned to think about it, which encourages the sense of isolation that people end up with," Galas has argued (Avena 182). The opening movement of "The Divine Punishment" (the first of the three parts that constitute *The Masque of the Red Death*), a piece that reappears in the *Plague Mass*, is a setting of Leviticus 15, titled "This Is the Law of the Plague." That law, Galas sings in a tone that both mocks and mimics such patriarchal pronouncements, is "To teach when it is clean / And when it is unclean." Epidemics present ideological opportunities by which power regulates persons and increasingly transforms private realms into public ones. Fear of disease becomes a vehicle of social control, for the reassertion of traditional binary identity categories (clean/unclean, monogamous/ promiscuous, heterosexual/homosexual) and for the construction of new identity categories ("innocent victim," "general population," "risk group"). In this way the repression, marginalization, and punishment of persons confined to penal categories like "risk group" can masquerade as the destiny arising "naturally" from a particular identity. Galas unmasks this masquerade by claiming repeatedly that AIDS is "homicide."

"When any man hath an issue out of his flesh, / Because of that issue he is unclean. / Every bed whereon he lieth is unclean," Galas sings, and these lines from Leviticus 15 about "unclean" issues from men's flesh call to mind another famous, but here unspoken, verse from Leviticus, the command in 18.22 that a man not lie with another man. The omission resonates for any listener familiar with the religious right's polemics against homosexuality. The *Plague Mass* reminds listeners that Leviticus is a founding text both for the ideological use of disease as an occasion for social division and control and for the West's discourse against homosexuality, a discourse that has allied it with sin, disease, and contagion. "The Divine Punishment" was first performed in 1986, a time when AIDS was consistently figured as a "gay disease" by the popular media and as a punishment for "sinful" sexual practices by the political and religious right. By quoting Leviticus, which figures disease as punishment for sin, Galas emphasizes that conservative and phobic discourses about AIDS in the early and mid eighties used the syndrome and the fear it generated to reinvigorate older discourses about the "sinfulness" and "pathology" of homosexuality and to argue for the punitive identification and quarantine of gay men as a "public health" measure.

Traditional *moirológia* are often structured antiphonally (for solo voice and chorus, for example) and the parts are often in antithetical relation. In some *moirológia* this structure is used to construct an imagined dialogue between the living and the dead (the personification of the voices of the dead is a convention of Greek dirges).[8] The *Plague Mass* mobilizes these conventions for its own ends. For example, in "This Is the Law of the Plague," the judging, excluding patriarchal voice of Leviticus is interrupted by responses from the suffering and dead, settings of Psalms 22 and 59 and a text written by Galas herself, which plead for deliverance and compassion and imply that the judging, Levitical voice is the voice of evil. This section is followed by a section of spoken dialogue, recitative, called "I Wake Up and See the Face of the Devil," which dramatizes an escalating exchange ("How do you feel today. . . . Are you sure you are facing things? . . . There's something unnatural about this thing") between a patient and another person or persons—physician, caretaker, visitor—which drives the patient to hysterical responses. A narrative is implied; roles are sung. Formally structured musical compositions (solo and technologically produced "choruses") alternate with passages of spoken dialogue. A liturgical form is transformed into a dramatic

form that takes up traditional operatic themes—death, madness, political resistance. Mass becomes opera. In the tradition of ACT-UP's 1989 demo and
die-in at St. Patrick's Cathedral in which Galas participated, Mass becomes
political action.

Epidemics, we noted, have long served as the pretexts for increased
social regulation, division, and surveillance—the means and ends of what
Galas has called the "quarantine mentality." What Foucault calls in *Discipline and Punish* "spectacles of enforcement" (public executions, for example) also function to regulate behavior and to divide persons from each
other.[9] Galas repeatedly describes AIDS as "homicide," and she opens the
Plague Mass with a composition called "Were You a Witness," which draws
an explicit parallel between the crucifixion of Christ and the deaths of persons with AIDS. The linkage is heavy with irony in a culture in which
AIDS is often figured as the wages of sin, where homosexual practices are
still in some places illegal, where some suspect that the government's slow
reaction to the epidemic was/is ideological, and where the PWA is so often
represented, like the criminal, as the person with whom identification is
forbidden. (Recall the many media images during the mid- and late eighties
of solitary and cadaverous PWAs hooked up to medical machinery—these
images served as monitory emblems, spectacles of enforcement, arguing
that a lonely and painful death was always the fate of gay persons and IV
drug users.) Exploiting the multiple senses of "witness" in legal and religious discourse, she sings to "you cowards and voyeurs" that "There are no
more tickets to the funeral / The funeral is crowded / Were you a witness /
Were you a witness." The singer some critics have called the "Diva of Disease" works to force her audience to give up its complacent ease over
AIDS.[10] While the *Plague Mass*, she argues, is *for* persons who are living
with AIDS, persons who have died of AIDS-related illnesses, and the
people who care about them and suffer with them, the work is *aimed* at, in
all senses of the word, the bigoted and the complacent. "This is not the music of a person who wants to play fairly with the forces against which she
aims her sonic assault. This is terrorism, pure and simple," writes her research assistant Michael Flanagan (161). Galas is not merely highlighting
the difference between passivity and action about AIDS here. By figuring
her audience as voyeurs, she draws a parallel between the masculinist gaze
that seeks to frame women in order to control them and the framing of
PWAs, the tendency to represent the HIV+ body as other and the PWA as
silent and monitory emblem of transgression punished.

Galas's genealogy of the plague mentality makes clear that representations of gays and PWAs are interested constructions. The work has another agenda as well, which it shares with *Wild Women, Vena Cava,* and her other compositions: to explore/express what it's like to be subject in/to a system of discursive oppositions that confine as they define (the speaker in *Vena Cava* repeatedly quotes the pedagogue's "boy, girl, boy, girl"). To this end Galas employs what might be called a strategic essentialism. In interviews, she claims repeatedly that the *Plague Mass* is the wound of the epidemic itself: "Most pop music is descriptive; it's *about* the thing, not the thing *itself.* Whereas my work is the thing itself, it *is* the sound of the plague" (Juno and Vale 14). This claim recalls her description of how she uses her voice, "extroversion of the soul, so to speak" (the qualification, we think, is significant). In other words, her work aspires to reproduce rather than represent, to express while circumventing cultural codes, to give a voice to those who are traditionally silenced and objectified in cultural discourse—women, gays, the mentally ill, PWAs. Of course Galas runs into the same difficulty feminists before her have found, how to make those who are constructed by the system as silent and objectified into speaking subjects within that system. Thus, we think, Galas's frequent use of glossolalia and the discourse of the mentally ill; their unintelligibility reminds listeners of the epistemological and representational limits of the discursive system (Galas figures glossolalia as a "space of freedom" ["Diamanda Galas" 18]). This is, perhaps, finally a utopian and nostalgic project, but we admire her insistence that there are real people who are suffering and dying and who therefore shouldn't be deconstructed away; "I'm talking about blood and muscle hanging from the cross and stinking up the room. Death by crucifixion is prolonged torture—the back breaks one vertebra at a time" (Gracie and Zarkov 78).

Not surprisingly, Galas's ironic use of biblical texts and liturgical forms ("You Must Be Certain of the Devil" closes not with a benediction but a "malediction") to represent persons living with and dying of AIDS as Christ-like martyrs to social bigotries has led to some religious hysteria. The Christian right in the United States has denounced her work as satanic, and during one of her European tours, Italian officials, in the tradition of Chrysostum's denunciation of earlier female dirge singers, accused Galas of blasphemy. Cast as demonic iconoclast, she appeals to tradition: "I was simply performing the mourning rituals of the old women of the south of Italy and Greece. . . . I don't think these old women would have been shocked at all" (Avena 193). In an interview she quotes an Italian editorial with pride, "After the fake scandal and fake blasphemy of Madonna, now we have a real blasphemer" (Polkow). Like Madonna, Galas takes female stereotypes—the hysteric, the vagina dentata, the phallic woman—to the limit in order to reclaim them for women's own interests.[11] (Like Annie Lennox, Galas repeatedly distances herself from Madonna: "And people like Madonna are only too willing to propagate the idea that, 'If you want to feel better about a terrible situation, you can dance'" [Juno and Vale 14]. Unlike Lennox, however, Galas wants to distance her work from pop music itself, which, she argues, "generally dilutes the subject [like AIDS] so that people live with it without confronting anything unpleasant" [Gracie and Zarkov 76]).

The spectacle of enforcement that was Christ's crucifixion was also, Christianity tells us, his sacrifice, and in her performances of the *Plague Mass* Galas presents herself as a sacrificial spectacle, covered in stage blood and naked to the waist. Her exposed and bloody breasts remind the audience that it occupies the discomfiting position of the voyeurs in "Were You a Witness," who either keep a passive and disengaged distance from the suffering they see or who find the suffering of others titillating. Here again the strategy of the critique is to display the extreme, to make the unspoken assumption and conventional mode of thought spectacularly obvious: "The People of the Catholic Church see suffering as something old—like the martyrs—by which they are voyeuristically thrilled and titillated. I'm talking about blood and muscle hanging from the cross and stinking up the room. . . . I'm not talking about pain as eroticism" (Gracie and Zarkov 78). The blood is Christ's sacrificial blood (in performance she pours blood on herself during the Consecration) and the infected blood of the PWA, but it also recalls the lamenting women of the *moirológi* tradition who draw their own blood and represent their dead as sacrificial victims. Galas likens her performances to sacrificial rites, and she finds her primary model for sacrifice not, as we might expect, in the mass or the tradition of the Levitical scapegoat, but in the *moirológi* tradition of vengeance: "Traditionally, they would sacrifice everything to avenge that person's death. So sacrificing one's public image, or sacrificing the intelligibility of the performance, when confounded by this intense emotional experience, is a small price to pay in comparison" (Avena 193–194).[12]

But what finally gets offered up, put at risk, is her voice. To hear Galas perform is to be constantly worried that what she is doing with/to her voice will ruin it, to hope that her extensive training, skill, and discipline will protect her instrument. In this, Galas seems to participate in a long tradition that includes Callas. As Koestenbaum makes clear, anxiety that the diva's voice might break is always a part of diva worship (we might call this a kind of "vocal voyeurism"). He argues further that some operas exploit this anxiety/expectation: "The audience is excited by the danger that hysterical or extreme parts pose to the voice: opera requires the preservation of a singing instrument, and yet opera also explodes the boundaried, obedient self, moving listeners and performers away from respectability and toward rage, even if the throat is silenced by the travail of speaking out" (*QT* 127). Here again Galas calls up and reworks the conventional diva narrative. Unlike most divas, Galas herself writes for her own voice; she knows where the outer reaches of safety are and can respect them. She exploits, in order finally to refuse, the romantic scenario of triumphant/tragic voice/lessness that opera, or at least Koestenbaum, finds thrilling; she makes us aware that she knows we expect everything to end in the silence of vocal rupture even as she refuses to be silent.

Galas links voice and rupture in another way. If every diva needs eye makeup to perform, so she needs a narrative of origins for her voice. The diva narrative that Galas constructs marks out rupture or discontinuity as the origin, rather than the potential climax, of hers.[13] Asked by an interviewer if there was "a break, when suddenly you were free to excavate the voice," Galas shies away from the depth metaphor of "excavate" (and the model of an essential and unified selfhood the metaphor implies) and locates origin instead in disruption: "*My* break happened shortly after living and working in a situation that had very little to do with art. It had to do with distrusting everything, distrusting every means of expression I had learned, so that all the means of my previous expression became too facile, like gestures. . . . I felt I was in search of a new vocabulary of expression. By no means was I alone in doing that" (Avena 180–181). But as she closes this decentering myth of origins, she decenters it in turn by providing another: "I often sang while working on the street; as a matter of fact, I discovered my voice. There I was with these queen sisters—in particular Miss Gina—saying, 'Do you know that you have a lovely voice, Miss Thing?' "Oh, why thank-you'" (Avena 182). Two elements of this tale are striking. In this narrative, the singer is a "whore," as the patriarchal voice has warned and as masculinist diva narratives repeatedly insist. Further, her first fans, and those who help her to recognize her voice, are transvestites (and thus themselves figures of disruption, as Garber makes clear). In this version, then, Galas "discovers" her voice in a world where boundaries are already blurred and identity categories already unsettled. As her early setting of Baudelaire's *Litanies of Satan* (1982) suggests, Galas is drawn to

the figure of the unrepentant outlaw and constructs her own self-represen-
tations along the same line, but she also illustrates here an important strategy of both her work and her politics: to proudly own the very traits/
identities the wider culture assigns and then uses to condemn, confine,
isolate.

As Madonna has been called a "pop diva," so we might call Galas a
"pomo diva." Critics have called her an "avant-garde diva," and she has
worked with avant garde and New Music composers and performers; Vinko
Globokar, for example, gave her the lead in his opera about Turkish women
tortured for treason, *Un Jour comme une autre*. Here too, perhaps disingenuously, she distances herself: "I don't think of my work as avant-garde
or bizarre, I think of it as natural expression. When you come from a place
like San Diego you don't know about the avant-garde" (Gaer 431). In the
bourgeois tradition to which many of the texts and singers we discuss in
this study belong, the voice is often figured (with some qualifications) as a
manifestation of—or the expressive vehicle for—a unique, unified, autonomous selfhood. Thea Kronberg's voice, remember, gives her a "sense of
wholeness." Galas, on the other hand, as techno-pomo diva deliberately
alienates her voice from her-/it-self; she distorts and multiplies her voice
electronically, a fitting strategy for works that, like *Wild Women*, *Plague
Mass*, and *Vena Cava*, assume a divided, fragmented, multiple human subject. *Vena Cava*, the voice of someone near death who is also suffering
from AIDS-related dementia or other mental illness, figures psychic life as
a tissue of quotations—we hear there the voices of parents and pedagogues
as well as quotations from the Mass, from Mozart and "Amazing Grace,"
obscenities, multiplication tables, bingo calling—from the discourses that
constitute us.

These multiple voices speak to a politics of multiple identification
that understands identity categories as fluid and constructed and understands gender and sexuality as performative. Speaking of the time she spent
as a sex worker in Oakland, Galas credits her transvestite coworkers with
not only encouraging her voice but educating her on womanhood: "I
learned a lot about *being a woman* from those black drag queens—the
power behind the role, how you can use it" (Juno and Vale 21). This may
sound retrograde to some ears, but we want to argue that at least part of the
power is a kind of freedom for multiple identification, an embrace of all
identities that subverts the (Levitical) notion of identity as fixed and essential and rejects the divisive identity politics that this model produces and
sustains. Significantly, Galas allies this politics of multiple identification

with her female voice: "From the Greeks onward, [the female] voice has always been a political instrument as well as a vehicle for transmission of occult knowledge or power. It's always been tied to witches and the shamanistic experience—the witch as transvestite/transsexual having the power of both male and female. People ask me, 'How do you feel as a woman onstage?' and I say, 'A *what*? Woman, man—I am a fucking nigger, a white person, lesbian, homosexual, witch, snake, vampire—whatever!' I don't think in any one of those terms—that's so limited!" (Juno and Vale 10–11). We have suggested that literary and historical divas of the revisionist tradition break down binary gender and sexuality categories through their "masculine" behavior and stance toward the world. Galas, as always, pushes further. By explicitly embracing all social positions and identity categories simultaneously, she seems to be trying to avoid—and perhaps this is an impossible, utopic, nostalgic project—reinscribing on another level both those categories and the binary structure that produces and depends on them.

This stress on the performative, and her sense of the political power of performance, should not, however, lead to the conclusion that Galas's politics are merely an exercise in striking a pose. Tattooed on her hand is the claim "We are all HIV+." "People always ask me why I am singing to a special interest group," Galas has complained; "I tell them I am the special interest group, *we all are*" (Gaer 432). Despite her protests, all this may leave Galas open, unfairly, to the charge of "fag-hagging." Gay male opera culture often identifies with the diva as a model of anguish and anger triumphant and as a model for the rejection of conventional gender behaviors; the archetype/object is Callas. Galas, an avowedly feminist diva, does what Callas never really managed—she publicly, and against the advice of many in the music business, identifies with gay men. Long before the opera scene in Jonathan Demme's *Philadelphia* (1993) linked divas (Callas), disease (AIDS), and gay men, Galas linked them. Long before the now alarming rise in the infection rates of women, Galas's work and public statements suggested that she understood that AIDS is an issue for feminists. As Constance Penley points out, like women, "gay men too inhabit bodies that are still a legal, moral, and religious battleground" (157). As the religious right's increased activism against gay rights legislation makes clear, the same forces that would legislate what women can and cannot do with their bodies seek to do the same to/for gay bodies. "That's what the whole trilogy is about," Galas argues, "the witch hunt" ("Diamanda Galas" 25).

Galas's electronic manipulation of her voice serves more than just her politics of multiple identification and her vision of a decentered human subject. Through technique and electronics she deliberately makes her voice—trained in the difficult art of *bel canto*, "beautiful singing"—unbeautiful; traditional aesthetic values, the strategy implies, are produced by and, in turn support, a conservative ideology. Similarly, Galas's embrace of technology to amplify, multiply, fragment, and deliberately distort her voice is at odds with conventional opinion in the opera world, where electronic amplification is feared as the distorter of the "real voice," a displacement of some pure, originary voice. Galas's privileging of technological mediation in both her performances and recordings reminds listeners that everything they hear is always already in some way mediated through the machinery of culture, a machinery that, for example, encourages us to hear women's anger as hysteria.

Part of a Galas performance is watching her control the equipment that produces and reproduces her voice(s). John MacKay has called the result a "woman-machine joint presence," a description that unsettlingly muddles agency and diminishes Galas's status as the power in control of the machines (72). As we have argued, Olympias and Trilbys have the status of tools or machines wielded, operated, and controlled by men. In *Diva*, technology is aligned with the masculine appropriation of women; Cynthia Hawkins knows that to record is to submit, to renounce her autonomy. Contemporary video biographies of opera singers, like London Weekend Television's *Cecilia Bartoli*, contain scenes of recording sessions that cut from the singer to a control room filled with men at machines who monitor, control, and shape her voice as it is recorded. Here again Galas reverses convention. In performance, she controls the microphones and machines, and when one looks up at her from the audience, the multiple microphones she uses seem to emanate from her head—a Medusa for the electronic age.

Coda: Dream Divas, Diva Dreams

*There's never been a sensible book about an
opera singer and the reason is it can't be done.*
—Of Lena Geyer

$\mathcal{M}$axine Hong Kingston concludes her category-defying work *The Woman Warrior* with the story of Ts'ai Yen, a singer and composer of second-century China. Captured by "barbarians" as a young woman, she spent twelve years fighting, bearing children, and struggling in an alien land. Her children, who did not speak Chinese, laughed at her voice and mimicked her mother tongue. The "barbarians" made music—disturbing to Ts'ai Yen—on whistling reed pipes. One night "out of Ts'ai Yen's tent . . . the barbarians heard a woman's voice singing, as if to her babies, a song so high and clear, it matched the flutes. Ts'ai sang about China and her family there. Her words seemed to be Chinese, but the barbarians understood their sadness and anger" (209). Not only did her children not laugh at her songs, they "eventually sang along." After her ransom, Ts'ai Yen "brought her songs back from the savage lands"; one of them, "A Song for a Barbarian Reed Pipe," becomes the title of *The Woman Warrior*'s final chapter. Now, the narrator says, the Chinese sing it "to their own instruments." The final words of the text refer to Ts'ai Yen's song: "It translated well."

The Woman Warrior is a book about voice. The narrator, a Chinese-American girl, daughter of a "champion-talker" mother, finds a voice both literally and figuratively. Often unable or unwilling to speak, she wonders if her mother's slicing of her frenum was an attempt to silence her altogether. Like her silence, the narrator's childhood paintings, completely black, disturb her Western teachers, but she sees them, "so black and full of possibilities," as stage curtains waiting to reveal "mighty operas" (164). Ts'ai Yen's story, then, is a mythical version of the narrator and her coming-to-voice among the barbarians, the "song so loud and clear" an analog to the text itself, mighty opera, the material manifestation of the unnamed narrator's newfound voice, of, finally, Hong Kingston's own voice. Like Willa Cather, Isak Dinesen, George Eliot, and many others before her, Kingston uses the figure of the singer to signify her coming-to-voice as a writer. Like the singer, the writer of this text—and in some sense every writer—is always translating and hoping that if readers do not literally understand the words (and who of us can really understand the words of another?) they understand at least "their sadness and anger." Ts'ai Yen, dream diva, bridge maker, translator, sings—in a utopian moment—to narrator, reader, and writer across cultures, countries, and centuries.

"*D*oña Diva Sings" is the title of both the signature painting and most elaborate performance piece of artist P. Dubroof. Doña Diva is part of the "secret society" paintings, a series that Dubroof uses to transform the characters of her everyday life—mothers, housewives, "bag ladies"—into larger-than-life, brighter-than-life figures on paper. Doña Diva is four-and-a-half feet wide and seven feet tall; she has big red lips, green hair with hands to match, a purple strapless gown. There is no doubt that she is a substantial, buxom woman. Her "triangular, solid composition," Dubroof says, is important: Doña Diva is "big and happy about it." A small woman herself, Dubroof sees Doña Diva as "the woman of my dreams." Her "rich, deep soprano" is always, effortlessly, on pitch, and "she doesn't have to think about getting there."

But Doña Diva is not just a dream woman; she is also, as Dubroof recognizes, a sort of self-portrait, a figure for Dubroof as artist, who in her painting strives for effortlessness and "meeting the pitch every time in color and composition." A big woman with a big voice—"she's pretty overwhelming"—Doña Diva becomes an emblem of the artist who works, consciously, on a larger-than-life scale. Doña Diva's big mouth is open wide.

A colleague, chemistry professor Janice Hicks, has a literal "dream" diva. When Hicks was a "frustrated" student midway through her graduate career, she had this dream: she and a friend have wonderful orchestra seats for a Met performance. Midway through the opera, there is a stir. The diva has taken ill! Hicks is summoned to replace her. She obediently takes the stage but, knowing neither words nor music, cannot sing.

A revised version appeared after she finished her graduate studies and was working in New York. The beginning of the dream is the same, but this time when she is called on to take the diva's place, beautiful sounds emerge from her open mouth. She not only sings the opera to completion but quickly becomes the toast of New York, her performance heralded in headlines in the *Daily News*, which also reports Kathleen Battle devastated that not she but Janice Hicks is now *the* diva of the Met.

$\mathcal{W}$e worry that our own dream diva/diva dream has become, like Professor Hicks's first version, a bit of a nightmare. We are haunted by eighteenth-century diva Brigitta Banti, "indolent and indifferent, rebellious and arrogant," who was, in spite of numerous fine teachers, a musical ignoramus (Pleasants 107). (But *we* can read notes, Rebecca.) Mozart's libretttist, Lorenzo da Ponte, condemned her as "free of speech, still freer of action, addicted to carousals, dissolute amusement and to the bottle" (Pleasants 108). (We don't drink *that* much, Susan, and we talk too much to carouse.) She was rumored—and this is the main source of our uneasiness—to have sung "da capo arias over and over again, not knowing how to end them" (107). Fearing an analogous fate (ourselves, perhaps, too "free of speech"), we let these dream divas talk—and sing—for themselves.

NOTES

Program Notes

1. Jones distinguishes the "bulletproof diva" from "that tired stereotype, the emasculating black bitch" (3). "Emasculating bitch" is certainly one way of describing the diva stereotype we elaborate in this study of opera divas as well. Most of these divas, however, are white, like the cultural stereotype itself. Until relatively recently black singers were rarely allowed on the opera stage, nor could the cultural imagination accommodate a black female as a figure of power and privilege.

2. A revised version of this dialogue appears in *Tulsa Studies in Women's Literature* 13 (1994).

Overture

1. This comedy joined a long tradition of comic works with theatrical settings that focused on conflicts between players. Grout places *The Impresario* in the tradition of "some of the early French *opéras comiques*, in which a rehearsal scene serves as a pretext to show off the paces of two rival women singers, who then fall to quarreling while a tenor tries to make peace" (289–290). Women singers have been the object of parody, it appears, nearly as long as they have been on stage.

2. We use here Lionel Salter's translation from the liner notes of the Philips Complete Mozart edition recording.

3. For Clément's reading of the opera, see *Opera, or the Undoing of Women*, 31–32. We agree with most of what Clément says but also see ways in which the opera critiques and complicates those stereotypes, ways that Clément ignores.

4. The opera is based on a novel by K. Čapek. We quote the libretto from the 1979 London Decca recording.

5. The pleasures and identifications possible in seeing the fat lady sing, command the stage, be the center of the action are not limited to gay men. Body size and image are issues in women's identity formation as well, of course. For an

example of how this works for particular women, see Clément on Callas and Montserrat Caballé (28–29).

6. We use the term "lesbian" here for a certain efficiency and accessibility with qualms and qualifications. We understand that terms like "lesbian" and "gay" are, and the identities to which they refer may be, of recent vintage, and that social constructions of gender and sexuality have changed across history. We have therefore tried to signal our sense that there is no transhistorical sexual subject in our discussions of texts and singers of the seventeenth-, eighteenth-, and early nineteenth centuries by using, for example, terms like "same-sex desire" or "homosexual practices" rather than talking about "homosexuals."

7. We could have chosen other texts to function as introductory set piece, Sand's *Conseulo* and its sequel *La Comtesse de Rudolstadt* or Flora Tristan's *Mephis* perhaps, but we have decided, both for reasons of space and because of our own training, to limit ourselves for the most part to Anglo-American writing about women singers.

8. The diva's voice functions this way in both "literary" and popular fiction. One of our favorite feminist detectives, Sara Paretsky's V. I. Warshawsky, is a hard-boiled sleuth, constantly accused—mostly by men—of mouthing off. V. I.'s inspiring Italian mother was an opera singer.

9. Speaking of theories about how fluids circulated in the one-sexed body of early anatomy, Thomas Laqueur summarizes Isidore of Seville:

> So too obese women (they transformed the normal plethora into fat), dancers (they used up the plethora in exercise) and women "engaged in singing contests" (in their bodies "the material is forced to move around and is utterly consumed") did not menstruate either and were thus generally infertile. The case of singers, moreover, illustrates once again the extent to which what we would take to be only metaphoric connections between organs were viewed as having causal consequences in the body as being real. Here the association is one between the throat or the neck through which air flows and the neck of the womb through which the menses passes; activity in one distracts from activity in another. (In fact, metaphorical connections between the throat and the cervix/vagina or buccal cavity and pudenda are legion in antiquity and still into the nineteenth century.) (36)

10. This point is not lost on divas themselves, and of course this loud voice links divas with other women who have aspired to a role and voice in the wider world. Jessye Norman, in a recent PBS special, introduced an aria from Tchaikovsky's *The Maid of Orleans* by noting that Church officials felt that Joan had raised her voice too loudly.

11. Another Freudian female seems akin to Armgart, though Freud treats her much differently than Eliot. Rosalia H., an aspiring singer, consults Freud about a constriction in her throat: "Every time she . . . forced herself to remain quiet in the face of some outrageous accusation [from an abusive uncle], she felt . . . a sense of constriction, a lack of voice . . . localized in her larynx and pharynx which now interfered with her singing" (242). Freud first tries to cure her by encouraging her to use her voice more, to speak her anger: "I made her abuse

her uncle, lecture him, tell him the unvarnished truth . . . and this treatment did her good" (243). But only after Freud uncovers childhood sexual abuse by her father do the symptoms, Freud implies, disappear. Clément reads Rosalia H. in conjunction with the stories of Manuel Garcia's physical abuse of his daughter Maria, later diva La Malibran, and concludes: "So this is the voice's source: paternal violation—the secret fantasy that gave . . . Malibran all her voice, that made sweet Antonia die, and that forever drives the imaginary figure of the prima donna" (33). For a reading of a handful of diva texts (mostly from what we are calling the masculinist tradition) that grows out of Clément's work and is more psychoanalytically oriented than our readings, see Bronfen.

12. In this Galas joins a handful of other diva-composers, like the Victorian diva Pauline Viardot. One of the earliest was Francesca Caccini (c. 1587–1640), singer and court composer for the Medici family. In her opera *La Liberazione di Ruggiero dall'Isola d'Alcina* (1625), recently retrieved from obscurity and recorded by the Ars Femina Ensemble, the knight Ruggiero is seduced from his duties by the singing sorceress Alcina and her sirens. Only when another woman, Melissa, "[breaks] Alcina's spell with her sweet singing," according to Susan Reigler's liner notes, does Ruggiero return to his responsibilities and is the island freed of Alcina's vile influence. Here, it appears, it is the proto-Micaela who wins the singing competition.

CHAPTER 1   *Pieces and Breeches*

1. Carlo Broschi (1705–1782), who sang under the name Farinelli, gained great fame in the 1720s and, in the 1730s, very high fees in London. Hogarth's *Rake's Progress* memorializes the praise of one lady of fashion, who enthused, "One God, One Farinelli." Hoping that Farinelli's voice might assuage her husband's profound melancholy, Elizabeth, wife of Philip V of Spain, invited Farinelli there at the height of his celebrity. Philip responded to Farinelli's voice and returned to his duties. Offered a fantastic salary, Farinelli stayed on and sang, according to legend, the same four songs for his royal audience of one every night for nearly a decade. He is said to have acquired a Rasputin-like influence over the court.

2. There are recordings of one of the last castrati, Alessandro Moreschi (1858–1922), a soprano in the Sistine Chapel choir. In an appendix to the 1974 reprint of the standard work on the history of castrati, Angus Heriot's *The Castrati in Opera* (1954), Desmond Shawe-Taylor suggests that the combination of Moreschi's voice and primitive recording techniques produces a sound that should not be heard as anything close to the sound produced by castrati in their great period, the seventeenth and eighteenth centuries. "The voice," he writes, "unquestionably a soprano, resembles that of neither a boy nor woman, being stronger than the one and less suave than the other. Chest notes are used freely. . . . Most people find the timbre, with its occasional suggestion of a whine, displeasing. . . . I find something distinctly fascinating about the unabashed, yet curiously disembodied, passion . . . of his singing. With a more

secure technique and a style less vitiated by the sentimental taste of his day, he might well please—on all but humanitarian grounds—a modern audience. But I am sure he is a long way from Farinelli" (226–227).

3. Working from Charles Burney and others, Lee summarizes the position of the castrati:

> He was received with open arms in every house; all his impertinence and caprice was tolerated; when he sang people remained silent and breathless, and occasionally fainted and went into hysterics; when he ceased the applause was perfectly frantic; everyone possessed his printed portrait with Latin distichs, Cupids, laurel-wreaths, &c; the ladies wore miniatures of him . . . ; all the wits of coffee-houses and lecture-rooms wrote sonnets in his honour. . . . The singer, meanwhile—usually a mere lad at the commencement of his career, of the lowest extraction, and who hitherto led the hardest, dullest life of musical routine—was placed in the most trying situation, and if the sudden change from the rusty cassock, the scanty food, and abundant blows of the *conservatorio*, to fine clothes, lacqueys, fashionable dinner-tables and great ladies' flatteries did turn his head and make him an intolerable, capricious, swaggering coxcomb, it was less his fault than that of society at large. But the satirists of the eighteenth century, embittered by this musical infatuation . . . fell upon the *virtuosi* with implacable rage. Parini denounced the singer as a base and ungrateful upstart, as a corrupter of morals; Passeroni abused him as a conceited imbecile; Baretti roared that of all living creatures the singer was the most abject. (*Studies* 119)

4. The era of castrati popularity was both preceded and followed by periods in which they were in the musical closet, as it were, and encouraged to pass as falsettists, as fully equipped men. According to Heriot, "In the late nineteenth century, propriety was so outraged by the persistence of the curious survivals that various absurd attempts were made to deny it or hush it up: the castrati were alleged to be merely falsettists, were given permission to marry . . . or were provided with medical certificates of the condition known as cryptorchidism" (22). Unable to reproduce, castrati had as a rule been denied permission to marry. The late-nineteenth-century medical certificates Heriot mentions recall the contentions of many eighteenth-century castrati that their condition was the result of an illness or accident—animal bites and falls from horses were especially popular explanations.

5. Scholars argue that most castrati were from families of poor or very modest means; many boys were sold by their families to teachers or other agents who made arrangements for the operation and vocal training. Many of the children, then, were rendered commodities even before the procedure by which, we might say, the castrato voice was manufactured. Rosselli sees the increasing numbers of castrated boys made available to the church and conservatories during the seventeenth century in the context of periods of economic crisis and deindustrialization on the Italian peninsula (35–36). Families knew that a castrated boy would find lifelong security in the church, and there was always the possibility that the child might go on to make huge sums by singing opera. The supply of castrated boys began to decline, he later notes, as economic conditions improved. In addition, he argues, we should not read an age when Chris-

tian asceticism was still highly valued through the filter of our own historical-cultural moment in which an individual's sexual fulfillment is more highly privileged (36).

6. The slippage and play between sex and gender (further complicated by the fact that these castrated men were, to some eyes, not "real" men) that cross-dressed castrati brought to opera remained an important feature of the art even after the decline of the castrati. Women took, and still take, early first man parts, and operas written after women were allowed to perform on all stages—Strauss's *Der Rosenkavalier,* for example—suggest with their trouser roles for women that the gender and sexual ambiguity generated by the castrati *en travesti* had a power and attraction that survived the expedient of males playing female roles because women were banned from the stage. Conrad argues that opera is an art devoted "to the definition and interchangeability of the sexes" (11). The phrase is an odd one, "definition" implying that opera works conservatively to reinforce normative gender difference, and the ambiguous "interchangeability" that in matters of gender there might not be any *there* there—the very worry that anti-castrato discourse during the eighteenth century wanted to address.

7. There were castrati whose desire and/or living arrangements approximated what we would now call "gay," although given that castrati were not allowed to marry, it is difficult to tell how many of the castrati who lived together and left their property to each other did so for practical, because their choices were limited, rather than affectional reasons.

8. In an essay on anti-castrato discourse in English writing and the links constructed there between castrati and women who "appropriated" male power, Campbell observes:

> The satiric reactions to the disruption a castrato creates along the boundary between masculine and feminine identity reveal some of the larger systems of oppositions normally stabilized by alignment with gender terms. Because the castrato's exception to masculine identity consists ultimately in the facts about his genitals, the castrati provided an occasion to literalize, to make explicit, the cultural significance of the phallus itself: in considering the castrato's loss, the satirists at times assume the phallus to be the guarantor of everything from moral discourse to English currency to English-ness. And in the real or imagined responses of women to them, the castrati provided a rare opening in the normally monolithic entity of masculinity in which to explore—whether with wishfulness, fear, or denunciation—complexities or contradictions in women's relation to the phallus. While some of the satiric material concentrated its ridicule on the castrati themselves, much of it . . . turned its satiric attention to the women interested in them, competing to articulate what it would mean for a woman to prefer a man without the use of his penis. (64)

9. For a reading of Ancillon's text as it participates in the attempts of anti-castrato discourse to construct masculinity and contain female sexuality, which also provides an analysis of the unpublished letters of castrato Gaspar Pacchierotti to novelist Fanny Burney (daughter of the well-known chronicler of the eighteenth-century music scene Dr. Charles Burney), see Kowaleski-Wallace.

10. Fielding, as Campbell shows, was especially interested in linking castrati, the

increasing freedoms women took in public, and women's contribution to a growing tendency for consumption of consumer goods.

11. In keeping with our focus on women's writing, we limit ourselves to a discussion of women's writing on castrati. Balzac's *Sarrasine* is perhaps the best known castrato narrative, thanks in part to Roland Barthes's virtuoso reading of it, *S/Z*. See also Lawrence Louis Goldman's novel *The Castrato* (1973) and Sven Delblanc's *The Castrati:A Romantic Tale* (1975).

12. Few critics have written on Lee's story. For a reading that places it in the context of Lee's theorizing on aesthetics, see Cabellero.

13. Narratives of the lives of courtesan-singers of early Italian comic opera take on a conventional quality, "a repetitive matter of affairs with nobles or ruffians or both, affrays, pregnancies, attempted elopements, male disguises, arrests, expulsions, brief and at times scandalous confinement in nunneries. They are documented because the police took a close interest," notes Rosselli, who speculates further that some of these women may have been "playing an expected part" or cultivating a reputation for transgression in order to better maintain their independence (63–64). Figures of disruption, threats to authority, divas have ever been spectacles on stage and objects of surveillance off stage.

14. If Tosi had specific targets in mind, they were probably Francesca Cuzzoni and Faustina Bordoni, whom Pleasants calls "the first prima donnas to achieve international fame and to hold their own with the greatest castrati of their generation" (96). Tosi gives them a backhanded compliment toward the close of his text: "What a beautiful Mixture would it be, if the Excellence of these two angelic Creatures could be united in one single Person!" (172). Two divas, it appears, equal one good castrato.

15. While it became easier for white women in Europe and America to get training and engagements, it remained difficult for African-American women who stayed in the United States. Story notes of African-American singer Elizabeth Taylor-Greenfield, "The world of American concert music in the middle nineteenth century denied Greenfield exposure and refused to train her, while reproaching her for remaining untrained" (24).

16. For an extended treatment of Victoria's interest in divas and her place in the history of female diva worship, see Castle (203–207).

17. The tradition of the diva constructed as anti-diva is a long and persistent one. Dawn Upshaw and interviewer Wayne Koestenbaum do an excellent job of such a construction in a recent *New York Times Magazine* piece called "This Diva Is Diffident." Upshaw tells Koestenbaum that she feels "kind of guilty" about "help" with housecleaning and assures him that she still cleans bathrooms and does "lots of scrubbing. I don't think of myself as some sort of queen. We have a very ordinary household." Koestenbaum gushes in response: "It is a mundanity whose miraculousness speaks in every warm, glassy note she sings" (16). We do not, of course, impute Lind-like motivations or machinations to one of our favorite divas.

For other twentieth-century divas who construct themselves or are constructed as anti-divas, see chapter 4 and the Annie Lennox section of chapter 7.

CHAPTER 2 *Singing His Mind Away*

1. In Joseph Machlis's *The Career of Magda V.*, the diva is also allied with the Nazis and tries to redeem herself by marrying an American. Although Magda is a much more sympathetic character than Lili, her choice to remain in Germany and sing for the Reich seems inextricably bound up with her divahood and New Woman–hood. When she refuses to leave the country with her Jewish lover, he says, "This is the problem of the modern woman—love versus career" (48), as though choosing a career were of a piece with becoming a Nazi sympathizer. This association seems especially ironic in view of the Nazi ideology of womanhood. The Nazi diva seems a particularly compelling theme: the makers of the film *The Accompanist* set it, unlike the original novel, in the Nazi era and imply the diva's collusion with the Reich.

2. That this "disorder" is so often constructed as "masculinization" in both masculinist and revisionary diva narratives is not surprising and is perhaps inevitable in a culture which limits itself to two genders and structures them as binary oppositions. Other figures of female power or unconventionality have long been similarly labeled.

3. In a novel written less than a decade later, F. Marion Crawford's *The Diva's Ruby*, the assumption that a married woman cannot perform on stage is challenged—appropriately enough by an American entrepreneur. British diva Margaret's friend and "guardian" asks the suitor, "If Margaret marries you, shall you want her to leave the stage?"

   "Why no . . . that wouldn't suit my plans at all. Besides, we're a Company, she and I" (408).

   Her other suitor, a European, has qualms about their engagement when he meets a lovely young Turk who "would much rather die than show herself on the stage in a very low dress before thousands of people and sing to them and take money for doing it" (413). Margaret's public voice is for the American a good investment, for the European both an irresistible attraction and an embarrassment.

4. The word "castrati" is not used in the text; by this time there were "officially" no castrati left. It was well known, however, that there were still castrati at the Vatican. What Evelyn actually remembers is "two grey-haired men in the Papal choir in Rome" (232).

5. This kind of separation is common. For example, the narrator of *The Diva's Ruby* remarks that "great singers develop a capacity for flying into rages, even if they have not been born with hot tempers" (Crawford 212). In other words, it is divahood itself that wreaks havoc with the natural woman.

6. Or the appropriation of her voice by God. An early example of the strategy whereby the female singer's voice is appropriated in the service of the masculine is a series of Latin poems Milton wrote in 1639 to Neapolitan singer Leonora Baroni. In the first, "Ad Leonoram Romae Canentem" ("To Leonora Singing in Rome"), Leonora's glory is greater than the angels':

   > For the music of your voice itself bespeaks the presence of God . . . mysteriously moving and graciously teaching mortal hearts how they may gradually

become accustomed to immortal tones. If God is all things and permeates all things, in you alone he speaks and possesses all His other creatures in silence.

The diva's throat is a conduit of the divine; the Holy Spirit inhabits it, and the music that comes from it is merely a precursor to heavenly sounds. Small wonder, then, that in the next poem Milton can quite explicitly reverse the siren narrative and speculate that the voice can cure: "Breathing peace into/ his diseased breast with your heart-stirring song," he writes of another Leonora, love for whom drove Tasso mad, "you might have restored him to himself." This looks forward to "The Solitary Reaper": the singer's voice brings the poet back to himself; to hear the voice is a means of returning to and reaffirming himself.

7. The several male mentors in Robertson Davies's *A Mixture of Frailties* have worse effects on aspiring diva Monica Gall. She is throughout the novel a man-made diva who finds happiness and fulfillment in "real woman" sex (106) and who wallows in "drudg[ing] for somebody far above me" (244), a male genius.

8. This novel is, of course, the source of the epithet "Svengali," sinister manipulator of an innocent victim. During the novel's wild popularity—it sold over a million copies—it generated as well "Trilby shoes, a nude foot scarf pin, socks, shoe laces, garters" (Berman 122), Trilby sausage, a city, Trilby, in Florida, and the Trilby hat. For years after its publication, it occasioned enormous controversy: the heroine was a fallen woman. But as Willa Cather, a defender, pointed out, Trilby is properly punished for her sins; the novel's force is a conservative one. Young women of the time, however, romanticized the charming diva and left home in droves hoping to live, like Trilby, an artistic life. For further details on *Trilby*'s reception, see Elaine Showalter's introduction to the Oxford University Press edition, which appeared shortly before this book went to press.

9. The diva Margaret in F. Marion Crawford's *The Diva's Ruby* and its sequel *Primadonna* is also (though less literally) "double," and, like Trilby/La Svengali, she has two names, "Madame Cordova and Miss Donne. Miss Donne thought Madame Cordova very showy. . . . The brilliantly successful Cordova thought Margaret Donne a good girl, but rather silly" (*PD* 75–76). The Italianate names—La Svengali, Cordova—seem to confer on both singers stereotypical diva characteristics.

10. A contemporary retelling, Sam Siciliano's 1994 *The Angel of the Opera*, even marries him off to a beautiful blind woman who cannot see his horrid face. The Phantom is, the text suggests, well rid of Christine; the male genius triumphs.

11. The trope of the excessive voice is ubiquitous in diva fictions. The protagonists' voices are seldom excellent, beautiful, or well trained but are instead heavenly, incredible, beyond any other voice. Mawrdew Czgowchwz's is so extraordinary that she creates for herself a new category—the "oltrano." Christine Daaé's voice is "seraphic"; Sandra Belloni has "the voice they hear in heaven" (450); La Svengali's rendition of Chopin's Impromptu in A flat is "not only the most divinely beautiful, but also the most astounding feat of musical utterance ever heard out of a human throat" (du Maurier 409). Cynthia Hawkins' voice takes listeners to "an unknown realm" (Delacorta 72).

CHAPTER 3   *The Sirens Avenged*

1. Among the critics who place Armgart in the context of female characters in Eliot's novels are Gilbert and Gubar, Blake, and Midler. Newton, on the other hand, places Armgart in the company of other Eliot egoists and pays little attention to gender issues. Carpenter does read Armgart in the context of Orpheus, but her critical interests are much different from ours.

2. Most of the biographical information we present here can be found in the standard biography of Viardot by FitzLyon. More recent, popular books on the diva, Christiansen's *Prima Donna* (1984) and Mordden's *Demented* (1984), add little that is new.

3. The story also features an early Eliot singer, but she is singing bird rather than diva. Caterina "passed her life as a little unobtrusive singing-bird . . . her heart beating only to the peaceful rhythm of love," but she began "to know the fierce palpitations of triumph and hatred" when the object of her love loves another woman ("Mr. Gilfil" 218). He dies. She feels she killed him because she wanted to. She eventually marries Gilfil, but dies after a few months, pregnant. Caterina's life is operatic; she dies, in effect, of love.

4. Christiansen speculates that Armgart is modeled on Viardot in "George Eliot, *Armgart*, and the Victorian Prima Donna." He is the only critic, music or literary, we have found who so speculates. He finds the Viardot connection interesting but not, as we do, important for a satisfying reading of *Armgart*.

5. Page references for *Armgart* are from volume 11 of *George Eliot's Works (Warwick Edition)* (Edinburgh: William Blackwood and Sons, 1906). For the sake of consistency, later citations from *Daniel Deronda* are from volumes 9 and 10 of the same edition of the *Works* (1911).

6. Carpenter argues that the trill "reveals both her ambition and her lack of artistic depth" (169), an argument that echoes Leo's and doesn't account for Leo's admission that Armgart's singing opens new doors, something mere "embellishment" generally doesn't do. In the background here is the movement away from florid singing in the nineteenth century. Mordden argues with others that while composers banned "wholesale revision and rude improvisation . . . they were not composing for robots" and thus expected each singer to "inflect" the music according to his or her own "distinctions of voice and approach" (*Demented* 44). Viardot was criticized for her florid singing in much the same terms Carpenter and Leo criticize Armgart, but she had defenders. Chorley writes of her Orpheus: "The chains of notes, unmeaning in themselves, were flung out with such exactness, limitless volubility, and majesty, so as to convert what was essentially a commonplace piece of parade, into one of those displays of passionate enthusiasm, to which nothing less florid could give scope.—As according relief and contrast, they are not merely pardonable—they are defensible; and thus, only to be dispensed by the indolence of the day, which, in obedience to false taste and narrow pedantry, has allowed one essential branch of the art to fall into disuse" (2:58).

7. We relish a final irony. Faithful to Eurydice, Orpheus refuses the attentions of the Bacchantes/Maenads—the frenzied fans of the original myth who are recast

in Eliot's drama as the archetypal angry women—who rip him limb from limb. His severed heads end up in, of all places, Lesbos.

8. Dinesen claimed that she *was* Pellegrina (Pelensky 132), and critics note the many links between her and her elusive diva. For an excellent reading of this story as "an explicit reflection on the meaning of her own creative project," see Aiken (50–61).

9. Such life-altering moments, common in diva narratives, may seem melodramatic and novelistic, but they have historical precedent. In *Mein Leben*, Wagner claims that after hearing diva Wilhelmine Schroder-Devrient, he wrote her "a letter in which I solemnly stated that, as of that day, my life had acquired its meaning" and that "on this evening she had made me what I herewith vowed to become" (quoted in Pleasants 152).

10. Recent fictions that plow relentlessly toward a predetermined end include Jane Smiley's *A Thousand Acres* and, more operatically, David Henry Hwang's *M. Butterfly* and Terrence McNally's *Lisbon Traviata*. What is particularly frustrating about these texts, and about *Tower of Ivory,* is that the tragic endings seem external and, ultimately, unfair. The historical case on which *M. Butterfly* is based had no such operatic conclusion, but in the play Butterfly must die because, well, Butterfly dies.

11. "Could I . . . continue to exalt you above your sex? . . . it is only in dreams that men are not fatally alike!" (463). In other words, she recognizes that the Ordham she loves is a dream, that the real Ordham is not an exceptional man in any way.

12. Significantly, Cather used the same language to write about her first meeting with Olive Fremstad: "Nothing, nothing . . . could equal the bliss of entering into the very skin of another human being" (72).

13. Cather's fictional divas often echo their real-life counterparts. Of Clara Butt, Cather wrote: "The girl has absolutely no musical intelligence; no musical memory, no musical taste" (Curtin 649). Cather is not the only woman writer interested in the lives of mediocre as well as brilliant singers. In Isabel Allende's "Tosca," a weak singer lives a fantasy of divahood; in Katherine Mansfield's "Pictures," an aging undistinguished diva, desperate for money, ends up going home with a "very stout gentleman" who "likes 'em firm and well-covered" (401). This move from diva manqué to prostitute suggests, of course, the tenuousness of divahood. Ellen Glasgow's *Phases of an Inferior Planet* features an aspiring singer who has "the artistic temperament without the art" (236). Even so, her mild ambition ruins a man and indirectly occasions her own death.

14. But see the following discussion of the married nightingale for a very different Cather sentiment. See also her 1913 interview ("Three Singers") with Louise Homer, Geraldine Farrar, and Olive Fremstad. Cather gives short shrift to Homer, mother of five and thoroughly domesticated diva, and is clearly much more interested in Farrar, who "does not believe that conjugal and maternal duties are easily compatible with artistic development" (36), and Fremstad, on whom Cather based her thoroughly undomesticated diva Thea Kronborg.

15. Divas disappear as protagonists in Cather's later fiction, although she revised

The Song of the Lark in 1934. In the 1935 novel *Lucy Gayheart*, the eponymous heroine is a musician but not a singer. She is also a much more passive figure than any of the middle-period divas and a figure involved much more inextricably in the heterosexual romance. For a reading of this text as a "simultaneous revision of and rigid adherence to a novelistic tradition of female failure," see Carlin (139 quoted).

16. Another diva "mined" by men is Domina in Harriet Prescott's *The Master Spirit*. Both the blind minister, who uses her to help him cure the sick, and Gratian, who wants to take her away from this life as a healer, in part because "there is a fortune in her throat" (94), exploit the developing diva's voice.

17. While the name directly suggests the mythical garden, it is also the title of a poem (1870) by Dante Gabriel Rossetti about Lilith.

18. We also read Cather's "The Double Birthday" (1929) as a *Trilby* antidote. It is less the story of the diva than of the Svengali figure; the young singer's death is not a punishment for *her* sins, perversions, and aspirations but for those of the man, significantly a physician, who wanted to "make" her. It is also a reverse "Solitary Reaper": Marguerite's voice constitutes for the doctor—and for the story itself—a center, a memory that informs not, as for Wordsworth's poet, his aesthetic life but his own decay. The singer lives on in the doctor's heart not to inspire but to censure, not to sustain but to blame.

19. In the preface to the revised edition (1937), Cather terms the title "unfortunate," because "many readers take it for granted that the 'lark song' refers to the vocal accomplishments of the heroine, which is altogether a mistake. Her song was not of the skylark order." She goes on to explain that the title comes from the painting Thea sees, *The Song of the Lark*, and its effect—"a young girl's awakening to something beautiful."

20. Again, we are here obviously speaking only of the Western operatic tradition. For example, in Chinese opera, as *M. Butterfly* and *Farewell, My Concubine* remind us, the tradition of the male diva has never died.

21. The controversy over racism in Cather's last novel, *Sapphira and the Slave Girl*, is briefly summarized in Carlin, note 12, 195.

22. Rosowski also notes other resemblances between *Song of the Lark* and male *Bildungsroman*: "Thea's two suitors, Ray Kennedy and Fred Ottenburg, assume roles complementary women ordinarily play: the older woman who provides money, the younger who initiates the hero into sexual passion, both prevented by plot manipulation from complicating the hero's development" ("Writing" 69).

23. It is also our personal favorite among these diva narratives, perhaps in part because we—enthusiastic cooks and eaters—find irresistible the diva with a hearty peasant appetite and a passionate appreciation of food. But the novel also combines an old-fashioned, riveting, well-told tale with a multilayered, narratively interesting structure, quirky but sympathetic characters, and fascinating gender politics.

24. Among the numerous similarities between Lena Geyer and Olive Fremstad, as she is portrayed in *The Rainbow Bridge* by Mary Watkins Cushing, Fremstad's companion for many years, is a "manly" stride, which Cushing describes as

"inimitable and challenging" (123). Geyer also shares Fremstad's hardy appetite, female entourage, and general philosophy: "A serious artist can't have lovers and still *think!*" (Cushing 184). See chapter 4 for a discussion of Fremstad in *The Rainbow Bridge.*

25. Elsie on her background: "If you have read Mrs. Wharton's novels . . . you will understand the type of family and position I was born into" (220). The intertextual allusion suggests the contrast between Wharton's novels and this one, the repressed, manipulative, marriage-bound protagonists here replaced with the vital, open, work-oriented Lena.

26. Given Willa Cather's same-sex predilections, it is worthy of note that her divas have few same-sex bonds. But this is perhaps not surprising, since Cather identified so often and so closely with men. See Sedgwick on Cather's "effeminiphobia" and "gender liminality." *The Song of the Lark* is dedicated to Isabelle McClung, one of Cather's very significant others.

27. Harriet Prescott's *A Master Spirit* also claims that men hinder divas's careers. The *dea ex machina* death of Domina's fiance, Gratian, frees her to follow Madama, her ex-diva mentor, into the exclusive service of Art.

28. By the time of their marriage Henry Loeffler is a widower, but it is perhaps significant that Lena was first attracted to his wife: "Not in many years had a person appealed to me so strongly" (335). It is possible to read the Geyer-Loeffler marriage as Lena's last kindness to Mrs. Loeffler, restoring her beloved husband to happiness.

29. Of her own mother's early death, Davenport writes, "I believe that for her having to stop singing was in certain ways to stop living, and that the secret frustration and sorrow of that fate were more than anything else responsible for her early death" (Paris 44).

CHAPTER 4   *Diva Truths, Diva Lies, Diva Lives*

1. Another diva novel that is largely "about" the fictionality of a diva (auto) biography and of memory itself is Margaret Kennedy's *A Long Time Ago*, published four years before *Of Lena Geyer*. In it, diva Elissa Koebel has just published *The Story of My Life*, which presents, in highly romantic language, an operatic episode of a passionate affair. Later in the novel, a character, Kerran, produces letters that tell quite a different version of the incident. These and Kerran's own version, much less romantic and operatic than Koebel's, suggest that the autobiography is a fiction by which the diva presents herself as romantic heroine. But the text ends with another character—significantly named Hope—calling into question as well the "truth" of the letters and Kerran's "objective" narrative.

2. Wood briefly discusses Styr but acknowledges neither the text's clear denial here of the lesbianism lightly suggested at the beginning of the novel nor the fact that Styr eventually kills herself out of love (sexual) for a man. Similarly, in her remarks on Thea Kronborg she emphasizes the feminine-maternal-matriarchal aspects of the Panther Canyon episode to the exclusion of Thea's heterosexual initiation in the same episode, and in the paragraphs on Lena Geyer

neglects to mention the duke or Lena's husband. These seem curious omissions in this otherwise stunning article.

3. This chapter limits itself to an exploration of how twentieth-century diva life narratives respond to these charges, but the charges, of course, predate these responses. An extreme and unusual accusation of unwomanliness occurred in a mid-nineteenth-century review of African-American diva Elizabeth Taylor-Greenfield, known as "the Black Swan," who had a three-and one-half octave range. The reviewer complained that the "idea of woman's voice is a feminine tone; anything below that is disgusting. It is as bad as a bride with a beard on her chin. . . . We hear a good deal about women's sphere. . . . [I]n music . . . it is the soprano region of the voice" (quoted in Story 22). The "disgust" here may, of course, be racial as well as sexual. Peterson notes that "Greenfield is invariably positioned . . . within a frame of radical Otherness" (122) and that the bodies of black female performers, perceived as "sexualized or grotesque" (124), are frequently as much at issue as the performances themselves. The "bride with a beard" is an especially vivid evocation of the kind of masculinity frequently attributed to divas and strenuously denied by divas themselves.

4. Marian Anderson's autobiography, *My Lord, What a Morning*, is a significant antecedent to these two narratives. When the response to Anderson's attempt to go to music school is "we don't take colored" (38), when Anderson is forbidden to sing in Constitution Hall, when, as Story points out, early African-American singers were criticized for having untrained voices and then denied the requisite training (24), it seems logical that issues of self-representation become, for African-American women, different from those of white women, even white women who have overcome serious obstacles to acquire their training.

5. The other exception to the divas' insistence on the importance of their personal lives is the object of Terry Castle's diva worship, Brigitte Fassbaender.

6. In this analysis of diva life narratives we are not at all suggesting that women like Lehmann and Farrar relegated their husbands to minor roles in their lives, only that they have relegated them to minor roles in their life stories. Likewise, the emphasis in recent diva life narratives on the importance of husbands may be equally far removed from "the facts." Renata Scotto inserts a rather lengthy biography of Lorenzo Anselmi, her husband, into her own text and laments that people do not recognize "how important he is." She states plainly "that without him I would not be where I am or who I am" (106).

7. The link between opera singer and nun is not confined to short admissions in diva autobiography. We discussed George Moore's two-volume narrative of the diva who enters a convent in a previous chapter. Mère Marie Brunel, singing teacher in the convent school in Kate O'Brien's *As Music and Splendour*, "had disappeared into Italy, with a singing voice of great promise, and an unusual intelligence about music. . . . But then, unexplained, unannounced, she reappeared—a nun" (14). Diva Clare Halvey in the same novel eschews marriage: "Married, me? Oh no. I *might* have gone to be a nun" (189). Lotte Lehmann recognizes that becoming a nun is, like becoming a great opera singer, one way of avoiding the prescriptions of marriage and family life. That these women did *not* become nuns suggests perhaps their realization that convents, like houses,

have walls. This sense of nunhood as a *chosen* alternative for divahood in nineteenth- and twentieth-century diva discourse contrasts with the lives of some historical singers in eighteenth-century Italy. Authorities sometimes gave particularly disorderly divas a choice between entering a convent or going to jail. Perhaps the convent alternative for later divas is a kind of self-punishment for their "disorderly" desires as well as an alternative to heterosexuality and domesticity.

8. Her chapter titles reflect this: "Prison and Sea Adventures," "Conquest of Mexico," "A Runaway Impresario"—*her* adventures, *her* conquest, *her* escape.

9. This interesting admission underlines the fictionality of this account. Tetrazzini, that is, does not record; she remembers. And she remembers from the vantage point of enormous success and in the context of an adventure narrative. Besides, as she later boasts of her operatic performances, "I like to improvise when I see an opportunity" (262).

10. The passing on of greatness from one diva to another is a common theme in these narratives as well as in the revisionary narratives of the previous chapters. One particularly interesting example is Renata Scotto's conviction that she is Maria Malibran's heir. Maria Malibran appears in a seance that Scotto attends early in her career, saying through the medium "that I must sing what she sang. . . . She seemed very sad and talked of dying young, of having wanted to go on singing forever" (42). Scotto romanticizes her predecessor, feels sad that she died during her first pregnancy. Scotto would perhaps be unhappy to read FitzLyon's claim that the pregnancy was by no means Malibran's first and that the riding accident in which she died may have been another attempt to abort.

11. While the diva's pride in her chosen profession is characteristic of diva narratives, it is important to remember that such pride may be in part defiance, in part defense against the very real shame that still attached to a public life for a woman. Alda's teacher—and the teacher of many other famous divas— Mathilde Marchesi writes in her autobiography *Marchesi and Music* that "the determined veto of my husband kept me from the stage then and for all time" (68). She taught, she wrote music, she sang in private settings, but this woman who knew, her students thought, everything about the human voice could not sing on stage.

12. The diva Frida Leider, writing at the end of the fifties, says that she thought seriously for a while about opera production but soon "came to the conclusion that, in addition to requiring years of experience, it is really a man's job, and rather too physically exhausting for a woman" (203).

13. In her biography of Malibran, FitzLyon claims that "as time went on . . . her ability to distinguish between real life and the operas she performed became less and less sure" (198). This psychological judgment is not one that divas make about themselves. They take pride in being not themselves but the character they portray; any confusion that ensues is part of the work, part of the art. They recognize the danger and embrace it. One of Lotte Lehmann's autobiographical works is titled, proudly, *My Many Lives.*

14. This casting of their intimacy in terms of childish play and adolescent enthusiasm reinscribes the conventional notions of the bourgeois patriarchal Freud (as

opposed to the more radical Freud who speculated that all humans might be bisexual and remarked that heterosexuality as well as homosexuality should be treated as a problem for thought and theory) of female homoeroticism as regressive, as a sign that a woman has not matured enough to withdraw her investments in mother and others like her and direct them instead toward the "proper" object, a man.

15. The issue of Callas's weight loss is an interesting one. Rumors abounded that she was so desperate, she swallowed a tapeworm. Tito Gobbi suggests that it was his insistence on her weighing herself that prompted a serious diet (193–194). Meneghini says that Callas *had* a tapeworm and that once it was expelled she simply lost an enormous amount of weight. Whatever the explanation, the change was dramatic.

16. FitzLyon is, of course, working here on the common heterosexist assumption that homosexuality has a cause and heterosexuality does not.

CHAPTER 5   *Divas, Death, and Detectives*

1. There is, of course, a great deal of speculation about the "real-life" identity of Irene Adler. Sherlockians have suggested numerous singers and actresses, including Giulia Ravogli, a contralto extravagantly praised by George Bernard Shaw for her Orfeo (Peschel and Peschel 85). Conan Doyle's second wife, Jean Leicke, was apparently herself a fine mezzo-soprano (87).

2. The sequel, which appeared after this manuscript left our hands, is less wonderful, in large part because it posits an unlikely romance between the revisionary hero Mary Russell and the aging Sherlock Holmes.

3. This sort of strategic cross-dressing does, however, have the conservative effect of reinscribing the male-female binary that the cross-dressing woman seeks to escape, as Marjorie Garber makes clear in another context (70). It is also important to remember that stage and street cross-dressing often have different political resonances and effects.

4. The pattern is repeated in *Irene's Last Waltz* when Adler resolves an international crisis (again, Holmes's forte) by attending to women's fashions. "I gather," she concludes, "that the foreign office now takes a greater interest in women's fashions than before?" Holmes responds "fervently": "As do I, Madam, as do I" (456).

5. Delacorta's *Diva*, might seem an obvious choice here, but because it follows few of the conventions of the British and American genres and because the diva, while central to the novel, is only tangentially part of the mystery, we have decided to discuss the film version (more complex and interesting, we think) instead. See chapter 6.

6. The association of divas with snakes is ubiquitous in diva narratives. We have already seen similar comments about Veda Pierce, for example, and Margaret Donne in F. Marion Crawford's *Primadonna* sings with feeling, in a moment of self-loathing, from *The Barber of Seville* : "*Una vipera sero!*" (147).

7. Fred Jarvis seems fond of this analogy. In *The Divas*, emerging diva Bonnie, "like the Fisherman's Wife, set her sights higher and goaded him [her husband]

into more egregious [deeds]" (380). The wife's fate in the fairy tale does not bode well for young Bonnie.

8. In *Murder at the Met*, with its garbled plot and ever-elusive characterization, the Italian divas *are* redeemable. Rita Quercia, once she disentangles herself from Millions, the "motherly octopus" (172), admits that she (Rita) "never had a real singer's blind sense of self-praise, of self-preservation" (173) and happily gives up singing for love. She thereby earns the praise of the inspector, who "realized in a flash that this was a remarkable girl. A girl with tremendous candor and intelligence" (174). Once, that is, she separates from her mother, learns humility, renounces her voice, and accepts her true role as a woman, she becomes an admirable person (or at least an admirable girl) in the eyes of the policing power, the figure of social authority and discipline. Even Amelita Dawson-Da Guerra turns out not to be the venomous rival all the characters— and the narrative itself—assumed: "Millicent had a vast talent and a thrilling voice, but I had a marvelous lover, and so I realized that things did balance out" (198). In other words, Da Guerra could be Millions's friend and a completely different person once her sexuality was firmly under control.

9. See, for example, *Miss Pym Disposes* (Josephine Tey), *Unnatural Death* (Dorothy L. Sayers), *Double* (Marcia Muller and Bill Pronzoni), and the detective film *Basic Instinct*.

10. An earlier text (which is actually a sort of proto–diva mystery complete with Scotland Yard detectives) that both respects the diva-flappers and recognizes the implicit class issue is F. Marion Crawford's *Primadonna*: "Then, too, she [Margaret Donne] has her 'following' of 'girls,' thousands of whom have her photograph, or her autograph. . . . They not only worship her, but many of them make real sacrifices to hear her sing; for most of them are anything but well off" (127).

11. An interesting "mystery" that features one diva murdering another is Louisa May Alcott's "The Rival Prima Donnas," presumably inspired by the rivalry between Jenny Lind and Henrietta Sontag. Diva Beatrice, seemingly a generous mentor to gifted young Theresa, ends up killing her. Her motive, however, seems less professional than personal rivalry: Beatrice's lover, Claude, really loves Theresa. But Beatrice's words as she murders Theresa with an iron crown render the situation less simple and less stereotypical: "Better to die *crushed with flowers* than to be what you [Claude] have rendered me" (20). The implication is that Beatrice, crazed by Claude's perfidy, seeks to spare Theresa a similar fate.

CHAPTER 6   *Divas Do the Movies*

1. This is a small example of the reverse influence of film on opera. For others, see Tambling, especially chapter 3.

2. In the early days of the film industry, famous stage actors were willing to appear in films but were unwilling to allow their names to appear on the billing for fear that film work would cheapen their reputations. Lasky rewarded Farrar's willingness to lend her prestige to film openly—"your prestige is such

that whatever you do, your public will accept it as right," he recalls arguing—by making her "the first personality in motion-picture history to receive what since has become known as 'the full treatment' [private rail car, furnished and staffed house, private bungalow dressing room, chauffeur, an orchestra on the set, etc.]" (MacCann 56, 57). The construction of film-star glamor begins with a diva or, rather, a diva who was a trooper: "She proved the most charming and gracious actress I ever brought to Hollywood, and was completely devoid of temperament, contrary to the tradition of prima donnas," Lasky wrote (MacCann 56).

3. Opera, figured as transcendent art untouched by the world of commerce, has long been used to sell products other than films. Early numbers of *Opera News*, for example, are filled with advertisements picturing divas listening raptly to their Victrolas, ads that foreshadow Kiri Te Kanawa's Rolex ads. Recent television commercials hawking cars and telephone books feature loud and demanding prima donnas.

4. For films about female performers, see Fischer. Fischer observes that one kind of female performer, the showgirl, has been "a privileged representation of the female from the very birth of cinema" (24) and grounds her work in Molly Haskell's contention that "the actress—whether as literal thespian. . . or as a symbol for the role-playing woman—is a key female figure throughout film history" (Fischer 64). Like so many other film theorists and critics, however, Fischer neglects the many films about female opera singers, some of which we discuss below.

5. For a detailed analysis of the parallel developments of film and sound technologies, see Lawrence's *Echo and Narcissus: Women's Voices in Classical Hollywood Cinema* (9–32). Lawrence shows that sound technology (radio, phonograph, telephone) was from its beginnings "fully inscribed within patriarchal ideology, its very invention replete with prescriptions about a speaking woman's voice" (71) and that these ideological assumptions were imported to film when sound was added to image in the late twenties. She uses the myth to epitomize the male/female and image/sound hierarchies of classic film and film theory and to illustrate her contention that in film, as in the myth, the speech of women is problematic and, further, that women in classic Hollywood film are constrained from speaking authoritatively. Lawrence is not especially interested in filmic women who speak and sing, and she doesn't mention the musical films, which we discuss below, that make explicit reference to Echo and Narcissus.

6. For more extended treatments of opera singers who made films that range beyond the thirties and include male singers, see Tambling and MacKay.

7. For a compendious survey of women's pictures and their conventions on which our own summary here depends, see Basinger. Like Lawrence, she ignores diva films.

8. This is not to say that diva films, with their portrayal of ambitious and professionally successful women who have a voice, were the most radical of thirties films to push at the boundaries of traditional gender and sexual roles. There is, for example, little questioning of the heterosexual imperative for women in

these films. Contrast this with other thirties films that privilege gender and sexual ambiguity: Dietrich's *Morocco* (1930), Garbo's *Queen Christina* (1933), and Hepburn's cross-dressing film *Sylvia Scarlett* (1936). For a reading of these films that stresses their potential for lesbian identification, see Weiss.

9. According to Basinger, the woman's film accepts female deception as a given of female life, as a necessary survival skill. The genre sends the message that women can deceive in order to fulfill their domestic destiny (65).

10. Annette's shift from artistic production to biological reproduction looks forward to the more relentlessly repressive pattern that Lawrence and Silverman examine in Hollywood films of the forties and later—the diminishment/punishment/confinement of women who would be speaking subjects by tying the voice back to body, image, and spectacle. One way these films do this, Silverman argues, is by confining women to an "inner textual space, such as a painting, a song-and-dance performance, or a film-within-a-film" (57).

11. For a more extended analysis of this film and of the entire elite versus popular art conflict in studio musicals, see Feuer.

12. For fertile readings of these and other forties films that turn on female speech and silence, see Lawrence (especially 109–145) and Silverman (especially 42–71).

13. For an analysis of the "rhapsodic atrocity [and] stylized excess" of Argento's films, see McDonagh.

14. Silverman sees a similar disciplinary strategy at work in American films from the forties to the eighties: "What the cinematic apparatus and a formidable branch of the theoretical apparatus will extract from her by whatever means are required—is involuntary sound, sound that escapes her own understanding, testifying only to the artistry of a superior force. . . . There is, of course, only one group of sounds capable of conforming precisely to these requirements—those emitted by a newborn baby. This, then, is the vocal position the female subject is called upon to occupy whenever (in film or in theory) she is identified with noise, babble, or the cry" (77–78).

15. Other recent films that feature divas include Schroeter's *The Death of Maria Malibran*, Bertolucci's *La Luna*, and Derek Jarmen's short film of an aria from *Louise* which focuses on an aging diva, *Depuis le jour*. Fellini's 1976 *E la Nave Va* takes place on a funeral ship bearing the ashes of a dead diva. The film version of Nina Berberova's short novel *The Accompanist* revolves around the love of a female accompanist for her diva.

16. Most critical readings of the film are psychoanalytic, arguing that the taping of the diva's voice is her forced entry into the realm of the Lacanian symbolic and that Jules's "loss" in the diva's voice is an "imaginary return to infantile plenitude or, to be more precise, . . . an imaginary return to the sonorous envelope of what is clearly (given the generational gap between Jules and the diva) the maternal voice" (Silverman 87).

17. This stress on the separability of women and their voices at first appears at odds with the general tendency of film to tie women's voices back to their bodies, as we have seen in *I Dream Too Much* and *Terror at the Opera*, but according to Mimi White this reversal ends up at the same place, the submission of

the woman with a voice: "The thematics of *Diva* thus alter the conventional signifying economy of sound/image relations in film. The holding of voice to body is figured as an idealized plenitude of non-divided female presence that resists male control. With the division of body and voice, women are inserted into the prevailing post-industrial, postmodern economies of international commodity circulation. In these terms *Diva* offers an allegory of women's submission to the ruling patriarchal order. . . . With its reversal of the status of sound in relation to gender, *Diva* ends up displacing but still repeating the problematic question of whether or how women can claim a place in cinema's signifying regime of sound and images" (38).

A Comic Interlude

1. These novels were published separately from 1920 to 1939. In 1977 an edition that includes all of them was published by Thomas Y. Crowell and reprinted by Harper and Row as *Make Way for Lucia*. We use here the Harper edition but also indicate the specific novel we cite: *QL = Queen Lucia, LL = Lucia in London, ML = Mapp and Lucia, MM = Miss Mapp, WL = The Worshipful Lucia, TL = Trouble for Lucia*.

CHAPTER 7 *Express Yourselves*

1. The material girl has, indeed, generated an enormous amount of material. Tetzlaff, for example, describes his approach to writing a piece on Madonna, "Metatextual Girl": "I thought I should make a thorough examination of Madonna coverage in the popular press. I gave up this idea very quickly. One might as well contemplate mapping the vastness of the cosmos as attempt to collect, let alone read, everything that has been written about Madonna" (239). It was, in fact, tempting not to write about her at all in this volume, given that so many other critics have already written, some of them quite brilliantly, about her. But even at the risk of being repetitious, we write on, hoping that readers will see Madonna's relevance to our project.
2. Madonna's own comments on her name repeat the diva-nun connection we have seen in other diva discourses: "How could I be anything else but what I am having been named Madonna? I would have ended up a nun or this" (Hirschberg 200).
3. Ellen Goodman, for example, wants Madonna to grow up: "If the business of adulthood is finding yourself, she creates as many selves as there are rooms in her video hotel" (165). If, indeed, the business of adulthood is finding yourself—surely an odious, boring, and, if the poststructuralists are correct, vain enterprise—we, too, opt for adolescence or at least for Madonna's many selves.
4. It is, in part at least, Madonna's continued identification with gay male communities and championship of AIDS causes that fuel persistent rumors that she has tested HIV-positive. Schulze, White, and Brown suggest that "making Madonna HIV-positive establishes her moral guilt and provides for her ultimate containment by death" (23). It is precisely Madonna's penchant for escaping and

evading containers that most rankles critics of every stripe. "Effeminate men intrigue me more than anything else in the world," Madonna remarked in a 1991 interview; "I see them as my alter egos" (Hirschberg 200). Given her defiant claims to both "feminine" and "masculine" behavior, such identification is hardly surprising and is, as we have seen, characteristic of literary divas of the revisionist tradition.

5. Schmuckler in *The Village Voice* in 1984 claimed that Madonna "materialized on black radio a year ago" (25). For two divergent academic analyses of Madonna's relationship to black audiences, see Ronald B. Scott's interesting (and interestingly puritanical) defense of Madonna's place in black communities, "Images of Race and Religion in Madonna's Video *Like a Prayer*," which suggests that Madonna is unusual in her appreciation of "the moral base, the black church, that serves as a foundation for the black community" (74) and bell hooks's "Madonna: Plantation Mistress or Soul Sister," which claims as "fact" that in the same video "this appropriative 'use' of [black religious] experience was offensive to many black folk" (223).

6. Not all of these "girls" are teenagers. Warner Brothers publicist Liz Rosenberg, for example, confessed in 1992, "I dream about her constantly" (Orth 300).

7. In an August 1994 piece in *Esquire*, "Norman Mailer on Madonna," Mailer comments that the breast cones Madonna wore on the Blond Ambition tour were ugly. Madonna replies, "The idea . . . is that breasts are these soft things that men rely on . . . so it's a way of saying 'Fuck off'" (48).

8. Pareles remarks on the occasion of the 1994 *Bedtime Stories* that "pop culture's ultimate chameleon is reinventing herself. Again" and refers to her "career whose only constant has been constant change."

9. Dita becomes the narrator of *Sex*. bell hooks takes exception to this persona: "Madonna's appropriation of the identity of the European actress Dita and of her Germanic couture is an obvious gesture connecting her to a culture of fascism, Nazism and white supremacy, particularly as it is linked to sexual hedonism" ("Power" 76). While hooks's point here is well taken and of significance in Madonna criticism, we think it's important to see "Dita" as well as only one of the many roles/selves Madonna constructs. (Who among whites does not have a white supremacist self?)

10. One of the other reasons is the pastiche of the past suggested by her reincarnations of the stars. As Evans suggests, "If *postmodern* more or less means the art of the deft rip-off, the canny revamping of styles, Madonna is our Postmodern Goddess—her every gesture is a shadow of some past vogue: the platinum blaze of Jean Harlow's hair; the hot boyishness of Louise Brooks; the dark, smoldering earth angels of Italian films. . . . Armoring herself with every wink and prop of the all-pro *femme fatale*, Madonna manufactures an elusive artwork self."

Her recognition and valuation of the performative is as well a reason that some queer theorists find her an irresistible subject. As Henderson explains, "Her image reincarnations connote the playful and painful liminalities of lesbian and gay life—always vigilant, always self-conscious, sometimes exposed, sometimes concealed" (109).

11. McClary offers extended *musical* analysis of "Live to Tell" and "Like a Prayer" in *Feminine Endings* (155–166). Music critics do not always agree with her. Christgau likes her work but claims that "because McClary comes out of academic musicology, she too ignores crucial stuff" (205). He also claims that music critics (as opposed to cultural/academic critics) have *not* been disparaging about Madonna's music. His article "Madonnathinking Madonnabout Madonnamusic," an excellent, thoughtful, and biting critique of academic critiques of Madonna, refers to many of the articles we've quoted here. If he reads this, he will doubtless bark at *our* misconceptions, historical inaccuracies, and musical incompetence.

12. Although the suggestion of a blow job seems clear in these lyrics, they have a much different spin in the church setting of the *Like a Prayer* video. Scott reads "there" as "a higher human and spiritual plane" (68), but we (and other critics) are less willing to separate the ostensibly religious from the erotic.

13. For striking confirmation of this perceived similarity, see the illustration from *The Science of Vocal Pedagogy* (1967) that Koestenbaum uses in his *The Queen's Throat* (160).

14. "As is the case in most pop, there is no single originary genius for this music. Yet the testimonies of co-workers and interviewers indicate that Madonna is very much in control of almost every dimension of her media persona and her career" (McClary, *Feminine Endings* 149). Critics by now take this very much for granted.

15. We don't mean by these ruminations to suggest that there haven't been plenty of liberal and left-wing critics who have consistently criticized Madonna on political grounds. Mandziuk, for example, calls *Truth or Dare* an "orgy of self-celebration" (167) and warns: "No matter how much fun Madonna's notion of voguing may appear, posturing cannot be allowed to replace politics" (181). Tetzlaff claims bitterly that Madonna "has won for herself an unlimited ticket for subcultural tourism—she can visit any exotic locale she likes, but she doesn't have to live there" (259). (An odd condemnation for an academic. Don't we make our livings on unlimited tickets for subcultural tourism?) On the other hand, Paglia's accusation that feminists have been "outrageously negative about Madonna from the start" (A37) is certainly an exaggeration. Kaplan counters that she has "never been able to locate these negative articles" (155).

16. The Agassi piece opens with sincere praise: "Mrs. Uri Frichtman, otherwise known as Annie Lennox, is a great soul." References to "Mrs. Sean Penn" could only have been made tongue-in-cheek.

17. One wonders why it's Madonna's and not, say, Michael Jackson's "power craving" that makes Lennox (and others) so tense. Bidini, among others, asks if it's perhaps because Madonna's a woman. "Like every great male rock upsetter before them [Sinead O'Connor and Madonna] their m.o. is ultimately to create scenes that threaten. . . . When Axl Rose does this, he's called a rebel. . . . When Madonna does, she's called a slut" (K11).

18. Whether the rich white girl here is Madonna, a generalized diva, or Lennox herself in an earlier incarnation, why should we listen to her? The mocking tone, that is, may call into question the rest of the lyrics. It's easy to croon, "I believe

in love alone," when you have everything else you could possibly want. The song as a whole, then, can be read not so much as a clichéd contrast between material and spiritual values but as an ironic meditation on the relationship between the diva and her audience.

19. The phrase is from "Legend in My Living Room." Critics seem to concur: Hunt says that Lennox has been dubbed "the Downer Diva" (45).

CHAPTER 8   *Diamanda Galas*

1. The epigraph to this chapter is found in Avena (194–195).

New Music soprano Dora Ohrenstein makes a similar argument in the liner notes to *Urban Diva,* her "one-woman, multi-character, music-theater piece": "Divas, it seems, were intended to love and lament. When confronted with anything more complex and threatening, a soprano's only option was to go mad. Despite my admiration of Verdi and Puccini, I found these 19th century notions cramping my style. What I wanted was the freedom . . . to express the emotions of *my* time, no matter how crude and impolite."

Galas prefigured Lorena Bobbitt's solution: "Ten years ago I came up with the concept of 'Black Leather Beavers,' a group of feminist diesel dykes who went around committing revenge on rapists. We had a veterinarian to perform the castrations, a tatoo artist to engrave 'BLB' on the rapists' foreheads, an arsonist to burn their houses down. . . . A girlfriend has formed a West Coast chapter in San Francisco, and I would encourage more women to do the same" (Juno and Vale 7).

2. Or, as Galas herself described the work in "Intravenal Song": "Theatrically, this diffraction of the mind is made infinite through a ceaseless navigation of the following variables: physical body effort & shape; changing light series which are choreographed; vocal timbre chains, incremental change of room reverberation; manipulation of sonic spatial coordinates and trajectories through the use of four microphones sent to a triphonic sound system. With the exception of the changing light series, the performer has control over all of the above during performance" (61).

3. *The Masque of the Red Death* was first released by Mute Records, a rock label, in three separate recordings: *The Divine Punishment* and *The Saint of the Pit* in 1986 and *You Must Be Certain of the Devil* in 1988. The *Plague Mass* (1991) contains new work as well as selections from the three parts of *The Masque* and is structured like a mass, with settings of scripture, a confessional, and a consecration. Galas sees her mass as an ongoing project that won't be finished until the epidemic is over. In this her work recalls the Names Project's Quilt, but it also illustrates her general rebellion against boundaries and against conventional aesthetic norms, values, and forms.

That she conceives of *The Masque* as an opera is important. Although she is often called a "performance artist," Galas rejects the term: "I use the word *auteur.* . . . I compose the music and I perform the music and I compose the libretto and I design the lights until I turn it over to a professional lighting designer. But Wagner did that, too! People who call this performance art do it out of sexism—any woman who organizes *Gesamkuntswerk* is condemned to this territory " (Gracie and Zarkov 79).

4. Galas's analysis of the PWA's position in relation to medical authority and the strategies and assumptions used to keep the PWA from having a voice in his/her own treatment parallels the cultural links between women, madness, and medicine: "Often people with AIDS dementia are seen as victims of atrophy of the brain, and 'incapable of making decisions.' So when a person with AIDS starts to act in a way that people don't understand, he may be classified as having AIDS dementia, which means that he is no longer listened to, no longer taken seriously. His treatment preferences are not taken into consideration. The person is demoralized by doctors and people around him. Induced madness" (Gracie and Zarkov 78).

5. Constructing a rhetoric to talk about these practices is difficult for us, who live in a culture where mourning practices are more sedate. "Wail," for example, seems pejorative. And is there a difference, we wonder, between grieving and performing grief? Both of us, Italian-Americans, can recall family funerals during which aunts or grandmothers cried and screamed at the grave of a husband whom—we had always thought—they hadn't liked very much. Behavior we saw then as extravagant, embarrassing (aspiring WASPS that we were), inauthentic, we now see as conventional; we now understand emotion as always mediated and expressed through convention; we no longer assume that grief performed is grief duplicitous.

6. For a survey of early civil and religious attempts to control funeral rites and, by extension, women's voices and a summary of possible reasons why, see Alexiou, especially 4–35.

7. This tradition of patriarchal discouragement of female singing continues. Like Chrysostum, Galas's father, a musician himself, tried to keep her from shifting from piano to voice by arguing that women singers were tone deaf and were "a bunch of whores. . . . As a Greek Orthodox, singing wasn't one of the things I was encouraged to do" (Gaer 431).

8. For an analysis of the conventions and themes of *moirológi*, see Danforth.

9. Foucault associates spectacles of enforcement with earlier forms of power since superseded by forms of power that work by more subtle disciplinary means; the occasion for this shift, he argues, was the plague of the late seventeenth century. The parallel Galas establishes between AIDS and crucifixion and her figuring of social and governmental indifference to AIDS as a kind of "homicide" (a genocidal cleansing of social "others" by conservative and homophobic forces, images of which are brought to us on the nightly news) call into question the marked shift from spectacular enforcement to disciplinary power in Foucault's reading of the history of power. For another important reading of how AIDS has unsettled Foucault's version of history, see Butler's "Sexual Inversions."

10. The heavily amplified vocal assault Galas unleashes on listeners during a performance is matched by her sometimes vehement and deliberately insulting offstage comments about the effect she hopes her work will have on those who see AIDS as an issue of/for "others." In a talk for the 1988 New Music Seminar she

claimed, "I've just completed a trilogy that is dedicated to my brothers and sisters, persons with AIDS who are now living and dying in Cadillacs, in hotel rooms, crucified in hospitals, and everywhere you don't think they are. And let me tell you something else . . . while you're sitting here having a good time, think about somebody who's lying in vomit bags, lying in perspiration and in dirty old sheets . . . and when you aren't too busy eating pussy and getting autographs, you might go to an ACT-UP meeting tomorrow night " (Flanagan 170– 171).

11. McClary comments on the risks and rewards of this strategy: "What Galas does is undeniably risky, given the tendency for women in Western culture always to be understood as excessive, sexually threatening, mad. She can be read as simply reaffirming the worst stereotypes available. But she can also be read as extremely courageous as she confronts these stereotypes head-on, appropriates them, and rechannels their violent energies in other directions. Her images enter into public circulation, challenging the premises of the prestigious male-constructed madwoman preserved within the musical canon and giving voice to what has always been represented as radically 'Other'" (*Feminine Endings* 111).

12. She also sacrifices conventional success and financial reward. In a number of interviews she recounts how often she has been advised that to be associated with AIDS is bad for her career.

13. We say "diva narrative" not only because she is, like most divas, conscious of herself as "diva" but also because the many interviews she has given to a variety of publications are beginning, when taken together, to constitute an autobiography in different versions. Despite significant changes in emphasis and tone, many of the same themes and events are repeated from interview to interview: her Greek heritage and Greek *moirológia*, her early success as a classical pianist, her interest in the free jazz movement, her days on the street, her shift from piano to voice (figured as a rebellion against the patriarch), her rigorous and disciplined vocal training, the reading and research she does for her compositions, the work on *The Masque of the Red Death* and *Plague Mass*.

WORKS CITED

Agassi, Tirzah. "Motherhood Sounds Good." *Jerusalem Post*, 14 May 1992.

Aiken, Susan Hardy. *Isak Dinesen and the Engendering of Narrative*. Chicago: U of Chicago P, 1990.

Alcott, Louisa May. "The Rival Prima Donnas." 1854. *Selected Fiction*. Ed. Daniel Shealy, Madeleine B. Stern, and Joel Myerson. Boston: Little, Brown, 1990. 10–20.

Alda, Frances. *Men, Women, and Tenors*. 1937. Freeport, NY: Books for Libraries Press, 1970.

Alexiou, Margaret. *The Ritual Lament in Greek Tradition*. Cambridge: Cambridge UP, 1974.

Alleman, Richard. "About Face." *Vogue*, Oct. 1992: 264, 266.

Allende, Isabel. "Tosca." *The Stories of Eva Luna*. Trans. Margaret Peden. New York: Macmillan, 1989.

Ancillon, Charles. *Eunuchism Display'd: Describing all the different Sorts of EU-NUCHS; the Esteem they have met with in the World; and how they can be made so*. London: E. Curl, 1718.

Andermahr, Sonya. "A Queer Love Affair?: Madonna and Lesbian and Gay Culture." *The Good, the Bad, and the Gorgeous*. Ed. Diane Hamer and Belinda Budge. New York: Pandora, 1994. 28–40.

Andersen, Christopher. *Madonna Unauthorized*. New York: Simon and Schuster, 1991.

Anderson, Marian. *My Lord, What a Morning*. 1956. Madison: U of Wisconsin P, 1992.

Atherton, Gertrude. *Tower of Ivory*. New York: Frederick Stokes, 1910.

Atkinson, Michael. "Virginity Preserved and the Secret Marriage of Sherlock Holmes." *Clue* 2.1 (1981): 62–69.

Avena, Thomas. "Interview with Diamanda Galas." *Life Sentences: Writers, Artists, and AIDS*. Ed. Thomas Avena. San Francisco: Mercury House, 1994. 177–196.

Babes in Arms. Dir. Busby Berkeley. 1939.

Baker, Janet. *Full Circle: An Autobiographical Journal*. New York: Franklin Watts, 1982.

Barnard, Robert. *Death on the High C's*. 1977. New York: Dell, 1988.

Basinger, Jeanine. *A Woman's View: How Hollywood Spoke to Women, 1930–1960*. New York: Knopf, 1993.

Benson, E. F. *Make Way for Lucia*. Contains the complete Lucia novels. 1920–1935. New York: Harper and Row, 1977.

Berberova, Nina. *The Accompanist*. Trans. Marian Schwartz. London: Collins, 1987.

Berman, Avis. "George du Maurier's *Trilby* Whipped Up a Worldwide Storm." *Smithsonian*, Dec. 1993: 110–126.

Bernstein, Jonathan. "Heavy Rotation." *Spin*, March 1994: 22.

Biancolli, Louis, ed. *The Flagstad Manuscript*. New York: Arno Press, 1977.

Bidini, Dave. "Is It Because They're Women?" *Toronto Star*, 28 Nov. 1992.

Blake, Kathleen. "*Armgart*—George Eliot on the Woman Artist." *Victorian Poetry* 18 (1980): 75–80.

Brittain, Vera. *The Dark Tide*. London: Grant Richards, 1923.

Bronfen, Elisabeth. "'Lasciatemi Morir': Representations of the Diva's Swan Song." *Modern Language Quarterly* 53 (1992): 427–448.

Brophy, Brigid. *The King of a Rainy Country*. London: Secker and Warburg, 1956.

Brown, Joe. "Galas's Screams of Suffering." *Washington Post*, 13 April 1991.

———. "With Songs of Rage." *Washington Post*, 7 April 1991.

Burney, Charles. *The Present State of Music in France and Italy*. 1773. New York: Broude Brothers, 1969.

Burney, Fanny. *Cecilia*. 1782. New York: Penguin, 1986.

Butler, Judith. *Bodies That Matter*. New York: Routledge, 1993.

———. *Gender Trouble*. New York: Routledge, 1990.

———. "Imitation and Gender Insubordination." *Inside Out: Lesbian Theories/Gay Theories*. Ed. Diana Fuss. New York: Routledge, 1991. 13–31.

———. "Sexual Inversions." *Discourses of Sexuality*. Ed. Domna C. Stanton. Ann Arbor: U of Michigan P, 1992. 344–361.

Byatt, A. S. "Introduction." Cather, *The Song of the Lark*. xiii–xix.

Caballero, Carlo. "'A Wicked Voice': On Vernon Lee, Wagner, and the Effects of Music." *Victorian Studies* 35 (1992): 385–408.

Caccini, Francesca. *La Liberazione di Ruggerio dall'Isola d'Alcina*. CD. Nannerl Recordings, 1994.

Cain, James M. *Mildred Pierce. Cain x Three*. 1941. New York: Knopf, 1969.

Calvé, Emma. *My Life*. 1922. Trans. Rosamond Gilder. New York: Arno Press, 1977.

Campbell, Jill. "'When Men Women Turn': Gender Reversal in Fielding's Plays." *Crossing the Stage: Controversies in Cross-Dressing*. Ed. Lesley Ferris. New York: Routledge, 1993. 58–79.

Carlin, Deborah. *Cather, Canon, and the Politics of Reading*. Amherst: U of Massachusetts P, 1992.

Carpenter, Mary Wilson. *George Eliot and the Landscape of Time*. Chapel Hill: U of North Carolina P, 1986.

Carr, C. *On Edge: Performance at the End of the Twentieth Century*. Hanover: UP of New England, 1993.

Castle, Terry. *The Apparitional Lesbian*. New York: Columbia UP, 1993.

Cather, Willa. *Alexander's Bridge*. 1912. *Stories, Poems, and Other Writings*. Ed. Sharon O'Brien. New York: Library of America, 1992.

———. "Coming, Aphrodite!" *Youth and the Bright Medusa*. New York: Vintage Books, 1975. 3–63.

———. "The Count of Crow's Nest." *Willa Cather's Collected Short Fiction 1892–1912*. Ed. Virginia Faulkner. Lincoln: U of Nebraska P, 1970. 449–471.

———. "A Death in the Desert." *The Troll Garden*. Ed. James Woodress. Lincoln: U of Nebraska P, 1983. 57–76.

———. "The Diamond Mine." *Youth and the Bright Medusa*. 67–120.

———. "The Double Birthday." *Uncle Valentine and Other Stories: Willa Cather's Uncollected Short Fiction 1915–1929*. Ed. Bernice Slote. Lincoln: U of Nebraska P, 1973. 41–63.

———. "Eric Hermannson's Soul." *Willa Cather's Collected Short Fiction 1892–1912*. 359–379.

———. "Flavia and Her Artists." *The Troll Garden*. 7–31.

———. "The Garden Lodge." *The Troll Garden*. 46–56.

———. "A Gold Slipper." *Youth and the Bright Medusa*. 123–148.

———. "Nanette: An Aside." *Willa Cather's Collected Short Fiction 1892–1912*. 405–410.

———. "Paul's Case." *Youth and the Bright Medusa*. 181–212.

———. "The Prodigies." *Willa Cather's Collected Short Fiction 1892–1912*. 411–423.

———. "Scandal." *Youth and the Bright Medusa*. 151–177.

———. *The Song of the Lark*. 1915. Rev. ed. 1937. London: Virago Press, 1982.

———. "A Singer's Romance." *Willa Cather's Collected Short Fiction 1892–1912*. 333–338.

———. "Three American Singers." *McClure's Magazine* 43 (Dec. 1913): 33–48.

———. "A Wagner Matinee." *Youth and the Bright Medusa*. 215–226.

Che, Cathay. "Wannabe." Frank and Smith 21–34.

Chin, Ong Soh. "Calmer Chameleon." *Straits Times*, 26 Aug. 1992.

Chorley, Henry F. *Thirty Years' Musical Recollections*. 1862. 2 vols. New York: Da Capo Press, 1984.

Christgau, Robert. "Madonnathinking Madonnabout Madonnamusic." Sexton 201–207.

Christiansen, Rupert. "George Eliot, *Armgart*, and the Victorian Prima Donna." *About the House* 7 (1986): 8–10.

———. *Prima Donna*. London: Bodley Head, 1984.

Clayton, Ellen Creathorne. *Queens of Song*. 1865. Freeport, NY: Books for Libraries Press, 1972.

Clément, Catherine. *Opera, or the Undoing of Women*. Trans. Betsy Wing. Minneapolis: U of Minnesota P, 1988.

Clover, Carol J. *Men, Women, and Chainsaws: Gender in the Modern Horror Film*. Princeton: Princeton UP, 1992.

Conrad, Peter. *A Song of Love and Death: The Meaning of Opera*. New York: Poseidon Press, 1987.

Corliss, Richard. "Angst for Art's Sake." *Time*, 25 May 1992: 70–71.

Crawford, F. Marion. *The Diva's Ruby*. New York: Macmillan, 1908.

———. *Primadonna*. New York: McKinlay, Stone and Mackenzie, 1907.

Crimp, Douglas. "AIDS: Cultural Analysis/Cultural Activism." *AIDS: Cultural Analysis/Cultural Activism*. Ed. Douglas Crimp. Cambridge: MIT Press, 1988. 3–16.

Crimp, Douglas, and Michael Warner. "No Sex in *Sex*." Schmuckler 93–110.

Cromelin, Richard. "Annie Lennox." *Los Angeles Times*, 12 July 1992.

Crutchfield, Will. "A Soprano Fascinated with the Past." *New York Times*, 29 Sept. 1985.

Curtin, William M. *The World and the Parish: Willa Cather's Articles and Reviews 1893–1902*. 2 vols. Lincoln: U of Nebraska P, 1970.

Cushing, Mary Watkins. *The Rainbow Bridge*. New York: Putnam, 1954.

Danforth, Loring M. *The Death Rituals of Ancient Greece*. Princeton: Princeton UP, 1982.

Davenport, Marcia. *Mozart*. New York: Scribner's, 1932.

———. *Of Lena Geyer*. New York: Grosset and Dunlap, 1936.

Davies, Robertson. *A Mixture of Frailties*. New York: Charles Scribner's Sons, 1958.

Davis, Kathryn. *The Girl Who Trod on a Loaf*. New York: Knopf, 1993.

Delacorta. *Diva*. 1979. Trans. Lowell Bair. New York: Ballentine, 1984.

Delblanc, Sven. *The Castrati: A Romantic Tale*. 1975. Trans. C. W. Williams. Ann Arbor: Karoma Publishers, 1979.

"Diamanda Galas: Tura Satana without Cleavage." *Forced Exposure* 15.5 (1989): 11–33.

Dinesen, Isak. "The Dreamers." *Seven Gothic Tales*. 1934. New York: Vintage Books, 1972: 269–355.

Diva. Dir. Jean-Jacques Beineix. 1992.

Dizikes, John. *Opera in America: A Cultural History*. New Haven: Yale UP, 1993.

Douglas, Carole Nelson. *Good Morning, Irene*. New York: Tom Doherty Associates, 1990.

———. *Good Night, Mr. Holmes*. New York: Tom Doherty Associates, 1990.

———. *Irene at Large*. New York: Tom Doherty Associates, 1992.

———. *Irene's Last Waltz*. New York: Tom Doherty Associates, 1994.

Doyle, Arthur Conan. *The Compete Sherlock Holmes*. New York: Doubleday, 1927.

Dubroof, P. Personal interview. June 1995.

Duckett, Chip. "Outfront." *Out*, Nov. 1993: 16.

Du Maurier, George. *Trilby*. London: Osgood, McIlvaine, 1895.

Dunnett, Dorothy. *Dolly and the Singing Bird*. 1968 (in U.S. as *The Photogenic Soprano*). New York: Vintage, 1982.

Edmonson, Roger. "Dyke Divas." *Advocate*, 2 Nov. 1993: 54.

Edwards, Anne. *La Divina*. New York: William Morrow, 1994.

Eliot, George. *Armgart*. *George Eliot's Works*, vol. 11. Edinburgh: Blackwood, 1906. 71–140.

———. *Daniel Deronda*. *George Eliot's Works*, vols. 9 and 10. Edinburgh: Blackwood, 1911.

———. *Essays of George Eliot.* Ed. Thomas Pinney. New York: Columbia UP, 1963.

———. *The George Eliot Letters.* Ed. Gordon S. Haight. New Haven: Yale UP, 1954.

———. "Mr. Gilfil's Love-Story." *George Eliot's Works,* vol. 5. Edinburgh: Blackwood, 1907. 125–336.

Ellison, Cori. "Breaking the Sound Barrier." *Opera* 57 (1992): 14–37.

Evans, Paul. "Diva." *Rolling Stone,* 25 June 1992: 41.

Farrar, Geraldine. *Such Sweet Compulsion.* 1938. Freeport, NY: Books for Libraries Press, 1970.

Feuer, Jane. *The Hollywood Musical.* 2d ed. Bloomington: Indiana UP, 1993.

Fillipenko, Cindy. "Opera for the Masses." *XTRA West!* 23 (1 July 1994): 27.

Fingleton, David. *Kiri.* London: Arrow Books, 1982.

Fischer, Lucy. *Shot/Countershot: Film Tradition and Women's Cinema.* Princeton: Princeton UP, 1989.

Fisher, Carrie. "True Confessions: Part One." *Rolling Stone,* 13 June 1991: 35–36, 39–40, 120.

———. "True Confessions: Part Two." *Rolling Stone,* 27 June 1991: 45–49, 78.

Fiske, John. "Madonna." Sexton 58–75.

FitzLyon, April. *Maria Malibran: Diva of the Romantic Age.* London: Souvenir Press, 1987.

———. *The Price of Genius: A Life of Pauline Viardot.* New York: Appleton-Century, 1964.

Flanagan, Michael. "Invoking Diamanda." Avena 161–175.

Foucault, Michel. *Discipline and Punish.* Trans. Alan Sheridan. New York: Vintage/Random House, 1979.

Frank, Lisa, and Paul Smith, eds. *Madonnarama: Essays on Sex and Popular Culture.* Pittsburgh: Cleis Press, 1993.

Freud, Sigmund. *Studies on Hysteria. The Pelican Freud Library,* vol. 3. Ed. and trans. James and Alix Strachey. Harmondsworth: Penguin, 1974.

Gaer, Jillian G. *She's a Rebel: The History of Women in Rock and Roll.* Seattle: Seal Press, 1992.

Galas, Diamanda. "Intravenal Song." *Perspectives of New Music* 20 (1981–1982): 59–62.

———. *Masque of the Red Death.* Parts 1, 2, 3. CD. Mute Records, 1988, 1989.

———. *Plague Mass.* CD. Live rec. 1984. Mute Records, 1991.

———. *Vena Cava.* CD. Mute Records, 1993.

Garber, Marjorie. *Vested Interests: Cross-Dressing and Cultural Anxiety.* New York: Routledge, 1992.

Garden, Mary, and Louis Biancolli. *Mary Garden's Story.* New York: Simon and Schuster, 1951.

Gates, David. "The Second Act of Annie." *Esquire,* July 1992: 82, 83.

Gehr, Richard. "Mourning in America: Diamanda Galas." *Artforum,* May 1989: 116–118.

Giannone, Richard. *Music in Willa Cather's Fiction.* Lincoln: U of Nebraska P, 1968.

Gilbert, Sandra M., and Susan Gubar. *The Madwoman in the Attic*. New Haven: Yale UP, 1979.

Gilmore, Mikal. "The Madonna Mystic." *Rolling Stone*, 10 Sept. 1987: 508.

Glasgow, Ellen. *Phases of an Inferior Planet*. New York: Harper and Brothers, 1898.

Goldman, Lawrence Louis. *The Castrato*. New York: John Day, 1973.

Goodman, Ellen. "Another Image in the Madonna Rolodex." Sexton 164–166.

Gould, Judith. *Forever*. New York: Dutton, 1992.

Gracie and Zarkov. "Killing Floor: The Harrowing Spirituals of Diamanda Galas." *Mondo 2000* 8 (1992): 75–79.

Grout, Donald Jay. *A Short History of Opera*. 2d ed. New York: Columbia University Press, 1965.

Hall, Trevor. *Sherlock Holmes: Ten Literary Studies*. New York: St. Martin's, 1970.

Halperin, David. *One Hundred Years of Homosexuality*. New York: Routledge, 1990.

Harris, Thomas Allen. "phallic momma/sell my pussy/make a dollar." Frank and Smith 35–46.

Henderson, Lisa. "Justify Our Love: Madonna and the Politics of Queer Sex." Schwichtenberg 107–128.

Heriot, Angus. *The Castrati in Opera*. 1956. New York: Da Capo Press, 1974.

Hilferty, Robert. "The Avenging Spirit of Diamanda Galas." *High Performance*, Spring 1990: 22–25.

Hirschberg, Lynn. "The Misfit." *Vanity Fair*, April 1991: 158–168, 196–202.

Holden, Stephen. "Diamanda Galas, Avant Garde Diva." *New York Times*, 19 July 1985.

Homer. *The Odyssey*. Trans. Robert Fitzgerald. New York: Anchor, 1963.

hooks, bell. "Madonna: Plantation Mistress or Soul Sister?" Sexton 218–226.

———. "Power to the Pussy: We Don't Wannabe Dicks in Drag." Frank and Smith 65–80.

Horne, Marilyn, and James Scovell. *My Life*. New York: Atheneum, 1983.

Huneker, James. *Painted Veils*. 1920. New York: Liveright, 1942.

Hunt, Dennis. "Annie Lennox, 'Diva Arista.'" *Los Angeles Times*, 24 May 1992.

Hwang, David Henry. *M. Butterfly*. New York: Plume, 1989.

I Dream Too Much. Dir. John Cromwell. 1935.

Jackson, Alan. "I was Besotted with Boys." *Times Newspapers Limited*, 2 May 1992, Features.

James, Henry. *Henry James Letters*. Ed. Leon Edel. Cambridge: Harvard UP, 1975.

Janáček, Leoš. *The Makropulos Case*. LP. London Decca, 1979.

Jann, Rosemary. "Sherlock Holmes Codes the Social Body." *ELH* 57.3 (Fall 1990): 685–708.

Jarvis, Fred G. *Murder at the Met*. New York: Coward-McCann, 1971.

Jarvis, Fred G., and Robert Merrill. *See* Merrill.

Johnson, Brian D. "Melancholy Baby." *Maclean's*, 11 May 1992: 54–57.

Jones, Lisa. *Bulletproof Diva: Tales of Race, Sex, and Hair*. New York: Doubleday, 1994.

The Joy Luck Club. Dir. Wayne Wang. 1993.

Joyce, Mike. "Anne Lennox as a Voluptuous 'Diva.'" *Washington Post*, 13 May 1992.

Juno, Andrea, and V. Vale. *Angry Women*. San Francisco: Re/Search Publications, 1991.

Kaplan, E. Ann. "Madonna Politics: Perversion, Repression, or Subversion? Or Masks and/as Master-y." Schwichtenberg 149–165.

Kennedy, Margaret. *A Long Time Ago*. New York: Doubleday, Doran, 1932.

Kingston, Maxine Hong. *The Woman Warrior*. New York: Knopf, 1976.

Koestenbaum, Wayne. *Double Talk: The Erotics of Male Literary Collabration*. New York: Routledge, 1989.

———. *The Queen's Throat: Opera, Homosexuality, and the Mystery of Desire*. New York: Poseidon Press, 1993.

———. "This Diva Is Diffident." *New York Times Magazine*, 23 July 1995: 14–18.

Kot, Greg. "Listen to Lennox." *Chicago Tribune*, 17 May 1992.

Kowaleski-Wallace, Beth. "Shunning the Bearded Kiss: Castrati and the Definition of Female Sexuality." *Prose Studies* 15 (1992): 153–170.

Laqueur, Thomas. *Making Sex: Body and Gender from the Greeks to Freud*. Cambridge: Harvard UP, 1990.

Lawrence, Amy. *Echo and Narcissus: Women's Voices in Classical Hollywood Cinema*. Berkeley: U of California P, 1971.

Lee, Vernon (Violet Paget). *Studies of the Eighteenth Century in Italy*. 1887. New York: Da Capo Press, 1978.

———. "A Wicked Voice." *Hauntings*. 1890. Freeport, NY: Books for Libraries Press, 1971.

Lehmann, Lilli. *My Path through Life*. Trans. Alice Benedict Seligman. New York: G. P. Putnam's Sons, 1914.

Lehmann, Lotte. *Midway in My Song*. 1938. Freeport, NY: Books for Libraries Press, 1970.

———. *My Many Lives*. 1948. Trans. Frances Holden. Westport, CT: Greenwood, 1974.

Leider, Frida. *Playing My Part*. 1959. Trans. Charles Osborne. New York: Meredith Press, 1966.

Lennox, Annie. *Diva*. CD. Arista, 1992.

Lentz, Kirsten Martha. "Chameleon, Vampire, Rich Slut." Frank and Smith 153–168.

Leon, Donna. *Death at La Fenice*. New York: HarperCollins, 1992.

Leonardi, Susan J. "To Have a Voice: The Politics of the Diva." *Perspectives on Contemporary Literature* 13 (1987): 65–72.

Leonardi, Susan J., and Rebecca Pope. "Screaming Divas: Collaboration as Feminist Practice." *Tulsa Studies in Women's Literature* 13 (1994): 259–270.

Leroux, Gaston. *The Phantom of the Opera*. 1911. New York: Penguin, 1987.

Lowe, David A., ed. *Callas as They Saw Her*. New York: Ungar, 1986.

MacCann, Richard Dyer. *The Stars Appear*. Metuchen, NJ: Scarecrow Press, 1992.

McClary, Susan. *Feminine Endings: Music, Gender, and Sexuality*. Minneapolis: U of Minnesota P, 1991.

———. "Foreword: The Undoing of Opera: Toward a Feminist Criticism of Music." Clément ix–xviii.

McCourt, James. *Mawrdew Czgowchwz*. New York: Farrar, Straus and Giroux, 1975.

McDonagh, Maitland. "The Elegant Brutality of Dario Argento." *Film Comment* 29 (1993): 55–58.

McNally, Terrence. *The Lisbon Traviata. Three Plays by Terrence McNally*. New York: Plume, 1990.

Machlis, Joseph. *The Career of Magda V*. New York: Norton, 1985.

MacKay, Harper. "Going Hollywood." *Opera News*, 13 April 1991: 10+.

MacKay, John. "The Orality Perspective: The Oral Mode in Contemporary Art and Culture—Voice and Performance." *Perspectives of New Music* 20 (1981–1982): 68–74.

McLellan, Joseph. "Carmen Can Wait." *Washington Post*, 25 March 1994.

Madonna. *The Immaculate Collection*, CD. Siren Records, 1990.

———. *Sex*. New York: Time Warner Books, 1992.

"Madonna Interview." From *Nightline*, 3 Dec. 1991. Sexton 277–287.

Mailer, Norman. "Norman Mailer on Madonna." *Esquire*, Aug. 1994: 41–56.

Mandziuk, Roseann M. "Feminist Politics and Postmodern Seductions: Madonna and the Struggle for Political Articulation." Schwicktenberg 167–188.

Mansfield, Katherine. "Pictures." *The Short Stories of Katherine Mansfield*. New York: Knopf, 1937. 393–401.

Marchesi, Mathilde. *Marchesi and Music*. New York: Harper and Brothers, 1897.

Marsh, Dave. "Girls Can't Do What the Guys Do: Madonna's Physical Attraction." Sexton 31–37.

Marsh, Ngaio. *Photo Finish*. New York: Jove, 1980.

Matheopoulos, Helena. *Diva: Great Sopranos and Mezzos Discuss Their Art*. London: Gollancz, 1991.

Meeting Venus. Dir. Istvan Szabo. 1990.

Meneghini, Giovanni Battista. *My Wife, Maria Callas*. Trans. Henry Wisneski. New York: Farrar, Straus and Giroux, 1982.

Menendez, Albert J. *The Subject Is Murder: A Selective Subject Guide to Mystery Fiction*. New York: Jove, 1983.

Meredith, George. *Sandra Belloni*. 1864 as *Emelia*. Boston: Roberts Brothers, 1894.

———. *Vittoria*. Cambridge, MA: J. S. Cushing, 1897.

Merrill, Robert, and Fred Jarvis. *The Divas*. New York: Simon and Schuster, 1978.

"Met Fires Temperamental Diva Battle." *Washington Post*, 8 Feb. 1994.

Michael, Dennis. "Singer Annie Lennox Scores with 'Diva.'" CNN transcript, 21 July 1992.

Midler, Marcia S. "George Eliot's Rebels: Portraits of the Artist as a Woman." *Women's Studies* 7 (1980): 97–108.

Milton, John. *Complete Poetry and Major Prose*. Ed. Merritt Y. Hughes. Indianapolis: Odyssey Press/Bobbs Merrill, 1957.

Moers, Ellen. *Literary Women*. New York: Doubleday, 1976.

Moon, Michael, and Eve Kosofsky Sedgwick. "Divinity: A Dossier, a Performance Piece, a Little Understood Emotion." *Tendencies*. Ed. Eve Kosofsky Sedgwick. Durham: Duke UP, 1993. 215–251.

Moore, George. *Evelyn Innes* and *Sister Teresa*. 1898, 1901. New York: Garland, 1975.

Mordden, Ethan. *Demented: The World of the Opera Diva*. New York: Franklin Watts, 1984.

———. *Opera Anecdotes*. New York: Oxford UP, 1985.

Morse, Steve. "Annie Lennox: From Duo to Diva." *Boston Globe*, 8 May 1992.

Morton, Melanie. "Don't Go for Second Sex, Baby!" Schwichtenberg 213–235.

Mozart, W. A. *Le Nozze di Figaro*. LP. London Decca, 1982.

———. *Zaide and Der Schauspieldirektor*. CD. Philips Classics, 1991.

Newton, K. M. *George Eliot: Romantic Humanist*. Totowa, NJ: Barnes and Noble, 1981.

Oberlin, Russell. "The Castrato: A Lost Vocal Phenomenon." *American Music Teacher* 40.2 (1990): 18–51.

O'Brien, Kate. *As Music and Splendour*. New York: Harper and Brothers, 1958.

O'Brien, Sharon. *Willa Cather: The Emerging Voice*. New York: Oxford UP, 1987.

Offenbach, Jacques. *Tales of Hoffman*. Libretto. *The Opera Libretto Library*. New York: Crown Publishers, 1980.

Ohrenstein, Dora. *Urban Diva*. CD. Composers Recordings, 1993.

Oldham, Todd. "Cover Girl." *Spin*, Nov. 1993: 42.

One Night of Love. Dir. Victor Schertzinger. 1934.

Orth, Maureen. "Madonna in Wonderland." *Vanity Fair*, April 1992: 298–306.

Paglia, Camille. "Madonna—Finally a Real Feminist." *New York Times*, 14 Dec. 1990.

Pareles, Jon. "Madonna's Return to Innocence." *New York Times*, 23 Oct. 1994.

Paris, Barry. "Unconquerable." Profile of Marcia Davenport. *New Yorker*, 22 April 1991: 42–88.

Patton, Cindy. "Embodying Subaltern Memory: Kinesthesia and the Problematics of Gender and Race." Schwichtenberg 81–105.

Paul, Barbara. *A Chorus of Detectives*. New York: Signet, 1988.

———. *Prima Donna at Large*. New York: Signet, 1987.

Pelensky, Olga Anastasia. *Isak Dinesen*. Athens: Ohio UP, 1991.

Penley, Constance. "Brownian Motion: Women, Tactics, and Technology." *Technoculture*. Ed. Constance Penley and Andrew Ross. Minneapolis: U of Minnesota P, 1991. 135–161.

Peschel, Enid Rhodes, and Richard E. Peschel. "Sherlock Holmes Foiled by an Opera Star." *Opera Quarterly* 7.3 (Fall 1990): 82–88.

Peterson, Carla L. *Doers of the Word: African-American Women Speakers and Writers in the North (1830–1880)*. New York: Oxford UP, 1995.

Phillips, Teresia Constantia. "The Happy Courtezan: Or, the Prude demolish'd. An Epistle from the Celebrated Mrs. C—— P——, to the Angelic Signior *Far—— n——li*." London: J. Roberts, 1735.

Pleasants, Henry. *The Great Singers: From the Dawn of Opera to Our Own Time*. New York: Simon and Schuster, 1966.

Polkow, Dennis. "Beating the Devil, Galas Tries to Face Reality of AIDS in her 'Plague Mass.'" *Chicago Tribune*, 3 April 1991.

Pope, Rebecca A. "The Diva Doesn't Die: George Eliot's *Armgart.*" *Criticism* 32 (1990): 469–483.

Porter, Dennis. "The Language of Detection." *Popular Fiction: Technology, Ideology, Production, Reading.* Ed. Tony Bennett. New York: Routledge, 1990. 81–93.

Pribram, E. Dierdre. "Seduction, Control, and the Search for Authenticity: Madonna's *Truth or Dare.*" Schwichtenberg 189–212.

Price, Walter. "Cecilia! Your're Breaking Our Hearts!" *Opera News,* Aug. 1993: 10–14, 46.

Queen, Carol A. "Talking about Sex." Frank and Smith 139–151.

Rasponi, Lanfranco. *The Last Prima Donnas.* New York: Knopf, 1982.

"Recent Releases." *Calgary Herald,* 26 April 1992.

Riccio, Richard, "'Diva' Is Simply Divine." *St. Petersburg Times,* 19 June 1992.

Rice, Anne. *Cry to Heaven.* 1982. New York: Ballantine, 1991.

Riches, Hester. "An Introspective Annie Lennox Confesses." *Vancouver Sun,* 16 May 1992.

Ringle, Ken. "The Met's Battle Royale." *Washington Post,* 9 Feb. 1994.

Robins, Wayne. "Annie Lennox' 'Diva' Complex." *Newsday,* 10 May 1992.

Robinson, Paul. "It's Not Over till the Soprano Dies." Review of *Opera, or the Undoing of Women,* by Catherine Clement. *New York Times Book Review,* 1 Jan. 1989: 3.

Rose Marie. Dir. W. S. Van Dyke. 1936.

Rosowski, Susan J. *The Voyage Perilous: Willa Cather's Romanticism.* Lincoln: U of Nebraska P, 1986.

———. "Writing against Silences: Female Adolescent Development in the Novels of Willa Cather." *Studies in the Novel* 21 (1989): 60–77.

Rosselli, John. *Singers of Italian Opera: The History of a Profession.* Cambridge: Cambridge UP, 1992.

Rothstein, Edward. "A Diva Makes a Cage Her Vehicle." *New York Times,* 10 July 1993.

St. Aubyn, Giles. *Queen Victoria: A Portrait.* New York: Atheneum, 1992.

San Francisco. Dir. W. S. Van Dyke. 1936.

Sand, George. *Consuelo.* Rpt. of London ed., 1876. New York: Lovell, Coryell, n.d.

Sarton, May. *Anger.* New York: Norton, 1982.

Schmuckler, Eric. "Madonnarama." Sexton 25–26.

Schulze, Laurie, Anne Barton White, and Jane D. Brown. "'A Sacred Monster in Her Prime': Audience Construction of Madonna as Low-Other." Schwichtenberg 15–37.

Schwartz, Deb. "Madonna and Sandra: Like We Care." Sexton 214–217.

Schweickert, William P. "The Better Man." *Baker Street Journal: An Irregular Quarterly of Sherlockiana* 39.2 (June 1989): 99–101.

Schwichtenberg, Cathy, ed. *The Madonna Connection.* Boulder: Westview Press, 1993.

Scott, Ronald B. "Images of Race and Religion in Madonna's Video *Like a Prayer*: Prayer and Praise." Schwichtenberg 57–77.

Scotto, Renata, and Octavio Roca. *Scotto: More than a Diva.* Garden City, NY: Doubleday, 1984.

Sedgwick, Eve Kosofsky. "Willa Cather's Others." *Tendencies.* Ed. Eve Kasofsky Sedgwick. Durham: Duke UP, 1993. 167–176.

Sexton, Adam, ed. *Desperately Seeking Madonna.* New York: Dell, 1993.

Shaviro, Steven. *The Cinematic Body.* Minneapolis: U of Minnesota, 1993.

Siciliano, Sam. *The Angel of the Opera.* New York: Macmillan, 1994.

Sills, Beverly, and Lawrence Linderman. *Beverly.* New York: Bantam, 1987.

Silverman, Kaja. *The Acoustic Mirror: The Female Voice in Psychoanalysis and Cinema.* Bloomington: Indiana UP, 1988.

Simon, John. "Immaterial Girl." Sexton 240–242.

Slote, Bernice. *The Kingdom of Art: Willa Cather's First Principles and Critical Statements 1893–1896.* Lincoln: U of Nebraska P, 1966.

Smith, Kay Nolte. *Elegy for a Soprano.* New York: Villard Books, 1985.

Smith-Rosenberg, Carroll. "Discourses of Sexuality and Subjectivity: The New Woman, 1870–1936." *Hidden from History: Reclaiming the Gay and Lesbian Past.* Ed. Martin Duberman, Martha Vicinus, and George Chauncey Jr. New York: Meridian, 1990. 264–280.

Söderström, Elisabeth. *In My Own Key.* Trans. Joan Tate. London: Hamish Hamilton, 1970.

Solomon, Alisa. "It's Never Too Late to Switch." *Crossing the Stage.* Ed. Lesley Ferris. New York: Routledge, 1993. 144–154.

Spofford, Harriet Prescott. *A Master Spirit.* New York: Charles Scribner's Sons, 1896.

Stasio, Marilyn. "Another Body, Another Show: Bravo for the Backstage Mystery." *New York Times Book Review,* 17 Oct 1993: 44–45.

Story, Rosalyn M. *And So I Sing: African-American Divas of Opera and Concert.* New York: Warner Books, 1990.

Tambling, Jeremy. *Opera, Ideology, and Film.* Manchester: Manchester UP, 1987.

Tenducci, Dorothy Maunsell. *A True and Genuine Narrative of Mr. and Mrs. Tenducci.* London: J. Pridden, 1768.

Terror at the Opera. Dir. Dario Argento. 1991.

Tetrazzini, Luisa. *My Life of Song.* Philadelphia: Dorrance, 1922.

Tetzlaff, David. "Metatextual Girl." Schwichtenberg 239–263.

That Girl from Paris. Dir. Leigh Jason. 1937.

Tippens, Elizabeth. "Madonna and Me." Sexton 262–274.

Tosi, Pier Francesco. *Observations on the Florid Song; or Sentiments on the Ancient and Modern Singers.* Trans. Mr. Galliord. London: Wilcox, 1743.

Truth or Dare. Dir. Alek Keshishian. 1991.

Weiss, Andrea. "A Queer Feeling When I Look at You: Hollywood Stars and Lesbian Spectatorship in the 1930s." *Stardom: Industry of Desire.* Ed. Christine Gledhill. London: Routledge, 1991.

White, Mimi. "They All Sing . . . : Voice, Body, and Representation in *Diva.*" *Literature and Psychology* 34 (1988): 33–42.

White, Timothy. "Annie Lennox Casts a Solo Spell." *Billboard*, 25 April 1992: 3.

Wood, Elizabeth. "Sapphonics." *Queering the Pitch: The New Gay and Lesbian Musicology*. Ed. Philip Brett, Gary Thomas, and Elizabeth Wood. New York: Routledge, 1994. 27–66.

Yarbro, C. Q. *False Notes*. 1977 as *Music When Sweet Voices Die*. New York: Jove, 1991.

INDEX

ABOUT THE AUTHORS

Overly-degreed and under-educated at prestigious institutions in the U.S. and abroad, Susan J. Leonardi and Rebecca A. Pope are the authors of articles, books, plays, and stories too varied, numerous, and clever to mention, though their publisher would not like them to omit Leonardi's *Dangerous by Degrees: Women at Oxford and the Somerville College Novelists* (Rutgers University Press, 1989). Whether their ostensible subject is recipes or mysteries, women's education or AIDS, divas or nuns, they, like most writers, write only about the curious meanderings of desire. No strangers to indulgence, self- or otherwise, they find their own desires, in (by?) middle age, much distilled: good food, lucid prose, a place in the sun (preferably a few choice acres in northern New Mexico). Currently they cook and write, without cats, in Bethesda, Maryland, and teach, respectively, at the University of Maryland and Georgetown University.